The Financial Times Guide to Business Start Up

The Financial Times Guide to Business Start Up 2008

Sara Williams

21st edition

Prentice Hall

FINANCIAL TIMES

An imprint of **Pearson Education**
Harlow, England • London • New York • Boston • San Francisco • Toronto • Sydney • Singapore • Hong Kong
Tokyo • Seoul • Taipei • New Delhi • Cape Town • Madrid • Mexico City • Amsterdam • Munich • Paris • Milan

PEARSON EDUCATION LIMITED

Edinburgh Gate
Harlow CM20 2JE
Tel: +44 (0)1279 623623
Fax: +44 (0)1279 431059
Website: www.pearsoned.co.uk

The *Financial Times Guide to Business Start Up* was previously published as the *Lloyds TSB Small Business Guide*

First published by Penguin Books 1987
Second edition 1988
Third edition 1989
Fourth edition 1990
Fifth edition 1991
Sixth edition 1992
Seventh edition 1993
Eighth edition 1994
Ninth edition 1995
Tenth edition 1996
Eleventh edition 1997
Twelfth edition 1998
Thirteenth edition 1999
Fourteenth edition 2000
Fifteenth edition published by Vitesse Media plc 2001
Sixteenth edition 2002
Seventeenth edition 2003
Eighteenth edition 2004
Nineteenth edition 2006
Twentieth edition published by Pearson Education in Great Britain 2007
Twenty-first edition 2008

© Sara Williams 1987 – 2002
© Vitesse Media plc 2003 – 2008

ISBN: 978-0-273-71487-3

British Library Cataloguing in Publication Data
A catalogue record for this book can be obtained from the British Library

10 9 8 7 6 5 4 3 2 1
11 10 09 08

Typeset in 9pt Stone Serif by 3
Printed and bound in Great Britain by Ashford Colour Press Ltd, Gosport, Hants

The Publisher's policy is to use paper manufactured from sustainable forests.

Contents

Acknowledgements / vii

Update for the *Financial Times Guide to Business Start Up* / ix

1 You and your ideas / 1

2 Who will buy? / 13

3 A spot of coaching / 27

4 Your business identity / 38

5 Are you sure? / 54

6 The business plan / 63

7 Timing the jump / 69

8 Less than 100 per cent / 74

9 Off the peg / 80

10 Franchises / 101

11 Beating the pirates / 119

12 The right name / 128

13 Getting the message across / 136

14 Getting new customers / 149

15 Building customer relationships / 163

16 How to set a price / 170

17 Choosing your workplace / 182

18 Information technology – and other equipment / 193

19 Professional back-up / 201

20 Getting the right staff / 210

21 Your rights and duties as an employer / 229

22 Insurance / 262

23 Forecasting / 269

24 Raising the money / 290

25 Staying afloat / 305

26 Moving ahead / 322

27 Not waving but drowning / 335

28 Keeping the record straight / 340

29 Tax / 350

30 VAT / 382

31 Pensions and retirement / 396

*References / 406

Index / 418

* An asterisk after the name of an organization or source in the text indicates that contact details are given in the Reference section.

Acknowledgements

The number of people who have helped me produce this comprehensive guide continues to grow. My debt to those who commented and supplied information for the original edition remains enormous; they helped me to improve the quality and content of the advice it contains to help you to get new enterprises up and running, and keep them that way. For the current edition, the third published by Pearson as the *Financial Times Guide to Business Start Up* but the twenty-first since it was first published as the *Lloyds TSB Small Business Guide*, the checking and updating was carried out with remarkable efficiency by Jonquil Lowe. I'd also like to thank all the team at Pearson Education for the work they have done in publishing the guide so successfully under its new title.

If you have any comments on the guide, please e-mail sbg@growth company.co.uk

Note

I have taken every care and effort to check the information and advice in this guide. Nevertheless, with a book as comprehensive as this one the odd slip may occur. Unfortunately, I regret that I cannot be responsible for any loss that you may suffer as a result of any omission or inaccuracy.

Free update for every reader!

The *Financial Times Guide to Business Start Up* went to press in October and to keep you up to date with what's happening in the small business world we are producing a free update. It will be available after the Budget next spring and will cover all the main changes in tax, law and the business environment.

If you would like to receive a copy of the free update:

- e-mail us at smallbusiness@vitessemedia.co.uk with your name and full postal address;
- fax us your name and full postal address, with a note asking for the *Free Small Business Update*, to 020 7250 7011;
- write to us at Business Start Up, Vitesse Media plc, Octavia House, 50 Banner Street, London EC1Y 8ST, enclosing a stamped A4 envelope.

Don't forget, you can also pick up a huge range of tips, ideas and links to useful services on our website www.smallbusiness.co.uk.

1

You and your ideas

As a way of earning a living, running your own business has two distinctive features. The first is that you do not submit yourself to a selection process; there is not, as there is with a job as an employee, a sifting carried out of possible applicants for a vacancy. There is no personnel manager wielding a battery of psychological tests or cunning interview questions to test your suitability for the job or the level of skills you have acquired.

You are the sole arbiter of your fitness to start and run your own business. This puts a very heavy responsibility on your self-knowledge, because without a doubt not everyone is suited to being an entrepreneur or being self-employed. The only external check on your fitness to found a business might occur if you need to raise money; in this case, a bank manager or other lender or investor judges you. But by the time you reach this stage, you may already have committed time and money to your project.

The answer to the dilemma of this self-selection process is self-analysis: know thyself. Additional insight can be provided by the opinion of colleagues, friends or family. But this can be fraught with emotional problems. Those you ask for an opinion may feel under pressure to give a favourable view for fear of offending. If an unbiased view cannot be expected, do not seek an opinion at all. Later in this book (p. 54), there is a checklist that you (and others) can use to carry out an assessment of your character and abilities. This should provide some assistance in answering the question 'Am I the right sort of person to succeed in my own business?' This chapter describes the type of person who makes the break. Some people talk over a number of years of running their own show but never take the ultimate step. Why do some people break the mould, while others only dream of it?

The second unusual characteristic of starting your own business to create your own income is that you decide what type of business it is and what market you will be selling to.

While you can select a salaried job in a firm of a particular size or selling to a particular market, you are restricted by the vacancies that are available. When it comes to establishing a business, in theory, the world is your oyster. A well-run business should succeed in any market. In practice, however, you can make success more likely by choosing your product and market carefully.

What is in this chapter?

The first section **you** focuses on individual characteristics and tries to answer these questions:

- who are you? (p. 3)
- what do you want? (p. 4)
- what will it be like? (p. 5)
- why will you succeed? (p. 7)
- why will you fail? (p. 8)
- how big a business? (p. 8)

The second section **your ideas** focuses on the business and your choice of business idea:

- what are your skills? (p. 9)
- which is the best market? (p. 10)
- no ideas at all? (p. 11)
- defining your ideas (p. 11).

You

The greatest determinant of the success of your business is you, your character and skills. This you must believe if your business is to have any chance of prospering. The type of person who blames external factors for failure and believes that their own decisions have little impact on the course of future events is not suited to building a business.

Who are you?

How frequently do you overhear, or partake in, conversations that run along the following lines: 'In a couple of years I would like to start off on my own if I can', 'I would love to have my own business but my financial commitments mean that I can't take the risk', or some other variant? Quite a number of people dream of running their own show, but not all take the plunge. A survey for the government found that 18 per cent of adults in England ran their own business. A further 12 per cent said they were thinking about it but, a year later, only one in seven of these 'thinkers' had become 'doers'.

In some ways, it is hardly surprising that few entrepreneurial dreamers take the final step. Lying ahead of them, maybe for a number of years, is the unknown: financial insecurity, long working hours, long-term financial obligations and, at the end of it all, possible failure. What is different about those who jump and those who only talk?

The conventional image of an entrepreneur is of a strong-minded, positive risk-taker with a sense of destiny, seizing the ever-present opportunities. Well, this may be a reasonably close approximation of some successful entrepreneurs and you may be that sort of person, but this still does not explain why you are starting your own business and why now. There are many people like this who stay employees for the rest of their lives; and many more who start a business 'accidentally' but make a great success of it.

One plausible explanation for why some start a business and others do not is that those who go solo have received a rude shock to their lives. Their previously cosy existence has been disrupted. This could be the result of, say, being made redundant or sacked, not being promoted as expected, having your ideas at work rejected, feeling undermined, having a new boss foisted on you, being transferred to a different job or location, retiring but finding you need extra money, reaching a milestone age and feeling you have yet to achieve anything worthwhile, or realizing that corporate life does not provide the security or sense of worth that perhaps it did thirty or so years ago. Another catalyst could be seeing a friend or colleague in similar circumstances to you successfully making the break into self-employment.

If you have experienced one of these shocks, the comfortable niche in life that you have created for yourself may suddenly feel restrictive and unsatisfactory. Your response may be to try to seize control of your own life by creating your own job.

Obviously, this shock theory does not explain everyone's decision. There are those for whom starting on their own is a positive, not a negative, move. Some have mapped out their lives to include starting their own business. There are others for whom being an entrepreneur seems commonplace, because most of their family are either self-employed or have started a business. But there is no doubt that the proverbial kick up the backside is the starting point for many a new venture.

Starting your own business is likely to become a more normal state of affairs. With the lack of security in corporate life and the focus on entrepreneurship in big companies, running your own business can even become part of your career plan for moving in and out and back into corporate existence. Starting your own business will become normal, not abnormal.

The conclusions that can be reached from this are that:

■ not everyone has the necessary ingredients for success.

■ there may be many people who live out their working lives as employees who possess the vital skills and characteristics in full, but fail to take advantage of them.

What do you want?

An important part of your self-analysis should include what it is you hope to achieve by starting a business. Motives may range from achieving monetary gain to enhancing status to establishing a comfortable working environment to combining work and home responsibilities. You could have a combination of business and personal objectives. It may be a helpful exercise to note what your objectives are under the following headings, which are not exhaustive:

■ *money*: how much? when? in what form? as much as possible? enough to live on?

■ *working hours*: number of hours? amount of holiday? flexibility?

■ *risks*: like a gamble? only low risk acceptable? prefer calculated risks?

■ *stress*: looking for lower levels of stress? can cope with stress?

■ *type of work*: want to be able to do the work you like? want to choose which work to do and which work to leave for others? want to concentrate on what you are good at? feel your skills are being wasted? want to achieve your full potential?

■ *independence*: fed up with being told what to do? no longer wish to explain your actions to your superiors? think you can do better?

■ *achievement*: want to have the feeling of satisfaction that building your own business can bring? like to set yourself standards to achieve? to see if you can do it where others fail?

■ *power*: looking for the sense of power that being the boss can give? want to enhance your reputation or status? want to do better than someone else?

■ *personal relations*: want to get away from the problems of having to coexist amicably with others? prefer the feeling of isolation? happier on your own, away from irritating workmates?

■ *any other objectives?*

Once you have drawn up a list of objectives that you hope to achieve from being your own boss, you need to assess how realistic these are. A number you will find fit ideally with the notion of being self-employed; others will be quite contradictory. Part of your self-analysis should be to see how good or how bad a match your objectives are to the reality.

What will it be like?

Most probably the answer is much worse than you can imagine. There are a few people who start out and find the whole operation flows smoothly from the beginning; there are others who pretend everything is going well, while the reality is quite different; and there are others who openly admit how hard it is. One of the more dispiriting aspects is that while you may expect hard work for one or two years, it could continue for several.

The government publishes survival rates for new businesses in the UK. The data show that, after one year, around one in ten new businesses has failed. After three years, three out of ten have ceased trading. Taking advice, such as counselling or training, is likely to improve your chance of success – research suggests you are 20 per cent more likely to still be in business after 2½ years if you have taken advice at the outset.

If you manage to survive, life will not always be easy. Your business life may follow this pattern:

■ *money*: your income can prove to be a problem. At the outset, if not later on, you may find you cannot draw as much income from your business as you would like. Initially, you will need extra funds to fall back on; it can be very helpful if you have a spouse or partner who is earning.

■ *working hours*: surveys show that nearly two-thirds of self-employed entrepreneurs and bosses running their own companies regularly use weekends to catch up on the paperwork and admin tasks that inevitably go with running a business. On average they work 55 hours a week, and three-quarters say they have to work even when ill. While, in theory, you can choose your working hours and be flexible, in practice you may find that you work all the hours possible. If your business is not going well, you will need dedication, drive and energy to overcome problems; even if the business starts off well, you may still find you cannot turn your back on it, because you want to make as much money as possible in case things start going wrong! You cannot win: until your business is well established you need to work long hours.

▪ *risks*: a gamble is an unlikely basis for a successful business; but if you only want to pursue low-risk ventures, you may be short of ideas to follow up. You stand the best chance if you are prepared to take calculated risks that allow you to make a sound estimate of the chances of success.

▪ *stress*: come what may, running your own business is a very stressful experience. You need to be able to cope with it or to seek advice on ways of overcoming it. Stress is not only caused by business problems; it may also occur in your domestic life as a result of allowing the business to overwhelm you. Your spouse/partner and close members of your family need to be very supportive and to be prepared for what is to come.

▪ *type of work*: you need to be a jack of all trades. Unless you are forming a partnership or hope to raise sufficient funds to allow you to employ someone who can complement your own skills, you will find you act as salesperson, technical expert, accountant, administrator or whatever. The wider the range of skills you possess, the greater your chance of success. Be honest about what you can do well and what you do badly. If there are gaps, consider being trained in the area of inadequacy (see Chapter 3, 'A spot of coaching') or try to make sure you can afford expert assistance.

▪ *independence*: you remain totally independent in your business decisions only if you never borrow or raise money. Once you have done that, you may find that you have to explain your actions, although not usually on a day-to-day basis.

▪ *achievement*: founding and controlling a successful business can yield a tremendous sense of achievement, but what happens if there are failures? What would be your reaction? To be a successful business manager, you need to be able to deal with failure. You must be able to accept failure without finding the effect devastating and yet to draw all the lessons possible from it, so that in future you will not make a similar mistake and your performance will be improved.

■ *power*: power can be a destructive influence in a business. There is no problem if you are a sole trader, but once you begin employing staff, you are trying to operate your business through others. Should the desire for power lead you to try to control employees in a way that is counterproductive for their work performance, your power will be a negative influence on the success of your business. Managing people properly is more important.

■ *personal relations*: one of the advantages of running your own show is that you select the people who work for you, and (provided you do not discriminate unlawfully – see Chapter 21) if you do not like them you do not need to employ them. But if you find it difficult to associate in a friendly manner with most people, you are unlikely to be a successful owner-manager. You need to be able to establish good relations with suppliers and customers, as well as with those you employ.

Why will you succeed?

The conventional view is that your business is more likely to be successful if it fulfils three criteria:

1 The people involved realistically assess their strengths and weaknesses and try to overcome shortcomings. This could apply to you alone if your business is as a sole trader. Or, if it is on a larger scale, it means you as the leading figure plus the rest of your management team should be balanced and with no obvious lack of skills. The quality of the management (you and others) is the most important criterion.
2 The idea and the market for it has the necessary growth potential and you have experience in that market.
3 Financing is sufficient to cover the shortfall of working capital (p. 293), especially in the early days.

If you cannot fulfil these criteria at the moment, do not accept defeat; you may be able to do so in the future. Most of the processes can be learned and acquired if your personality allows for realistic self-assessment. At this stage in the chapter, you should already have some self-knowledge about your strengths and weaknesses as an owner-manager. In Chapter 5, 'Are you sure?', the information is drawn together in a checklist (p. 54), which you can use as a quick test of where you stand.

Why will you fail?

You will fail if your operation does not match up well to the three criteria mentioned above. But some more specific problems are:

- overestimating sales and underestimating how long to achieve them.
- underestimating costs.
- failing to control costs ruthlessly.
- losing control over cash, that is, carrying too much stock, allowing customers too long to pay, paying suppliers too promptly.
- failing to identify your market because of inadequate market research.
- failing to adapt your product to meet customer needs and wants and failing to retain customers.
- lacking sufficient skills in one of the following areas: selling and marketing, financial, production, technical.
- failing to build a team that is compatible and complementary, if your business is on a larger scale.
- taking unnecessary risks.
- underpricing.

Many of these causes of failure are a result of lack of skills. Running your own business does not mean you have to be an expert at everything; but you do have to appreciate the importance of all these aspects so that you can control your business properly. Try to acquire an appreciation of the crucial factors to watch out for by seeking training or advice from others in those areas in which you are weak. Use this book as a starting point. If more help is needed, there are training courses and advice agencies (pp. 27, 31).

How big a business?

One factor to consider at an early stage is which track you are in – the fast-growth, medium-growth or slow-growth lane. You may know, from the assessment of your skills and character, that the most you aspire to is being a one-person business, pottering along steadily, making a good income for yourself. Or your analysis may convince you that, with the right funds and the right management team, you have the potential to look for swift growth. Your plans about raising money are determined by this consideration.

Your ideas

Frequently, the reason given for failing to take the step and start on your own is that you lack an idea of what you can produce and sell. This may be because there is a misconception about what is needed for a business to be successful. Your idea does not have to be novel, original or revolutionary. If it is, it may be helpful; but equally, it could be a hindrance. Trying to sell a product or service that has not been available previously can be an uphill struggle. Being first is not always best. The first to offer such a product has to educate a market and possibly establish a distribution structure. The second or third into a market can capitalize on all the effort and investment made by their predecessors. The moral is that you should not veer away from an idea because it is not original.

However, it does not follow that you can offer something identical to another business. If you do, how can the potential customer choose? It could only be on the basis of price (p. 170), which suggests that you will struggle to make a profit unless you can sell in volume. The ideal product or service to choose as a basis for your business is one that you can distinguish from the competition by including some additional feature or benefit that is not available in other products.

If you are starting from scratch, how do you come up with a business idea? The first stage is to draw up a shortlist of two, three or four ideas that you can define and research before selecting the one to run with.

There are two possible ways of choosing an idea:

1 Using an established skill, product or knowledge; in general, this gives you the greatest chance of success.
2 Identifying a market that looks ripe for development by your business and acquiring the necessary technique and knowledge.

In reality, the approaches must be closely interlinked; your business will not succeed if you have the skill or product but not the market, and vice versa.

What are your skills?

The logical business idea for most people is to choose an area in which they already have considerable expertise. Many self-employed people are simply practising their own acquired knowledge, such as engineers, solicitors, design consultants. Your expertise may be acquired as a result of your education or training on the job. If you have been employed as a manager of a supermarket, one obvious idea is to do the same but on your own. Or you may have worked in the computer industry and so possess considerable knowledge about products, the market and distribution.

Many people also opt to begin a business using a skill that they have acquired in their spare time as a hobby. Obvious examples are the craft-type business, such as jewellery-making and pottery. The disadvantage with these is that you have not acquired any of the business knowledge needed to turn hobbies into a living. You will not know the suppliers or the distribution network, for example. However, given determination, this disadvantage should not be insuperable. A more serious problem may emerge later: you may have decided to base your business on a pastime because you found it enjoyable; but a few months of struggling to keep your head above water can soon turn a pleasure into a chore.

Which is the best market?

An alternative to choosing an idea based on your existing skills and knowledge would be to research some markets in which you believe there are profitable opportunities. The ideal market to base your business in is one that:

- is growing or is large.
- is supplied by businesses that are not efficient or are outdated.
- has a niche or sector (p. 14) that you can exploit.
- is not heavily dependent on price to help consumers to select one product rather than another.
- is not already supplied by products that are heavily branded; that is, there is not considerable customer loyalty to products from one or more businesses.
- is not dominated by two or three very large suppliers but instead has a number of smaller would-be competitors.

In practice, there is only a remote chance of finding such a market; and if you did, so would many other businesses, which would make it very competitive. But it would be unwise to base your business in a market that does not come up with some of these positive indicators. The moral is, do not be afraid of competitors; they prove that there is business there to get.

It is difficult to enter a market if you have none of the technical skills or industry knowledge necessary. In particular, if you need to raise money, the decision-makers will want to see some, if not considerable, knowledge and experience in that market. If you do not have it, you have to concentrate instead on demonstrating your all-round business skills and experience, the strength offered by your character and abilities, and the research you have undertaken into your chosen market.

No ideas at all?

If you cannot come up with an idea on your own, do not despair. Try organizing what is called a brainstorming session. Ask two or three colleagues, friends or relations to join a discussion. Hold it as a proper meeting in peace and quiet, with paper and pencil in front of you. Spend a couple of minutes outlining the sort of idea you are after and what you have already considered but dismissed and why. Ask for their reactions and cross your fingers that some ideas will emerge. A brainstorming session need not last a long time. Probably a quarter or half an hour will be sufficient.

Defining your ideas

At this stage, you may not have focused on just one idea but still be considering two or more. Whether it is only one or several, your next step is to draw up a pen portrait of each idea. Clearly, some of the aspects will be nothing more than wild guesses; you will need to carry out research before encapsulating your final choice in a detailed business plan with realistic forecasts. The brief sketch should define the following points:

■ a description of the product or service.

■ an indication of why it will sell.

■ a description of the intended market: UK, Europe or global.

■ your estimate of the approximate price.

■ how you think it will be sold.

■ a first stab at the amount of sales you can make.

■ how it will be made, if it is a product.

■ its approximate cost.

■ whether revenues are likely to be more than costs.

Having drawn up these broad-brush definitions of a couple of the most promising ideas, you will find that during the detailed estimation and calculation stage, one idea will emerge as the favourite. You can concentrate on developing this one into your business plan.

Summary

1 An unusual aspect of starting your own business is that you make the decision yourself that you have the necessary qualities and abilities to make a success of it.

2 Analyse what you expect and hope to achieve from your own business.

3 Do not underestimate the problems and difficulties that emerge for business owners.

4 Use the checklists in Chapter 5, 'Are you sure?' (pp. 54, 56, 57, 61), to identify your weaknesses and strengths.

5 Use the many training courses and advice agencies listed in Chapter 3, 'A spot of coaching' (p. 27), to help to improve those weaknesses.

6 Do not be dissuaded from launching a business because you do not have an original idea. With the right management and a promising marketplace, a well-worn idea can be successful.

7 The market can be crucial in determining success or failure (rated second most important factor after management by providers of finance). Carry out detailed market research following the advice in Chapter 2, 'Who will buy?' (p. 13).

8 Develop brief descriptions of a couple of ideas before researching more thoroughly. Select the favourite and make up a detailed business plan before setting up the business.

Other chapters to read

2 Who will buy? (p. 13); 5 Are you sure? (p. 54); 7 Timing the jump (p. 69).

2

Who will buy?

By now you have probably narrowed down your shortlist of ideas. You may know which market you want to enter; you may have got your eye on a product that you think has potential. What you must do next is to study your prospective marketplace in detail. Researching the marketplace comes before raising money, making profit and cash flow forecasts, finding premises or any of the other steps you have to take to form your business.

This is especially true if you need to raise money for your proposed business and have to produce a business plan. You will not obtain financial backing unless you can show with confidence that you understand the structure of your market and have a clear idea of where your product will be positioned compared with the competition. The crucial questions are who will be your customers, why will they buy from you and how much can you sell.

Knowing the number of customers is not the only information yielded by studying the marketplace. More importantly, you should be able to obtain information about what your potential customer needs. This, in turn, should aid you to angle your product or service to satisfy the greatest demand.

It is much easier to persuade people to purchase something they already want; educating a market to buy your product if the market has expressed no great desire for it can be a long haul.

An asterisk (*) after the name of an organization or source indicates that contact details are given in the Reference section.

What is in this chapter?

This chapter is about market research and how you can proceed to find out about your particular market. But the first part of the chapter concentrates on what it is you need to know, rather than how to carry out the research.

First, the chapter helps you to define the bit (or segment) of the market you are specifically going for, *who will buy?* (p. 14): which are your customers and what are their common characteristics?

The next section, *why will they buy?* (p. 17), helps you to form your sales proposition to your target market. What are the main features and benefits that your potential customers are looking for? Can your product supply them? This process helps you to define your service or product specifically, and in relation to the competition, so that your product is differentiated from the run-of-the-mill.

The third section, *how much will they buy?* (p. 19), leads into how you can utilize the information to make realistic sales forecasts.

The final section, *how to do the research* (p. 22), looks at the nitty-gritty of carrying out the market research needed. How is it done? What sources do you use? Are some more important than others?

Who will buy?

Knowing which market and which product is only the start of the work you need to do before you will be able to begin selling. First, you have to research the market. You are not simply looking for lots of statistics to blind potential backers. You need the details to help you to plan your business strategy.

It would be a mistake to assume that you have an equal chance of selling to every customer in your market. If it is that sort of market, it implies that you are looking for volume sales. In turn, this suggests a market that is very sensitive to price levels and in which it is difficult to sort out one product from another. If this is the sort of business you are planning, think carefully. Few small businesses have the resources to make a success of this.

Basically, you should be looking for a niche in your proposed market that allows you to charge a reasonable price and so maintain reasonable profit margins. To achieve this, your product needs to be clearly distinguishable from the competition (called product differentiation).

The purpose of your research at this stage is to look for that niche. This process is called market segmentation. In everyday language, it means looking for a group of customers within your target market that has common characteristics, tastes and features. If you can find such a group, it allows you to tailor your product to meet its particular needs. Your search for a market segment need not be confined to the UK – extend your horizons and see if you can identify a market segment running across Europe or even the world. With the development of the Internet as a sales distribution channel, the world has shrunk and even small businesses can sell worldwide.

Once you have sorted out the groups, you must look at the competitive position. Are there already suppliers to that group of people? The existence of competition does not mean that you should not try to enter the market, but it does mean that you need to be able to offer customers some additional benefit in your service or product, and it must be a benefit they want.

For a small firm, a strong attraction of using this market segment approach to sales is that you may be able to achieve a dominant position in that segment. This could mean becoming the market leader, with its attendant advantages of selling more at a higher price (p. 177).

If your business is on a smaller scale (perhaps only yourself or a couple of employees), it still makes sense to look for a niche, because of the advantages of being able to keep your prices above rock-bottom.

There are several different ways of grouping people. You could group people according to where they live, what kind of work they do or what their hobbies are. Other interesting characteristics to identify include behaviour in purchasing. Is price the key factor, for example?

What makes a useful market grouping?

The fact that you can identify a group of people with similar tastes in your target market does not necessarily mean that you have unlocked a source of sales. To be useful, a market grouping needs to have certain characteristics. First, the segment needs to be big enough to give you the living you require. You must also be able to differentiate it from other groups, so that its size can be measured. Another necessary characteristic is that the segment must be easy to reach. If not, you will experience problems getting your message across or supplying the product because of location. Finally, the group must have common features that actually lead to similar buying decisions.

A step-by-step analysis to identifying market groupings

1 Is your target market a consumer market? Or is it an industrial or professional market? If it is a consumer one, go to 2; if it is industrial or professional, go to 9.

2 Look at family and personal factors. Would age, sex, family size or marital status form the basis of different groups?

3 Is your product the sort that relies on supplying a local area? Location may be an important feature of a group.

4 Look at social class. Could this be important for your product?

5 Can you distinguish groups of potential customers on the basis of how much or how little they use or buy your product? Could your product be tailored to appeal to heavy or light users?

6 Are there psychological or social factors at work? Could the product appeal to those wishing to 'better themselves'? Is lifestyle important? Would prospective customers be likely to 'follow the crowd' or want to be seen as stylish? Could there be snob or prestige appeal?

7 Price could be a feature that distinguishes one group from another. Is there an element of value for money in a target group's make-up? Some people go for the cheapest, no matter what. Most customers would say that they want good value for the money they spend.

8 How do the potential customers buy? Local shop, large supermarket or store? Mail order? The Web? Can you create a niche out of distribution methods? Now go to 14.

9 What type of industry will you be selling into? You could specialize in one industry or profession (called vertical marketing).

10 How big are the companies or businesses you are likely to sell to? Size can mean different procedures in buying and in frequency of purchasing. Can you create a distinguishing product benefit from the need to satisfy large, medium or small businesses?

11 Will one group of potential customers require quicker or more frequent deliveries than others?

12 Price could well create different market segments in industrial or professional users.

13 Will one group of customers be looking for a higher level of after-sales care or maintenance? Could this be your distinguishing product feature?

14 Consider what other categories might apply to your market. Each market will have its own specialized characteristics apart from the general ones listed above.

15 Now look to see if there is a group with more than one of the characteristics listed above. This could define your target group.

What do you know about your likely customers?

To help you to understand your potential customers, and to help you to sell to them, you need to know a range of information about them. If it is a business you are selling to, you need to have information on the organization and buying policies. Investigate the other suppliers to your customers and acquire and analyse information on the products bought by them.

Databases are the key. Set up a database for information about your potential customers and gather and collate as much as you can within the legal limits allowed. Interrogating databases will help you to target potential customers more effectively.

Why will they buy?

Before you can answer this question, you have to find out what your customer wants. What are the benefits and features of a service or product that your target group rates most highly? Research is essential (p. 22).

Once you have the framework of your customer needs, you can begin to vary your service or product with the aim of meeting those customer wants and needs more successfully than any other supplier. There are a number of ways in which your sales package (that is, your product/service plus a range of other sales features of your business) can be altered to achieve the desired objective. These include:

■ *appearance*: what material is the product made of? Does it look stylish? How about the colour? How is it packaged or presented? All these can be changed to match your target customer profile. If appearance is an important feature for your target group, it may be worth using a designer to help you to achieve this (p. 207).

■ *delivery time*: if speed or reliability of delivery is important to your potential customers, concentrate on how you can improve or stabilize your delivery times.

■ *maintenance*: does your target market look for prompt attention to faults? Or frequent maintenance visits? Adjust your strategy to allow for this.

■ *performance*: identify the main requirement – for example, it may be speed, reliability or a low level of noise. This sort of consideration should be taken into account when you specify your product. If it is already past the specification stage, can it be altered?

■ *quality*: this is rather an ethereal topic, as quality can be subjective, existing in the eye of the beholder. Or it can be objective, for example the evenness of the stitching. You can create an impression of quality by building up the image or reputation of the product to suggest this (p. 129). The appearance of quality tends to depend on all the variables of a product: appearance, service, packaging, reliability, performance and so on.

By adjusting your service/product in this way to meet the wants and needs of your target market, you are trying to establish that you have at least one unique feature that your competitors don't. Use this as the basis of your selling message to persuade people to buy. Your target market will buy if you convince them that it meets a need, conscious or unconscious. If your competitors already meet these needs, it is difficult to see what additional benefit your product can offer, but usually there is something.

It would be a mistake to believe that buyers act in a rational way, comparing products and choosing their purchase on the basis of some organized assessment. Even in an industrial market, buyers are affected by a number of emotional factors, sometimes not openly admitted. These can include wanting to be like someone else, to be considered stylish or a leader, or to be liked. Your potential customers may also want the best, a change, or to improve their personal standing. They may be trying to outdo the competition or to gain revenge on another person or business. So, if your product can't be differentiated in practical benefits, can it be distinguished in emotional ways?

One possible way you could think about your target market is to consider how it would match up to the range of cars available. Each car model has tried to establish its own niche, and it is possible to categorize your target buyers by the car you imagine they might buy. For example, if your market is likely to buy a Ford Fiesta, you can picture them as young, wanting something cheap and cheerful and not minding the lack of comfort. If it is a Rolls-Royce, your customers are looking for the ultimate in prestige, comfort and specification. A BMW is an executive car, indicating business success and achievement; the car is stylish and luxurious. And so on.

Once you have a mental picture of what your target group is looking for in a car, you might be able to use this picture to adapt your service or product to meet those same needs.

How much will they buy?

This is the third question that market research should help you to answer. You cannot plan your business unless you have some estimate of how much you are going to sell and when that is likely to happen. You need this data to help you to formulate your sales and cash forecasts.

The level of sales you can make over the years depends on:

■ the market size.

■ the market structure.

■ the market share you can establish (and the competition you face).

■ the market trends; that is, whether it is growing, static or declining.

■ the investment in time and money to sell your product.

You need to be able to forecast how much you need to put in to get sales established and how long this will take. Many business failures occur because this is underestimated. And many businesses would not start at all if the development period was accurately forecast at the outset.

Market size

The first step is knowing the market size. This could be either its monetary value or the number of units sold. Beyond this you need an estimate of the market potential, which is unlikely to be the same figure as market size because it is unlikely that everyone in the market will buy your, or an equivalent, product. Obviously, if you have the figure for the overall market but have decided to concentrate your business resources on a particular market segment, your next step is to assess the size of that particular segment. Even then, this may not give you your estimated market potential (the amount of sales you stand some chance of being able to make over a period of years).

Market structure

This is the process by which a product is sold to the end-consumer. Market structures constantly evolve, and the world economy is currently undergoing a rapid restructuring with the development of the Internet as a tool to sell products on a global basis direct to end-consumers. Over the last twenty years, distribution has moved away from face-to-face selling to selling by direct mail, telephone, Internet. A key stage in selling used to be the role of intermediaries, businesses were placed somewhere between the end-consumer and the end-producer. Intermediaries include agents, distributors and brokers. But the restructuring of the global economy is squeezing this sector as a distribution channel. Nowadays intermediaries need to offer more than just a range of products: service is crucial.

The routes for direct selling include direct mail, telephone, e-mail, Internet, through your own web site, face to face, in person and retail outlets.

But not all markets can be reached by direct selling, and small businesses may find that selling through others, or a chain of others, is still a lower-cost alternative. These can include distributors, agents, brokers, through an Internet portal or someone else's web site.

If you sell through others, you have to pay them a royalty or commission or sell to them at a lower price than you would sell to the end-consumer.

Market share

Unless you are supplying a completely new product or service, you are going to share the market with other businesses. To be in a dominant position (that is, the supplier of 25 per cent or more of the market) would be very rare for a small business.

To be able to forecast your sales you are going to need some idea of what share of the market your competitors have. You also need information about your competitors' businesses and products to enable you to position and price your own offering. Knowing the market shares gives you a measure of how successful the other businesses have been.

Monopolies are unusual, but there may be a duopoly (two businesses supplying 25 per cent or more of the market each) or an oligopoly (three, four or five businesses dominating it). However, many small businesses are likely to face a fragmented supply position, where there are lots of suppliers and one business is unlikely to achieve more than 5 per cent of the market. This is particularly true if it is a new industry or market.

Measuring market share is one thing, achieving it another. But there are some ways of influencing the share you can seize. On the whole, it is helpful to build a reputation for good, consistent quality. For this to be translated into market share, a second influence is maintaining a reasonable level of marketing activity: PR, advertising and sales activity. A third influence is if your product is recognized as being ahead of the competition in performance, design or whatever.

Look at your competitors in a detailed fashion. The data it would be helpful to have include:

■ what are the competing products and how much do they sell?

■ how well have they done in the last few years?

■ how is the company organized?

■ how is its selling carried out?

■ if it produces goods, how is it done and what are the facilities?

■ who are the main customers?

■ what is the pricing policy and what sort of delivery is offered?

Market trends

Market size, market structure and market shares do not remain the same. What happens today may be totally irrelevant to what is happening in one, two or three years' time. The usual method of deciding what is going to happen in the future is to look at what has happened in the past and project it forwards. This approach is fraught with dangers. At the very least, you need to adjust the figures for changes that may occur or are forecast to occur.

On a general level, anticipated changes in the economy can affect the buying patterns of individual markets. There may be changes forecast in tax or other laws that will influence purchasing decisions. New information may emerge on the effect of certain items (for example, health hazards).

On a more specific level, there may be changes caused by government or local authority policy. And so on. You need to look closely at your market to guess what changes will occur that might affect the market trends. In any conversations with people already operating in the market, remember to ask what likely changes they think are on the cards. You may be better able to take advantage of them as a new entrant with no constraints from existing products, methods of operating or overheads.

Investment needed in sales

You need to make realistic forecasts of how much you will sell, when you will be able to do it and what you need to spend on selling and promotion to achieve it. Inevitably, if you are starting your own business, you are optimistic, but do not let optimism blind you to the uncertainty of making sales.

If you are in any doubt, a rule of thumb is to double the length of time you expect it will take you to achieve a certain level of sales. In this way, you will organize sufficient funds to keep the business going until you reach break-even. The danger of this rule of thumb is that your business may not seem sufficiently attractive to lenders and investors. Keep a balance.

It might be possible to obtain a more reliable estimate of sales by carrying out tests (p. 25) on a limited basis, though this is tricky for a small business.

How to do the research

There are a number of techniques for researching a market. The ways open to a small business are likely to be fewer than to a larger organization, simply because of money. In many cases, it will be you, the owner, who does the research. The basic research methods for small businesses include:

- web research, studying competitor's web sites and looking for market and industry information.
- desk research, studying directories and other literature.
- interviews with customers, suppliers, competitors, distributors and ex-employees of competitors.
- tests.

Web research

With a computer and a modem, you have an enormous treasury of information at your fingertips in the Internet. If you do not have your own Internet access, bear in mind that you can now log on at most public libraries, through many community facilities, such as adult learning centres, and at cyber cafés. The World Wide Web lets you tap into computers around the world to gather a diverse range of data and ideas. However, there is so much information out there that it is easy to get bogged down. You need to use a good 'search engine' to help you to find your way around. A search engine is a piece of software within the Internet that searches for items on the Web by keyword or key phrase. Different search engines are better suited to different tasks, for example:

- *Google* is rapid and comprehensive. Hone down the very large number of entries you'll probably get by using precise, multiple keywords.
- *alltheweb.com*, owned by Yahoo!, includes advanced search tools to help you to hone your search.

■ *webcrawler.com* aims to improve coverage by combining the best results from several search engines, including Google, Yahoo! and Ask.com.

■ *www.yell.com* is the Internet version of *Yellow Pages* and lets you search by business type and location.

A lot of useful information from different government departments, such as the Department for Business, Enterprise and Regulatory Reform* and Her Majesty's Revenue & Customs*, can be found on the web sites of these departments or on the government's general site at *http://www.direct.gov.uk*.

Desk research

The main sources of information are:

■ directories.

■ government information.

■ information from within your own business, if already up and running – keep good sales records and encourage your employees to be on the look-out for market information.

■ trade associations.

■ the trade press and special features in the quality papers.

■ competitors' literature.

■ published statistics and reports.

■ former colleagues.

Your starting point for a lot of information can be your local lending library or the reference library. You will need to organize your research in a systematic way, because the danger is that you may end up with too much information, a lot of it irrelevant, and with no way of being able to gain quick and easy access to the data that matters.

If you plan to sell locally, your local authority might be a source of useful reports and survey statistics. You could also try your local chamber of trade or commerce, though these vary greatly in size and resources.

There are also the trade sources of information. Find out which are the trade magazines and, if they are not free, take out subscriptions. Organize cuttings files. Contact the relevant trade association and obtain information about its members. Check out their web sites. Use trade exhibitions as an opportunity to pick up literature about your competitors and talk to potential customers about the market, the suppliers, the products and the gaps.

A useful background resource is HM Revenue & Customs' range of 'Tactical and Information Packages' (TIPs). These are detailed profiles of particular business sectors (that tax officers use to help them decide whether profits are being correctly declared). You can find TIPs on the Revenue web site (*www.hmrc.gov.uk/tips/index.htm*). In spring 2007, the following sectors were available, though more were due to be added: estate agents; mortgage brokers; franchises; confectioners, tobacconists and newsagents; and waste disposal and landfill sites.

Interviews

The term 'interview' can cover anything from a chat at an exhibition to a brief telephone call, to a long face-to-face discussion in private. The main point is that you can pick up a lot of information simply by talking.

Whether you have started your business or not, good sources of information are customers, potential or actual. If you have access to a list, properly gathered and complying with the Data Protection Act, you could carry out a telephone survey, limiting each interview to ten minutes, say. It would help you to analyse the information if you had prepared a questionnaire sheet. On the whole, you will find that most customers are usually ready to cooperate, as it may mean you develop a product more suited to their needs. Carry on the number of telephone interviews until you begin to feel that you are learning nothing new, because the same points are being repeated.

If you want detailed information, you will find that the telephone is not the best method of acquiring it. Instead, try to carry out a number of in-depth interviews.

If you are researching a consumer market, you should try to talk to the distributors and retailers as well as to the end-users. Most people are flattered to be asked their 'professional' opinion. Talking to the final consumers can be a bit of a problem because you may not know who these are. Perhaps a retailer will allow you to spend a day in the shop talking to customers? Asking people in the street outside the store is another possibility.

If your product is likely to be exhibited at trade fairs for the consumer, spend some time there asking about the market and product. Use a brief questionnaire to ensure that you ask the same questions so that the information can be analysed.

Interviewing competitors may sound an odd idea, but there is no harm in it and it can help you to understand what are common problems. If you come across any ex-employees of competitors, it is always worth a discussion, although you have to bear in mind that their view may not be entirely objective if they did not part with the business on good terms. And the information may be out of date.

Before you start your business, you could carry out some discreet research into how the competition organizes their businesses by pretending to be a prospective customer. In this way you can gain some idea of the literature, prices, the way telephone queries are dealt with, selling methods or even how your potential competitors quote. It may seem unfair, but it is an unrivalled source of information and you may rest assured that once you are in business others will do it to you.

Tests

It would be a great help to you if you could test-market your product, especially if you will be setting up production facilities or ordering very large quantities. If you can try out a few before you make the substantial investment needed, you would be able to refine the product, satisfy yourself that the demand does exist and define the likely sales cycle (the length of time from first contact to purchase). To test this, buyers of the trial product need to be followed up and interviewed.

If you are selling by phone or direct mail, you can test your product and your offer before launching into selling in volume. A pilot mail shot to say 5,000 potential customers can give you a huge amount of information about the likely response and sales.

Summary

1 Market research that is undirected is not very useful; it needs to concentrate on who will buy, why they will buy and how much they will buy.
2 It is much easier to sell a product that meets some already perceived need rather than to try to educate a market to buy a new, perhaps revolutionary, product or service.
3 Look for groups within your target market that you think you can sell to, either because no one is currently selling to them or because you can adapt your product to meet their needs.
4 Use the step-by-step analysis (p. 16) to identify a suitable market group.
5 Rational and emotional factors affect your target group's willingness to buy. Research these and alter your product or sales approach to match.

6 Knowing how much customers will buy is crucial to your business planning. You need to research market size, market structure, market share, the competition and market trends.

7 Try to carry out your research in a systematic way so that it can be properly analysed. Use desk research, interviews and test trials, if possible.

Other chapters to read

12 The right name (p. 128); **13** Getting the message across (p. 136); **14** Getting new customers (p. 149); **15** Building customer relationships (p. 163); **16** How to set a price (p. 170).

3

A spot of coaching

'I don't have the time' might be the instant reaction of a budding entrepreneur if it is suggested that training or asking for advice would be beneficial. At the other end of the spectrum, there may be people who could make a success of self-employment but 'don't know how to start'.

Training, counselling and seeking advice can all improve your chances of success, so do not dismiss the idea. If you have not yet started on your own, try to fit in some sort of training before you do so. If you are already under way, look around to see what training or help is available to fit in with your schedule – and don't wait until things are going wrong. Give yourself the greatest chance of success and consider it now.

There are an extraordinary number of organizations able to help new or small businesses – the network of Business Links*, local enterprise agencies (LEAs)*, local enterprise companies (LECs)* in Scotland, the Department for Education and Lifelong Learning and Skills (DELLS)* in Wales, Learn Direct*, local chambers of commerce*, economic development units of local authorities, banks, accountants and local colleges. However, you can tap into the vast majority of sources of help through your local Business Link* (Business Gateway* and Highlands and Islands Enterprise* in Scotland, Business Eye* in Wales or InvestNI* in Northern Ireland).

Training courses

Obviously, the main purpose of attending a training course is to learn new skills and techniques. But a secondary purpose is that it gives you an opportunity to meet people with similar problems and possibly meet potential partners, suppliers and customers.

The diversity of courses available makes it difficult to describe an average course. On the other hand, this very diversity should ensure that you will find a course run somewhere that meets your needs and suits your personality, although obviously you do not want to travel too far.

How long is a course?

The length of courses available varies. There may be a one- or two-day taster. Or there could be a series of short modular courses, attended part-time (say, at weekends, in the evenings or spread over several weeks or months). Learn Direct* offers a wide array of courses which you can complete over the Internet at your own pace.

What topics are covered?

The content of most of the general self-employment or small business courses leans heavily on the financial side. Topics such as cash flows, business plans and sources of finance, financial control, tax and book-keeping are covered. There should also be a substantial content on selling and marketing. Apart from these key areas, other topics that may be covered include premises, information technology, employment law, recruiting, time management, exporting, and other legal aspects of business and insurance.

As well as general courses, some organizations run more specialized ones, for example a two-day course concentrating on finance or marketing. If you feel fairly confident in general about your business expertise, this sort of course could help you to brush up your knowledge in your weakest area.

What sort of training?

Inevitably, with a fair number of courses, quite a lot of the information and training is given in a fairly traditional classroom format. However, in all courses there should be discussion and questions. The success of the course can depend as much on the quality and interest of the participants as the trainers. Before you choose a course, try to find out a bit about the type of participants attending the course to gauge if it is the right level for you.

An increasing number of courses are trying to introduce a 'hands-on' approach. Your business plan will be presented to a trainer and the other course participants for discussion, suggestion and improvement. On a few courses, there may be an opportunity to present your plan to someone from a bank or other source of funds. This could simply be a training exercise. However, if you present your case well, the bank may want to discuss your business idea in more detail.

Attending a course in person is often the best route because of the chance to network with other people. But if this would be difficult – for example, you can't take time away from business during the day – an alternative is online learning. You study over the Internet at times convenient to you and at the pace of your own choosing. One of the biggest providers of courses over the Internet is the government through its Learn Direct* initiative, which offers a large range of courses designed for small businesses. If you don't have access to a computer at home, you can study from a learning centre, typically based in local schools, colleges and community centres.

Who runs the courses?

Courses are run by a wide variety of organizations, including training and enterprise councils, local enterprise agencies or colleges of further education or technology. The ideal trainer for a small business course is someone who has had experience of running a business and is a trained tutor. Before you choose a course, look at the backgrounds of the people running it.

One ingredient for successful business training can be the support that you can get before and after the training course itself. To maximize the benefit from the time you spend, look for an organization running the course that can provide counselling or has close links with one that does.

How to find a course

You can go direct to any of the sources listed below to find out about courses being run in your area. The Business Link* web site includes a good search tool to help you find workshops and seminars throughout the UK (follow the link to Training). Learn Direct* runs a helpline and Web-based directory that searches over 900,000 courses (face-to-face and distance learning) available throughout the UK. You search by postcode, type of course and/or venue, but results are a bit patchy, so don't assume a negative result means there is nothing available in your area. See the Reference section for how to find your nearest Learn Direct* centre, or to study from your own computer log on to *www.learndirect-business.com*.

How to choose a course

1 If you don't know whether training will meet your needs, ask for advice from your local LEC, LEA or DELLS or contact Learn Direct.
2 Decide whether you want a general or specialized course.
3 Try to find out about the trainers. Is there a good mix of practical business knowledge and teaching experience?
4 Find out about the kind of participants for whom the course is designed and, if possible, the individuals who will be on the course with you.
5 Ask if the training is mainly classroom based. Go for courses with practical emphasis on business plans, especially if there can be a mock presentation for raising finance.
6 See if pre- and post-course counselling is provided or easily arranged.
7 Check the cost – there may be training allowances available.
8 Check whether you can get tax relief on the cost. If the course is connected to your business and involves updating your skills, you should be able to deduct the cost as an allowable trading expense (see p. 356). If you are acquiring new skills, claim capital allowances or, from 2008, the new annual investment allowance (see p. 361).
9 Check the hours of the course and, if applicable, find out the childcare facilities. If you cannot get to a course, check out Learn Direct.

Counselling and consultancy

Help and advice on a one-to-one basis is given by counsellors. You could approach a variety of advice agencies at any stage of starting a business. Initially, counsellors can help by discussing your idea, and its strengths and weaknesses, and suggesting ways of carrying out market research.

At a later stage, counsellors can help you to prepare a business plan, including cash flows; you may even find a counsellor prepared to approach a bank manager with you. And counsellors will spend time with you if your business is hitting a sticky patch or if you feel you have a weakness in a particular area of your business and need fresh ideas or guidance.

The background of counsellors can vary a lot. All of them should be able to help in discussing your business idea, finding out about markets, preparing plans and budgets, advising on finance and helping you to find your way around the business world. If you need specialist advice or have more detailed problems, your counsellor will be able to help or will know who can.

Advice agencies very often will also provide an information service. So if you need to know a particular business fact and do not have the information at your fingertips, try ringing your local advice agency.

For established businesses, there may be a need for consultancy on specific topics: design, marketing, quality systems, manufacturing processes and so on. Agencies can signpost you to consultants and may be able to offer help at a 'fair' rate.

Who provides counselling or consultancy?

There are several sources:

1 *Business Link**. This network has changed substantially in recent years. It is being developed as a single, one-stop portal for all support for small businesses in England. In the past, Business Link provided its own advice and consultancy services, but now acts as a broker recommending and signposting you to appropriate agencies for the services you need. For example, you might be directed to your local enterprise agency (see below).
2 *Business Eye** is the Welsh equivalent of Business Link. It provides information and acts as a conduit, putting businesses seeking advice in contact with suitable agencies, such as your local enterprise agency (see below).
3 *Local enterprise agencies* (LEAs)*. This is a network of agencies operating throughout England and also Wales. There is no standard agency: they are dissimilar in name, size, how they are funded and what they can do for you. But they are all independent, not-for-profit bodies that share the common aim of supporting small and growing businesses. You can find your local LEA in England either through Business Link or by contacting the National Federation of Enterprise Agencies (NFEA)*. The NFEA itself runs the Small Business Advice Service which is an Internet-based scheme providing free and confidential advice in response to queries you submit. You can find Welsh LEAs through Business Eye.
4 *Business Gateway**. This is a network, providing a one-stop shop for new and growing businesses and delivering some of the services of Scottish Enterprise*, one of the two economic development agencies for Scotland. Business Gateway services include free one-to-one support from a business adviser.
5 *Local enterprise company* (LEC)*. Highlands & Islands Enterprise* is the other economic development agency for Scotland and delivers its business support services through its network of LECs. Services include free access to business advisers and counsellors.

6 *Invest NI** is the economic development agency for Northern Ireland. It offers various programmes to support businesses, but focuses on those that meet certain criteria. To become an Invest NI client, you need to be able to show that over the next three years your business will have sales over £100,000 a year with more than a quarter of your sales being to markets outside Northern Ireland. If your business is not eligible, you may still be able to use some of the advice and information services, for example, to help you develop export markets.

7 *Chambers of commerce**. Local chambers vary greatly in size and the resources they can offer. To find your local branch, see the phone book or contact the British Chambers of Commerce (BCC)*.

8 Other *ad hoc* agencies providing support for small businesses, such as Natural England*, English Heritage* and local authorities, which offer advice and sometimes grants to businesses where this helps also to achieve the particular aims of the agency.

9 *Banks*. Many banks offer specialist services for small businesses and have a network of small business centres or advisers. They can direct you to appropriate counselling organizations and information services.

Sharing problems with others

The business problem you are currently struggling with is unlikely to be unique; other businesses may have faced similar dilemmas. Picking someone else's brains can be a useful source of ideas and advice – if you can find the right brains, that is. One way of meeting other business people is to find out if there is a chamber of trade or commerce or a small business club operating in your area. Try asking in your local library or LEA (some enterprise agencies also run small business clubs).

The aims of clubs like these are variously to promote the growth of small business in a particular area or field, to keep small businesses informed of relevant information and legislation, to provide a social situation in which business can be discussed, to act as a voice for small businesses both locally and nationally and, possibly, to promote trade between members.

You may also find that there are web sites with chat forums, where you may find useful suggestions if you raise a problem.

If one of your problems is being too small to undertake effective marketing of your products, you could consider working with other businesses by forming a joint venture or consortium. This is sometimes called a purchasing or marketing cooperative. Contact your local Business Link*,

Business Gateway*, LEC* or Business Eye* to see if they can provide further information and assistance.

The media, books and exhibitions

Some of the national newspapers devote some space specifically to the small business sector. The *Financial Times*, the *Daily Express*, the *Guardian* and *The Times*, for example, have pages which include business-to-business ads for businesses offering or wanting services, products or money, or businesses to buy and sell or franchises available – but see p. 80 for how to find a business to buy. The pages also have some editorial. There may be an article on the experience of one small business, but there are also usually up-to-date bits of information, for example about training courses, exhibitions, books and new finance packages.

There are quite a number of books written for small businesses. Some of them aim to be comprehensive, such as this one; others are more selective in particular areas. You could contact your local library, whose staff can be very helpful on suggesting sources of information. The Internet contains numerous sites offering general business advice, including Business Link* and Small Business Advice Service* sites. Use the search engines (see p. 22) to track down other sites covering areas in which you are particularly interested.

At an early stage of your business planning, wandering around business exhibitions can give you some ideas and useful literature. These are also an opportunity to speak to some potential customers and competitors. Ask your Local Enterprise Agency* if there is soon to be a local exhibition or check out the directory of events on the Business Link* web site (follow the link to Training).

Other organizations

There are many trade associations covering different sectors – and you may gain information or support by joining one of them. There are also four well-known small business organizations that can lobby at a national level.

1. The Federation of Small Businesses*

This is the largest small business organization in the UK, representing over 205,000 small and medium-sized businesses. Its primary role is to act as a lobbying group promoting and protecting the interests of its members. But there are direct membership benefits too, including access to a business banking package and legal benefits service. Members also get two magazines and a range of special offers for insurance, debt collection, factoring and so on. The yearly membership is £100 for a sole trader working alone and £140 for businesses with one to four employees, increasing after that on a sliding scale according to the number of employees. There is also a £30 registration fee in the first year.

2. The Forum of Private Business*

The UK's leading pressure group, influencing laws and policies that affect private businesses, providing members with the support they need to grow profitably, and representing members' views to MPs and MEPs. The FPB represents 25,000 UK businesses and has campaigned on issues such as banking, late payments, employment law and red tape. Members can buy information guides at discounted rates, usually get free legal expenses insurance and are eligible for discounts on a range of business services. Membership costs start at £150 a year for a sole trader or business with up to ten employees.

3. The Small Business Bureau*

This is a group that lobbies Parliament on behalf of small and medium-sized companies. It produces a quarterly newspaper. The yearly subscription is £115 (including VAT). The subscription is reduced to £58.75 if you pay by standing order.

4. Professional Contractors Group*

PCG represents the freelance small business community. Its members include professional freelancers, contractors and consultants in, for example, IT, management, finance, engineering, oil and gas, telecoms and accounting. PCG campaigns on issues such as taxation, agency regulations and e-commerce regulations. Membership benefits include professional expenses insurance (to cover the fees of professionals employed during tax enquiries, VAT disputes, and so on), access to free tax and legal helplines, a contract vetting service, manuals to aid tax analysis and preferential rates from a range of suppliers. It also maintains a fighting fund to back suitable legal cases to establish important principles in tax and employment law. Standard membership starts at £120 + VAT for a sole trader or company with one fee-earner.

Advice aimed at specific groups

If you are relatively young and thinking of starting a business, or if you are unemployed with little prospect of obtaining employment, or a woman or from an ethnic minority, or an older person, you are often able to choose more specialized counselling or advice.

If you are from an ethnic minority, you may find that there is a local agency in your area especially to help members of ethnic minorities who start small businesses. Many other agencies now recognize that you may prefer to see a counsellor from an ethnic minority.

Here is some information on three specialist national organizations:

1. Instant Muscle*

Instant Muscle is a national charity and training provider that helps people who are disadvantaged and unemployed back into the labour market. Instant Muscle has over 30 centres across the UK. It provides mainstream support for people seeking work including one-to-one enterprise coun-selling and training to help people to set up their own small businesses. Instant Muscle specializes in helping economically, socially and physically disadvantaged individuals and its services are available to anyone regardless of their age, race, gender or circumstance.

Instant Muscle helps people to think about and plan a viable business start up. Clients are encouraged to identify their own skills and to look at the commercial possibilities of being self-employed. Training is geared towards producing a quality business plan. Advisers can also help you to approach organizations that may have funds available for the financing of the busi-ness and will help you to access facilities you may require to get started.

If, after preparing the business plan, self-employment does not look like the right option after all, Instant Muscle can provide professional job search guidance as an alternative.

2. Shell *Live*WIRE*

Shell *Live*WIRE is a UK-wide community investment programme funded by Shell UK Limited to stimulate young people aged 16–30 to explore the option of starting or developing their own business. As well as being active throughout the UK, *Live*WIRE programmes are now established in 24 coun-tries worldwide.

Through the web site or a hotline, young people can get free information tailored to them: for example, using the Start a Business Toolkit and Finance Action Planner, networking with other entrepreneurs, putting questions to online mentors and finding out where to get further business advice in their local area. Shell *Live*WIRE encourages sound business planning and continual monitoring of the business. The Shell *Live*WIRE Young Entrepreneur of the Year Awards Competition provides a £10,000 top prize to young owner-managers.

Shell *Live*WIRE operates through a UK-wide network of over 100 local co-ordinators, each of whom has been identified as a focal point for youth enterprise development.

3. The Prince's Trust*

The Prince's Trust helps 18 to 30-year-olds (18 to 25 in Scotland) to set up and run their own businesses, providing low-interest loans of up to £4,000 (sole trader) or £5,000 (partners), grants in specific cases of up to £1,500 for individuals or up to £3,000 for groups, test-marketing grants of up to £250, business advice and sales opportunities. To qualify for Trust support the young person must be unemployed or under-employed, have a viable business idea and be unable to raise the finance elsewhere.

Each new business is assigned its own volunteer business mentor – someone with suitable business experience – who offers advice to the business during the first three years of trading.

The work of the Trust is carried out through area offices. Each office has its own board made up of volunteers from the business community who decide who shall receive funding. A huge range of businesses are supported by the Trust – everything from hairdressers to farmers, computer experts to musicians.

4. The Prince's Initiative for Mature Enterprise (PRIME)*

PRIME is a not-for-profit organization linked to Age Concern that helps people over 50 start up in business. It offers free information and help, workshops, business networking events and, through partner organizations, free business advice. It can also provide loans of last resort (in other words, if a normal bank has turned you down). PRIME also lobbies government to remove barriers to older people's employment.

PRIME operates in England and Northern Ireland and, through PRIME-Cymru, in Wales.

Summary

1 A great deal of help and assistance is available to businesses in the UK, much of it free. Please make use of it, as it can help you to avoid mistakes.

2 Business Link provides a centralized source of information about what help is available. It is often your best starting point.

3 Choose your training course carefully. Check that it is a practical course with emphasis on your own business plans.

4 Counselling can be a useful source of advice, not just when you start but also when you have been in business for some time.

5 Other business people can provide help and contacts – see if there is a small business club in your area.

4

Your business identity

An important decision to make early on is to decide what legal form your business will take. Whatever you decide is not irrevocable, but it will take time and money to undo mistakes. You can choose between:

- sole trader.
- limited company.
- partnership (or limited liability partnership).
- cooperative.

If you want to work on your own, your choice is either sole trader or limited company. If you want to work with others, your choice is between partnership, limited liability partnership, limited company or cooperative (or a sole trader if you intend to employ others, rather than work with them).

The form you choose can hinge on emotional factors, as well as objective ones. If you choose a cooperative as your form, this may be because of political, social or ethical reasons. If you choose a partnership, this may be because you have a close colleague with whom you work well. However, the choice between a sole trader and limited company will probably be made for monetary reasons.

What is in this chapter?

This chapter compares the pros and cons of becoming a sole trader, a partnership, a limited liability partnership or a limited company. Next, the chapter shows you how to set up each of these legal forms. Finally, it looks briefly at forming a cooperative.

Which type of business form

There are twelve elements you have to look at so that you can weigh up the pros and cons of each legal form.

1. The credibility of the business

There is probably very little to choose between a sole trader and a conventional partnership when it comes to credibility. On the whole, it is thought that a limited company may give your business added credibility, but this may not work if a customer researches your company and finds, for example, that it has a paid-up capital of £100, which is typical for a very small business. An LLP (limited liability partnership) may also give an air of credibility to your venture, as it means you have to meet certain commitments at Companies House.

If you want to acquire a greater air of credibility, you could set your company up as a PLC (a public company), but this is much more expensive (see p. 49) and more onerous in legal requirements.

Summary

On balance, if you are going to be selling to large companies, forming a company or LLP will probably have the edge on credibility.

2. What happens with money you owe

If you are a sole trader, you are liable for all the money your business owes (your liability is unlimited). Your own personal assets, such as your house, furniture and car, can be seized to pay your business debts; in the final breakdown, you can be made bankrupt.

This unlimited liability also applies to a conventional partnership, with a further drawback: you are liable for your partner's share of the debts.

By contrast, the concept of limited liability appears very attractive and applies to both an LLP and a limited company. Shareholders' liability for debt is, in most cases, limited to the amount they paid for their shares. The personal assets of directors can be touched only if that company has been trading fraudulently or when the directors knew it was insolvent. But this protection for your personal assets may be illusory. When you are starting in business, it is common for you as a director to be asked for personal guarantees for a bank overdraft, leasing agreements, rent or credit from suppliers. However, once you have become established you may be able to shed your personal guarantees; a sole trader or partner cannot shed unlimited liability.

An LLP is a separate legal identity, like a limited company. The firm itself and negligent members of the LLP will be liable for debts with all their assets, but other members of the partnership will not.

Summary

If yours is the sort of business that buys materials or services from other businesses, needs a small overdraft or has to operate from rented premises, forming yourself as a limited company or LLP has the edge. You may be able to get away without guaranteeing all of these debts; it is certainly worth negotiating to avoid doing so.

3. What you do to start up

It is very easy to start up as a sole trader. Simply register with Her Majesty's Revenue & Customs (HMRC)* within three months of the month you start up. They will also then send you the form you need if you decide to register for VAT (see Chapter 30).

In theory, it is equally simple to start a conventional partnership, as you do not have to get a written partnership agreement. But this would not be a sensible or businesslike approach. Partners argue, including members of the same family; you should accept that this may be so, no matter how unlikely it appears at the start. Get a solicitor to draw up a written agreement that covers things like profits split, work split, tax split and partner changes. See p. 48 for more on what should be in the partnership agreement.

An LLP can be formed by registering a name at Companies House* for a fee of £20, or £50 if you opt for same-day registration. You need two or more people (a minimum of two people must be designated members and responsible for getting the accounts audited, sending an annual return to Companies House and so on).

You can set up a limited company yourself. This involves filling in various forms and drawing up certain documents (which can be adapted from standard formats). The company must be registered with Companies House. For a new company, this costs £20 (or £15 if you register online) or £50 for a same-day service (or £30 if you register online). Alternatively, you can enlist the help of a solicitor, accountant or specialist company formation agent either to form your company from scratch or to supply an 'off-the-peg' company (i.e. one that already has a name and has already been registered).

For a standard company, expect to pay between £50 and £200, including the Companies House fee. You can change the name of an off-the-peg company. There are some brief formalities and the change must be registered with Companies House for a fee of £10, or £50 for a same-day service. If you use an agent to change the name, £25 to £30 is a normal charge. A private company must have a minimum of one person as director. There must also be a company secretary, who does not need any specific qualifications. You can be both a director and the company secretary provided you are not the sole director. If you are the only director, you will currently need someone else to be your company secretary. This could be, say, a relative or close friend. Solicitors, accountants and specialist agents usually offer a company secretary service, which could cost around £150 a year. Under the Companies Act 2006, from April 2008, it will become optional for private companies to have a company secretary. The Act also introduces a number of other simplifications that will make it easier to run a private company, for example, in most cases you will no longer have to hold an annual general meeting. For details, see the free guide, *Companies Act 2006. A summary of what it means for private companies* from the Department for Business, Enterprise and Regulatory Reform*.

You must also meet the disclosure requirements set out in the Companies Acts if you form a limited company. This includes sending in an annual return, accounts and changes in the company's directors and secretary plus other information. Companies House publishes free online guidance, including GBF1 *Company formation*, GBA1 *Directors and secretaries guide*, GBA2 *Annual return*, GBA3 *Accounts and accounting reference dates* and GBLLPI *Limited Liability partnerships, formation and names.* These can be viewed and downloaded from its web site, *www.companieshouse.co.uk.* Companies House* also holds regional seminars to help companies to understand their legal obligations.

Summary
Setting up as a sole trader involves the least work and fewest formalities.

4. Your accounts
As a sole trader and a conventional partnership, your accounts must follow accepted accounting practice to give a true and fair picture. But the exact form of the accounts is not laid down by law. In practice, this means you do not have to produce a balance sheet. It would, however, be advisable to do so to impress your tax office or bank manager and to help you to keep a proper check on the financial position of your business. (See p. 280 for

what a balance sheet is.) It is possible to do your own accounts rather than employ an accountant. If your business is very simple, you could set up your own accounting system using a spreadsheet, but generally it is better to use an off-the-shelf software package or paper-based accounting system – computer and book shops offer a wide range. (On tax returns, some self-employed people have to provide only a three-line summary of their accounts, but they must still keep full and proper accounts to back up the summary.)

In contrast, the form of accounts for a limited company and limited liability partnership is laid down by law and must comply with detailed accounting standards. The accounts have to be filed at Companies House: any member of the public can inspect them. A small company or small LLP can file a short-ened balance sheet and special auditors report if it chooses. The definition of 'small' is having two of the following: sales of £5.6 million or less, balance sheet total of £2.8 million or less, fifty or fewer employees on average.

There are penalties if you file your accounts late, even one day late. For private companies and LLPs, the potential fine ranges from £100 to £1,000.

Summary

The rules about your accounts are more onerous if you set up as a limited company or LLP.

5. Getting your accounts audited

As a sole trader or conventional partnership, you do not have to get your accounts audited if you do not want to. You may want to consider doing so, if the cost would not be too exorbitant, as it can help in dealings with your tax office. It may also help you if you need confirmation of income from your business – for example, to get a mortgage to buy a house or to help teenage offspring claim student loans.

If your business form is a limited company or LLP, you may have to get your accounts audited by an accountant. If your company has sales of less than £5.6 million and a balance sheet total of no more than £2.8 million, you will not need to do so. (The limits are £1 million and £1.4 million for financial periods ending before 1 April 2004.)

Summary

Small private companies and small LLPs have similar audit requirements to sole traders. Rules for other companies and LLPs are more onerous.

6. Paying tax and National Insurance

As a sole trader or partner (including in an LLP) you pay two types of National Insurance contribution (NIC). If your earnings are above a lower threshold, you pay flat-rate Class 2 contributions of £2.20 a week in 2007–8. In addition, you pay Class 4 contributions as a percentage. In 2007–8, Class 4 NICs are 8 per cent of profits between £5,225 and £34,840 and an additional contribution of 1 per cent of profits above the upper profit limit.

The business of a sole trader or partner does not have a separate identity from the individual concerned. So your profits are added to any other taxable income you have and subject to income tax if the total comes to more than your personal allowance (usually £5,225 in 2007–8).

A company does have a separate identity from its owners (the shareholders) and directors (who are employees of the company). Corporation tax is charged on the profits of the company. Companies with profits under £300,000 in 2007–8 pay tax at the small companies rate of 20 per cent. Before 1 April 2007, the small companies rate was 19 per cent but it was announced in the 2007 Budget that it will be raised by 1 per cent each year until it reaches 22 per cent from 2009–10 onwards. The increases are designed to remove any tax incentive to choose operating as a company rather than as a sole trader or partnership.

Profits are worked out after deducting any salary you pay yourself. On earnings above a certain limit, Class 1 NICs are paid by both you as employee and by the company as your employer. You normally pay at a rate of 11 per cent of your pay above £5,225 up to £34,840 in 2007–8 and 1 per cent on earnings above the upper earnings limit. Your employer pays 12.8 per cent on all your earnings above £5,225 (without any upper earnings limit). But, provided your salary is no more than £5,225, there is neither employee nor employer NICs to pay.

Instead of or as well as paying you a salary, your company may pay out some or all of the profits in the form of dividends to the shareholder(s) – i.e. you. There are no NICs to pay on dividends. The dividend is paid with an income tax credit of 10 per cent, which satisfies any liability for income tax at less than the higher rate. There is only extra tax to pay if, when added to any other income you have, you are a higher-rate taxpayer.

You may be able to minimize your overall tax and National Insurance bill by paying yourself just a small salary and the rest of your income in the form of dividends. But HMRC have been attacking this arrangement in an increasing number of ways:

■ *personal service companies and partnerships*: you may be charged tax and National Insurance on a 'notional salary' even though it was actually paid to you in dividends.

■ *husband and wife shareholders*: HMRC may try to tax dividends paid to a shareholding spouse, who does little or no work for the company, as income of the main worker. This is a controversial interpretation of the law and is being tested in the courts. At the time of writing, the Court of Appeal had said that HMRC's view is wrong but the House of Lords is due to review the judgment in summer 2007 and might overturn it.

■ *shares acquired on or after 2 December 2004*: if HMRC can show that the main purpose, or one of the main purposes, of issuing the shares is to avoid paying tax or National Insurance, dividends from the shares can be taxed as if they are earnings.

■ *managed service companies*: under tax avoidance measures introduced in the 2007 Budget, if you are a shareholder in a company that is managed for you by someone else, any income you get from the company will be taxed as salary even if it is paid to you in the form of dividends. The managed service company should deduct the correct tax before handing the money over to you.

See Chapter 29 for more information about tax.

Summary

By choosing the right combination of salary and dividends, many businesses can cut their overall NICs and tax bill by opting for a company structure rather than self-employment or partnership. However, this will not apply in all cases and is being increasingly attacked by HMRC.

7. Claiming state benefits

Class 2 NICs paid by sole traders and partners entitle you to claim certain state benefits. These are the state basic retirement pension, maternity allowance and incapacity benefit (or employment and support allowance which is due to replace incapacity benefit from April 2008). They also entitle your widow or widower to bereavement benefits. Class 4 NICs do not give you any benefit entitlement.

Employees (including directors) who have earnings at least equal to a lower earnings limit (£4,524 a year in 2007–8) are entitled to all state benefits listed above. In addition, they can also claim contributory jobseeker's allowance and are building up the state second pension. Note that employees entitled to these benefits may be earning less than the limit (£5,225 in 2007–8) at which Class 1 NICs become payable.

Summary

Provided you pay yourself a salary of at least £4,524 a year, you are entitled to more state benefits as a director of a company than you would be as a sole trader or partner. This is the case even if your salary is below the limit at which Class 1 NICs become payable.

8. When you pay tax

If you are in business as a sole trader or a partner (including an LLP), you will pay tax on your profits for the accounting year ending in the tax year in up to three instalments: interim payments on 31 January and 31 July and final payment (or repayment) on 31 January the following year.

With a limited company, on your salary you pay tax each month under the PAYE system. On the profits of the company, you pay tax nine months after the end of the accounting year.

Summary

There is little to choose between business forms.

9. What you can do with losses

If you are a sole trader or in a partnership (including an LLP), you can normally deduct losses from:

■ future profits of the same trade.

■ other income or capital gains either in the year of the loss or the year before. This includes any personal income you may have.

■ other income in the previous three years if the losses occur in the first four years of the business.

If you form a limited company, the relief is not so generous. You can deduct losses from company profits of the previous year, future profits of the company and any capital gains the company makes.

Summary

If you are likely to make losses in the first year or so, you would be better organizing your business as a sole trader or partnership, if you have another source of income.

10. Providing yourself with a pension

From 6 April 2006, new simplified rules for pension schemes came into effect. These allow you to get tax relief on contributions equal to the higher of £3,600 a year or the whole of your UK earnings paid into any type of, or combination of, pension schemes. There is also an overall annual limit on your contributions of £225,000 a year in 2007–8. Therefore, provided you have reasonably high UK earnings (which includes profits from self-employment or salary as a director, but not dividend income), you have the scope to make substantial pension savings whatever form your business takes. See Chapter 31 for more information.

If you organize your business as a company, the company (your employer) can make broadly unlimited contributions to a scheme on your behalf. These contributions qualify for relief from corporation tax provided the contributions are 'wholly and exclusively' for the purpose of the business. In practice this means that your whole remuneration package, including salary and pension, must be in proportion to the value of the work you do for the company. If you would prefer to take a large proportion of your remuneration in the form of pension contributions rather than pay, you could arrange a 'salary sacrifice' where you formally give up part of your pay in return for pension benefits.

Self-invested personal pensions (SIPPs), which can be taken out by anyone, and small self-administered schemes (SSASs), which can be set up by a company for its employee(s), can be used to invest in a wide range of assets including, for example, the premises from which your business operates. This can have tax advantages but it is a complex area so get advice from an independent financial adviser (IFA)*.

Summary

There is little to choose between business forms.

11. Raising money

As a sole trader, your options for raising money for your business are fairly limited and are basically getting an overdraft from your existing bank or a loan from your own or another bank. As an outside possibility, you may find an individual to lend you the money. In a partnership, you may be able to find a new partner to bring in some extra capital.

But if you form a company (and it must be a PLC if you wish to raise money from the public), the choice is wider. You may find a business angel willing to invest money for part of the business. On a larger scale, you may be able to raise venture capital from a fund or a venture capital trust. Or you may be able to raise funds under the enterprise investment scheme. You may also be able to raise money from your bank secured with what is known as a floating charge on your assets. For more about these methods of raising money, see pp. 295–303.

Summary

Your choices for raising money are wider if you form a limited company.

12. Selling part of your business

This can be slightly tricky if you are a sole trader or in a partnership. One way of solving this could be to take on a partner (or a further partner), but this obviously means you must have trust in the person. If part of your business is easily separated, you might be able to sell it as a going concern on its own.

It should be somewhat easier to sell part of your business if it is in the form of a limited company. You could sell some of your shares, although it can be difficult selling shares in a private company.

Summary

Selling part of your business may be easier if it is a limited company.

How to set up as a sole trader

It is really very easy and straightforward. You need to:

■ register for National Insurance with the HMRC* by filling in form CWF1 in the back of HMRC* leaflet SE1 *Thinking of working for yourself?* or by phoning the Newly Self-Employed Helpline*. With just a few exceptions, you'll face a fine of £100 if you fail to do this within three months of the end of the month in which your business starts. On the plus side, once registered, you'll be sent a guide on starting up in a business and have access to an HMRC local Business Support Team.

■ check with the Planning Officer* that your workplace is suitable (p. 192).

■ if you decide to trade under a name different from your own, you must put your own name on your headed paper (p. 133).

■ consider whether you have to, or whether you should ask to, register for VAT (p. 383).

How to set up as a partnership

The fundamental drawback of a conventional partnership is that each partner is jointly liable with the other partners for all the debts and obligations that each partner incurs. This financial responsibility can include all your own personal assets, which could be seized to pay partnership debts (which might have happened as a result not of your actions but of your partner's).

You must be able to trust your partners. Do not drift into an informal partnership. Make sure you and your partners have discussed difficult problems right at the start and come to some clear agreement.

There are several different sorts of partner, but only two are suitable for consideration in a business partnership:

1 A full partner, who will share in the profits and losses in an agreed proportion and will be part of the management.
2 A sleeping partner, who will have no part in the management of the business but will still be held responsible for the debts. (But see p. 374 for how loss relief is restricted for this type of partner.)

The partnership agreement

This is a job for a solicitor (and find out about the Lawyers for Your Business Scheme*, on p. 205). The agreement and its details, whether for a conventional partnership or a limited liability one, can be kept private. Briefly, an agreement should include among other points:

■ the names of the partners, the name of the business and its activity.

■ the date the partnership starts and how long it will last.

■ the capital and the interest on it.

■ the profits split.

■ management and control of the business.

■ holidays.

■ what happens on retirement, on death and if one of the partners leaves.

Forming a limited liability partnership

You need to submit an Incorporation Document (form LLP2) to Companies House*. This requires:

■ the limited liability partnership's name.

■ the location of the registered office (England, Wales or Scotland).

■ the address of the registered office.

■ the name, full address and date of birth of each member.

■ which of these members are the designated members or that all members are designated members.

A designated member has certain duties, such as appointing an auditor, signing the accounts, delivering the accounts and annual return to Companies House, and notifying Companies House of changes to the members, registered office addresses or name of the LLP.

There are certain rules about displaying information. The name of the LLP must be displayed outside every place of business and on all its notices. On all its letters and order forms must be shown the LLP's place of registration and registration number, the fact that it is a limited liability partnership and the address of its registered office.

How to set up as a company

You can set up a company yourself, in which case get a 'starter pack' from Companies House*. But it's simpler to pass the job to a solicitor, accountant or specialist company formation agent. Forming a company from scratch can take several weeks, although there is now a fast-track one-day registration service. You could form a public company – this would mean you must put PLC after its name. It must have an authorized share capital of at least £50,000, and at least one-quarter must be paid on each share, plus any premium. This means you need at least £12,500 to form it. Or you can form a private company (which is any company that is not a public company). A public company must have at least two directors and a private company one. At present, every company must have a secretary, and a sole director cannot act as a secretary. However, from April 2008, it will become optional for a private company to have a secretary.

A company cannot start to trade until registered with the Registrar of Companies at Companies House. If you use a solicitor, accountant or other agent, they will handle this for you. Otherwise, you currently need to send in:

- memorandum of association. Among other requirements, this should state the name of the company, the intended location of the registered office and the objects of the company.

- articles of association. This should have the detailed rules about internal management of the company. If you don't draw up your own articles, the standard format set out in the Companies Act will be adopted. You can also buy a memorandum and articles of association from law stationers.

- form 10 – notification of the first directors and secretary and the intended location of the registered office. You should also send in details of any director's business occupation, nationality and other directorships held within the last five years.

- form 12 – declaration of compliance.

- in the case of a public company, form 117 – which you have to send in to obtain a certificate required before the company starts trading.

- registration fee of £20, or £50 if you are using the same-day service (or £15 or £30, respectively, if you register online), made payable to 'Companies House'.

From October 2008, the memorandum of association will simply become a historic document setting out the facts at the time the company was formed. The important document for registration will be the articles of association and private companies will be able to opt to use a simple, standardized format. It will no longer be necessary for either the memorandum or the articles to set out the objects of the company, so (unless it chooses otherwise) there will be no restrictions on the company's activities.

Instead of forming a company from scratch, you can buy a ready-made one. This is a quicker process, but it may take three or more weeks to change its name to whatever you want to call your business, but if there is no problem with the name it normally takes about five working days. If you are willing to pay extra, you can even be up and running within 24 hours. To change a company's name you need to convene an annual general meeting or extraordinary general meeting and pass a special resolution. A signed copy of the resolution should be sent to Companies House with a registration fee of £10. Companies House offers a same-day name change service, though the fee for this is higher at £50.

There are certain rules about displaying information. For example, the Certificate of Incorporation and the registration date need to be displayed publicly. On your stationery, web site, e-mails and order forms for example, you need to show the full registered name of your company, either all or none of the names of the directors, the place of registration (for example, registered in England and Wales), the registration number, and the registered office address (marked as such) as well as the trading address of the company. You must put the company name outside your office premises.

There are rules on what name you can give your company – see Chapter 12, 'The right name', on p. 128.

What directors must do

In practice, a director's general obligations are not much worse than those for a sole trader or partner, and indeed they can be better. This is because by forming a company you can separate your own assets from the business assets (in theory at any rate). But this separation is conditional on what could be called, in layperson's terms, responsible business behaviour. However, a director also has to cope with some technical, more detailed requirements, for example sending in your accounts, which aren't there to trip up a sole trader.

Some of a director's duties, responsibilities and potential liabilities are:

- to act in good faith in the interests of the company – this includes carrying out duties diligently and honestly.

- not to carry on the business of the company with intent to defraud creditors or for any fraudulent purpose.

- not knowingly to allow the company to trade while insolvent ('wrongful trading') – directors who do so may have to pay for the debts incurred by the company while insolvent.

- not to deceive shareholders.

- to have a regard for the interests of employees in general.

- to comply with the requirements of the Companies Acts, such as providing what is needed in accounting records or filing accounts.

■ the Companies Act 2006 introduces a new duty, from October 2007 onwards, for directors to promote the company's success.

If a company is insolvent, and the directors have failed in their duties and obligations, they could be declared 'unfit' and disqualified from being a director of any other company for up to fifteen years.

Most of the big firms of accountants and the Institute of Directors* have booklets explaining what a director's responsibilities are. You can also get insurance to protect yourself, Directors' and Officers' Liability. Ask your insurance broker*, see p. 262.

Forming a cooperative

A cooperative is a group of people operating through a jointly owned and democratically run organization. The type of cooperative varies. For example, this could be a group of workers who own the organization they work for, or consumers who join together to buy more efficiently, or an agricultural cooperative where farmers join forces to strengthen their bargaining power. Cooperatives are underpinned by strong values, such as self-help, democracy and equity. To foster these, most cooperatives adhere to seven principles:

1 Voluntary and open membership.
2 Democratic member control. Many adhere to one member, one vote.
3 Member economic participation. Members all contribute to the organization's capital and democratically control its use in the business. Often the capital itself cannot be distributed to individual members and, even on winding up, would be given to charity or put to some community use. Profits may be distributed to members, kept within the business or used in some other way agreed on by the members.
4 Autonomy and independence. Cooperatives can enter into agreements with other organizations and raise money from external sources, provided the democratic control of the members is maintained.
5 Education, training and information. These are provided by the cooperative to its members so they can contribute effectively to its development. The cooperative also has a duty to inform the public about the nature and benefits of cooperation.
6 Cooperation among cooperatives (through local, regional, national and international bodies).
7 Concern for the community.

You will need to get legal registration or incorporation for the cooperative. There are four possible legal forms.

First, you could form a partnership. The disadvantage with this is that there is no limited liability. And the business could be sold for the benefit of its members; this is not in keeping with a fundamental principle of a cooperative. On the other hand, you can form a partnership with only two people, whereas to form a cooperative society (see below), you need seven.

Second, you could form a limited company; but the aims of a company run counter to some of the basic principles of a cooperative, so it would be difficult to organize.

Third, you could seek registration with the Financial Services Authority* as a cooperative society under the Industrial and Provident Societies Act 1965. You will need seven founder members. You will find registration will be quicker if you apply through a 'promoting body', such as the Cooperative Union* (which now incorporates the Industrial Common Ownership Movement). The Cooperative Union can help with setting up a new cooperative.

Finally, you could organize the cooperative as a company limited by guarantee. This needs only two people to form it.

Summary

1 A limited company has several advantages: limited liability, greater credibility, lower tax, better pension rules, more avenues for raising finance and easier disposal of part of your business.

2 Sole trader and partnership have much simpler admin arrangements, less onerous rules about accounts and better tax treatment of losses.

3 If you are forming a partnership, get a solicitor's help to draw up a written partnership agreement.

4 The simplest way of all to start a business is to begin as a sole trader.

Other chapters to read

12 The right name (p. 128); **24** Raising the money (p. 290); **28** Keeping the record straight (p. 340); **29** Tax (p. 350).

5

Are you sure?

Every would-be entrepreneur should take stock before undertaking the final commitment; reassessments are a vital part of the decision process. Are you the right person? Have you got the necessary skills? Will you be able to earn enough to live on? Is your idea the best one?

What is in this chapter?

This chapter draws together all the key points made in the previous four chapters, presenting them in a series of four checklists. This should allow you to reconsider previous decisions to confirm that you are on the right road. The checklists are you (p. 54), your family (p. 56), your skills (p. 57) and your idea (p. 61).

Checklist: you

Underline the word in each answer that best describes how you fit each question. You can also ask friends, colleagues or relatives to fill in the checklist about you, so that you can obtain an external view of your character and fitness for self-employment.

1 Can you work long hours?
(1) Always   (2) Sometimes   (3) Occasionally   (4) Never

2 Do you have persistence and stamina?
(1) Always   (2) Most of the time   (3) Occasionally   (4) Rarely

3 Is this business more important than, for example, leisure or family?
(1) Completely   (2) Much more   (3) As important   (4) Less important

4 If the business struggled for five years, would you keep going?
(1) Yes, easily   (2) Yes, fairly easily   (3) Yes, with difficulty   (4) No

5 Is financial success your main guide to what you have achieved?
(1) Completely   (2) Mainly   (3) Partially   (4) Not at all

6 Are you thought of as a survivor?
(1) Always   (2) Usually   (3) Occasionally   (4) Never

7 If you were in a tight corner, would you be able to come up with an original way out?
(1) Frequently   (2) Sometimes   (3) Rarely   (4) Never

8 Do you keep going until a task is completed?
(1) Always   (2) Usually   (3) Sometimes   (4) Occasionally

9 Are problems a challenge?
(1) Always   (2) Usually   (3) Sometimes   (4) Never

10 Can you live with insecurity about job and income?
(1) Yes, easily   (2) Yes, fairly easily   (3) Yes, with difficulty   (4) No

11 Are you self-confident?
(1) Yes, always   (2) Yes, usually   (3) Sometimes lack confidence   (4) No

12 How do you view failure?
(1) Opportunity to learn   (2) A disappointment   (3) A setback
(4) A disaster

13 Can you take criticism?
(1) Always listen; may reject   (2) Always accept   (3) Don't like it
(4) Always reject

14 Do you ask for comments on your performance so that you can do something better next time?
(1) Always   (2) Usually   (3) Sometimes   (4) Rarely

15 Do you believe your success will be dependent on outside factors?
(1) Strongly disagree   (2) Disagree   (3) Agree sometimes
(4) Agree always

16 Do you like being the leader in situations where you can be assessed?
(1) Very much   (2) Quite a lot   (3) Not really   (4) Not at all

17 Are you good at finding the right person or source to help you to achieve what you want?
(1) Very good   (2) Quite good   (3) Not very good   (4) Poor

18 Do you recognize when you need help?
(1) Always   (2) Usually   (3) Sometimes   (4) Never

19 Do you set your own high standards to compete against?
(1) Always   (2) Usually   (3) Sometimes   (4) Never

20 In the past, which sort of risks have you preferred taking?
(1) Calculated   (2) High risks   (3) Low risks   (4) Seldom take risks

21 Can you identify which decisions are important and which not?
(1) Yes, always   (2) Yes, usually   (3) Yes, sometimes   (4) No

22 Can you delegate to others?
(1) Yes, when appropriate   (2) Yes, sometimes   (3) With difficulty
(4) No

23 How is your health?
(1) Very good   (2) Good   (3) Quite good   (4) Poor

When you have completed the checklist, look at the pattern of underlined words. The more underlined answers 1 and 2, the greater your probable success as a business owner.

Checklist: your family

If you are single, you may not need to consider this section. But if you have a husband, wife, partner and/or children, involving them in the decision to go it alone is important. Starting a business is an all-embracing existence, and your family life is unlikely to remain the same after taking the plunge. They will need to understand that the home atmosphere should be very supportive, particularly during the early business problems.

Your family may also turn out to be an important business resource. They can provide extra input in all you do: clerical, manual, problem solving, for example. With a family, deciding to found an enterprise is likely to be more successful as a family decision. Having said that, many succeed without the support of their families; but, in this case, the strain can be severe. In the extreme, the choice may be your business or your relationship.

In the following checklist, cross out whichever is inapplicable:

1 Have you discussed your thoughts about starting a business
with your family?   *yes   no*

2 Are they willing to help out if necessary?   *yes   no*

3 Will they live easily with job or financial insecurity?   *yes   no*

4 Have they accepted that there may be a permanent drop in
living standards?   *yes   no*

5 If you need to raise money using your home as security, do
they understand the full implications?   *yes   no*

6 Is your family self-sufficient, that is, can they manage without
you to do the shopping, gardening, decorating?   *yes   no*

7 Does one of the members of the family earn a living in another
way, which can be used to tide the whole family over?   *yes   no*

8 Have you worked out a family budget to see how you will cope?
If you have not, the *pro forma* cash flow below may help you.
Remember to use conservative estimates of your likely income
and allow for all the costs.   *yes   no*

9 Have you talked to your bank manager about your intended
business and shown him your cash flow to demonstrate how
you hope to cope in domestic finance?   *yes   no*

When you have completed your family checklist, the more times you have
answered 'yes' the better prepared you are for starting your business.

Pro forma cash flow

Month	1	2	–	11	12
Balance at bank at start of month	. . .	. . .	–	. . .	. . .
Income					
Estimated from business	. . .	. . .	–	. . .	. . .
Other family	. . .	. . .	–	. . .	. . .
Total income	. . .	. . .	–	. . .	. . .
Expenses					
Mortgage/rent	. . .	. . .	–	. . .	. . .
Loan interest	. . .	. . .	–	. . .	. . .
Council tax	. . .	. . .	–	. . .	. . .
Pension	. . .	. . .	–	. . .	. . .
Life insurance	. . .	. . .	–	. . .	. . .
Tax on business income	. . .	. . .	–	. . .	. . .

Month	1	2	–	11	12
Electricity/gas/phone/fuel	. . .	. . .	–	. . .	. . .
Travel/car	. . .	. . .	–	. . .	. . .
House: insurance/repairs	. . .	. . .	–	. . .	. . .
Food	. . .	. . .	–	. . .	. . .
Clothes	. . .	. . .	–	. . .	. . .
Subscriptions/newspapers/magazines	. . .	. . .	–	. . .	. . .
Other:					
. . . .	. . .	. . .	–	. . .	. . .
. . . .	. . .	. . .	–	. . .	. . .
. . . .	. . .	. . .	–	. . .	. . .
Total expenses	. . .	. . .	–	. . .	. . .
Balance in bank at end of month	. . .	. . .	–	. . .	. . .

Checklist: your skills

This checklist should help you to look honestly at what you can do well and what you do badly. If there are skills you lack, this does not mean that you cannot go ahead. But you need to compensate:

- be trained or seek advice from an enterprise agency or other advice body.
- fund the business so you can employ those skills that are lacking.
- use professional advisers, if appropriate.

Financial

As you answer each question, underline the appropriate word or words:

1 Have you kept accounting books, for example sales and purchases day-books, cash books (see p. 341) or used a simple software program?
many times   *on a few occasions*   *not at all*

2 Have you had to chase bad debts owed by your customers (p. 317)?
yes, frequently   *yes, sometimes*   *no, not at all*

3 Have you ever installed a system of credit control (p. 314)?
yes   *no*

4 Have you ever negotiated credit terms with a supplier (p. 315)?
yes   *no*

5 What is your experience of drawing up cash flows (p. 270)?

extensive   *a little*   *none at all*

6 Do you understand the importance of controlling cash (p. 311)?

yes   *no*

7 What is your experience of drawing up budgets (p. 310)?

extensive   *a little*   *none at all*

8 Is break-even analysis a technique you have used before (p. 307)?

yes, frequently   *yes, sometimes*   *no, not at all*

9 Do you know when and how you would use:

(a) An overdraft (p. 293)?   *yes*   *no*

(b) Leasing (p. 199)?   *yes*   *no*

(c) Factoring (p. 318)?   *yes*   *no*

10 What is your experience of estimating and raising long-term financial needs (p. 291)?

extensive   *a little*   *none at all*

11 Do you know what are the sources of long-term funds, for example venture capital (p. 300)?

yes   *no*

12 What is your experience of drawing up business plans (p. 63)?

extensive   *a little*   *none at all*

13 What is your experience of presenting your plan to financiers (p. 303)?

extensive   *a little*   *none at all*

Marketing

14 Do you understand the different ways you can establish prices (p. 174)?

yes   *no*

15 Do you know how to analyse market sectors (p. 14)?

yes   *no*

16 What is your experience of identifying product benefits (p. 17)?

extensive   *a little*   *none at all*

17 What is your experience of:

(a) Direct-response advertising (p. 139)?

extensive   *a little*   *none at all*

(b) Public relations (p. 144)?

extensive   *a little*   *none at all*

(c) Face-to-face selling (p. 154)?

extensive   *a little*   *none at all*

(d) Direct mail (p. 150)?

extensive   *a little*   *none at all*

(e) Telephone selling (p. 153)?

extensive   *a little*   *none at all*

(f) Marketing through the Internet (p. 145)?

extensive   *a little*   *none at all*

18 Do you understand how to build relationships with customers (p. 163)?

yes   *no*

Operational

19 Do you know how to introduce a stock control system?

yes   *no*

20 Do you understand all the ins and outs of your product; that is, how it works, what it does?

yes, very well   *yes, somewhat*   *no, not very well*

21 Do you understand the effect that control of costs can have on profits (p. 323)?

yes, very well   *yes, somewhat*   *no, not very well*

22 Do you understand the manufacturing process of your product (if applicable)?

yes, very well   *yes, somewhat*   *no, not very well*

23 Do you know how to use a database to gather information?

yes, very well   *yes, somewhat*   *no, not very well*

24 Do you understand how to integrate the use of information technology in your business?

yes, very well   *yes, somewhat*   *no, not very well*

General management

25 What is your experience of staff recruitment (p. 210)?

extensive   *a little*   *none at all*

26 What is your understanding of employment law (p. 229)?

extensive   *a little*   *none at all*

27 Do you know how to set goals and objectives for employees?

yes   *no*

28 What is your experience of project management?
extensive   *a little*   *none at all*

Once you have finished assessing your skills and abilities, you will have some indication of what improvements you should make. A first step is reading the relevant chapters of this book.

Checklist: your idea

This is an opportunity to have a final check on your idea before you start becoming involved in the actual formalities and expense of forming your business. Note that where the word 'product' is used, this could also be 'service' or 'skill'.

	yes	*no*	*does not apply*
1 Have you defined your product ideas?	. . .	. . .	. . .
2 Have you carried out market research into your idea?	. . .	. . .	. . .
3 Have you discerned a market sector or niche that you will sell to?	. . .	. . .	. . .
4 Is that segment big enough for you to build a business on it?	. . .	. . .	. . .
5 Have you researched the characteristics of your likely customers?	. . .	. . .	. . .
6 Have you identified what are the benefits and advantages not yet available to that segment?	. . .	. . .	. . .
7 Will you be able to supply a product that meets those needs?	. . .	. . .	. . .
8 Do you know how your product will be different from the competitors'?	. . .	. . .	. . .
9 Have you estimated how much your likely customers will buy and when that will be?	. . .	. . .	. . .
10 Have you found out how the product will be sold, for example e-commerce, direct mail, direct selling, retail, distributors?	. . .	. . .	. . .
11 Have you made a realistic forecast of the market share you can attain?	. . .	. . .	. . .
12 Is the market likely to grow in the next few years?	. . .	. . .	. . .
13 Have you talked to potential customers, and do they like your product?	. . .	. . .	. . .

	yes	no	does not apply
14 Have you carried out any test-selling and has it confirmed your estimates of sales?	. . .	. . .	. . .
15 Will the product live up to the reputation you intend to project?	. . .	. . .	. . .
16 Have you estimated a price you can sell for?	. . .	. . .	. . .
17 Do you know how the product will be made?	. . .	. . .	. . .
18 Can you work out an approximate cost?	. . .	. . .	. . .
19 Do you have an initial idea of overheads for the business, for example rent, telephone, heating and lighting?	. . .	. . .	. . .
20 Have you made an approximate guess at the profits and when they will be earned?	. . .	. . .	. . .
21 Will this give you an income you can live on?	. . .	. . .	. . .
22 Will you need to raise money, and is this a realistic amount?	. . .	. . .	. . .
23 Have you thought carefully about what the principal risks are to your business?	. . .	. . .	. . .
24 Can you put an estimate on the likelihood of these risks occurring?	. . .	. . .	. . .

Now you have completed this checklist; the more times you answered 'yes', the better prepared you are and the greater the chance of success.

What next?

If you have worked carefully through these four checklists, you are now faced with one of three options:

1 Give up because you are not the right person to be self-employed or start a business or the idea is not suitable.
2 Carry out further research or training or seek a better idea.
3 Proceed.

To proceed, you need to make several decisions and carry out actions. These include choosing advisers, formulating a detailed business plan, deciding the form of your business, working on what your business or product will be called. Chapter 7, 'Timing the jump' (p. 69), should guide you through the maze.

Other chapters to read

1 You and your ideas (p. 1); **2** Who will buy? (p. 13); **6** The business plan (p. 63).

6

The business plan

Life can be very chaotic when you are starting or running a small business. The telephone calls to make, the letters to write, the decisions to take – all the day-to-day emergencies can push aside the long-term strategic planning that is essential to keep your enterprise on the right track. Do not let short-term problems divert you from your longer-term objectives.

Writing a business plan is merely encapsulating your longer-term objectives, estimates and forecasts on paper. Once you have put down your plan, do not necessarily accept that it is set in concrete. Forecasts and objectives change as new bits of information and your better experience emerge. The important point is to incorporate your best estimate, given your current state of information. There is nothing like writing something down to help to clarify your mind and reveal your uncertainties and weaknesses.

What is in this chapter?

- the objectives of the plan (p. 63)
- how many plans? (p. 64)
- who should do the plan? (p. 65)
- what should be in the plan? (p. 65)

The objectives of the plan

The two most important reasons for producing a written plan are:

1 To show to outsiders to help to raise money.

2 To use within the business to keep yourself on your planned course or to alert you to things that are not going according to your strategy. This use is discussed in more detail in Chapter 25, 'Staying afloat' (p. 305).

To persuade someone to lend or invest enough money in your business to enable you to achieve your strategy, you will need to:

- show that the lender or investor stands a good chance of being paid back or getting a good return on their investment.

- instil confidence about your abilities to manage the business and, if applicable, show that you already have the beginnings of an experienced management team.

- demonstrate that there is a good market for your product or service.

To achieve these objectives you must bring out what is exciting about the prospects of your business, combined with a thoroughly prepared presentation of the back-up figures and research.

Beware of filling your plan with nothing but turgid facts and figures; you must allow the reader of your plan to see instantly what is so interesting about your business. You need to do this to persuade your reader that it is worthwhile studying the detailed forecasts, which can be very time-consuming. Lenders and investors can be presented with so many plans for consideration that unless yours grabs the reader's attention it could be consigned to the bin before your carefully prepared figures are looked at.

How many plans?

As there are two reasons for having a written plan, will one plan suffice? The answer to this depends on who is advising you. A bank manager, or other financial backer, may say there should be only one plan, as they would like to know the absolute truth about what is happening in your business. But some small businesses adopt a different strategy and have two plans. One is for outsiders; this plan must be one that will not fail, so it will be fairly conservative about projected sales and costs. The reason for adopting a conservative approach with outsiders is that you must not be seen to fail as this can erode confidence in you and your judgement. This could make it difficult to keep the support of your bank manager when you need it later. If your plan is being used to raise money, your figures must achieve a balance between optimism and realism if you are to persuade banks and others that your business will be successful and so worthy of a loan or an investment. You must always remain confident that the figures are achievable; if you are misleading the lenders and investors, you are also misleading yourself.

The second plan is for your own use and will set higher targets, although you must believe you can do that level of business. If you pitch the figures too low, you might not achieve as much as is possible. The well-known fleas-in-the-box analogy applies to your plan; if you put a lid on the box, the fleas learn to jump to that height only, but, if there is no lid, they jump as high as they are capable of doing. Your plan should set that lid higher.

Who should do the plan?

It is your job. You will know the product and the market better than anyone else. You have to be prepared to present the plan to banks or other sources of finance, so you need to be fully confident about all the statements and forecasts. You will have that confidence if you have provided the data.

However, as it is so important for your plan to look professional, consider seeking advice and help on its production. This is available from:

■ Business Links* and training courses. Many counsellors can help you put your plan together (see Chapter 3). This help is often free.

■ accountants* or financial advisers* can help you to prepare the figures (see Chapter 19).

Use a computer program to help you to produce forecasts and to examine the effect changes will have on the results. Computerized spreadsheets can make short work of a lengthy task and let you investigate different scenarios.

What should be in the plan?

1 Summary of your plan (one to two pages).
Highlighting the attractions of your business.

   a) What is the business?
   b) What is the market?
   c) Potential for business.
   d) Forecast profit figures.
   e) How much money is needed?
   f) Prospects for the investor/lender.

2 The past (one page plus an appendix).
   a) When the business started.
   b) Summary of past performance (last three years' accounts in appendix).
   c) Indication of how relevant or not past performance is to future progress.

3 Management (as many pages as are needed).
   This is the crucial section.

   a) Your past employment and business record. Identify achievements, not just a chronological statement.
   b) The record of other people working with you.
   c) If there are obvious weaknesses in management, how you'll deal with them.

4 The product or service (two pages plus an appendix).
   a) A simple description of what it does. Avoid technical words – if essential, technical descriptions can go in the appendix.
   b) Why the product is unique or distinct.
   c) Brief survey of the competition.
   d) How the products will be developed, what new products are being considered, when replacement will be needed for the existing product range, what competitive products may emerge.
   e) Any patents applied for.

5 Marketing (three or four pages with detailed statistics in an appendix). The market:

   a) Its size, its past and future growth.
   b) Analysis of market into sectors; identify sector your business is aimed at.
   c) Likely customers: who, type (industrial or consumer), size, how they buy.
   d) Your competitors: who, their size, position in market, likely response to your challenge.

   Selling:

   a) How you will sell (Internet, direct mail, phone, intermediaries, and so on).
   b) Who will sell.
   c) Some idea of your sales pitch (for example, benefits of your product).
   d) How you will price.

6 Operational details (length depends on nature of business).
   a) Where you will be based – location, premises.
   b) Suppliers.
   c) Manufacturing facilities.
   d) Equipment needed.
   e) Information technology strategy.

7 Financial analysis (two to three pages; data in optional appendix).
   a) Summary of forecasts.
   b) Monthly profit and loss forecast for two years.
   c) Profit forecast for further three years.
   d) Monthly cash flow forecast for two years.
   e) Cash flow forecast for further three years (optional).
   f) Forecast balance sheet for two years.
   g) Audited accounts for last three years (if available).
   h) The assumptions behind your forecasts.
   i) What are the principal risks that could affect figures?
   j) SWOT analysis – strengths, weaknesses, opportunities and threats.

8 The prospects (one or two pages).
   a) Your objectives – short-term, long-term.
   b) The finance needed and what it is needed for.
   c) Shareholdings suggested (if appropriate).
   d) Prospects for the investor or lender (if appropriate, including possible value of business if floated on the stock market or sold, so investors may cash in).

The length of the plan

In the outline above, suggested maximum lengths for each section are given. If your need for finance is small (£25,000, say) and your business simple, these would be too long. Probably all you will need for your bank manager is two or three pages plus the financial forecasts – a bit more if it is not your own bank manager. However, if you need a large sum of money, you may have to put rather more in than the above suggestions. But keep at the forefront of your mind that you need to get across to your reader what is interesting about your business.

One possible way around the conundrum of giving all the necessary information without boring a potential investor would be to include a note of what other figures and data are available, if requested.

Presenting your plan

Financiers will assume that if your presentation to them is unsatisfactory, your presentation to customers is equally unsatisfactory. So while it may seem obvious, your plan will look better if it is given a clear layout and presented in a smart folder. The information will also be easier to understand if you do not try to cram too much on one page. How you should present your plan and who you should approach for money are covered in Chapter 24.

Summary

1 If you want to raise money for your business you will need to have a well-presented, carefully researched business plan to support your request.

2 Producing a business plan also helps you to keep control of your business by allowing you to look at how your actual performance differs from your forecast performance – and forcing you to explain the differences.

3 Preparing the plan can help you to clarify your thoughts about the success or failure of your business venture. It can also help to highlight in your mind the important steps that need to be taken.

4 Consider whether one plan will suffice for outsiders and inside use, or if two plans will be more helpful to you.

5 Your plan must get across to readers what is interesting about your business. Stress your management ability and demonstrate carefully the market for your product.

6 An ideal format for your plan for outside use is to have between three and ten pages of text that draw out the important points, plus a series of financial figures. Excessive detail should be confined to appendices.

7 You can get help to produce the plan from an advice agency or an accountant. It is crucial to try out your plan on someone independent before you try it out on the financiers.

8 Use the checklist starting on p. 65 to help you to decide what should be in your business plan.

9 Your plan should be typed and neatly presented in a folder.

10 Include cash flow forecasts, profit forecasts, and possibly a balance sheet forecast. The more money you wish to raise the more detail your forecasts need to have and the greater period they should cover.

Other chapters to read

23 Forecasting (p. 269); **24** Raising the money (p. 290).

7

Timing the jump

Starting a business can be a confusing operation: so many decisions to take, so many actions to carry out. It can be important to keep to the right path. If you fail to take one step when it is necessary, this can delay your start.

What is in this chapter?

This chapter should help you to keep to the critical path. It sets out sixty steps. Not all will apply to every business – decide which are critical for yours and which you can ignore. You might find it convenient to combine two steps even though one does not need to be done until later. But, in general, carry out the steps in the approximate order given. The steps are divided into four sections:

1 Initial preparation (p. 69).
2 Getting into greater detail (p. 70).
3 Setting up (p. 72).
4 Ready to trade (p. 72).

Initial preparation

1 Carry on in your job, if you are in paid employment; carry on drawing jobseekers' allowance, if unemployed. You can undertake the initial preparation and research while still doing this.
2 Analyse your character and abilities. Are you the right person to start on your own (p. 54)?
3 Discuss with your family the possibility of starting a business. Are they aware of what it will mean to family life? Will they be committed (p. 56)?

4 Come up with a shortlist of ideas for a business. Do you have the necessary skills? Does the market look promising (p. 59)?

5 Briefly define product ideas (p. 11).

6 Brush up inadequate skills. Apart from reading the relevant sections of this book, consider training courses and counselling (pp. 27, 30).

7 Consider whether you should start the business with someone who has complementary skills, that is, who is strong in those skills in which you are weak. Negotiate who gets what share.

8 Decide how big a business you want. Will it be large- or small-scale? How much growth potential do your business ideas have? Do you have the essential management skills to opt for a fast-growth route?

9 Did your self-analysis suggest that you needed ongoing help? Or have you been unable to come up with a sound business idea? What about a franchise? You need at least one-third of the purchase price (p. 101).

10 Investigate the possibilities of buying a business if you have the necessary funds or can raise them (p. 80).

11 Carry out detailed market research into a shortlist of ideas (p. 14). Do this whether you are starting from scratch, buying a franchise or buying a business.

12 Identify a market sector (p. 15). Establish what will be different about your product (p. 17). Estimate all of these: market size, market share, market structure, market trends (p. 19). Investigate competition and their products (p. 20).

13 In steps 11 and 12, narrow down possible ideas to a leading prospect.

14 Work out your principal selling method – e-commerce, direct mail, intermediaries, for example.

15 Forecast amount and timing of sales.

16 Review yourself, your skills, your family, your idea (p. 54). Take the decision to proceed, do further work or abandon. It is better to drop the idea now than carry on with doubts.

Getting into greater detail

17 Draw up an initial business plan. Forecast sales, costs, cash flows. At this stage, figures will be very approximate (p. 269).

18 Make a preliminary decision about your need to raise money. Roughly, how much will you need? Who is the likeliest lender (p. 295)?

19 Discuss with your family what you will be able to invest. Consider what security you can offer (pp. 59, 295).

20 Seek out and employ the advisers you need. These could include solic-itor, accountant, bank, design consultant, IT specialist, database experts, web designers (p. 201).

21 Decide how much you will spend setting up, but keep a margin of safety. Tailor the amount to how much you are willing to risk yourself, as the funds you can raise will be a multiple of what you can invest.

22 If you are currently employed, are you able to give the necessary effort to get the business going? Or do you need the extra income? Consider giving up work.

23 Test your product to confirm its performance. Test-market your product or service, if possible (p. 25).

24 Apply for a patent to protect the product or register the design or trade mark, if applicable (p. 119).

25 What form will your business take: for example, sole trader, partnership or limited company (p. 38)?

26 Decide your IT strategy – consider your needs for hardware and soft-ware: accounts package, spreadsheet, e-mail, database and so on.

27 Name your product and business (p. 128). Keep in mind your sector of the market and the product's benefits. The name is part of your selling effort.

28 Register the company name, or change the name if buying a ready-made company (p. 48). Check there is no other company with that name. Sole traders and partnerships need take no action.

29 Draw up a partnership agreement, if applicable (p. 48).

30 Come up with some initial ideas about letterheads or consider those put forward by a designer (p. 207).

31 Develop ideas about how to sell your product or service. Identify the product benefits and advantages. What means will you use to get your message across: leaflets, brochures, etc. (p. 138)?

32 Identify possible suppliers. Begin your negotiations.

33 Develop a pricing strategy (p. 170).

34 Refine a business plan (p. 63). Be pessimistic about sales and costs.

35 Ask an adviser or colleague to go through the plan with you, chal-lenging all the assumptions and figures. Have you identified the principal risks?

36 Review the plan yet again. Does the business look viable? Will you go ahead, research further or abandon? All the momentum is to push forward because of all the work and commitment put in so far. But if the idea does not hold water, the right decision is not to proceed but to research something else.

Setting up

37 Consider what equipment your business will need. Investigate how to pay for it: cash, hire purchase or leasing (p. 198).

38 Establish guidelines on what credit to offer, what credit to take from suppliers, how you will control cash (pp. 311–21).

39 Find out what insurance you will need for your business (p. 262).

40 Estimate the amount of initial stock and production run.

41 Make first approaches about raising money.

42 Decide if you will start trading before you raise the money or if you will wait until you have finalized. Remember with complicated finance, it can take several months.

43 Register for VAT if you are forced to and, if not, consider whether it would be beneficial (pp. 383, 387).

44 Set up a simple accounting record system (p. 342).

45 Work out what your accounting period should be. There is some advantage in a year end early in the tax year if profits are rising (p. 353).

46 Consider the virtues of trading from home, even if several of you are joining together to start the business. E-mail can help you to communicate from several locations. Otherwise, start the search for premises.

47 Finalize decisions about letterheads and order stationery, once you have found premises and know your business address.

48 If you will need staff when you start trading, start the search now.

49 Carry on developing your ideas about image (p. 138), how to sell (p. 149) and how to get your message across (p. 136).

50 Draw up terms and conditions of sale, if applicable. Set up your database for actual and potential customers.

51 If you will be selling direct yourself, develop a sales dialogue. Train by carrying out role-play with your spouse or a colleague (p. 157).

52 Set up a financial control system, that is, how you will compare actual performance with budgeted performance as drawn from your business plan.

53 Finalize your decisions about brochures, literature mailers, phone scripts.

54 Draw up contracts of employment for any staff.

Ready to trade

55 Finalize premises, fitting out, employing staff, sales methods.

56 If you are still employed, hand in your notice. If you are unemployed, contact your local Business Link* or Jobcentre Plus* to find out whether you can get any financial assistance from the start of trading.

57 Tell Her Majesty's Revenue & Customs (HMRC)* if you are to be a sole trader or partner (p. 45).

58 If you are forming a company or taking on staff, ask HMRC for information on how to operate the PAYE tax system (p. 240).

59 Set up a reporting system for your staff.

60 Plan the opening.

Summary

1 Use this step-by-step guide to help to start your business in the right way.

2 The guide is in approximate order; in particular, actions may vary depending on whether you decide to postpone trading until you have raised the money you need.

8

Less than 100 per cent

Businesses don't have to be all-consuming. Many self-employed and small businesses are run on a part-time or less than full-time basis. The increase in the number of these sorts of enterprise reflects the restructuring in society and the economy that has occurred over the last couple of decades. There are a number of typical scenarios.

First, you might have some sort of business idea but be uncertain whether you want to give up your relatively secure paid employment to commit yourself to surviving on the idea. It may strike you as sensible to test the water a little bit in your spare time or to find out more about the idea before you commit yourself further.

Second, you could be a permanent toe-dipper. Perhaps you have to stay at home, for example to look after dependants, children or elderly parents and you are looking to make some money on the side. The amount of time you can devote to your enterprise might be fairly limited, and you need to select your business idea with care.

Third, you may come into the category of 'greys' who have taken early retirement or redundancy and you are looking to establish a business that will supplement your other income without taking away all your spare time.

Fourth, at the other end of the age scale, you might be a young person starting a business while still in full-time education.

Fifth, a number of businesses are being set up that are 'virtual' businesses. People are opting for a different lifestyle from the driven corporate existence and choosing to establish businesses based around the home, possibly with others in a similar position, for example forming a network of consultants.

Finally, it is very common nowadays for individuals to establish themselves as self-employed with a portfolio of work based around their contacts from their experience in corporate life.

What is in this chapter?

- testing the water (p. 75).
- toe-dipping (see p. 76).
- a 'grey' business (p. 77).
- a 'virtual' business (p. 78).
- portfolio work (p. 78).

Testing the water

There are drawbacks to trying out your business idea without devoting all your time to it. If you are in full-time employment, you will be trying to carry out your business in the evenings or weekends, when you are tired. The result may be that you give up simply because you are too weary.

The second drawback is closely linked. Because you do not have the time your business idea needs, you will not carry it out successfully; you will assess it a failure because it has not achieved what you hoped. The real reason may be that you have not stoked the fire enough.

The third drawback is that there are not very many businesses that you can start only in the evenings and weekends, because they are not natural business hours for anyone else. Telephone answering machines, call diversion, mobile phones and e-mail do not always provide the solution.

The big advantage of toe-dipping is that you carry on earning money from your job while you are starting up. This may be essential if you have no other income, as your business is unlikely to make profits for some time.

The model way of testing the water is not necessarily to start full trading while still employed elsewhere, but to use your spare time to carry out all your market research and prepare your business plan during this period. When the initial preparation is completed, you should be able to assess whether your business idea will work and have some idea of when you should be generating an income to live on. Now would be the time to cease full-time employment. One possibility at that point is to try to raise some money to fund the business, but obviously this is not a step to be taken lightly.

Toe-dipping

Your motivation may be quite different; you may not be attempting to start a full-time business at all. You may simply want to earn more money on the side. You may be in full-time employment or you may have domestic responsibilities. In either case, the number of hours available for business is limited. And that is the way it is going to stay, at least in the foreseeable future.

You will need a very special sort of business idea. The ideal trade should allow you to fit the work into odd or irregular hours and should not need a permanent presence. Suitable ideas include:

- *fashion, health and beauty*: hairdressing, beauty therapy, dressmaking, fashion design, knitting, invisible mending and alterations, massage, aromatherapy, physiotherapy, chiropody, acupuncture, reflexology, personal fitness training.
- *office services*: book-keeping, word processing and desktop publishing, duplicating, addressing and stuffing envelopes, data preparation, printing.
- *writing*: books and articles, translating, copy-editing, proof-reading, indexing, copywriting.
- *arts and crafts*: drawing, illustrating, photography, picture framing, candlemaking, glass engraving, jewellery, pottery, soft toys and dolls, design work.
- *home-based activities*: catering and cooking, upholstery, childminding, curtain making, garden produce, taking lodgers, rearing animals (goats, poultry, bees, rabbits), boarding animals.
- *assembly work*: toys, lampshades, clothes, Christmas crackers, fire extinguishers, watch straps, jewellery and so on.
- *design work*: graphic design, interior design, web design.
- *property*: dealing, buy-to-rent.
- *miscellaneous*: consultancy, teaching (music, exam coaching), repairing (bicycles, china, clocks), agents (mail order, party plan organizer, telephone selling), dealing, building, decorating, electrical repairs, car maintenance, light removals, odd jobs.

A 'grey' business

There are legions of people in their late 40s and 50s, far too young to cease an active economic life but pushed out from their established role by companies 'downsizing', 'restructuring', 'retreating to core activities' or simply being replaced by the march of technology. In addition, around one person in ten over state pension age currently chooses to carry on working.

Such people may not be looking to set up in a full-time business, because the package offered by their previous employer has given them a pension or other financial help. But they may be looking to supplement their income and, more importantly, remain economically and socially involved.

'Greys' can set up sound businesses. They have a number of advantages:

■ they are not looking to derive a huge financial return.

■ they have years of business or work experience behind them.

■ they are very motivated.

■ they may have some initial capital to start the business off and may not need to draw money from it until it is well established.

The disadvantage is that what might start out as a well-controlled economic activity could end up dominating their lives at a time when 'brain' work should be more important than 'brawn' work. It may also be hard to find good working space (but see p. 186 about working from home).

Young business

'Schoolboy entrepreneur nets millions' is sufficiently unusual to make headlines. But some school and university students do start their own businesses and this number could increase as a result of government policies to teach enterprise in schools. Many student businesses are Internet-based which can fit well around school hours, the demands of university and limited capital availability. There are also educational initiatives – particularly those run by Young Enterprise UK* – which enable school pupils to set up and run their own company.

There is no limit on the age at which you can start up as a self-employed person. At the time of writing, children of any age can be directors of companies but from October 2008 there will be a minimum age of 16. This will apply to both new and existing directors. Even at age 16, you might find it hard to gain acceptance as a credible business because of your youth (though with an Internet-based business your age will not necessarily be apparent). You will normally be unable to get trade credit or external funding if you are below the age of 18.

A 'virtual' business

Information technology has transformed the way business can be carried out. Businesses can seriously be run and grown without infrastructure and without employee overheads. Such a business fits neatly into a lifestyle for someone looking to spend less than 100 per cent of their time developing it. You could develop, say, a network of consultants, which operates without an office and without employees. Communications can be by e-mail; meetings can be held via the Internet or conference telephone; demonstrations or presentations can be given using the phone and the Internet. Meetings with clients can be held at their offices, in coffee shops, or in a hired room.

The advantages of a 'virtual' business are that the overheads are low, the lifestyle is flexible, the work is home-based, and the content is mostly intellectual, with a minimum of time devoted to administration and low-quality work. The disadvantages are those typical of a home-based business: face-to-face contact can be missed, self-discipline is required to work, and meetings with clients are not in ideal situations.

Portfolio work

Typically the person who retires early from middle or senior management might look to build a portfolio of work. A good start for such a life of enterprise might be to obtain a contract from your previous employer. This gives you a good base income but now gives you the freedom to organize your time in the way you want to. This also gives you the opportunity to start using your network of contacts to produce further work. A portfolio approach to business might include the following elements:

- consultancy.
- non-executive directorships or chairmanships.
- project work.
- buying and renovating property to sell or to let.

The advantages of portfolio work are that the income can be relatively secure (especially if the first contract is with your former employer), the diversity of contracts also adds a quality to your earnings, the work is varied and the lifestyle is flexible. However, be careful of your employment status when you first set out on this course. Her Majesty's Revenue & Customs (HMRC) has clamped down on people who leave an employer one day and return the next claiming to be 'consultants' either working through their own company or on a self-employed basis. Expect HMRC to look carefully at your status – see p. 372. If it decides you are, in reality, still an employee, you will be charged tax and National Insurance on that basis.

Summary

1 Trying to start a business while still in a job can lead to failure. Instead, use the time while you are employed to do the basic research about the market and your likely sales and costs. After this, decide whether to take the plunge or not.
2 If you know that you only want spare-time earnings, not a full-time business, choose your business idea carefully to allow you to fit it in with other commitments.
3 Older people starting businesses have a number of factors in their favour.
4 Think about how you can set up a business keeping the overheads and infrastructure as low as possible. Use modern technology to enable you to do this.
5 Starting out with a contract from a former employer gives you a head-start in building a portfolio of work.

Other chapters to read

17 Choosing your workplace (p. 182); 18 Information technology – and other equipment (p. 193); 29 Tax (p. 350).

9

Off the peg

At some stage in thinking about your business ideas, it probably flickers across your mind that it would be simpler if you could buy a ready-made business. Your reasoning might be that this would get you off to a flying start and cut down the period needed to establish a business from scratch.

But would it? The truth is that there is no easy way to having your own business. Either you must accept that there is a hard slog ahead of you, building up your own business, or, if you decide to buy an established business, you must expect to pay for someone else's work in having built it up successfully. What is more, if you decide to buy, you might end up paying too much for a business that still needs you to work very long hours. If you want to buy a ready-made business because you think it will be easier, you should seriously examine your motives in wanting to take on a business.

The real temptation to buy a business from someone else is that you might buy a bargain, perhaps because the owner is desperate to sell, or because the business has been run badly and you can see a few easily applied steps that could transform its profitability.

There are three main ways you can get yourself off to a flying start: you can buy a franchise (p. 101), buy into a partnership (p. 86) or buy an established business.

What is in this chapter?

This chapter looks closely at buying the whole or part of an established business or buying into a partnership. Franchises are dealt with separately in the next chapter.

There are several ways to buy into an existing business (a 'going concern'). The first part of the chapter looks at buying outright and managing the business yourself. It considers:

■ search for a business, a guide (p. 81).

■ the business profile you want (p. 81).

■ finding a business for sale (p. 82).

■ investigation (p. 84).

■ changing the business (p. 93).

■ setting a price (p. 93).

■ tips on negotiation (p. 96).

Alternatively, you could invest as a 'business angel' in someone else's business. This is looked at on p. 98. Finally, you could buy into a business with funds raised from a venture capital organization through a management buy-in (MBI) or, as an employee, a management buy-out (MBO). These are considered on p. 99.

Search for a business, a guide

1 If you are already in business, pinpoint your overall objectives, the missing factors in your present business and what is holding back growth.
2 Develop a profile of the sort of business you are interested in acquiring – either all of it or a stake (p. 81).
3 Carry out the same market research as you would do if starting a business from scratch (p. 13).
4 Research the businesses available for sale (see p. 82) and produce a short-list of the likely contenders.
5 Investigate the shortlist of businesses carefully (p. 84).
6 Consider what effect your purchase would have on the business (p. 93).
7 Establish a price for the business; or, better still, a price to open the negotiation and a maximum price you would consider paying (p. 93).
8 Plan the negotiation carefully (p. 96).

The business profile you want

You should try to avoid the random search for a business to buy or a good deal to make. If you were starting your own business, you would set out your thoughts and ideas. This is exactly what you should do when considering which sort of business you could run successfully if you were to buy one already set up.

To help to clarify your thoughts, it is a good idea to write down in specific terms a profile of the ideal business. This should include the following, among other points:

- the ideal market (or even more specifically, the segment). This choice should follow from a review of your own skills (p. 54), coupled with some market research, which should enable you to pinpoint a market providing you with the opportunities any successful business needs (see Chapter 2).
- the products or services that fulfil this marketing strategy.
- the main factors in a business that could enable you to be successful.
- the price of the business, the maximum you could pay and how that would be financed.
- the ideal size of the business you are looking for.
- where it would best be located (for business and personal reasons).
- whether the business needs to be successful already or whether you are looking to make it profitable through your extra management skills.
- the minimum level of profitability you could accept and the minimum level of income you require from the business.

Once you have drawn up this profile, you should use it to judge the suitability and likelihood of success of all the prospective businesses you see.

On the whole, do not be tempted to abandon the principles enshrined in your profile because you see what you think will be a bargain. It is safer to adhere to the outline you elucidated in a calm, rational manner when you were not under any pressure to do a deal.

Finding a business for sale

There are two basic (but not mutually exclusive) approaches you can adopt:

1 Look at businesses that the owner is advertising for sale.
2 Search out suitable businesses that the owner may not have decided to sell, but that fit your profile.

The advantage of the second method is that you may be more likely to find the business you want; the disadvantage is that you may not be able to persuade the owner to sell, certainly at a realistic price. If you carry out this research, be prepared for several false starts.

Where are businesses advertised for sale?

Newspapers and magazines can be a good source. The business pages of the *Financial Times*, *The Times* and the *Sunday Times* include many businesses for sale. If you are looking locally, your local newspaper may have a section for this. Other possible sources include *Dalton's Weekly* and *Exchange and Mart*. If you know the business area you want to trade in, also take a look at trade journals for that sector. There are also numerous web sites advertising businesses for sale. Try, for example, *www.businessforsale.com*, *www.daltonsbusiness.com* or *www.exchangeandmart.co.uk*. Many web site services let you search for free, but others charge a subscription or fee.

The details given in the advertisements will be very brief; it may only include the market, the general location and some indication of the income from a business. Note that a number of the advertisers may be the receivers of the business, trying to sell it as a going concern. If the advertisement is by a liquidator, the aim will be to sell off the assets or bits of the business, as it will not be possible to sell it as a going concern because there is no goodwill.

Another source to try is business transfer agents and estate agents. They carry details of small businesses for sale; estate agents will be mainly concerned with retail businesses. You can find the names and addresses of agents in the area you are interested in by looking in *Yellow Pages* or using the 'Search for a transfer agent' facility on the *www.ukbusinessbase.com* web site. These agents are not independent advisers but are acting on behalf of the business being sold.

Finally, try asking around in the area you want. Try accountants*, solicitors* and banks. These sometimes maintain a register of businesses for sale. You can also try someone already in the industry for ideas of what might be for sale. Advertise in the local newspaper or trade magazine for a business you want.

Conducting a search for a business

You may be able to identify other possible businesses not yet put up for sale by studying the market segment you want to enter. Carry out market research into that sector, identify the competitors and investigate the backgrounds. You may well find that the businesses already for sale are the worst buys. On the whole, go for what you want and not for what is available. There are also a number of organizations specializing in helping you to find acquisitions. These include some of the big firms of accountants. Other useful sources include:

- the membership lists of relevant trade associations.

- *Yellow Pages* and *Business Pages*.

- databases that include unlisted companies, such as Extel Cards and ICC Company Information – try business or academic libraries.

- trade exhibitions and trade journals.

Investigation

Once you have a shortlist of two or three businesses you could be interested in, the next step is to investigate thoroughly and then to investigate all over again. It is crucial to be absolutely confident that you know all the pitfalls as well as the good points of the business you are buying. Do not be hurried into an acquisition for fear of losing that so-called bargain.

Investigation is largely a question of using your common sense and being very distrustful about what you are buying. Guidance in this section is very much of the 'Don't forget to do this or that' or 'Look out for', but it cannot be an exhaustive list of what you must do. There are also specific investigations that need to be made for each business you look at; some of these will be exclusive to that business.

What help can you get with an investigation?

It would be wise to employ an independent adviser to help you to analyse a potential purchase. The most likely candidate for the role of adviser will be an accountant*, as a considerable part of the investigation will be analysing existing accounts and assessing asset values. However, accountants may be expert at the quantitative aspects of a business but miss the qualitative aspects, such as how crucial present employees are to the business. Help and advice from someone in the industry can be invaluable.

Why is the business being sold?

This can be difficult to establish satisfactorily. For example, if it is being sold because the present owner doubts that it will prove to be profitable in the future, you are not likely to be told this. Your investigation of the business prospects must try to identify this sort of reason.

The most likely cause of a sale is that the owner wishes to retire. If this is the case, you need to keep your eyes open for signs that the business is running out of steam as the owner's retirement nears. It is also possible that the business and its equipment are now out of date.

Sometimes you may come across small businesses that are being sold by larger companies. The reason given may be that it does not fit with the strategy or pattern of the larger business. The real reason may be because the large company cannot make it profitable, so you need to look for the warning signs. Look carefully at the past history and the accounting policies used.

If the business is in the hands of a receiver, it will be advertised for sale as a going concern. You cannot take for granted that this is so. Investigation needs to pinpoint whether the assets are actually owned by the owner, whether any genuine goodwill exists and, obviously, the reasons for the financial difficulties.

A sale for any of these reasons may present opportunities for the right business person. The ability to turn round a run-down or unprofitable business is a management and business skill, which you may possess. The important point in acquisition is to know the real reason for the sale before you negotiate to buy. Then you can price the business correctly and assess the impact you could make, post-purchase.

What is being sold?

What you are buying depends on the legal form of the business. If you want to buy a business operated by a sole trader or partnership, you are strictly buying its assets, excluding what the previous owner owed and was owed. You could buy all or only some of the assets. If the business has traded under a different name, not the owner's personal name, you might consider buying the right to carry on using this. This is a wise decision only if there is some goodwill attached to the business name. Your agreement should be very specific about the assets you buy and the price you pay.

On the other hand, if the business is a limited company it has a life of its own, separate from the shareholders. In this case, you could be buying only assets or you could be buying the company itself. If it is the latter, as the new owner you will acquire a business that has obligations and liabilities, such as contracts and debts, as well as assets.

Partnerships

An added ingredient if you are buying a share in a partnership is the necessity to investigate the prospective partner (or partners). All the other business aspects – for example, track record, business prospects, assets – need careful study, but it is also essential to find out what you can about the partners. This is for two reasons.

First, as a partner you are jointly and severally liable for the debts of the partnership. In practice, what this means is that if there are bills to be paid and your partners do not pay up their share, either because they do not have the assets to cover the debts or because they refuse, you can be made to pay for the whole debt, not just your share of it. You must satisfy yourself that the new partners hold some assets that would cover the likely value of their share of any debts and find out their track record of paying bills. A history of unpaid bills or lack of assets of any value (for example, a house) might raise question marks in your mind about their suitability as partners.

Second, the ability to coexist amicably in a partnership is crucial. Personality conflicts can be crippling and may mean, whatever the economic sense of the partnership, the future of the business would be in jeopardy.

If you are buying a share in a partnership in which there are already two or more partners, be prepared for the negotiation to take a long time. Two or more people have to agree; it is not just one person deciding, as would be the case if you were buying from a sole trader.

Use a solicitor* to help you to draw up a written partnership agreement or to vet the one offered to you by the partnership (see p. 48 for an idea of what needs to be covered). It might be wise to attach a note to the partnership agreement that would cover areas such as how the business is to be run, who has responsibility for what, what is the extent of the decision-making for each partner and so on. These are not strictly part of a written formal agreement, but it is crucial that each of you has a clear understanding of how the business will be run.

The accounts

The past accounts of the business are written evidence of what has happened in the last few years. But how good is the evidence? The minimum you should insist on seeing is the accounts for the last three years; these should be handed over to your accountant for stringent analysis. However, there are some points you should bear in mind. If the business is a sole trader, partnership or small company (see p. 38), accounts do not have to be audited. Indeed, the only reason that accounts need to be prepared is for tax purposes, and the accounts need only be a statement of sales and expenses; a balance sheet is not necessarily required. The evidence about the track record could be decidedly patchy and even inaccurate.

The fact that the accounts are prepared for tax purposes may suggest that the sales are understated; indeed, vendors may claim just that. But you should be wary of accepting that profits are really higher than stated in the accounts.

As well as published accounts, ask to see all the management accounts and accounting books, debtors' and creditors' lists and bank statements.

Once your accountant has examined the accounts thoroughly, you should begin questioning whether there are any specific reasons why, for example, the profits were high during the period reviewed. Was there no competition? If so, is there now? If the business is retail, has the pattern of shopping facilities altered to make the location less attractive now than formerly? Will there be a rent review, with a likely increase in rent, which will make a dent in future profits? And so on. Query anything that you think might have affected the results of the present owner, favourably or unfavourably.

Land and buildings

With land and buildings you need to consider the following points:

■ *position*: this is particularly important for shops. You need to study a shop's location very carefully. What are the other shops in the immediate area selling? Direct competition need not be a disadvantage, as customers sometimes like to have a choice and will go to a location with two or more shops selling similar products. The population of the shop's immediate catchment area could be crucial to the success of the business; you should not assume that you can persuade people to travel far to your particular store. What sort of population lives near by?

Is there high unemployment? Are inhabitants likely to have high purchasing power?

The future plans for the area, if any, need to be discovered. Are any redevelopments planned? Any road changes mooted? Has planning permission been given for facilities that might undermine your trade – for example, a superstore nearby – or enhance it – say, a new leisure centre that might draw extra trade to the area, or a large new housing estate. The effect of these needs to be considered.

An important consideration for many types of retail business is how many potential customers will pass the shop each day, for example on the way to work or to do other shopping. Test this out for yourself by standing outside the shop on days that are likely to be busy for the business and on days likely to be quiet.

- *tenure*: if the property is not freehold, what are the terms of the lease? For how much longer does the present lease run? When is the next rent review due, and is there any indication of the likely increase? Who has the responsibility for maintaining the exterior of the building? Check that the seller has the right to transfer the lease. Would you be able to sell or sublet at some future date? With a freehold property, bear in mind that the current owner might own it outright. If you'll have to borrow, you would need a higher level of profits than the current owner to make the business viable, because you'll have interest payments to cover.

- *business rates*: these are based on the property's estimated rentable value not the profits you generate. Make sure they seem reasonable given the level of trade you are likely to attract. For example, rateable values for shops in a run-down High Street are often still assessed on the basis that this is a prime retail area even if the bulk of trade has moved elsewhere. If the property's rateable value is less than £15,000 (or £21,500 in London), you may be able to claim Small Business Rate Relief – see Chapter 29.

- *condition*: pay for a survey to be carried out to establish the extent of your likely bills for the property. Run your eye over the decoration and shop or office fittings. Are there any improvements you could make that would improve the potential of the property, and what would these cost?

- *space*: what is the useful selling space? Is this sufficient to stock the quantity and range of goods you intend to carry? Will there be any surplus space? Could this be used profitably – by you or some other business?

- *insurance*: what insurance currently covers the property? Is this relatively expensive or cheap?

- *valuation*: take expert advice on the value of the property. You should also ask your solicitor to check the title, any covenants that apply and the likelihood of planning changes.

Plant and equipment

With plant and equipment you need to cover the following points at least:

■ *condition*: is the plant and equipment old or badly maintained? Is the technology outdated? What volume of business or production levels could the equipment deal with? Can it cope with periods of maximum demand?

■ *value*: this can be a problem to establish to both vendor's and buyer's satisfaction. The vendor may well seek to be paid a value based on the cost of the equipment. As a potential buyer, you need to look closely at the market value, as this may well be less than cost. Indeed, if the equipment can be used in that business only, the market value may be very low, although the value to this business may well be higher than that. You will have to negotiate a price.

■ *future commitments*: if you are buying a company, you should investigate what capital expenditure has been contracted for which you would be responsible. This may also apply to any advertising expenditure to which the company is committed.

Stock

Stock is likely to be the major area of disappointment after a purchase. Opt for ruthless reductions in the value in the accounts or make an agreement to buy, subject to certain conditions being met, if you can. At least, check:

■ *how much*: first of all, establish that the amount of stock in the business agrees with the figure in the accounts (particularly if you are buying the business, not just selected assets). Once you have established how much stock there is, you need to analyse whether this is the right amount and the right sort for that business. Get guidance on the mix of stock from an expert in the industry. Be wary of buying too much stock, even at apparent bargain prices. Keep an eye out for any outdated or damaged stock as well. You should also check if the business has had a proper stock control system. If it has not, this should raise questions about quoted amounts. It can also be worthwhile to find out whether it is possible to return any stock items to suppliers.

■ *value*: as with plant and equipment, it is likely that the seller will hope to be paid the higher of cost or market value for the business stock. You, on the other hand, may only be willing to settle for the lower of cost or market value (and that may be a very low figure indeed). You should not deviate far from your value of the stock.

Debtors: the customers who owe you money

Your investigation should cover:

- *how old?* your main query about debtors must be: 'Will they pay and when?' Ask the seller for what is known as an age analysis of debts. This should show how much is owed and how long it has been owing. Very old bills may suggest they will not be paid or simply that the owner is very dilatory about collecting money. You need to know which.

- *credit rating*: the analysis of debtors should pinpoint which customers owe the larger sums. Assuming that you were to keep these customers if you purchased the business, it is worth checking the credit backgrounds of those businesses (p. 314). You do not want to buy a business that relies heavily on a few customers who are bad payers.

- *credit collection*: investigate how the existing owner collected debts. An improvement in this could enhance the profitability of the business.

- *value*: once you have made a careful analysis of unlikely payers and allowed for the cost of collecting the debts, you should be able to arrive at an estimate of the value of the debtors.

Other assets

There are a range of other assets that the business may hold:

- *cash*: confirm the level with the bank or wherever the cash is held.

- *patents, trade marks, etc.*: investigate their status; for example, is the trade mark registered? You should find out what would happen to these 'intangible assets' if the business should fail. They may prove to be unrealizable assets if the rights revert to their original owner, for example.

- *investments*: if the business holds investments, perhaps in other companies, your accountant should ensure that an appropriate value is placed on them.

- *goodwill*: the price you will eventually fix is unlikely to be the sum of the values you set on the individual assets. Negotiation may result in a price above the asset value. The surplus is known as goodwill. Goodwill can also be described as the reputation of the business and what you are paying to acquire that reputation. Valuing goodwill is a very uncertain process. Will the goodwill disappear once the present owner is no longer part of the business? Will customers and suppliers stay with the business on the same terms, assuming those to be satisfactory?

Liabilities: what the business owes

The main liabilities to be investigated are:

■ *loans, debentures and overdrafts*: establish the amount, the conditions, the period of the loans and the interest rate.

■ *creditors*: an examination of an age analysis of creditors should give you some idea of the sort of credit periods suppliers have been extending to the business in the past. If the business has paid very slowly, it may suggest that its reputation with suppliers is fairly low.

Sales

To estimate the potential of the business, you will need to look carefully at the sales figures. Carry out a product or service analysis. Does one product account for the vast bulk of the sales? What is the profit margin on this product? Does your analysis suggest scope for streamlining the product list?

Your study of the debtors will also have thrown up information about the customer structure. Does the business rely on one or a few customers? Do those customers account for the major portion of the profits as well as the sales? An over-reliance on a few can mean the business may be fairly risky and prone to sudden downturns should a customer cease using the product.

Crucial information about sales potential can be ascertained by talks with the major customers. These may throw light on the quality and reputation of the business and product. Further evidence can be obtained by a study of the level and nature of credit notes and a study of the percentage of sub-standard goods produced.

Look for any special relationships that exist with major customers, such as an extended credit or returns arrangement.

Other aspects of the sales figures you should study include:

■ the element of windfall sales that are unlikely to be repeated.

■ the sales by territory or area.

■ the pricing and discount structure, including the existence of fixed-price or fixed-volume contracts, particularly if buying a company.

■ the distribution of the product.

■ competition.

■ the seasonality.

The products

If the business is the manufacture or distribution of a product, you will need to find out more about it. The areas you should concentrate on are:

■ *cost*: ask yourself if there are any reasons why the costs should rise or fall in the near future. Have there been any changes in the prices of raw materials, and are there seasonal variations? Is there a shortage of skilled labour to make the product? Are any changes likely among the suppliers? Are there any key supplies that need careful management?

■ *profit margin*: an examination should also be made of the cost of each individual product compared with its price. Do all the products cover direct costs and make a contribution to overheads? Which gives the highest contribution and which the lowest? What is the pricing policy? Have discounts been offered? Turn to Chapter 26 for information about profit margins, contribution and overheads and Chapter 16 for pricing.

■ *orders*: if it is a company, what is the quantity of advance orders? Will these all be retained if ownership of the company changes hands?

Employees

If the present owner has staff, you will have to find out what your obligations will be to them. If the owner is a sole trader and you are buying some of the assets, there will probably be no legal obligation to offer continued employment; but there may be if you are carrying on the business. If the business is a company, you will most likely have legal obligations to the employees. This is particularly important if it is your intention to replace the staff or make them redundant. You will need to ask your solicitor* for advice.

Even more crucial than the legal responsibilities for employees can be the extent to which the business relies on key personnel. You need to understand their calibre, attitudes and responsibilities – before the deal. It is vital to sustain their enthusiasm and commitment through the period of ownership change.

Changing the business

Finding out what has happened in the business in the last few years and what changes are likely to occur as a result of external factors does not give you a complete picture. It ignores the fact that you intend buying the business and have some ideas of how it could be improved. You need to consider what changes you would like to impose on the business, what they might cost and what improvement in profits you estimate they would make.

Realistically, you should also recognize that a change in ownership may mean lower profits rather than higher. This might occur if the business is heavily dependent on personal contacts. The previous owner may have established an extensive network of relationships, which means that, in a shop, for example, a substantial proportion of the customers come because of the owner's personality rather than because of its location, its prices or its range of goods. No matter how confident you are that you will handle customers courteously and cheerfully, you may not have that magic ingredient your predecessor possessed and some customers may drift away.

On the other hand, you may estimate that, in a business where personality is important, the previous owner has not been ideally suited to the nature of the work and that you will be able to bring a change for the better because of your own character.

Other changes you may introduce are more tangible, and you will be able to estimate the effect and cost of their introduction. The three main ways you can increase profits are by cutting costs, increasing prices or selling more. See Chapter 26 for some ideas.

Bear in mind that you may need planning permission if you intend to change the use of the premises. If the change of use might be controversial – for example, opening a workshop in a primarily residential area – it could be a good idea to apply for permission before deciding to buy.

Some changes may involve you spending money: for example, redecorating or refitting a shop, reorganizing the production facilities, buying new equipment, restocking. Include these in the cost of acquiring the business. This allows you to set a realistic price that you can pay for the business.

Setting a price

The right price for any business does not exist as a theoretical calculation. The only price that is 'right' is the price that both the buyer will pay and the seller will accept. It is all down to negotiation. This may bear no relation to the prices calculated as a result of the value of the assets or the earnings potential that the business gives you. The first step is to jettison all notions about real value. The second step is to throw out of the window all notions that the price given in the agent's details, for example, is the price you will have to pay. Negotiation is everything.

However, you should enter any negotiation with two prices in mind. If you are the buyer, the lower price will be the price you use to open the negotiation; the higher price is the maximum you will be willing to pay. You should not start negotiating unless you have a clear idea of this maximum price. If you are the seller, the lower price is the minimum you will accept for the business and the higher price the one you adopt initially.

Nevertheless, it is vital to have used a number of methods of arriving at a price. These can give you a benchmark for establishing lower and upper prices. You must have a base point to work from. The accountant who is advising you should carry out these calculations for you, but you should know the basis for the figures. You can set a value by asset value, earnings multiple, or return on capital employed.

Example 1

George Gabriel is interested in buying a health food store.

The details he has been given are:

Price for the freehold of the shop and flat	£160,000
Price for the stock	£9,500
Goodwill	£6,000
In total, he is being asked to pay	£175,500

George needs to carry out his own investigation. First, he looks at the shop. The size is reasonable (500 sq. ft) for a specialized business and the location is excellent. However, the shop has been fitted in an idiosyncratic way, not especially suitable for the type of business. Although the condition of the fittings is good, George would want to replace them; in particular, he would like to include facilities for serving take-away food, including hot food, which the shop does not have at present. He estimates that the cost of these alterations will be about £36,000, £18,000 of which is for the additional food facilities.

When it comes to the living accommodation, this seems in reasonable condition. He asks a valuer to give some idea of what an alternative two-bedroom flat would cost in the area and is given an estimate of £90,000 to £110,000.

A close examination of the stock reveals that some of it is damaged but, most importantly, there are very big stocks of a few slow-moving items. George would place a value of only £4,000 on the stock acceptable to him. Nor is he convinced that there is that much goodwill associated with the business; the present owner's odd personality has militated against this.

George's value for the business based on asset values would be £160,000 less £18,000 fittings that need replacing plus £4,000 for the stock. This makes £146,000 for the business, rather than the £175,500 asked.

Example 2

George Gabriel (see Example 1) now works out a value for the business based on an earnings multiple. He has been told that the present owner derived an income of £30,000 a year from the business. George estimates that, with the improvements he intends, he can increase this figure to £35,000 in the first year; he hopes to push it up to £40,000 subsequently.

George has £100,000 of his own; he intends to spend £5,000 on extra stock plus £36,000 on improvements. This leaves £59,000 towards the purchase of the business. He'll have to borrow the rest of the purchase price – an additional £87,000 if he buys the business for the valuation above. At an interest rate of 8 per cent a year, this means interest charges of, say, £6,960 a year (exact amount depends on amount borrowed, which will vary with the purchase price).

So George's approximate earnings figure for the last year would be:

$$£30,000 - £6,960 = £23,040$$

And for the current year:

$$£35,000 - £6,960 = £28,040$$

And once the shop has reached its full potential:

$$£40,000 - £6,960 = £33,040$$

These figures give the following values of the business:

2 times multiple: £46,000, £56,000, £66,000

3 times multiple: £69,000, £84,000, £99,000

For negotiation, George should refer to the past year's earnings figure only and go for the two times multiple. This gives a much lower figure for valuation than the asset value basis does. In fact, the range of values he obtains suggests that, on the whole, the asset value basis will result in a figure that is too high for him to get the return he needs on his investment. From these figures, his negotiation should start at £46,000 and go up to £69,000, say.

There are a couple of other factors that might influence his decision; one increases the value he would be willing to pay, the other lowers it. These are:

■ the savings he will obtain from living above the shop, for example rent or mortgage payments.

■ the loss of interest his £100,000 was earning.

Asset value

Your investigation will have helped you to set values for individual assets. If you are buying the whole business or it is a company, the figure you are interested in is the net asset value, that is, value of the assets less the value of the liabilities. There is no rule on whether you should use the cost of the asset or its market value as a basis for your price estimate, although you will be wise to choose the lower of the two.

The final value agreed upon is unlikely to be a simple sum of the individual assets; any additional value is called goodwill.

If property forms a major part of the business, you may automatically think that the price you pay is asset value. However, it is very important to look at what sort of profits those assets will be able to earn for you. See Example 1 in the box on p. 94.

Earnings multiple

A second way of valuing a business is to apply some multiple to the earnings from the business, perhaps two or three times. Clearly, you will not take the present owner's figures for earnings at face value; apart from investigating whether they are a fair reflection of what has happened, you also need to take into account in your calculations what interest charges you would be paying after the purchase of the business. This should include loans for any improvements you intend making. See Example 2 on p. 95.

Return on capital employed

To assess value on this basis you need to decide in advance on a rate of return that you require on the money you invest. This should certainly be more than the rate of interest you could get from leaving your money in a building society account. Once you have decided, you work out what the income before interest and tax is as a percentage of the capital invested. If the figure you get as a result of this calculation is less than your required rate, you would decide not to buy or to lower the figure you were prepared to pay.

Tips on negotiation

The negotiation is the key to future prosperity. This may well be the only time you are involved in negotiating to buy a business, so there is no opportunity to practise negotiating skills. But negotiation must be done if you are to buy the business at the right price for you. Follow these tips:

1 An obvious point, but do not agree to the price first quoted.

2 Open the negotiation at the lowest price you can. This price must be one that you can back up with credible reasons, so a good deal of planning is needed before negotiation begins. A shock opening bid can lower the seller's expectations and undermine resolve.

3 Look carefully at apparent bargains. If the seller accepts your first low bid, perhaps given the seller's better knowledge, your opening price was too high. Think again.

4 During the negotiation, you can undermine the opposition's confidence by asking a lot of 'what if' questions. For example, 'What if the government changes?' 'What if your major customer goes bankrupt?'

5 Do not fall into the trap of making a concession for the sake of the goodwill of the negotiation. The opposition will most likely strengthen his or her resolve to hold out for the highest price possible.

6 Do not answer questions of how much you can afford to pay, at least until you wish to use it as a negotiating tactic at an appropriate time. Answering the question at the timing of the seller's choice may lead you into discussion of helping you to foot the bill by loans or easy instalments. Later you can use what you can afford as a limit on price.

7 Sometimes, you will find that if you start out as a tough negotiator, the reaction from the other side is a soft response. A tough reply to a tough opener is more unusual.

8 Never be offensive and over-critical; it draws a defensive response.

9 Keep your reactions very low-key; never indicate whether the news is good or bad. Keep calm.

10 If the other side makes a concession, do not feel you must respond in kind. Stay tough. There is no law that if you make an agreement with the seller, the agreement should be midway between the two initial positions. On the contrary, the purpose of negotiation is to try to make sure the pendulum swings your way.

11 If you are probing for solutions that will allow you and the seller to agree, always begin your possible concessions with 'If'.

12 Planning your arguments and rehearsing them before the negotiation will give you confidence in the strength of your bargaining power.

13 Try role-playing before the negotiation occurs with a colleague or spouse acting as an objectionable seller.

14 Whatever the treatment meted out by the seller, do not let it get to you and your confidence in your own bargaining position. Do not be affected by the other's apparent wealth, status, success or attitude.

15 The best way to counter any threat is to indicate that you are indifferent to its being carried out. Making threats yourself can be unproductive.

16 If it is possible to produce some outside authority who limits your bargaining position, do so. This could be your spouse, your partner or the person lending you money.

17 Keep in mind whether the goodwill of the previous owner is needed after the change of ownership.

18 It is often useful to link part of the price to future performance. This reduces the risk of failure against forecast.

Business angels and agreements

If you don't want to purchase the whole of a business and be responsible for running it yourself, an alternative is to be a business angel. A business angel is looking to invest money in a private company, but an angel is not the main driving force of a business. The angel is looking to invest risk capital (not usually a loan) in exchange for owning part of the business (becoming a shareholder). An angel is also usually looking to work in the business, bringing additional skill, contacts and experience.

Before you invest as a business angel, you will need to carry out all the investigation spelt out earlier in this chapter. In addition, you need to negotiate your role in the company and a shareholder agreement to give you some protection in the event of disagreement. You need the protection because it is likely that you will be a minority shareholder (own less than half the shares) and thus could have little power over how your investment is spent or your role in the business. The agreement should cover:

■ what the business activity is and what it can be in the future.

■ no competing business to be carried on by the management.

■ the issue of further shares to other shareholders and the right to buy the shares of any other shareholder who wants to sell.

■ what happens if the existing shareholder gets into financial or legal difficulties.

■ board meetings and who is on the board of directors.

■ ensuring that the management cannot move assets out of the business.

- level of management salaries and how much time management gives to the business.
- your right to look at financial information.
- who can sign cheques and up to what amount.

As you can see, a solicitor* should carry out drawing up a shareholder agreement. But don't get bogged down in legal niceties and remember that you want to work with the management after you have reached an agreement. A shareholder agreement is just to protect yourself from an unscrupulous management and should not divert you from your prime aim, which is to make the business more successful with an investment by you.

Brief guide to management buy-ins and buy-outs

In recent years, there has been a growing number of management teams buying into another business and buying out and running the business in which they were previously employed. Buying into another business is known as a management buy-in (MBI), and the purchase of the business will be funded by a venture capital organization, in addition to your own money.

You can make an MBI on your own or with one or more members of a team. You need to get the backing of one or more venture capital organizations before you can go ahead. Backing is only likely to be there if you have solid management experience, usually in a large company.

A management team buying out a company that they already work for is known as a management buy-out (MBO). There are three main occasions when this occurs.

First, a large organization decides to sell or close down a subsidiary. This could be because:

- the business does not fit the strategy of the organization.
- the business does not give the rate of return required by the organization, or it could even be unprofitable.
- the parent company does not have the resources to provide the funds needed by the business or it simply needs to raise cash.

Second, a private company may want to sell out *in toto*. This may be for personal reasons, such as the family not wanting to run the business any longer or the need for cash.

Third, the company may have gone into receivership. There may be a part of the business that could be profitable if separated.

Raising money is likely to be the major problem for a management buy-out, as the management team may not be able to finance more than 10–20 per cent of the business. There is also a need to raise the money quickly before the opportunity slips. Lenders and investors will want to go through the same process as with any investment or lending decision (see Chapter 24). A large proportion of the money put up to buy the business will be interest-bearing loans, which can be an onerous burden for a company.

Some MBOs opt to organize as cooperatives with all the workers contributing part of the capital needed and all participating democratically in the way the business is run (see p. 52).

Summary

1 Do not be tempted into paying too much to buy a ready-made business because you want your business life to get off to a flying start.
2 Clarify your thoughts about the market you want to enter, the size of business you want to run, the type of product or service you want to offer and how much you want to pay before you start searching for a business to buy. Summarize it in a business profile.
3 Consider seeking out a business that fits your profile as well as investigating all those currently advertised for sale.
4 Use advisers to help you to investigate a partnership or business.
5 Adopt a sceptical approach to investigation; query and question everything about the business.
6 Be realistic about the effect of a change in ownership; there could be changes for the worse as well as the better.
7 Set two prices before you go into negotiation; the lower one with which you start the bidding, a higher price beyond which you will not go.
8 Negotiation is everything. There are no rules; there is no right price for any business. It is up to you to summon your facts and marshal your arguments to keep the price as low as possible.
9 Use the negotiation tips listed on p. 97.

Other chapters to read

1 You and your ideas (p. 1); 2 Who will buy? (p. 13); 10 Franchises (p. 101); 24 Raising the money (p. 290).

10

Franchises

It would be lovely if there was a way you could start your own business with a much greater chance of survival than most people. And this is just what is claimed by the franchising industry. The statistics seem to back this up, although they are rather patchy. What information is available suggests that a franchised business has a much greater chance of surviving the first three years (the danger years) than other new businesses.

Clearly, you don't get something for nothing. The price of choosing the franchised route can be high. It is up to you to weigh up the costs of buying a franchise and the risks of starting from scratch.

Some of the costs are obvious; you may have to pay a lump sum at the outset as well as paying an amount each year to the person selling the franchise. Less obvious is the cost if you buy a franchise in which you have to buy products from the seller's company at a price determined by it; in this way, you cannot benefit from shopping around to buy your supplies at the lowest possible price.

One of the economic theories behind the success of franchising is that the franchised business can earn for the product as a whole higher-than-normal profits. The intention of the seller of the franchise is to cream off the above-normal bit of the profits, for example by charging a percentage of sales each year, leaving only the normal bit of the profit for the person who buys the franchise. These higher-than-normal profits can build up a brand image for the product or business by carefully positioning the product in the market and using advertising and PR to promote it. In this way, the end-user of the product, the consumer, will pay higher prices than for an equivalent product.

What is in this chapter?

This chapter looks mainly at what happens if you buy a franchise (become a franchisee) and only briefly touches on how to form a franchise to sell to others (become a franchisor). It concentrates on what is called *business format franchising*. This sort of franchising is where you buy a complete business system or way of trading. All the franchisees trade under a common name, appearing to be branches of one large firm, rather than a whole series of independent businesses. The chapter includes:

- a brief guide to franchises (p. 102).
- the pluses and minuses (see p. 103).
- a guide to choosing a franchise (p. 105).
- how a franchise works in detail (p. 106).
- the contract (p. 114).
- setting up as a franchisor (p. 117).

A brief guide to franchises

This brief guide to a typical franchise describes what happens in the different stages of a well-organized and properly developed franchise; occasionally, there may be a franchise that is not developed in a model fashion, and you should beware of buying one of these. Use the guide on p. 105 to sort out the wheat from the chaff.

In the first step, a business is developed or set up. It could be based on a novel or revolutionary product, a comprehensive and well-organized business method, particular marketing style and so on. The business (or pilot) will have run for a couple of years, so that all initial problems have been sorted out. Preferably there should be more than one pilot, which demonstrates that the business idea can be repeated.

Next, the owner of the business (the franchisor) decides to expand, not necessarily by creating more branches but by selling franchises to the business format already developed in the pilot operation. Note that the two forms of expansion, selling franchises and opening branches, can be carried on at the same time. The franchisor develops the franchise operation, which should be a mirror of the successful pilot. The franchisor should produce an operating manual to show how each franchise should be set up and run.

Once the format has been developed, the franchisor will try to find suitable people to buy the franchise (a franchisee) for a particular territory. There will be careful investigation by the franchisor to make sure that the franchise is sold to a suitable person who will develop the particular territory successfully. A prospective buyer should investigate the franchise, the pilot operation, the contract, operations manual and so on to ensure that the franchise will be worth buying. Mutual suspicion should rule.

When the franchise is bought, the contract (p. 114) will be signed and the buyer will usually pay an initial fee to the franchisor. After opening, the franchisor should continue to provide advice and should advertise and market the product name. The franchisee will normally pay a fee each month. The product will usually be purchased from the franchisor, which may be another way that the franchisor makes his or her profit instead of the percentage on sales. The franchisor has the right to make visits to the franchisee's business to examine the accounting records. At the end of the contract, which lasts five or ten years or more, the franchisee can usually renew, subject to the franchisor being satisfied with performance.

The pluses and minuses

Your main consideration before buying any particular franchise is whether it will work as a business for you and provide you with the sort of living you require. Assuming that you have found such a franchise, there are advantages and disadvantages of which you should be aware.

The pluses

1 It is your own business.
2 If the business format has been well worked out and tested in the pilot operation, many of the problems experienced in setting up a business can be sidestepped. This reduces your risk.
3 You receive ongoing advice and support.
4 You hope you are buying a product with a recognized brand name. To create a brand image all by yourself can involve considerable resources. But in the case of a franchise, the franchisor should carry on promoting it, using the management service fee (or royalties) or possibly an advertising levy (p. 108), which all the franchisees will pay. So the brand name of your business will be getting a bigger selling push than could be achieved by each franchisee's individual contribution.

5 In the case of many franchises, you need no knowledge of the industry before you start your business. The training given by the franchisor should be sufficient to overcome any ignorance.

6 Franchisors, because of size, have greater negotiating power with suppliers than you do on your own, although not all of them pass this benefit on to the franchisees.

The minuses

1 While it is your own business, you are expected to act in the best interests of other franchisees and the franchisor. You could find this irritating and restrictive.

2 As well as the initial fee, part of your profits will have to go each year in a payment to the franchisor. You might find this galling.

3 Often the continuing fee to the franchisor is based on your sales rather than profits. This could lead to problems if you are struggling to make profits, perhaps because the costs are too high. This will not be reflected in the level of the fee.

4 The franchisor has the right to demand that you send in sales statistics and other documents promptly, plus the right to come to your business premises and inspect your records. This might seem intrusive.

5 You have to adhere to the methods laid down in the franchisor's operating manual. This could be restrictive and allow little room for you to exercise your own initiative and enterprise.

6 You may have to purchase all your stocks from the franchisor. This allows little room for you to seek competitive alternatives. Again, you could find this stifling if you want to run your own business.

7 Should the franchisor fail to maintain the brand name by promotion or fail to meet commitments about training and the search for better products, frankly there is little you can do about it. If this is all buttoned down in the contract, however, you may be able to get somewhere.

8 If you want to sell the franchise before the end of your contract, the franchisor has to agree.

9 The franchise runs for a certain number of years. Normally, if your performance is satisfactory (whatever that means, see p. 115), you will be able to renew for another period; but you may have to commit to spending more money on refurbishment and more modern equipment. What happens about further renewals is not always clear. You should assess the return on the money you invest over the first period of the franchise only. If, for some reason, you are not able to renew, you may have little to sell, because you cannot sell the name or the goodwill.

A guide to choosing a franchise

1 Be sceptical about franchises, franchisors and franchise specialists.

2 Make your own choice of advisers; do not use those suggested by the franchisor. The most unbiased advisers are likely to be a High Street bank – some of which have specialized franchise units giving independent advice – and the solicitor* and accountant* you employ to advise you.

3 Get your accountant to examine the forecasts given to you by the franchisor and to advise you on how realistic they are.

4 Ask your solicitor to go through any contract carefully to bring out clearly the restrictions and also the ways in which the franchisor will be making money. A legal affiliate to the British Franchise Association* will have specialist experience.

5 Find out how many franchises have already been sold and how long they have been going.

6 Find out, visit and talk to existing franchisees. Do not allow yourself to be restricted only to the franchisor's choice of references.

7 Be particularly careful if the franchise you are interested in is one of the first to be sold. You will need to study the pilot operation with a fine-tooth comb. Does it mirror your likely business? Does the manager of the pilot have the same sort of knowledge and skill as you? Are the premises and their location much the same? Is the stock identical?

8 Watch out if the initial fee is relatively large and the continuing fee relatively small. It is essential for the franchisor that the business continue to be promoted and properly managed. The success of your business depends on how effective the franchisor is in marketing and purchasing.

9 Look carefully at the arrangements for purchasing equipment and stock. You do not want to be forced to buy new equipment if unnecessary; nor do you want an arrangement in which the franchisor can increase the mark-up on products sold to you. Can you buy from alternative sources?

10 Investigate the franchisor. The continued existence of the franchisor's business is important to you, because it carries out the marketing, purchasing and other centrally organized functions. Get references and credit ratings. Ask the franchisor to give you a copy of the latest accounts and ask your accountant to study them.

11 Be careful about buying a franchise from a franchisor who is not a member of the British Franchise Association*. Membership does not guarantee the success of your business or the franchisor's business. And

a number of quite reputable franchisors do not belong to the association. However, members agree to abide by a code of ethics. Ask a franchisor why it is not a member, if it is not.

12 Check that your territory is properly marked out (and you receive a clearly defined map of it). What market research has been done to ensure the territory is promising enough to provide the estimated sales? Do your own analysis – don't rely on the franchisor.

13 Examine what will happen if you die, want to sell your franchise, disagree with your franchisor or want to renew the franchise (see p. 114).

14 What sort of product is it? It must have a useful life of at least the length of the franchise that you are purchasing.

15 Carry out market research in exactly the same way as if you were setting up the business on your own. Chapter 2 should help you to do this. Do not rely on market statistics or views passed on by the franchisor.

16 Check that the product has been patented or the name registered as a trade mark, otherwise the franchise you buy could be worthless.

17 How will the advertising levels be maintained? Does the franchisor contract to spend certain amounts on promoting the brand name?

18 What is the quality of the field force run by the franchisor? How often will they visit? Are they competent to give sound business advice? What will happen if your business runs into difficulties?

19 The relationship between franchisee and franchisor may, in a few cases, prove difficult to maintain at a harmonious level. What are the lines of communication? Do you think that you will be able to build a good relationship with this particular franchisor?

20 If it is a good franchise, you will face competition from other would-be franchisees. So you should expect a grilling. If you are not closely investigated, this may indicate that the franchisor is short of buyers.

21 Many points on which you need information before you tie up an agreement with a franchisor are listed in this chapter. Make sure you cover them in your discussions, and check the franchisor's response.

How a franchise works in detail

Cost

The cost to you could be made up of one or more of the following. There will be the initial cost of a franchise, including the initial fee, and most likely there will be a continuing fee (also called royalty or service fee). There may also be an advertising levy, a mark-up paid on goods or equipment supplied by the franchisor and a mark-up if you lease premises from the franchisor.

You also need to look out for any hidden costs of financing, which may occur if the franchisor obtains a commission on introducing you to a business providing finance or to a leasing company, if you lease equipment. It is only a cost to you if you could have arranged cheaper finance elsewhere.

■ *initial cost*: the range of prices for all franchises is wide; it could be less than £10,000, for example, or as much as £5 million, but typically £200,000. Usually, the initial fee is between 5 and 10 per cent of the total investment but can be as much as 40 or 50 per cent.

There is no typical start-up package, but below is an example of the sort of items that could be included in the initial cost:

Shopfitting	£13,000
Equipment	£15,000
Initial stock	£8,000
Initial franchise fee	£4,000
TOTAL	£40,000

The initial fee is what you are paying to be given the right to use the brand name within a certain territory and to be trained and provided with advice.

■ *service fee*: the service fee payable can also vary quite a lot, from nil up to 20 per cent of sales, but is probably on average around 7–8 per cent. The service fee could be paid weekly or monthly. The fact that the service fee is nil does not necessarily mean that all you are paying will be the initial start-up cost. Franchisors can also be paid by using mark-ups on products and equipment.

A low service fee is not necessarily an advantage for you. It is crucial that the franchisor retains an ongoing interest in promotion and improvement of the business format, and that will only be achieved by the reliance on some sort of continuing payment from the franchisee.

The franchisor prefers to base the service fee on sales rather than profits. This is because monitoring the franchisee accounts to ensure that the franchisor is receiving the proper amount can be time-consuming and expensive. If the fee is based on profits rather than sales, the monitoring has to apply to costs as well as sales, doubling the difficulty of the task.

However, a fee based on sales can be disadvantageous to the franchisee. If the costs of the enterprise prove to be higher than forecast, paying the service fee could be an onerous burden for the franchisee.

You should not underestimate the size of the service fee, because it is based on sales not profits. If, for example, your costs are 60 per cent of your sales value, a service fee of 10 per cent of sales translates into a service fee of a quarter of the profits you make. Work out the figures before you sign.

One point to watch out for is what happens at the end of the original franchise contract if you want to renew. Does the contract allow the franchisor to increase the size of the service fee? Try to negotiate on this, as you do not want a bigger percentage of your hard work to be passed over to the franchisor.

■ *advertising levy*: a number of franchise packages charge an advertising levy as well as the service fee. This is usually calculated as a percentage of sales and paid at the same time as the service fee. The existence of an advertising levy could be regarded as an advantage for a franchise if promotion of the brand name is a very important part of the franchise success. If an advertising levy is made, look to see if this will be audited separately in the franchisor's accounts so that you can see that it has indeed been used for that purpose and that alone, not just disappeared into the franchisor's pocket. If there is no separate advertising levy, the franchisor may undertake to spend a certain proportion of the service fee each year. The other common alternative for advertising is that the franchisor will undertake to advertise as and when needed. With some franchises, the franchisee is expected to advertise as well as, or even instead of, the franchisor. This could lead to promotions that are at odds with each other – and may mean that the prestige of the franchise name deteriorates.

■ *mark-ups*: one apparent advantage of grouping together can be that buying in greater bulk can mean bigger discounts and cheaper supplies. This should also apply to franchises, where supplies are often an important part of the cost of the enterprise. However, some franchisors put on mark-ups that deprive the franchisees of any benefit from bulk purchase.

■ *hidden costs of financing*: it is not unusual for companies to pay commission to someone who introduces a new customer to them. This does not necessarily mean that you will get a bad deal if your franchisor helps you to arrange finance. But it does mean that you should shop around to satisfy yourself that you cannot organize a more attractive deal elsewhere. In practice, you may find it difficult to arrange finance except through the franchisor, but you should examine the possibility.

Finance

Raising money to finance the purchase of a franchise is treated in the same way as raising money to start any new business. All the clearing banks have specialist franchise units and, on the whole, they appear to look more favourably upon the average franchise application than on the average start-up. This is because a franchise is believed to offer a lower risk to a lender.

However, any bank will require that a prospective franchisee contributes a proportion of the start-up capital, around 40 per cent. The remaining 60 per cent could be financed by the bank. Don't forget that the lower the level of your borrowing the greater the chance of your business surviving.

A loan will need to be repaid by the end of the franchise term; however, there may be some leeway on the initial repayments of capital. For example, a repayment holiday could be arranged until the business is in profit.

If the bank requires security, this could be provided by a charge on the business assets, such as premises or equipment, but only if you run the franchise as a limited company. If you remain a sole trader, a mortgage on your house may be acceptable.

Territory

The interests of the franchisor and franchisee may clash when it comes to the allocation of territory. The franchisor would like the option to introduce another franchisee to the area to maximize sales and profits. The franchisee, on the other hand, does not want to be competing with another business on the same patch, selling identical goods.

Whatever is granted in terms of rights, it is important to have clear identification of the territory. Check that it is clearly specified in the contract. The delineation of the territory should also be relevant to the particular trade. If it is a shop, perhaps a certain number of miles from the site would be relevant. If it is a service franchise, perhaps a *Yellow Pages* division of territories would be more suitable.

It is also important to ensure that the territory is large enough to support a business of the type proposed. If you have any doubts, do not buy.

Premises

There is no set practice on whether the premises are owned or leased by the franchisor and sublet to the franchisee or the premises are owned and leased by the franchisee. It varies from franchise to franchise. Controlling the premises has advantages either way. If the franchisor owns the site, and if the franchise is not renewed, a valuable, well-placed site is not lost, as far as the franchisor is concerned. Conversely, if you are the franchisee and the premises are in your name, when it comes to renewal, you can use the site for another business if you would prefer.

Whatever the position about tenure, the location of a site, especially if it is for a shop, needs to be examined carefully, in exactly the same way as for any other business (p. 183). Do not take the franchisor's word for it.

Operations manual

This is where the franchisor puts all the know-how of the business; it should incorporate the essence of the business format you are buying. One of the terms in the contract will be that you must adhere to the manual.

It should include details on everything: accounting systems, recruitment, how to carry out the actual process of the business (for example, grill a hamburger, print a leaflet or unblock a drain), reporting systems and so on. You should see a copy of the manual before you buy. Make sure you understand what is in there; it is how you will have to behave in your business while you own the franchise.

An indicator of the ongoing interest of the franchisor can be how frequently the manual is updated. Ask how often this has been done.

Training

Training is an important part of what a franchisor is offering. Before you sign the contract, you need a clear idea of how much training there will be and how long it will take. You should expect training in all the basic business skills you will need to run a business. This includes financial methods, stock levels, operating the equipment, carrying out the process of the business, working out accounts and PAYE, employment law, VAT and so on *ad infinitum*.

Opening

The franchisor should help you to start your business. If it is a retail business, once the premises have been found, the franchisor will help organize the shopfitting. Indeed, it may be part of the agreement, as it may be that the shopfitting has to conform to the brand image: the colours, style of counter, type of shelves and so on.

Additionally, advice will be available (it may even be a requirement to follow it) on the equipment and amount and mix of opening stock you should have. Find out before you sign what the franchisor's policy is on this and satisfy yourself that you are not being cornered into a policy of over-equipping and over-stocking.

To have a successful opening, you need publicity and perhaps an opening ceremony; you should get help and advice on how to advertise and arrange media coverage. Find out the franchisor's level of commitment on this.

Ongoing support and supervision

This could consist of six elements:

1 Refresher training (see p. 110).
2 Product research and development (see p. 111).
3 Troubleshooters and supervisors who pay regular visits (see p. 112).
4 Updated operations manual (see p. 110).
5 Advertising the brand as a whole (p. 112).
6 Advice on an individual level about promotion (see p. 112).

Products do not last for ever. So for any business there needs to be continuous assessment of the product to see how well it meets its customers' needs, not just in the past, but now and in the future. Any market trends need to be taken into account, and the product may need altering over the years to meet the new criteria. Or a completely new product may need to be evolved. For a franchise to be successful, the franchisor should devote some energy to this. Check what your franchisor's policy will be on this before buying.

The downside to this is that any innovations or alterations could end up being costly for the franchisee. Try to establish what the future plans of the franchisor will be and check what the agreement says about implementation of any new developments.

Another element of support and supervision by the franchisor is the help available if you or the business are in difficulties; for example, are there troubleshooters to provide guidance? The sort of questions you want the franchisor to answer include:

- how often will support visits be made, and what is the calibre of the support staff?
- if the business is struggling to break even, does the franchisor have special troubleshooters? If not, what sort of help will be available?
- what happens if the equipment does not work properly? Are there maintenance facilities, and what is the response time?
- if you are ill, is an emergency staff team available to take over?

As well as the positive side of providing support, you must recognize that the supervisory team also fulfil the role of monitor for the franchisor. You will have to accept that they will want to examine your records and books on a regular basis, check that you are not understating sales (or whatever it is that the service fee is based on) and ensure that the service fee is paid on time.

A final element of support that you need to investigate before you buy is the advice available on promotion of your business. While it is a better arrangement for the franchisor to carry out the advertising and promotion of the product name on a national basis, you may feel that there are opportunities that allow you to boost your business by advertising and promoting locally. The franchisor may be able to advise on this. In fact, the franchisor may insist as part of the agreement that you promote locally. For example, is the amount of expenditure specified, and will it prove onerous?

Franchising and pyramid selling

You need to check that the franchise does not get caught by the Trading Schemes Act 1996, which is intended to curb pyramid selling. The two main caveats that would exclude a franchise from the terms of the Act are:

1 If all the franchisees are registered for VAT; or
2 The franchise operates through a single tier only. For example, if there is a single franchisor for the UK and all franchisees are recruited by that single master franchisor, the scheme could be exempt. But if there is a layer of several different franchisors for different regions of the UK who each recruit franchisees, the scheme would be caught by the Act. Similarly, if the franchisees themselves recruit further franchisees or even if they contract self-employed people to carry out their work, the scheme would be caught by the Act.

Finding and buying a franchise

There are several hundred different franchises. There are 141 full members of the British Franchise Association*, 78 registered associates and 113 companies with a provisional listing. Associate members have begun franchising but do not yet have a track record; full members are longer-established franchisors. Companies that are new to franchising can get a provisional listing as long as they can show that they are taking all reasonable steps to develop their business properly and test its viability for franchising.

To start your search for a franchise you could write to the association. It has a Franchisee Information Pack, which provides advice on how to evaluate a franchise, together with a list of franchisor members and affiliated professional advisers. The pack costs £29, including postage and packing. The British Franchise Association also organizes free introductory evening seminars on becoming a franchisee at various locations across England and Scotland. For more in-depth information, you can sign up for a one-day seminar (£75 plus VAT).

There are a number of organizations operating as franchise consultants that say they will give advice on finding a franchise. Before you use one, be absolutely certain that it is not an organization concerned solely, or even mainly, with finding franchisees for one or two franchise companies. If this is the case, the impartiality of the advice can be discounted. There are a couple of franchise directories* that may give you a head start. Web sites advertising businesses for sale – for example, *www.businessforsale.com* or *www.daltonsbusiness.com* – usually include franchises.

Work out some rough guidelines for the sort of business you would be happy to be in and the sorts of areas of the country you would be prepared to move to. Estimate the sort of price you could pay, bearing in mind that you should be able to invest at least one-third, while borrowing the remaining two-thirds is a possibility.

Write to a shortlist of five or six franchise companies, asking them to send you the details you need. This should include projections of the likely level of business and a draft contract, as well as the areas where the company currently has a franchisee vacancy.

Once you have received the information, the hard work begins. Consult your solicitor* and accountant*. Carry out your own very thorough research investigating, among other aspects, marketing, advertising, product lines, financial aspects and supervision. Use the guide on p. 105 to assess each franchise. It is important to remember that if the franchise is a good one, the franchisor will be able to pick and choose from applicants. Treat the negotiation with the franchisor from two points of view:

1 The need to investigate and assess the worth of the franchise.

2 The need to sell yourself as an ideal applicant to the franchisor.

For a good franchise, you will need to provide references along with much more information about your suitability as a franchisee.

While you are negotiating, you may be able to reserve a particular territory by placing a deposit. The amount of the deposit and whether it is partially refundable or not varies from franchise to franchise. Sometimes the deposit is set against the initial fee on signing. Check the terms and the franchisor's references before you pay it.

The contract

This is the kernel of all franchises. Once you have signed it, it will rule your life. Do not skimp on independent legal advice, although it is unlikely to be negotiable as the franchisor will want to ensure that the same conditions apply to all franchisees.

The contract will attempt to ensure that you run the business along the lines specified by the franchisor. The contract should cover these areas:

- the type of business, its name and the use to which it can be put.
- the territory where the franchisee has the right to use the name.
- how long the franchise will run.
- what the franchisee will have to pay (the initial fee and service fee).
- if the franchisee wants to sell.
- if either the franchisee or franchisor wants to end the agreement.
- what both the franchisor and franchisee have agreed to do.

The type of business, its name

This part of the contract will describe the franchise. It will indicate that the franchisor has registered any relevant trade mark or patented any invention. The franchisee will probably have to agree not to handle any trade mark, product or service belonging to a competitor of the franchisor.

The territory

The contract may specify a right to carry out your business in a particular area, defined by a map or postal code, for example. Unfortunately, it is very difficult to stop another franchisor, or indeed any competitor, encroaching upon your particular area.

How long the franchise will run

The typical length of a franchise could be five years or could be ten. But it could be as short as three or as long as twenty. Normally, you can renew the franchise at the end of the original agreed period, but this may be subject to satisfactory performance. You should certainly want an option to renew and you should try to ensure that the legal wording about what constitutes a 'satisfactory performance' is clear to you, fair to you and can be enforced by you. This is essential, because unless you have the lease on the premises, you would have very little to show for your work at the end of the initial franchise period. You would not be able to sell the business as a going concern, because you would no longer have the rights to the name or to use the business format, and without these there is little goodwill to be attached to the business.

Some contracts specify that if you do not wish to renew, the franchisor will buy the business from you, including a value for goodwill. The value put on the business will be set by an independent accountant.

If you have an option to renew, the contract may specify that certain sums of money are spent to update the premises and smarten the business. The details of this commitment need to be buttoned down in the contract. In any case, the option to renew may well be to renew on the terms currently on offer to franchisees; these may be less favourable to a franchisee than the terms on which you originally signed.

If you have decided not to look for another agreement with the franchisor, the contract may restrict your activities. It may specify that you cannot carry on a similar or competing business for a certain length of time.

What the franchisee will have to pay

The contract will specify the amount and the nature of the fees that will be paid: that is, the initial fee, the service fee (or royalty) and, if applicable, the advertising levy.

If the franchisee wants to sell

Most agreements include some arrangement whereby the franchisee can sell the business during the course of the term. The contract may specify that the franchisor will be entitled to first refusal. Additionally, one of the conditions will be that the franchisor has to agree that your buyer is properly qualified to run it. Your buyer will have to receive training and probably have to be prepared to sign a new agreement. However, it will be difficult to give the same sort of rigorous vetting that the franchisor can do for the initial holder.

Watch out for the sort of agreement that allows the franchisor to charge high transfer (or other) fees on a sale. This sort of condition could effectively block any sale you might make, except to the franchisor on poor terms.

A contract should also include the terms and conditions that apply if you die during the agreed period of the franchise.

If franchisee or franchisor wants to end the agreement

It is possible that you want to end the agreement, if you find that the business is hard going, for example. In those circumstances, it may be difficult to find a buyer. On the other hand, it is not especially in the franchisor's interests to insist on keeping you to the agreement if you are not making a success of it. The contract should deal with what can be done in these circumstances. You need to satisfy yourself that the contract would treat you fairly.

The contract will also specify the conditions under which the franchisor can end the agreement. This could occur if you break the agreement that you sign and fail to meet your obligations under it. Conditions might include:

- minimum performance target.
- agreement to purchase minimum amounts of goods and merchandise.
- the requirement to bring your unit up to standard, if necessary.

Experience is now indicating that, with a good franchisor, renewals are made and some are now on their third or fourth term.

What franchisee and franchisor have agreed to do

The contract will stipulate what both of you must do to keep your side of the bargain. For example, for the franchisor the rules about training, supervision, advertising, support and maintenance and management services should be specified.

The franchisee will have to operate according to the manual and allow the franchisor's staff to monitor the business activities. There will be a requirement not to handle the trade marks, products and services belonging to any competing business of the franchisor's or possibly to trade in any other area allocated to another franchisee.

Setting up as a franchisor

This aspect of franchising is beyond the scope of the guide, although your interests can be interpreted from what is said about the franchisee's interests. Here are a few brief guidelines:

■ you need to have proved in practice that the business format works. This is done by establishing a pilot operation, which should be run exactly along the same lines as the proposed franchise. All the systems and products should be tried out here and all the wrinkles ironed out before selling any franchises. Ideally, the pilot should have run for two years. It goes almost without saying that the pilot has to be successful, otherwise you will not be able to sell any franchises.

■ the business format needs to be distinctive in its image and/or its way of operating.

■ it must be possible to pass on the format successfully to others.

■ the format needs to be capable of earning high enough profits to give both the franchisee and franchisor an adequate living.

The British Franchise Association* has a *Franchisor's Guide*, which costs £55 (including postage and packing) and provides advice on franchising an existing business.

Summary

1 The main advantage of starting a business by buying a franchise is that a lot of the initial start-up problems have already been sorted out; this means there should be a greater chance of survival than starting a business from scratch yourself.

2 The main disadvantages are that there is a loss of independence because of your commitments to a franchisor; you also lose the possibility of

earning exceptionally high profits, because the profits are divided between the two of you.

3 Use the guide to choosing a franchise on p. 105 to help you to sort out the good from the bad.

4 The franchisor should provide support and development throughout the franchise.

5 Because of uncertainty about what will happen at the end of the initial agreed period of the franchise, your decision to buy or not should be based on the initial period only.

6 Use your own advisers, for example bank, solicitor and accountant, and carry out your own research into finance, the market, the product, the franchisor, the location and the detailed terms of the franchise. Do not rely on the word of the franchisor.

Other chapters to read

2 Who will buy? (p. 13); **5** Are you sure? (p. 54); **24** Raising the money (p. 290).

11

Beating the pirates

Successful small businesses do not need to be founded on an invention or an original design. A much more important factor is that there is a market that wants to buy your product. The ultimate in good indicators for success would be a strong market and an original product. But often there is not a ready-built marketplace waiting for inventions. You may need to educate customers. This can be expensive as well as time-consuming.

However, if you have thought of an invention, a trade mark or an original design that could form the kernel of a successful small business, it is worth trying to protect it with the law. For example, if the idea can be turned into profits, someone else may try to copy it and you should obtain the best protection you can, so that you make the profits, not the imitator.

The law cannot protect alone. First, you have to be vigilant in watching out for infringements. Second, and more importantly, the best protection of all is guaranteed by carrying out effective marketing: this can turn a product based on an invention, for example, into the market leader (p. 138).

What is in this chapter?

- what to do with an invention (p. 120).
- what to do with a design (p. 122).
- what to do with a trade mark (p. 124).

What to do with an invention

What is an invention that can be patented?

There are four requirements for something to be regarded as an invention for patent purposes. These are that it must:

1 *Be new*: it must not have been published or made known anywhere in the world previously.
2 *Involve an inventive step*: by and large this means that it must not be obvious to another person with knowledge of that particular subject.
3 *Be capable of industrial application*: an idea that cannot be made or used will not be counted as an invention.
4 *Not be excluded*: there are various categories that are excluded by law. These include something that is a discovery (that is, you found out about it, but did not invent it), scientific theory or mathematical method, mental process, literary, artistic or aesthetic creation, playing a game, presentation of information or a computer program. Also anything that would be regarded as encouraging offensive, immoral or antisocial behaviour, a new animal or plant variety or a method of diagnosis or surgery for animals or humans.

What is a patent?

A patent of invention is granted by a government body. It gives the owner of an invention the right to take legal action against others who may be trying to take commercial advantage of the invention without getting the owner's permission. This right is granted in return for complete disclosure by the owner of his invention.

The body that grants the UK patent is the UK Intellectual Property Office*. A UK patent can last up to twenty years from the date on which you first hand over documents to the Patent Office. After the first four years, you have to pay a yearly fee to keep it in force. Note that the four years start from the date you first applied for the patent. A national patent gives protection only for the country in which it is granted.

If your invention is of a type that you believe you may want to exploit throughout Europe, not just in the UK, it could be cheaper to take advantage of the European Patent Convention. This allows you to obtain patent rights in a number of European countries. You need to make only one application (still to the UK Intellectual Property Office*), whereas if you applied for a UK patent first, you would then need to apply for patents in each of the individual countries you thought important.

Can you get a patent?

The main criterion for granting a patent is whether or not the invention meets the four guidelines about what an invention is (see p. 120).

One area you have to be particularly careful about is not telling anyone (apart from in confidence a patent agent*, which would be a good idea) or publishing information about your invention before you file your application at the UK Intellectual Property Office. If your invention is not kept secret, it may mean that, even if no one else has thought of it, you will not get a patent.

Occasionally, even if you have been granted a patent, you may find that someone challenges it. This could be on the grounds that someone else had already thought of the invention and had made details of it public before you filed your application for your patent. The other person may have decided not to bother to apply for a patent. Making details of it public would include describing it in a trade journal or exhibiting it or selling it.

What does it cost?

When you first file your application, there is no fee. Within a year, you will have to pay a fee of £130 for a preliminary search and examination. If you go ahead with your application there is another fee of £70. To keep the patent in force for up to twenty years, there is a yearly fee, which increases. For the fifth year it starts at £50 and rises to £400 for the final year.

You'll pay more if you want to patent your product in other countries as well. Because the UK has international agreements with European and many other countries, the cheapest route is often to obtain a UK patent first and within twelve months file applications to extend your rights abroad.

However, many inventors use a patent agent* to help with the application. You would have to check the fees before employing one.

A guide to obtaining a UK patent

1 Keep mum about your invention, unless to a patent agent.
2 Complete and file patents form 1/77 in the UK Intellectual Property Office (there is no fee unless you are also applying for a search). With the form should be sent a description of the invention drafted in accordance with UK Intellectual Property Office rules, which specify the exact format. It must describe the invention fully and clearly enough so that a competent person could follow the description and build it or carry out the process. Enclose two copies, preferably typed and on A4-size paper.

3 You will receive a receipt with the date of filing and a number. This gives you your priority date, which gives you precedence over the same invention being filed later. But this is no guarantee that the same invention has not already been publicized elsewhere by another person (see p. 121).

4 During the next year, examine the commercial possibilities and decide whether to press on with your application or let it lapse.

5 If you make an improvement to your invention, you cannot add it to your first application but would have to file a new one. However, as long as you do this within a year of the priority date, that date will apply to whatever is in the new application that was also in the first application. The first application can now be allowed to lapse.

6 Within a year of the priority date you need to file a request for a preliminary search and examination on patents form 9/77, together with the required fee. If you do not do this, your application lapses. You will also need to file the patent 'claims', which define in words the monopoly sought and an 'abstract', a short summary of the invention.

7 Once the search has been carried out by a UK Intellectual Property Office examiner, a search report will be issued. This is a list of relevant documents so you can compare your invention with others and decide whether your application is likely to be successful.

8 If you do not withdraw your application at this stage, your application will be published by the UK Intellectual Property Office without any changes.

9 Within six months of publication of the application, you have to file the next form (form 10/77), plus the required fee. There is now a much more detailed examination of your invention.

10 As a result of this substantive examination, amendments may be required by the examiner. If these are carried out satisfactorily and within the required time, the patent will be granted. Typically, it takes two to three years from application to grant of patent.

What to do with a design

Sometimes the success or failure of a product depends not only on how it works but also on what it looks like. The outward shape or decorative appearance of a product can also be protected, either by:

■ relying on the automatic protection of design right; or by

■ registering the design, by applying to the UK Intellectual Property Office*. This gives stronger protection, but not all designs can be registered – and it takes time and money to register.

What protection does design right give you?

Design right means someone else cannot copy the shape or configuration of an article if it is an original, non-commonplace design. Design right does not apply, for example, to items like wallpapers or textiles (but these may still be protected by copyright and you may be able to register them).

Design right protection lasts for the shorter of ten years from the end of the year in which you first start selling articles made to the design, or fifteen years from the end of the year in which you created the design.

You have an exclusive right for the first five years after you start selling the articles, and in the remaining five years others can obtain a licence to the design – but you don't have to hand over drawings or know-how.

The limits to design right are that something you design to fit or match an article designed by someone else won't get protection, and design right protection applies in the UK only. However, some countries accept UK registration as equivalent to a registration in their country too or as establishing a priority date for a local application.

What is a registered design?

Registering a design gives you a monopoly right for the 'look' of an article or set of articles manufactured from the design. The protection lasts for twenty-five years, but you must renew it every five years.

You can't register a design either if the outward appearance of the article is not important or if the shape of the article is determined by the shape of another item. And the design must be 'new', otherwise registration won't be granted. For this reason, it is important to keep the details of the design secret before you register; if you have not done so, it will not count as new.

What does it cost?

To register a design as soon as possible, you pay £60 for the first design and £40 for each subsequent design applied for on the same form. If you are happy to defer the publication of your design(s) by up to 12 months, the costs are reduced to £40 for the first design and £20 for each subsequent one. You can register a design for protection throughout the European Union via the Office for Harmonization in the Internal Market*. Registration lasts a maximum of twenty-five years. The initial fees are €230 (registration fee) plus €120 (publication fee).

A guide to registration of a design

1 Keep mum about your design, except in confidence to a patent agent.
2 Tell the UK Intellectual Property Office what the design is and what is going to be made from it. You must do this with a copy of the design, for example a drawing or a photograph, in accordance with the rules laid down by the Patent Office. Remember to send the required fee.
3 The UK Intellectual Property Office carries out searches and assesses whether the design is original and new. If it is, registration is granted.

What to do with a trade mark

What is a mark?

A trade mark is something that identifies a product in the eyes of the consumer. The consumer will know who has manufactured the goods or who is selling them. Trade marks are closely linked with the idea of building loyalty among customers, so that they will choose your product or service over another similar one.

A trade mark can be a word or a symbol, such as a logo. Since 1994, distinctive smells and three-dimensional shapes can also be registered as trade marks. Obviously, what you use as your trade mark should be carefully considered, as it needs to fit in with the image of your product and business that you are trying to put across.

In the past, you have not usually been able to register your own name as a trade mark if it is a fairly common name. But, in a recent case, the European Court of Justice found no reason to treat names any differently from other trade mark applications. As a result, an application to register a name as a trade mark will be judged on criteria specific to the sector in which it is to be used.

How can you protect it?

You can register a trade mark with the UK Intellectual Property Office*. To be eligible for registration, the mark must be distinctive. A made-up word or a new symbol would be considered distinctive. Ordinary words would not; although after a number of years, with the advertising you put behind such a trade mark and the reputation for the product and business that you build up, the mark can acquire distinctiveness. Consumers will now recognize what was formerly an everyday word or name as identifying your product.

Registration entitles you, and only you, to use the mark. It gives you the right to take action against someone else to prevent their using it.

You can also obtain an EU-wide trade mark effective in all the member states of the EU by applying to the Office for Harmonization in the Internal Market*.

There are also some simple steps you can take to help to protect the mark yourself. For example, put TM beside the mark when you use it in advertisements or sales literature. It can also help to include a sentence like 'Microtops is the trade mark of Matthews Computer Stores'.

What does registration cost?

The cost will be £200 but could be more if anyone challenges the mark. However, this would only be for one class of goods, and there are 45 altogether. If you intend to use your mark on more than one product, you may need to apply for registration in more than one class at £50 per extra class.

A guide to registering a mark

1 Consider whether the mark will distinguish your product from another. Is it similar to another mark? Could it confuse consumers about the nature of the product or service? Even if the mark is an ordinary word or name, do you believe that your reputation has built it up into a distinguishing feature for your product or service?
2 Apply to have the mark filed at the Registry. Include the required fee and a description of the goods on which your mark will be used.
3 The Registry considers the application; if there are any objections you will be told, so that you can decide what to do.
4 After about fifteen months from the application, the Registry will advertise the mark in the *Trade Marks Journal*. If there is no opposition, the trade mark is registered.

What to do with copyright

What is copyright?

Generally, you have copyright in any creative literary, musical or artistic work you create. This can include not just books, films, photographs, recording, and so on but also, for example, content you create for your web site, computer programs and databases you create if they have an original element. Copyright is automatic – there is no need to register – and usually lasts from the time the work is created until 70 years after the year in which the author dies. (Databases can also be protected by database right which is similar to copyright but lasts only 15 years.)

Copyright gives you the economic right to benefit commercially from the work you have created. The benefit might come from your own use of the work. Alternatively, you might sell (assign) your copyright or, for a fee, license others to use your work. Copyright usually also gives you moral rights to be identified as the author of the work and to be protected from misuse of the work that would damage your reputation.

How can you protect it?

There is no official register for copyright and no need to register it at all. Some private firms run their own registers and offer to register your work for a fee, but there is little advantage for you in using these services unless the firm offers extras, such as legal help defending your right.

Wherever you use the work, it is sensible to mark it with the copyright symbol (©) followed by your name and the date the work was created.

Copyright is private right and, if someone else uses your work without permission, it is up to you to decide what remedies to take. You could go to court but this is generally costly and time-consuming. The best first step might be to write a strongly worded letter to the offender, requiring them to stop using your material, with the threat of legal action if they do not. If the offender has used your work on a web site, print off the relevant screens so you have a record of the offence even if the web site is subsequently changed.

If someone disputes your claim to be author of the work, you may need to provide evidence that you are. You can establish the date at which the copyright material was created by posting yourself a copy using special delivery and leaving the package unopened. However, this does not prove you were the creator, so you should also keep drafts and any other evidence that supports your claim to be the author.

What does it cost?

Nothing. Copyright is automatic without any need to register or pay fees.

Summary

1 The strongest way of protecting an invention, design or trade mark is to use effective marketing (Chapters 2, 11 and 13).

2 Patents and registration provide protection; but the law cannot achieve this alone. You need to follow up infringements of your rights.

3 With inventions and designs it is crucial to keep quiet about them before you apply for a patent or design registration.

4 Mark original work you create with the © symbol and be prepared to challenge anyone who uses it without your permission.

Other chapters to read

2 Who will buy? (p. 13); 12 The right name (p. 128); 13 Getting the message across (p. 136).

12

The right name

At an early stage in your planning, the question will come up: 'What am I going to call my business?' or 'What am I going to call my product?' You may be tempted to plump for your own name or your initials and quickly move on to other tasks. But this would be a mistake.

Choosing a name is a long-term decision, which is all wrapped up with working out what you are trying to sell and identifying why customers will buy from you rather than your competitors. Your company or product name should encapsulate a message to potential or existing customers. This will not happen overnight; it takes many years to build up a name to carry the message you want. But one thing is for sure, you cannot change horses mid-stream. The name you plump for now should be the name you still have in five or ten years' time.

Choosing a name

Before you start the search for a name, there is quite a lot of background thinking to do about your marketplace, competitors and product.

Why do people buy from you?

If you analyse why people buy a particular product or service, the list might include things like it is cheaper, the product has a special feature that others do not have, the service is near by and is very convenient, its running costs or maintenance are less, and there is 24-hour guaranteed service. These are all rational reasons, capable of proof. If your product or service has one feature, or more, that are like this you have a primary benefit. You may be able to achieve your sales on this alone.

The list of reasons why people buy a product might also include it is better, it looks good, the quality of the service is high, it is believed to be very reliable, it is better value for money, and the design is excellent. These are all emotional reasons, which may be real or imagined. But they reflect how customers feel about a product.

A combination of the emotional and the rational reasons gives a product its reputation (or brand image).

How does your product rate?

Your product may have some unique element; if so, you are probably unusual. The chances are that there is nothing that much different or better about what you are going to do than your competitors. But that does not mean you will not be more profitable, make more sales and get a bigger share of the market than someone with a product that does have unique features.

Creating a 'good feeling' among buyers about your product can give you a better general reputation and can make you better thought of and more widely known. Giving your business an identity can make you successful.

However, creating an image of quality and reliability for a utilitarian product can lead to a downfall if your product or service does not live up to it. The product must be good even if it is not the best; the service must be reliable even if not the most reliable.

Where does name come in?

You want the name of your business or product to summarize all the emotional and rational feelings about the product. So if a potential customer hears the name, it instantly gives a good connotation. On day one of your business, this will not happen. You must plan to achieve it over a number of years.

Your first step is to select a name that does not, by itself, cause any feeling of antipathy. Ideally, the name on its own should give a clue to your image. You should at least aim for the name to generate neutral feelings in the early stages, until you have built the image from scratch.

One name or two?

Should your business and product share the same name? There is no clear-cut answer to this one, and for a small business it may not be very important. You will not have the resources to create two brand images, one for the product and one for your business. In any case, it could be confusing. So even with separate names, you will be promoting only one.

If I'm selling to industry, do I bother with image?

Yes. You may be selling to a buyer from an industrial firm but, with the other hat on, the buyer is also a normal human being. This means that he or she will probably have the same number of prejudices as a member of the general public buying soap. It is as important to create a good feeling about your product with an industrial customer as with a domestic one.

If my product has a unique feature, do I have to bother with image?

Yes. You may have some original feature, but once you have launched it on the market, your competitors will be beavering away to make sure that it does not stay unique for very long. And, on the whole, you cannot patent an idea, only a mechanism, so you may not be able to rely on protection (p. 119). If you do not concentrate on the image of your product, and your competitive advantage is subsequently eroded because other products are improved, the future of your business may not look so rosy. Building an image for your product is a low-risk safety route.

What image do you want to create?

This is all linked up with the market research you will have done (p. 14), a crucial stage of your planning. You will have found that there are sectors within the market. For example, if you were considering opening a picture-framing business, you might find the following sectors: do-it-yourself, speedy service, mail order, high-quality frames, and a service with advice from a designer or artist.

Your research will identify the size and growth of each sector, where the competition lies, and what are the prime demands by customers in each sector. In turn, your decisions will be to go for one or more sectors, to look at your service compared with the competitors and to focus on what your customer wants. This will give you guidance on what sort of image to build for your business.

Logo – a no-go?

A logo or logotype may be nothing more than a word, the name of your company or product, always shown in the same typeface or in the same colour, or, perhaps, within a simple shape. It could also include an unusual or memorable shape; one that people will recognize quickly and eventually come to associate with all their perceptions of your product.

Using a logo can emphasize your name and get greater customer awareness. If you can afford to do it, do it. But do not rely on your printer. Paying a designer may be worthwhile (p. 207). In your dealings with your designer, specify that the logo must be cheap to reproduce, as once you have got it, you will use it on everything you can. So you do not want to end up with a beautiful logo that costs you an arm and a leg every time you want new quantities of stationery.

Do not make snap decisions on logos; if you can, try a little bit of market research on potential buyers to assess their reaction or possibly ask colleagues, family or friends.

Tips on choosing a name

1 Made-up words can make good product or business names. They may not arouse any positive feelings about your business, but they are also unlikely to create negative ones. If you are going to register that name as a trade mark, you will stand a greater chance of success in doing so if it is a made-up word (p. 124).
2 If you are going to use an existing word, if possible try it out on potential buyers to check that you will not create a bad impression simply because of the name.
3 Use brainstorming sessions with family and friends as well as colleagues to produce a list of names for consideration.
4 Check that the name you prefer is not used by another product or business in the same or similar market.
5 Avoid initials: it is difficult in the short term to create a comfortable feeling about a business or product with initials.
6 If you think that some of your business will come through *Yellow Pages* or other alphabetic listings, choose names beginning with A.
7 Check that the name you choose does not mean anything nasty in a foreign language (for example, look it up in dictionaries in the library). If you are interested in selling throughout Europe, consider whether your proposed name is suitable.

8 Very complicated words need careful consideration. If a customer has to ask you to spell the word when it is first mentioned, this can be a positive reinforcement for recognition in future. But if it is just too difficult, it may be a disadvantage.

9 A name that uses all capital letters, for example FLAG, can stand out in a chunk of written text, giving the name prominence.

10 Finally, ask yourself if the name seems right for the image you want to project.

What the law says about names

With a limited company or a limited liability partnership (LLP) (see p. 39), you will not be allowed to register names:

- that are considered the same as that of an existing company or LLP. You can check this by looking at the index at Companies House*.

- contains 'limited' or its equivalent anywhere else in your company name but at the end.

- could be considered offensive or illegal.

And you're unlikely to be able to register a name that could give the impression of a connection with the government or local authority. There is also a range of words that require the agreement of the Secretary of State or various other bodies before you can use them. Examples are Abortion, British, Charity, Royal, Windsor, National and English. There are around 145 of these words altogether. There are other rules about company and LLP names, so advice from your solicitor* would be helpful.

If you are a sole trader and want to use a business name other than your own surname, there are certain rules you have to observe, and the same names which are prohibited or sensitive for company or LLP use (see above) also apply in this context. You are not required to register your business name anywhere, but you must disclose your own name in various ways. You must put your own name and address legibly on all business letters, on written orders for goods and services, on invoices and on written demands for payments of debts. You must display your name and address prominently at your business premises or at any place to which your customers and suppliers have access. And if anyone with whom you are discussing business asks you to disclose your own name and address, you must do so immediately in writing.

If you are going to trade under a name that is not your own, consider registering it as a trade mark (see p. 124). You won't be able to register a name that is descriptive of your product or service (because this would be too restrictive for other businesses), but if you choose a name that is made up or unusual you may be able to do so. And registering it as a trade mark would give you some sort of protection for the investment you are making to build a brand image.

If you will be trading under your own name, you could apply to trade mark it. This might be especially worth doing if you have built up a reputation that would enhance the image of your business – say, you are a sports personality selling sports equipment. Following a European Court ruling, an application to register a name as a trade mark is now more likely to be successful than in the past, even if it is a relatively common name.

Companies and sole traders can get free advice on business names from Companies House*.

Building your reputation

Once you have selected your business or product name, your next strategy is to devise means of getting your name noticed by as many of your target customers as you can. Obviously, you do not want your name to be associated with any bad news, so you may find that you do not want to take up every opportunity to publicize your business name. What you should aim for is that your business or product name comes instantly to mind in your potential buyers, but with a favourable impression.

Letterheads

This is the single most important way for most of the self-employed and small businesses to create some sort of image about themselves. Poor-quality paper suggests cheap, poor-quality service. Spend more on the paper to create that good impression.

It is tempting, especially if you know little about marketing or design, to play safe and choose white paper with black type for your letterheads. But consider experimenting with some draft versions before making your choice; it may cost a little extra, but if it helps to create the image you are seeking you should do it. Your local instant print or photocopying shop can be very helpful, either printing small-run samples of different types or positions or at least letting you rearrange elements (name, logo, address) and photocopying the permutations. Consider:

- different colour paper.
- different colour type.
- different positions for your business name (for example, the centre or to the right).
- different typefaces for name and address.
- big- or small-sized typefaces.
- adding a line to give a more finished appearance.

Once you have settled on your letterhead, look carefully at your other stationery needs. If your work is the type where you send out few invoices for large sums of money, you may not need separate invoices but can use ordinary stationery. Will you need compliments slips, or will business cards suffice if you will only need them for a few occasions? Whatever stationery you do require, the colour and typeface should be uniform throughout the range. If you have a logo, it should be included on all your stationery.

If you are in retailing, you may decide that letterheads are not an important tool for you in creating an image. While this may be so with customers, letterheads are still needed to create that right image with suppliers, on whom you rely for credit.

Labels and stickers

If you can see any opportunity for using labels and stickers on your products, seize it. These can also carry the message you want. There must be continuity with your chosen letterheads: colour, style, typeface and logo – if you have one – all identical to your stationery. In a shop, you might consider having price stickers. On garments or other material items like rugs, tableware and so on, labels should be sewn in.

Packaging

The package says lots about the goods, so take the opportunity to reinforce the message you are sending to customers. The style of the packaging should be consistent with all the other items for promoting your image, and with your chosen image itself. Packaging is an extension or even an integral part of your products.

Your own web site

You may decide to have your own web site or to rent space on someone else's. Branding on your web site should be an extension of the branding on your product, letterheads and so on. And the address for your web site (the site name or URL) ideally should be the name of your product or company to strengthen your branding further. Web site names are registered with Nominet UK*.

Other ideas

These can all help to build your reputation:

- advertising.
- public relations.
- appearance of salespeople.
- how you answer the telephone.
- vehicles: their cleanliness and livery, that is, the colour or markings on them.

Summary

1 People buy particular products for rational and emotional reasons.
2 You should aim to create a 'good feeling', a brand image, a reputation, about your product among customers. Make sure that your product can live up to this.
3 Industrial or unique products still need brand images.
4 Analyse your market and customer requirements to decide on an image.
5 A business or product name will be built up over the years to summarize what your image is all about.
6 If you can afford it, have a logo designed for you.
7 Try to encapsulate as many pleasant (or positive) associations in your name as you can.
8 Letterheads are a most important way of projecting messages about your business. Keep the style consistent with web site, labels, stickers and packaging.

Other chapters to read

2 Who will buy? (p. 13); 4 Your business identity (p. 38); 13 Getting the message across (p. 136); 14 Getting new customers (p. 149); 15 Building customer relationships (p. 163).

13

Getting the message across

Do you know what message you want to say about yourself, your product and your business? If you do not, how can your customers know? But knowing the message is not the end of the story. You have to decide who to send it to and how you are going to do it. If your message is not received loud and clear, your customers will not understand why they should buy from you or what it is they are getting. If they do not know the reason for buying, there will be no sales; if they have the wrong reason for buying, there will be dissatisfaction.

If you do not manage to communicate effectively the benefits of your product or service, your business will fail. The message, and getting it across, is crucial. Broadly, marketing is all about getting your message across. But marketing can be a very expensive habit if it is undirected, too ethereal and without a clear purpose. Small businesses need to market, but more and more the marketing should be focused on generating direct responses, on building communications with your target group of customers rather than broad-brush image generation.

What is in this chapter?

This chapter focuses on how you can get potential customers to be responsive to your business message: to soften them up until you can close the sale. It covers:

- the message: who, what, how? (p. 137).
- building up your brand (p. 138).
- direct-response advertising (p. 139).

■ public relations (p. 144).

■ marketing through the Internet (p. 145).

The message: who, what, how?

Who is the message to?

If you do not know what your target market is, you really do not deserve to succeed. You need this information at your fingertips from a very early stage of planning your business (see Chapter 2). Defining the target market necessitates sorting out its characteristics: the number, the location, the spending power and the class structure (if consumer).

Knowledge of the target market is needed to help to refine the message and select the most useful way of communicating it to that particular group.

What is your message?

You need to work out what message you want to send to customers. The two main constituents of your message are:

1 *The long-term reputation* you want to build for your product or business. This can be things like good quality, reliability, quick service and good value. There is more about reputation in Chapter 12.

2 *The specific message* you want to get across now. This may simply be part of building your reputation, as above. Or it could be that you want to describe your product, giving customers information to make a buying decision. Or it could be some specific offer you have available. Or it could be an item of good news about your business. The list is endless.

How to send the message

There are numerous ways of trying to get across your message to your target market. The trick is to select the most cost-effective way of reaching your group. The cost of communication should be measured by what you have to spend to reach each potential customer or, if possible, by the number of sales leads each pound spent generates. Obviously, any cost-conscious small business has to look at the total figure too. But it would not make good sense to plump for a way of sending the message on the grounds that the overall cost is least, if few customers are reached. What matters is how many possible buyers receive the message compared to the total expense. Very broadly, you can communicate with your customers by:

- *writing the message*: this includes direct mail, advertising, web sites, press releases and materials such as brochures.

- *speaking the message*: this includes telephone selling, carrying out demonstrations, attending exhibitions and face-to-face selling.

- *implying the message*: this does not give any specific details but gives an impression about your business or product. For example, the quality and design of your letterhead, a business gift or van sign send an implied message to anyone who sees them. You should recognize that all ways of communicating the message, such as selling and advertising, also include an element of this. An advertisement does not simply have a picture and some words describing a benefit; the whole adds up to more than this, or it should. It should build up the general impression you want.

Building up your brand

All the means you use to get your message across contribute to building up your brand. The methods described above for writing, speaking and implying your message build up the strength of your brand. The aim should be to receive instant recognition of your product (or company) name and an understanding of and favourable reaction to your business among your potential customers. This is explained in more detail in Chapter 12.

Brochures, leaflets, flyers and data sheets

These can be used to send out in response to sales enquiries or possibly mailings to generate interest. But beware the unfocused, general, corporate brochure that has no specific product to sell. If it is not informative and specific, such a brochure may simply be consigned to the bin.

Brochures can be relatively cheap, and there is no need to make them glossy or over-complicated. You can use a brochure to describe your product as well as drawing attention to the benefits. But while you need to be careful not to make it too general, you also need to avoid filling a brochure with a mass of technical details. If the only recipients are going to be highly technical people, consider cheaper forms of product information, such as leaflets or data sheets. Or keep the brochure jargon-free and tuck a one-page technical sheet in the back.

Leaflets are cheaper still, as they may be only one or two pages or a foldover. But again, the style should be consistent, and the leaflet should not look low-quality. A leaflet can be used more widely than brochures, given out at exhibitions, sent out in mail shots or dropped through letterboxes. A leaflet should try to attract attention and increase awareness for your name and product. What is likely to catch a target reader's eye will be a benefit from your product that is something your target customer is interested in.

Flyers are a good, sensible option for small businesses. You could have an A5 one-page flyer, or an A4 flyer folded into three to fit into a standard DL envelope. The flyer could be four-colour one side to incorporate your logo or illustrations of your product, and mono on the reverse to give the details.

Data sheets are simpler still, can be printed at your office, and supply product details without a big selling message. They are for information.

You need to work out your costings very carefully before going for a full-blown brochure. Instead, look closely at the options of flyers, leaflets and data sheets. A cheaper alternative to a brochure may still generate as much interest and so be much more cost-effective.

Direct-response advertising

What can you expect advertising to do for you? Sell more. Unfortunately, it does not seem to work quite like this. The direct link between spending money on advertising and generating more sales is sometimes difficult to establish; the linkage is there, but measurement can be fraught with problems. General advertising is an investment decision, as are all the other ways of trying to get your message across. Spend money now in the hope of more sales later; but the outcome and the return are not certain.

Your advertising strategy should aim to move the potential customer from ignorance about your product to purchasing it. It should:

■ get attention for your product.

■ help them to understand the product or service.

■ get them to believe in the benefits.

■ establish a desire for the product.

■ generate action.

■ improve the reputation and general impression of the product.

You should not expect one particular form of advertising carried out at one particular time to achieve all this. To expect it might be counterproductive if it leads you to cram too many objectives into one small piece of advertising. Your strategy should be to use a mix of different forms to achieve these aims over a long period of time.

If you can sell as much as you want by personal contact, do not waste money on advertisements, PR or literature. With large-value items sold to a few buyers, spending more on direct selling might be a better use of money.

Apart from the obvious form of advertising – advertisements in newspapers and magazines – there are other forms that small businesses will probably find more useful.

Generating a direct response

The sort of general corporate advertising that large blue-chip companies indulge in is not an option for small businesses. You need to focus on how you can generate a response from the reader because you want details of that reader in your database of potential customers. You may also be able to sell products off the page by generating enough interest so that they phone up and purchase direct (you will need to have organized credit card facilities to achieve a proper off-the-page sales plan). Here are some ideas for generating response:

- use eye-catching headlines.
- offer some incentive for people to contact you, such as a sample copy or version of the product.
- offer a discount.

Using a media buyer

If your product has a national market and if you would advertise in national papers, or even in specialist publications with a national reader-ship, consider using a media buyer. This is a business that specializes in buying advertising space. A media buyer can get much cheaper space from publications than you can buying direct and is paid by the publication rather than by you. Discounts of up to two-thirds of the rate card advertised by the publication can be obtained by media buyers.

If you are going to advertise, you may need to have copies of your adver-tisement ready for the publication and produced on film or bromide. Your agency can advise you.

Publications may have very cheap slots available at the last minute. A media buyer could advise you to have advertisements made up and ready so that if a slot comes up you could send over your file, film or bromide at once to catch the empty (and very cheap) space.

Where can you advertise?

You can advertise in:

■ local newspapers and directories.

■ technical or special interest magazines.

■ local radio, cinema or TV.

■ local shops, pubs and so on.

■ national newspapers and magazines.

■ reference handbooks and trade directories.

TV advertising will be too expensive for most small businesses and would be appropriate only if you are looking for volume sales nationwide. You can often target a national audience more effectively and more cheaply if you pick a specialist publication aimed at your target audience. If you run a locally based business, local advertising is clearly most appropriate and there may be numerous opportunities – for example, sponsoring the printing of raffle tickets for a local school or charity in return for your ad on the back of all tickets, ads on boxes used by a local video library, special features in your local newspapers. Clearly, which form of advertising suits you will depend crucially on the nature and scale of your business.

Before embarking on an advertisement, every small business has to decide:

1 Which newspaper or magazine?
2 What size and position of advertisement?
3 What goes in the advertisement?
4 When do you advertise?
5 How often do you run this, or any other, ad?
6 How do you get the ad drawn up?

1. Which newspaper, magazine, directory?

Choosing the right place to put your advertisement is crucial. To be cost-effective, the ad must be placed where it reaches the biggest possible section of your potential customers. The journal or paper must be read by the people or businesses you want to talk to and by people at the right level in the organizations or in the right class grouping in the population.

Two important statistics you need to find are the number of copies sold and the readership. Larger magazines have their circulation figures independently audited by the Audit Bureau of Circulations (ABC)*, although it may be necessary to rely on publishers' claims for smaller magazines. Rates charged for space usually bear some sort of relationship to circulation. Do not assume that the cheapest or the most expensive will be the best bet. Try to estimate the cost per reader for any ad you want to put in.

A listing of magazines and journals accepting advertising, together with the prices charged for space, can be found in British Rate and Data (BRAD) or its online version *www.intellagencia.com*. Look in your local reference library for the hard copy version.

It may be important in your type of business to pay for entries in various directories, the commonest of which is *Yellow Pages*. Before you commit yourself to paying for an entry, investigate how many copies of the directory are sold and to whom. The longer-established directories may be the ones with the biggest usage by potential customers. If you expect to find most of your customers locally, there might be a town directory (check with the library or chamber of commerce) that would be suitable – often a simple listing is free, and charges for display ads may be modest. Directories tend to be published once a year, and entries need advance planning. Some towns have community magazines published, say, monthly or bi-monthly that carry display ads and go to every household.

2. What size and position of ad?

Clearly, the cost of your ad is affected by its size and its position; the bigger the ad and the better the position, the more expensive it will be. For example, an ad on the front page will be seen by more readers and an ad that does not have to compete with others on the same page will be more easily seen too. There is no clear-cut advice that can be given about whether to go for bigger and better. In a trade magazine, a good rule of thumb is:

- in the first third of the magazine.
- on a news or editorial page.
- on a right-hand page.
- one-third the size of the page.

3. What goes in the ad?

Here are some general guidelines, none of which is sacrosanct:

- have a clear, straightforward message.
- do not be afraid of white space in an ad.
- use as few words as you can to get your message across, unless you are trying to sell off the page.
- steer clear of humour; readers may not share your sense of what is, or is not, funny.
- do not copy other people's ideas.
- remember that you are speaking to your customers, and to no one else.
- the reader is more interested in the message than in your name, so do not put your name at the top of the ad.
- an ad is easier to read if the words go left to right and top to bottom.
- make sure your ad complies with relevant voluntary codes of practice and any legal requirements – see below.

4. When do you put the ad in?

There may be seasonal fluctuations in your business, and an advertising strategy may need to take this into account, using ads at the start of the summer for summer goods and at the start of the winter for winter ones.

5. How often do you run this, or any other, ad?

One isolated ad on its own may, frankly, achieve little. If that is all you can afford, you may be better concentrating on the other ways of getting your message across. To achieve objectives such as increasing awareness, generating further action or reminding existing buyers, an ad may need to be repeated several times. A different ad may be required to follow the first one to consolidate the improvement in awareness and, ultimately, in sales.

6. How do you get the ad drawn up?

If you want help producing the ad (the copy, design and layout), you may want to use an advertising agency. There are lots of small agencies or free-lancers willing to work for small businesses.

Keeping it legal

There are few formal legal controls on general advertising in the UK, but there are several voluntary codes. The most important of these are the

British Codes of Advertising and Sales Promotion published and enforced by the Advertising Standards Authority*. As well as a general requirement for all advertisements and promotions to be 'legal, decent, honest and truthful', the codes contain sections dealing with specific areas, such as health products, financial products, children and tobacco.

If you are involved in particular types of business, such as providing credit, your advertisements may also be subject to legal requirements, for example under the Consumer Credit Act 2006. The sale of and advice about many financial products, including investments, mortgages and insurance, are subject to advertising and promotion rules set by the Financial Services Authority*.

If you plan to target your customers with direct mail shots, consider joining the Direct Marketing Association*. Its members are required to comply with a code of practice. You must also comply with the Consumer Protection (Distance Selling) Regulations 2000. Among other things, these require you to give customers all the relevant information they need and to fulfil orders within 30 days. Your customers have a statutory right to cancel an order and receive a refund within seven days of receipt. Further details are available from the Office of Fair Trading*.

Public relations

This can be a low-cost method of getting across a message to the marketplace, although it can be time-consuming. The basic aim is to get information or news about your business into magazines or newspapers in the form of an article or news item. If you can achieve this, such items are seen as very credible and 'true', in a way that advertising is not, because readers place greater trust in the objectivity of journalists. Sometimes the newspaper or magazine will accept editorial material only if it is accompanied by an advertisement, which obviously you have to pay for. If it is obvious that you have paid for an ad to get a placing for some editorial, it dilutes the effect of the editorial.

The main ways of achieving this use of the press are to:

■ *issue press releases* when there is a news item. You will have to write this yourself, or pay someone else to do it. If you do the latter, you are losing one of the benefits of public relations, which is its low cost.

To write a press release yourself, keep to the facts, brief and salient. The length of the press release should be as short as possible and summarize all that you want to say in the first paragraph, as this may be all there is room for in the journal. Somewhere in the press release, put your name and telephone number, where editors and journalists can speak to you.

If there is a good quote that you can include from yourself or the person in your business responsible for this item, this can be an excellent way of lightening the copy and making it more readable. If there is any other personal or human angle that might appeal to the public, do not forget to introduce that. Do not be too optimistic about the chances of getting your press release in – hundreds will be sent each week.

Press releases stand a better chance of publication if there is a photograph attached. It can be a good investment to have some interesting photos of you and the business, which can be appended to the release.

■ *get to know the editor or journalist*: in this way, if you have a story, you could ring your contact before issuing a press release, to see if they would be interested because it is 'exclusive'. This may well be a more successful way of publicizing your story than issuing press releases.

■ *try writing suitable small articles*: for example for trade or technical papers, and sending them in.

Marketing through the Internet

It can be very tempting when everyone else is rushing around putting up web sites to think that you should have your own web site too. It's worth going carefully over the pros and cons before you decide that you need to be up on the Internet.

First of all, ask yourself why anyone would want to come to your web site. Customers would come only if:

■ they know your web site exists.

■ your web site is interesting.

■ your web site is a convenient way of purchasing your product.

The major problem for most small businesses is making potential customers aware of the existence of your business and your product. If you throw in your web site as well, you now have a third element that you have to promote and market. So setting up your own web site could simply increase your costs and increase the amount of effort that you need to put into marketing rather than be the source of a lot of extra revenue.

The argument goes that by browsing, potential customers will find your web site and visit it. But the visit won't last more than one second if your site is not interesting. Your site could interest customers if there is some free and useful information on it. But don't forget that someone has to spend the time producing that information – and to keep the site accurate and interesting the information needs to be updated. This could be a major extra cost of a web site, not immediately apparent to you.

Promoting your web site

If you are convinced that a web site would be a crucial element in your business, you need to work out how to bring it to people's attention. First of all, you have to get it onto what are known as search engines. These are sifting software programs that will give you a list of sites of interest if a customer types in a topic. Depending on how the search engine works, you may need to include keywords on your site, send a summary to the engine editors and/or pay a fee.

Another way of promoting a web site is to establish links with other web sites. Somewhere on another web site there could be a reference (words, logo, web address) that is activated. A visitor to the web site could click on that reference and be directed to your site. However, you have to remember that most sites would only agree to a link if there was a reasonable chance that some traffic would come through from your web site to theirs. So you are back with the problem of encouraging traffic to your site, either by promoting it or by offering something free and interesting to browsers. If you market your products or services locally, you might be able to establish a link from your local authority's or tourist information centre's web site.

You can promote your web site by putting a reference to it on all your literature, including your letterheads. But you should be more anxious to promote your product rather than your web site.

However, a certain proportion of your potential customers could prefer to access information about your products on the Web, so a web site could be your 'shop window'.

Other ways of marketing through the Internet

You could consider advertising on someone else's web site. But take care, as browsers and users of the Internet find advertisements irritating and turn them off, so you may pay on the basis of a number of visitors but find that your ad is not seen by the number you expect.

You could take space in someone else's web site. For example, there are sites devoted to people wanting to buy second-hand cars or organize travel arrangements. The owners of the site are faced with the problem of promoting and marketing the site and ensuring that there are enough visitors, and you may pay for a page or an entry or whatever. If the site really does generate the audience claimed, this could be your most satisfactory way of marketing on the Internet.

Take the claimed number of page impressions with a pinch of salt. Look carefully to see how the claim is made up. Dissect the claims before estimating how many people are likely to see your particular page. You can work out how cost-effective the entry is.

If you are marketing locally, you might be able to get a link to your site from your local authority's web site or any online local directories.

Designing your site

If you have decided that your own site is important, consider these points:

■ *visitors to the site don't want to waste time*: usually they have come for information. Illustrations and graphics simply slow the site down, and many net users turn them off. Focus on your site being quick rather than over-elaborate.

■ *enable visitors to enter your site easily*: don't block them by requiring them to register first.

■ *encourage visitors to register at a later point in the site*: for example by offering them an e-mail newsletter or advance notice of special offers. In this way, you can gather information about your site visitors, including their e-mail addresses, and you may be able to use this for direct mail.

■ to be of any value to potential and existing customers, your site needs to offer real service and real value (and this is a cost you should quantify and allow for in your business plan).

■ if you want customers to be able to buy your goods or services through your web site, you'll need to think about how to receive payments. Specialist companies can either help you to design secure links for accepting payments direct or link you up with third parties who can handle the payment side of things for you.

Summary

1 To communicate your message about your product's benefits, you need to know who you want to talk to, what your message is and the best way of getting your message across.

2 Look at flyers, leaflets and data sheets as a way you can convey information about the benefits of your product to your target customers.

3 Advertising can create attention, inform, remind, prompt sales and improve the image of your product. But the return from advertising is uncertain. It costs more and takes longer than you think.

4 Focus on direct-response advertising, which encourages readers to contact you about your product. You can enter details in your marketing database and send offers to them until you convert them to customers.

5 Do not rely on one form of advertising to achieve your objectives. If you can afford it, use a mixture and try to organize a spread of advertising over a period of time (unless you need specific timing for your product).

6 Advertising must be consistent with the impressions of your product and business that you are endeavouring to foster among potential buyers.

7 Think carefully before you set up a web site. You may spend as much time and effort marketing the web site as you do marketing your product.

Other chapters to read

2 Who will buy? (p. 13); **12** The right name (p. 128); **14** Getting new customers (p. 149); **15** Building customer relationships (p. 163).

14

Getting new customers

The simple truth is that if you do not make any sales, you do not have a business. This chapter looks at how you get new customers by selling direct.

Every part of your business will be involved in selling, in the search for more customers. This extends from answering the telephone to your notepaper and literature, to any person or activity in your business that may one day come into contact with an existing or potential customer. Train everyone who answers the telephone the correct way to do it: they must be prompt, polite, friendly and helpful. If necessary, provide them with a script to follow. But also read Chapter 12, which gives lots of useful tips on building your reputation: from choosing the right name to the right notepaper. Chapter 13 gives some simple and cheap ways of getting your company or product message across to potential buyers.

The first step in gaining sales is to plan and organize. The key to gaining new customers is to gather data and information about people who fit the profile that would be interested in your product. Databases are fundamental to the development of sales, so you need to select database software and work out how to design it to meet your needs.

What is in this chapter?

- direct mail (p. 150).
- telephone selling (p. 153).
- face-to-face selling (p. 154).
- indirect selling (p. 161).

Direct mail

An increasing amount of sales activity takes place by direct mail, either by post, by fax or now by e-mail – see pp. 143 and 167 to check out the law. Even if you will close the sale by a face-to-face meeting, direct mail will be the first stage in the sales process to filter and screen the prospects.

However, many products can be sold simply by direct mail without any follow-up stage. The key to a successful direct mail campaign to attract new customers is to have a very clear idea of your likely customer and to select a mailing list to match that profile. The second most important factor is to be careful about the letter or mailer that you send, the offer that you make, the envelope, even the postage that you use. All these details can be incredibly important in raising or lowering response rate.

The trick with any list, any offer and any mailer is to test first, before you roll it out on a larger scale. A minimum test to be economic is probably 5,000 names. But you can start lower if you print and fulfil in-house.

The list

You can compile lists yourself from different sources, carefully chosen to include what you believe to be potential customers. Or you can buy a licence to use lists from list owners or through list brokers. In this case, you are buying the right to use the list usually either just once in a 12-month period or multiple times during a specified period. Increasingly you can buy lists online for immediate download from web sites such as *www.marketingfile.com* (consumer and business lists) and *www.businessmailing.co.uk* (business lists).

Try to make sure that any list you buy is responsive: that is, the people on it are proved to have bought previously as a result of direct mail. The list should also be recent; lists over 6–12 months old decline in responsiveness.

The price for a consumer list that is recent and responsive might typically be around 16p to 22p per entry for single use (so £160 to £220 for every 1,000 names) and, say, 28p to 44p per entry for multiple use. But watch out, because list owners tuck in all sorts of other expenses and selections that increase the price.

Response rates of 1 or 2 per cent for mailing a list that you have bought or compiled would be good.

Lists should be regularly cleaned and the names of people who have died, moved away or have asked for their names to be taken off should be deleted. When you buy a list, if you find that the number of returns is over 2 per cent, say, you should be able to get a refund. Unfortunately, the amount of the refund is likely only to be for the names, not the wasted postage or mailer.

The offer

Typically, you devise some sort of offer that makes what you want to sell look attractive. For example, you might be able to offer a discount. Or you might be able to offer some sort of extra. The idea is to give recipients some sort of feeling that this offer is particularly good and not likely to be bettered.

You might also offer a free product or sample of something if the recipient responds within a number of days, say 7, 14 or 21. The difficulty with direct mail is to generate action by the person receiving it. So the notion that something extra is on offer for a prompt reply is attractive.

The mailer

Gradually, you will find out what style of mailer best fits your target market. But it could be something simple like a letter with a flyer. Or it could be much more elaborate.

There needs to be some sort of strapline to attract the reader's attention and prompt your mailer to be read. Otherwise, it might be consigned to the bin, like the other 99 per cent. And the copy can be highlighted to emphasize particular words.

The envelope

Some mailers include messages on envelopes to encourage people to open them rather than stick them in the bin. You could mail using stamps or franking to give your mailer more of a personal touch, but this is expensive. The Royal Mail* and the other 17 firms now licensed to deliver UK post offer a variety of cheaper mailing options. For example, you may get discounts if you pre-sort your mail shot into postcode areas.

Mailing services are cheaper if envelopes are not personalized or individually addressed. But this might lower the response rate. You have to weigh up what is more important for you.

The web site of Postcomm* (*www.psc.gov.uk*), the mail regulator, has a useful list of mail industry suppliers, outlining the direct mail and other services they offer, with links to their web sites.

The law

Anyone collecting or using data lists needs to establish whether they need to register with the Information Commissioner*. You will not have to register if you collect data or buy data lists solely for the purpose of marketing your own goods and services. But, regardless of whether you need to register, you must comply with the principles of data protection – see p. 167 for more information.

Steps to help you to organize a mail shot

1 Build up your mailing list from all past, present and potential customers. You can get names from personal contacts, through existing customers, following up requests for information, from exhibitions and so on.

2 Add to your mailing list by checking trade directories, members of trade associations, in fact, any likely place for finding potential members of your target market.

3 Consider renting or exchanging mailing lists with other organizations. If you can buy a list it means you can use it as often as you like, but few organizations sell them. If you are going to rent or exchange, the other organization may insist on using a specialist mailing service, so you cannot copy the list. The organization may also want to see what you are going to send out, so that they can approve what is going to their customers. If necessary, ask a list broker to help to find suitable lists for a fee. Always test a list first. If the test works, on the second occasion you use the list, don't use more than three times the size of the initial test.

4 Weed out all 'gone aways', 'cannot be founds' and 'died' from your mailing list. To achieve this, you need to keep working on your mailing list on a regular basis and feeding in any information that comes in. But keep a separate note of old sales leads in case they resurface.

5 Find out the name of the most suitable individual to receive your message. If you are sending to businesses, do not simply send to a company or to a position, for example the chief accountant. Finding out names may mean telephoning the company first.

6 Always include a letter addressed to the individual and, if possible, signed personally by yourself or someone in your business, not pp'd (that is, signed by someone else on your behalf).

7 Remember what image you are trying to build. Choose good-quality literature, paper and envelopes.

8 Look carefully at what you are sending. If it is a letter, do not make it too long; probably one or two pages is the maximum. Nor should it be too cluttered with jargon. Try to grab your reader's attention in the opening sentence or headline. Make sure that the letter ties up with any other material, such as leaflets or catalogues.

9 Consider how you can increase the response. Would reply cards or coupons be a good idea? Could you use, say, Royal Mail* Freepost for replies? The charge for the standard pre-printed handwritten Freepost service is postage for the replies you receive, plus a yearly licence fee of £70.55 and deposit of £41.50.

10 Test your mailer first, if you think it necessary. Learn from your mistakes and improve your full mail shot.

11 Work out the cost. Try to assess your likely response rate. Only 1 or 2 per cent is considered to be a good response. A poor mailing list could mean even fewer enquiries. Calculate the cost for each response by dividing total expenses by number of likely enquiries or follow-ups. Is this a cost-effective way of reaching potential customers?

12 Do not forget to find out about any cheap rates on offer to new businesses and for large postings from Royal Mail or other business delivery services.

Telephone selling

The last few years have seen a huge growth in the amount of telephone selling (and call handling generally). More and more tasks are being handed over to telephone operators – fixing up insurance policies, giving details about bank accounts and so on.

Face-to-face selling is partially being superseded by the use of the telephone. Face-to-face selling is being made more effective by the qualifying of prospects by telephone before appointments are made. People's time is one of the most valuable resources for a business. Anything that reduces the wastage of that time is beneficial.

If you have not sold by telephone, and even if you don't intend to be selling yourself by telephone, it makes good sense for you to be trained in how to do it. The trick is to try to establish a relationship with the person at the other end of the phone.

Telephone selling requires you to have carried out the research into your prospect, preferably to have already sent a letter or an e-mail setting out your proposal, and ensuring that the specific offer you are making is likely to be of some interest to the person you are calling, perhaps because it helps to meet some sort of business objective.

The stages of a sale are the same as for face-to-face selling: opening stage, building the sale and closing the sale; see p. 158.

Face-to-face selling

The first stage in acquiring new customers is to work out a possible list by market research and other methods. You may, for example, start with the raw list that you use for doing mailings. But you could not possibly follow up and sell direct to everyone on this list; your efforts would not be effective, because you would not be pinpointing those most likely to buy. So the list needs narrowing. This is done in many ways:

- *following leads*: leads are those people who have approached you, either as a result of your advertising or mailers or having seen your business at an exhibition. They may have asked for your literature or for a demonstration or simply expressed interest.

- *using referrals*: ask your existing customers if they know of other businesses that might be interested in your product or service. On the whole, referrals are more likely to lead to a successful sale than a lead, because you have several advantages. You already have an introduction, you know something about the person, and your existing customer may have already expressed satisfaction with your business.

- *by qualifying potential customers*: when you are starting up your business, you may not have any referrals or leads to follow. All you may have is a list you have built up from market research. To reduce the list to the best prospect for you, you need to qualify. Find out the name and position of the decision-taker. Look for information about the potential customer's business. Work out what are likely to be the main factors that mean a business is likely to buy your product or service. You also need to know if the potential customer is considering buying a product like yours or has recently bought one.

Two important aspects of sales organization are:

1 Recording the information you have about each potential customer.
2 Devising a strategy for following up at regular intervals those potential customers who are not interested now but may be in the future.

There are two possibilities to carry out direct face-to-face selling: you, directly as a salesperson, or using a sales representative.

You

When you are starting your business, or if it is a very small one, it is more than likely that you yourself will be selling. If you have not previously worked in this role, the prospect may be fairly daunting. But you are likely to start with one major advantage – complete product knowledge – which is very important for selling. It is possible to acquire and develop many of the personal selling skills that you need, and many courses are available. If you are doing the selling, it would be a mistake to think that you do not need to organize and plan because you have stored it all in your head. You need the same information, sales systems and records as any sales rep.

If yours is a very small business, you might include your mobile phone number in your advertisements. This is fine if you do not expect a high volume of enquiries, but you'll find it hard to get on with your job if you're constantly being interrupted by phone calls. Bear in mind that you will need to hand some means of noting down the callers' details.

Sales representative

At some stage, you may decide to employ someone else to carry out or help with the selling. To enable a sales rep to work effectively, you need to make several decisions:

■ how will the rep be paid?
■ how much training is needed?
■ what sort of back-up organization and systems will be needed?
■ how to control the rep's activities.

Pay

Most salespeople will have an element of business-related remuneration. The purpose is twofold. First, commission or bonuses can be a motivator for salespeople to achieve greater sales. Second, it allows you to keep your overheads lower by not having to pay a greater fixed salary.

Three of the possible combinations of salary and commission are:

1 Basic salary, plus commission on all the sales the rep makes. The rate of commission could vary depending on the volume of business already achieved, that is, the more sold the greater the rate. Commission could be based on value of sales, or if there is some discretion on pricing, possibly the amount of gross profit achieved by each sale.

2 Basic salary, plus commission on sales once a certain level (or quota) has been achieved.

3 Commission only, that is, no basic salary and every sale made triggering commission payments.

Training

Unless you yourself as the business owner are a sales specialist, it would be unusual for a small business to take on someone who needs basic training in selling skills. If you do employ a trainee, you need to be prepared to wait for a long period before the person is achieving a good level of sales.

However, even if you employ only experienced salespeople, you may find it difficult to employ someone who knows your particular market and product in great detail. You must be prepared to provide good product training, plus detailed analysis of the strengths and weaknesses of competitive products. If you fail to do this, your sales are likely to be disappointing.

Back-up organization

There need to be a number of systems and records in place to enable the sales effort to work effectively.

1 Sales staff spend a lot of time out of the office. This is incompatible with the need for existing and potential customers, as well as new leads, to be in contact. You should have a well-organized way of recording phone calls: for example, name, position and company of caller; date and time call received; brief message about purpose of call and what response was promised at your end. Any good sales rep will keep in touch with your office to ask what calls have been received and follow those up.

2 Every sales rep needs a comprehensive and up-to-date price list, plus copies of any literature, press releases and publicity material.

3 If yours is the sort of business that has to issue quotes to customers, try to standardize these as much as possible. This cuts down the amount of time the rep has to spend on paperwork. This also applies to any other sales job that can be standardized. Sales letters, follow-ups to those not currently buying, and terms and conditions of the sale can be standardized. Terms and conditions can be printed on the back of the order form.

Control

You need to exercise effective control over your sales staff. This can be difficult if they spend most of the time out of the office. You must insist on a weekly sales meeting with prepared information, such as number of phone calls or sales visits made, demonstrations carried out, quotes issued and orders received. The sales rep should be able to give you an estimate of the probability of receiving an order from each potential customer and when it is likely to be received.

The information provided by salespeople is crucial in helping you to plan your business. You may be able to produce 'conversion ratios' to help you to predict your likely level of sales. This would be something like a percentage of initial phone calls that become a sales visit, a percentage of sales visits that move to the quote stage, or a percentage of quotes that turn into orders.

Personal selling skills

Many people regard salespeople as liars, cheats and commercial vultures. Some salespeople may be like this, while others can be more successful by being honest and responsible, and by paying attention to every small detail and developing their own selling style to match the product, as well as their own character.

What you need to do to improve your selling skills is develop a sales strategy, which can be simple but which should be applied to every sale. One approach is to produce a series of lists. These should include:

- main features of your product.
- major benefits it offers.
- most likely objections and your planned response.
- advantages and weaknesses of competitive products.
- the key characteristics of your potential customer.
- in what ways your product meets the customer's needs or wants.

There are also simple rules you can follow that will vastly improve your selling ability:

- know your product.
- listen to your buyer.
- relate what you are selling to your customer's needs and wants.

■ plan your sales strategy for each prospective customer so that you know what you want to achieve at each stage of the negotiation.

■ have clear and well-worked-out sales presentations, demonstrations or telephone calls.

■ make sure at all times that you know who the decision-maker is in your prospective client's business.

Developing your own sales approach

The first time you try out your selling approach should not be in a potential customer's office. It is important to feel confident in your dialogue and handling of the client. This means practice. Ask a relative or a colleague to take part in a role-playing session. The best practice for you will be obtained if the customer is played by your relative or colleague as hostile, vindictive and uncooperative. Try to carry out role-playing sessions many times before you come face to face with a genuine customer so that you can develop confidence in your style.

The stages of a sale

There are three stages to making the sale:

1 Opening stage (often a telephone call making an appointment to visit).
2 Building the sale (including sales presentations, demonstrations and dealing with objections).
3 Closing the sale (recognizing buying signals and asking for the order).

Opening stage

Your objective at this stage will usually be to make an appointment to visit a prospective buyer of your product and commence the negotiation. Obviously, you do not want to spend the time doing this unless you have already qualified this potential customer and satisfied yourself that there is a chance of selling your product.

The most efficient way of arranging appointments is to do so by telephone. The first hurdle may be to get past the buyer's secretary. Do not allow your name and phone number to be taken with a promise of ringing back. Instead, ask when your prospect will be free to take a telephone call.

The purpose of the phone call is to make the appointment, not sell your product at this stage. Try to keep it fairly brief and plan ahead what you are going to say. It may run along these lines:

■ an opening statement.

■ any qualifying questions you would like to put (such as 'Are you likely to buy this product in the next three months if it meets your requirements?' or 'What is your budget?').

■ why your prospective customer should arrange a meeting to see you and your product.

■ be prepared with a list of answers to the possible objections your prospect might throw out.

■ offer alternative times for the appointment.

■ finish the phone call.

Jot down the important parts of the conversation while you are speaking on the phone or straight afterwards.

Building the sale

You must plan in advance any sales call, presentation or demonstration. Carefully analyse your potential customer's needs and requirements and decide the relevance of your product or service to these.

The opening phase is important. First impressions are important, so make sure that your appearance fits in with your customer's, as well as being neat and clean. Do not waste too long on social trivialities but establish why you are there and awaken your listener's interest in your product. Before making your detailed sales pitch, ask about the customer's needs, so you can sell to these.

Important points you want to communicate to your listener are:

■ the good reputation of your business, product and yourself.

■ the benefit your potential buyer will gain if your product or service is purchased.

This suggests that you are talking while your possible buyer is listening. But this is unlikely to achieve your sale. Salespeople have a tendency to talk too much. Instead, you should spend over half the sales call listening to your prospective customer. If you do not do this, you cannot judge the chance of making the sale and you cannot relate your product to the customer's needs. You must be able to see yourself, your product and your company through your prospective customer's eyes. This involves listening.

It also implies that your prospective customer will talk. Some try not to, which can be disconcerting. Prepare a number of open questions that you can put during the sales call. An open question is one that cannot be answered by 'yes' or 'no'.

References to other customers who are already dealing with you can be very powerful, as long as your buyer sees the reference as relevant. So the reference must be to a comparable business and use.

At some stage, the subject of your competitors may be raised by your buyer. The traditional stand-by advice is 'Don't knock the competition!' On the whole, the advice is sound; criticizing the competition may have an adverse effect on your listener, because it tends to make you sound rather weak. However, do emphasize any benefits that you know your competitors do not have, as long as they are important to your buyer.

Demonstrations can be an effective selling device but need careful preparation. Make sure everything works before you leave your office for the appointment. Handle the equipment carefully during the demo and if possible involve the buyer in using and handling it during the demo.

With some products or services, quite a lot of investigation needs to be done by you before you can suggest a solution and give a quote. If yours is this sort of complicated sale, before you make a proposal you should carry out the following steps:

- make sure you are investigating the right problem.
- ensure you have all the facts you need by speaking to everyone involved.
- keep an open mind about the solution you will propose.
- keep in touch with the decision-maker and talk through your proposed solution before committing yourself to paper.

The sales proposal should be a restatement of what has already been said. Little has been said so far of your potential client's reactions. If there is to be any chance of making a sale, at some stage objections will be raised. Do not view these negatively as a nuisance. An objection displays that your listener is interested in the negotiation process. An objection should be treated as a request for more information. It would be a mistake to respond to sales resistance by becoming too persistent or pressuring too much.

There are some general guidelines to follow:

- do not contradict or argue and remain calm at all times.
- do not allow the objection to become too important by spending too long replying to it or making several attempts to reply.

■ if possible, anticipate the objections and prepare a response.

■ the best way of dealing with an objection is to turn it into a sales benefit or to agree with the prospect, but counter with a benefit.

Closing the sale

It is important to ask for the order at the right psychological moment. This could be after overcoming an objection or if your potential buyer is showing buying signals. These might include asking about delivery terms or financial terms, arguing about price or asking about extras available.

If your prospective customer is hesitating, extra pressure is unlikely to be effective. Instead, try to create a relaxed atmosphere to have a discussion and assume the decision will go your way. Talk about what will happen in the future and assume that there will be a continuing relationship between the two businesses.

Once you have got the order verbally, do not relax – you can still lose it. Do not count it as an order until you have received written confirmation; in particular, do not order materials until you have the order in writing. If it is a new customer, it is financially prudent to take up references or find out credit ratings before you accept the order. The last thing you want is to do all the work and find that you will not be paid.

Indirect selling

Your particular industry may still use various intermediaries to make sales. The advantage from your point of view is that it is a management problem passed to someone else. The disadvantage is that you are far more concerned about revenue of your products than some outside firm.

Agent

Agents are not employees. They are in business on their own. They are likely to be agents for several products, but you should insist that they are not agents for any competing products. They work for commission on each sale, often between 7½ and 15 per cent. The agent does not buy the product from you; instead, you invoice the customer direct.

The advantage of an agent is that you do not have to fund the overheads: no salary, car, office space and so on. The disadvantage is that you may find it difficult to control the agent's activities. If you have a continuing responsibility for your product, be careful the agent does not sell to unsuitable customers.

To mitigate the disadvantages, you need a written agreement, which you should enforce carefully. The agreement should include the details on territory, products, type of customer, commission and the duration of the agreement.

Distributors

Wholesalers and distributors are not the same as agents. They are your customers. They buy direct from you. When they sell on to their customers, they expect to be able to put on a mark-up of at least 30 per cent, if not more. If you choose this route for your business, it cuts out most of the costs of direct selling, as you will probably deal with only a few distributors. However, you have no control over their selling effort.

Summary

1 Direct mail can be an effective way to sell some products. Test your lists, offers and mailers before mailing in volume.
2 Telephone selling is an increasingly important sales means. Consider being trained yourself for your own calls.
3 Qualify all potential customers to avoid wasting time and effort. Narrow down your list to those most likely to buy from you.
4 If you employ salespeople, you will need some back-up organization and system. You need to be able to record information about customers to help with negotiations and to help you to plan, control and forecast.
5 If you are doing the selling, try to develop personal selling skills. There are some hints about starting sales negotiations, developing them and closing the sales on pp. 158–61.

Other chapters to read

2 Who will buy? (p. 13); 12 The right name (p. 128); 13 Getting the message across (p. 136); 15 Building customer relationships (p. 163).

15

Building customer relationships

Who is more likely to buy from you? An existing customer? Or a passer-by on the street who has never heard of you, your business or your product? The answer to this is pretty obvious. An existing customer is many more times likely to buy.

For a business to be secure and to produce high-quality long-term earnings (and provide you with a good, steady income), it needs to focus on retaining its customers. It also suggests that this should be part of your initial strategic thinking. A business that relies on one-off purchases is building a steeper cliff to climb than a business that targets a group of customers and develops products that can be sold more than once and has much spin-off potential.

Clearly, when a business is starting, every customer is a new one. Potential customers need to be sold to in a number of different ways to generate confidence in your product. But once your business is up and running and has been going for some time, sufficient for your product to be known, to be tested and to be liked, your organization needs to be ready to cope with the next part of your strategy, customer retention. Any well-run small business should have as its motto, 'Once a customer, always a customer'.

What is in this chapter?

- customer care (see p. 164).
- data gathering (p. 166).
- new offers, new products and repeat purchases (p. 168).

Customer care

It's all too easy when you're struggling with the finances, the production or the employees to regard customers as 'just another problem', 'a nuisance' or 'getting in the way'. But you need to drag yourself back to reality. Without customers, you have no business, no matter how slick your financial control or how good your man-management.

Put yourself in your customer's shoes. What would you expect if you were buying this product? How would you want to be treated over the phone if you are phoning with a query? You won't be able to satisfy all customers, but you should struggle to satisfy all reasonable customers, because you want them to carry on buying from you.

When a new customer signs an order, this is not the end of the selling story. You should aim to build up a long-term relationship, because, in most businesses, you will be hoping for repeat orders or for additions to the original order. These will not come to fruition if you do not follow up orders, see they are delivered on time, or, if they are going to be late, warn your customer in advance. You need to give prompt attention to any problems or criticisms.

If your business depends on a few sizeable customers, establish a network of contacts in the customer's business, not just the buyer.

Response times

As a starting point, set up response times for the care of your customers. How quickly is the phone picked up? Within one ring? Two? Four? Or longer? A phone line dedicated to customers that avoids the switchboard or general business line would provide a better service. It would mean that customers get directly through to the correct person to deal with queries or complaints. You could even look at providing an 0800 number for customers.

Also set up required response times for replying to letters, e-mails or faxes.

Complaints handling

In some industries, money-back guarantees are commonplace – and in any case if you sell your products by credit card, you will find that if a consumer complains to the credit card company, the money will almost always be refunded to the customer to your cost. Distance selling means that a customer is legally entitled to a seven-day cooling-off period in which payment has to be refunded.

Perhaps you could adopt a money-back guarantee or some sort of guarantee of customer satisfaction. Businesses are happy to offer these guarantees, because the number of complaints or people who ask for refunds is usually tiny, but it encourages more people to buy from you in the first place.

If your sort of business cannot offer this sort of customer guarantee, you will need a clear policy and procedure on complaints and how they will be handled. Depending on the number of customers, there are also software programs developed specifically to deal with customer complaints. In some industries – for example, if you are an insurance or mortgage intermediary – you must comply with regulations that require you, among other things, to have a formal complaints procedure and to belong to an independent complaints handling body.

As a basic premise, you should follow the policy that a customer who has complained but has been dealt with satisfactorily can turn into one of your most loyal and supportive customers. The ability to solve problems well can be impressive. A survey in 2001 found that 90 per cent of customers would do business again with a firm that had successfully resolved a complaint, and 97 per cent of these would tell others about their positive experience.

Developing the concept of a club

If you can convince customers that their input and opinion matter, they will feel as if they belong to a select group or a club. This feeling of belonging can help to increase the responsiveness from your customers to anything else they might be offered by you. So work on ideas that can reassure them of their value to you – special letters, special offers, or inducements offered only to them as one of your valued customers.

Customer referrals

Another important reason for building up a good working relationship with your present customers is that they can often be the source of your new business too. They may be able to suggest others in the same line of business who may be considering buying a product or service similar to yours. They may even be willing for you to use their name as an introduction. If the customer is very satisfied with your service or product, they may be willing to act as a reference for you, although obviously you must ask first. A reference means that you can give their name to potential customers and they will be prepared to discuss your business with them.

Data gathering

A very important part of building relationships with customers is data gathering. Databases are the key foundation for any business trying to put the emphasis on customer retention. All communications with customers (or potential customers) should be recorded.

If you get an enquiry from someone not yet a customer, it should be logged, along with name, mailing address, e-mail address, phone number and any other details that come up. A note of the communication should be made. Thus whenever this person subsequently contacts you, you need only to ask for their surname and postcode and you can find that record and build on it.

When someone becomes a customer, you may be able to build a little more information, such as age or occupation, although you can't constantly bombard people with demands for information that appear to them to be irrelevant and intrusive.

The basic premise, though, is to gather and capture whatever data and information you can about potential and existing customers. As you gain more experience, building up a picture of your current customers allows you to select lists to mail to attract new customers with greater certainty for a higher response.

Data warehousing and data mining are two jargon phrases used by the data and direct mail industry. Warehousing is putting together lots of names with appropriate information, for example from the electoral rolls or from shareholder registers, which are lists that have to be available legally to the public. Data mining is searching through those names to target those that match your customer profile.

Individual records

The record will need to be tailored to your individual business or product, but more than likely it should include:

- name, address, e-mail address, telephone number mailing.
- customer's type of business (if any).
- what the customer has bought from you, how frequently and in what quantities.
- the name of the decision-taker and the names of other contacts and their positions.

■ the customer's credit rating or information about paying.

■ any complaints and how they were resolved.

Checking out the law

The gathering and holding of personal data is tightly regulated. You are required by law to comply with the following eight principles. Data must be:

1 Fairly and lawfully processed. This means you must have a person's consent – usually this is done by including a tick box on any forms that gather data. Unless the information is sensitive, it is usually enough to give a person the right to opt out of your data lists. But where the information you collect is sensitive (for example, ethnic origin, political or religious beliefs) you must have the person's express consent to be included. Fair processing includes observing people's rights to confidentiality.

2 Processed for limited purposes. This means using data only in ways that are compatible with the purpose for which you collected the data.

3 Adequate, relevant and not excessive. In other words, you should stick strictly to the data you need for your purpose.

4 Accurate. You must ensure the data you keep are accurate and up to date.

5 Not kept longer than necessary. If you don't need a person's details or a particular category of information any more, delete it from your list.

6 Processed in accordance with the data subject's rights. This includes preventing processing if a person has indicated this could be damaging or distressing, and preventing processing for direct mailing purposes if the person has requested this.

7 Secure. You must have adequate measures to prevent unauthorized use of the data and to guard against loss or destruction.

8 Not transferable to countries without adequate protection. If you intend to transfer data to countries outside the European Economic Area, you must first check that the country has adequate data protection measures.

These principles apply to all databases, whether held on computer or manually. If you hold a computer database, you may in addition be required to notify the Information Commissioner* so that your name can be added to a public register of data controllers. There are exemptions from notification, including the processing of data only for the marketing purposes of your own business. Failure to register if you do need to is a criminal offence. If you hold manual data lists, you do not need to register, but you can do so voluntarily. Registration costs £35 a year.

There are bodies with which people can register if they do not want to receive unsolicited mail, phone calls, e-mails or faxes. Becoming a member of the Preference Service (Mailing*, Telephone*, E-mail* or Fax*) allows you to check their lists and so eliminate from your database those people who will not welcome your unsolicited advance. Under the data protection legislation, you do not have to belong to any of these bodies, but the Information Commissioner strongly encourages membership. If you belong to a direct marketing trade body, you may well find that its rules require you to be a member of the Mailing Preference Service* or its equivalent bodies.

Using questionnaires

You could try sending around a simple questionnaire for your customers to complete. Don't make it too elaborate or too long (not more than two sides), and offer an incentive to encourage people to complete it, for example a prize draw for a free product. Questionnaires can give you a huge amount of information about your customer base, what they are really looking for from your product and other general information. Responses of 10 per cent of your customer base would be very good and would be considered a sound basis for making decisions.

New offers, new products and repeat purchases

This is where the real benefit to your business will emerge from adopting a proper customer care policy and being ruthlessly efficient at data gathering.

New offers

If you mail a list of existing customers with a new offer, you should expect a much higher response rate than from a list of people who have never heard from you before. A response of 1 per cent would be good to bring in new customers; but to sell something to existing customers you might look for a response of 3 or 4 per cent. A very targeted and specific offer might bring in a higher response than that, up to 10 per cent say. What this means is that your business suddenly becomes much more profitable.

New products

Successful customer care and data gathering should mean that the launch of new products can be infinitely less risky and more successful if you have a good existing customer base. For a start, you would choose your new products to appeal to your existing customers, as well as targeting other potential purchasers. Indeed, you might offer different products to different sections of your customer base.

The benefits of this should be obvious. Launching new products may even become cash flow positive. At any rate, the period between launch and the product becoming profitable should be considerably shortened.

Repeat purchases

A much higher proportion from a list of existing customers will make second or further orders of the same product (assuming it is a product that has a life of more than one purchase) compared with first orders from a list of potential customers. For example, a magazine or publication that has succeeded in getting a response rate of 1 per cent on the initial direct mail campaign could get a second-year subscription rate of between 25 and 75 per cent, say, without any marketing or selling costs.

Summary

1 Develop a long-term strategy of building sales with recurring purchases to existing customers.
2 Develop policies on response times and complaint handling to improve customer care.
3 Make data gathering and data capture a priority.
4 Making very specific offers to existing customers should be very profitable.
5 New products should become profitable after a much shorter period if you target an existing customer base.

Other chapters to read

2 Who will buy? (p. 13); 13 Getting the message across (p. 136); 14 Getting new customers (p. 149); 26 Moving ahead (p. 322).

16

How to set a price

There are four ways you can increase your profits. You can cut your costs, you can sell more, you can change your product mix or you can increase your prices. Clearly, your aim should be to set your prices initially at the level that gives you your highest profits possible. Needless to say, as with everything else to do with your business, it is easier said than done. There is no clear-cut or agreed method of establishing a price for your product.

Some people use the level of costs as a way of fixing price. This may seem a straightforward calculation, but it has drawbacks. For example, if your costs are very low, does it automatically mean that your prices should be low too? And even working out the cost can be fraught with possible errors.

Other people argue that the price should be set by what the market can bear. But there are no quick and simple calculations that can tell you what this should be. Instead, you have to establish the price by looking at the market you are in and the particular part of it your product appeals to. How does your product rate against others competing in the same marketplace? There are also different strategies you can adopt depending on whether your product is a new or old one. Often overriding all your plans can be the effect that your competitors' pricing policy has on yours.

It is probably more realistic to think in terms of a range of prices. The lowest price you should consider setting will be fixed by the cost. You should not go below this price; if you have to, it would be better not to be in business at all. There are a couple of exceptions, where temporarily it may make sense (p. 178). The highest price will be the highest the market can bear without sales disappearing altogether. Between the two will be the price that will give the highest possible profits.

What is in this chapter?

- the price range (p. 171).
- setting a price (p. 174).
- pricing with more than one product (p. 180).

The price range

There is a range of prices open to you to charge for your product or service. Your aim should be to get as near as possible to the price that is going to give you the biggest profit. But this is a long-term strategy; there may be short-term considerations that imply another price is appropriate.

The highest price

This strategy means you have decided to go for the cream at the top of the market. In marketing jargon, it is called price skimming or prestige pricing. You are pricing your product to appeal to those of your potential customers with the highest incomes or those seeking the snob value of a high-priced item. You can also carry out price skimming if you have a product with a genuine technical advantage or if it has novelty value.

Adopting a price-skimming policy usually implies that you are accepting that you could make bigger profits if you lowered the price, because you would sell correspondingly more. Nevertheless, this strategy can be very appealing to small businesses. To sell more you may need to invest in bigger production facilities or employ more staff. This could involve raising funds to be able to do so. And you may find that this bigger business is harder for you to control. Creating a specialist niche could be ideal for the self-employed and small business owner. While it may not give the highest possible profits, it could make you a very acceptable living.

A pitfall to watch out for is that high prices attract competitors. Your profitable niche may soon be invaded by those offering lower prices or a better service or product. You need to allow for this competition in a price-skimming strategy. This applies particularly if you are adopting a price-skimming policy because your product is new with a technical innovation. It is unlikely to remain unique for long. Your strategy needs to involve either reducing prices in the longer term or concentrating on other advantages or benefits so that your product establishes its own image. This allows it to carry on commanding a higher price even when the technical advantage no longer exists.

The lowest price

The lowest price you should consider accepting for your product is the one that covers your direct costs and contributes something to the cost of your overheads. But this must be regarded as a last resort and not to be accepted if you can obtain business at a higher price.

How is it worked out?

You need to find the direct costs of your product or service. Direct costs are the costs that you would not have if you were not producing that particular item. Your business will also have other costs, indirect costs or overheads. You will still have to pay these whether you produce the item or not.

Example

Sidney Smith knows that the cost of producing his stationery pads is as follows:

Direct materials (paper, glue)	10 pence
Direct labour	5 pence
Total direct costs	15 pence

Lowest price Sidney should consider accepting for his stationery pads is 15 pence plus something towards the costs of overheads, for example, 16 pence a pad.

Note that the terms direct costs, indirect costs and contribution to overheads are explained in much more detail in the section 'break-even point' on p. 306.

When should you use this price?

As little as possible must be the answer. You would need to sell very large volumes of your product to have enough contribution to cover the cost of your overheads, never mind make a profit.

The main circumstance in which you can justify selling as cheaply as this is if you have spare capacity, with very little prospect of using it for product or services selling at a higher price. If this is the case, anything you sell that helps to contribute to the cost of your overheads should be considered.

However, making this decision can have longer-term effects that must be considered. If you are operating in a market that is very competitive or in one in which your customers tend to be in contact, you may find that you are being forced to sell all your products or services at this very low price.

Raising or maintaining your prices can be very difficult in these circumstances.

Selling your product at the lowest price, even on a one-off basis, can have an even worse effect on your business if it triggers off price-cutting by your competitors. This could well occur if customers use your low price to force the competition to lower their prices.

The moral is only sell something at this contribution price if it is a one-off product, perhaps not part of your normal range of goods, and if you are very confident that it will not lead to secondary effects on your other products or the competition. You must only consider this price if you have spare capacity. If you do not have any spare capacity, choose the price that gives you the biggest contribution.

Can you go lower than this price?

Only in exceptional cases, such as if you need to clear excess stocks or low-selling lines. If this is the case, try to clear these outside your main selling channels so that it can have no counter-effect on your normal selling activity.

Why you should not use cost as a basis for establishing your normal price

Many businesses work out their prices by calculating what it costs to make the product or service and adding on what they consider a suitable profit margin. But this approach is not satisfactory for two reasons:

1 It is surprisingly difficult to work out what it costs to produce an item.
2 The cost of an item tells you nothing about whether customers will buy it at that price at all or whether they would have paid much more.

There are various different ways of working out the cost of something, but very often businesses use some variation of a standard costing system. Typically, it looks something like this:

Direct materials	£100.00
Direct labour	£75.00
Indirect materials (50 per cent of direct materials, say)	£50.00
Indirect labour (30 per cent of direct labour, say)	£22.50
General overhead (40 per cent of direct labour, say)	£30.00

▶

Total cost	£277.50
Profit margin (add 50 per cent)	£138.75
Price	£416.25

Of course, various discounts may be offered on this price.

The problem with this system is the difficulty of working out how much of the indirect costs and overheads should be added to each product to work out the cost. To attribute a certain percentage to the product, you need:

- some idea or forecast of the total amount of overheads and indirect costs for the year and

- some idea of the total amount of product you will sell during the year.

In other words, a pricing system based on cost is based on your best forecasts. Obviously, forecasts can be wrong. You may find that you have not sold at a price high enough to cover the cost of overheads, because either your sales are lower or your overhead costs higher than your forecast.

The problem is multiplied if you have more than one product or service. How do you decide how much of the indirect costs and overheads should be apportioned to each product? There is no clear-cut answer.

Setting a price

There are several influences that will determine how near the top or how near the bottom end of the price range your product should be placed:

- how your product compares with competing products.
- the life-cycle of the product, that is, how new or mature.
- how price-sensitive your customers are.
- what price conveys to your customers.
- what position your product has in the market.

How your product compares with competing products

Assuming that you face competition in your chosen market, it is realistic to assume that the price you can place on your product will, to a certain extent, depend on the competition. This does not mean that if your competitors price very low, you have to follow suit. But it does mean that you should analyse your product carefully in relation to the others. The sort of characteristics you should look at include:

- what your product looks like and how it compares with the others.
- how it is packaged and presented.
- what the availability is.
- whether your delivery and after-sales service is better or worse than that offered by your competitors.
- how customers pay.
- whether your product has a better image or reputation.

If your product compares favourably with the others, you may be able to justify a higher price than the competition, even if you are relatively new into the market. Do not be afraid of putting a higher price than the competition. If your product really does have benefits, such as better delivery and service, or a better image, the marketplace may well accept that your price should be higher.

Stage in the product life-cycle?

If it is a new product, one not before produced, as flat-screen plasma and LCD TVs are at present, there are two possible strategies to adopt. One possibility is a price-skimming policy (p. 171), which goes for a high initial price. The other possibility is to try to secure a very large share of the market for your product before the competition appears on the scene. This would be achieved by setting a low price, known as penetration policy (p. 178).

How price-sensitive your customers are

If you put up your prices, do you have any idea how many of your existing customers would switch to another supplier? Or if you dropped your prices how many new customers you would acquire? How great an effect change in prices has on the amount you sell is called price sensitivity (or elasticity of demand). If customer response to price changes in your product is not that great, you can push nearer the upper end of the price range.

Broadly speaking, if your product is not bought that frequently, that is, one purchase will last quite a long time, the sales of it will not be so sensitive to price changes. On the other hand, if it is bought at regular intervals, sales may react much more strongly.

If it is difficult to differentiate one product from another in your market, this also implies that it will react much more strongly to price changes. If, on the other hand, your product can be differentiated from others by perceived benefits such as image and delivery, sales will be more resistant to price changes.

What price conveys to your customers

Price alone can conjure up ideas about your product in your potential customers' minds. The consumer often associates higher quality with a higher price; paradoxically, a high price can help the image or reputation of your product. If this applies to your market, a lower price will not generate more sales.

In general terms, a product that has the greatest market share is unlikely to be the cheapest. These products may generate high sales, because despite their high price they are thought by consumers to offer the best package of benefits (or best value for money).

What position in the market?

Often, your ability to set prices may be limited by the market in which you operate. There may be a going rate established in the market, and unless your product becomes the market leader (see opposite) or is definitely a better product, it may be difficult to establish any other price.

The price of your product needs to fit the market position planned for it. This is the place that the product occupies, compared with competitive products, in the eyes of your existing or potential customers.

A guide to setting prices

1 Analyse the position your product holds in the market. Are your target customers those who are looking for reliability? Has your product already achieved an established image in the eyes of the market? Do buyers view it as good quality, prompt service, stylish, say?

2 Analyse your product. Are you planning modifications or alterations that could alter its reputation or relative position in the marketplace?

3 Analyse the competition. How do their products rate against yours? What is the relative price structure in the market?

4 Decide your pricing strategy. Where in the price range are you going to pitch your price? Is it going to be average for the market, 5 per cent less than the average, 5 per cent above the average or a premium price, 25 per cent above the average?

5 Choose some specific prices. Estimate volume of sales, profit margin and costs to forecast the level of profits for each price.

6 Choose your price.

7 Would you be able to test-market the price in a small area of your market? This would allow you to gauge customer reactions.

Price near the top of the range

There are two possible reasons why you may be able to justify a price near the top end of the range:

1 The product is the market leader.

2 The product is set apart from the competition by non-price benefits.

Market leader

The market leader will be the biggest-selling product in the market. There are several advantages to being the market leader, so it is a position worth aspiring to. The advantages include being able to charge a higher price than the average, making greater sales, having more power over your suppliers and competitors, and being less risky in poor economic conditions.

There is no easy way to become the market leader. Some of the guidelines to achieve the premier position are:

■ try to be one of the earliest entrants into the market (not necessarily the first).

■ develop, by careful marketing, selling and advertising, what is different about your product or business.

■ be ruthless about efficiency and costs.

■ be sensitive to changes in the market.

■ compete intensively on all sales.

■ look for profits over a long period, not the short-term fast buck – so lengthen your horizon.

Non-price benefits

The price you put on the product tells prospective customers something about it. On the whole, a higher price implies high quality, a lower price low quality. You are unlikely to build a business offering a low-quality product at a high price; on the other hand, you are throwing away profits if you offer high quality at a low price. You have to decide where your product is placed in the market compared with competitors and price accordingly.

You will be able to justify a higher price, near the top end of the range, if you decide to offer a high-quality product. You must not be frightened into thinking that the only thing that matters to buyers is price; they are interested in other aspects of your product too.

In your marketing and selling, build an image or reputation for quality, efficient service, reliability, prompt delivery, and effective sales and technical literature. This will allow you to raise prices and generate higher profits.

Price near the bottom of the range

There are three main reasons why your pricing policy might be near the bottom end of the range:

1 Fear (because you mistakenly believe that the main factor in buying is price – but see above).
2 A strategy of grabbing market share.
3 Severe price competition.

Market share

A legitimate strategy for a business is to sacrifice the level of profits in return for an increased market share. To achieve this, you would pitch the price near the low end of the possible price range (in marketing jargon, a penetration price) in return for selling more of the product. The intention in the strategy is to increase your market share, to consolidate your position and to increase your prices gradually while retaining the share you have established. Essentially, the aim is eventually to become the market leader with higher unit sales at a higher price. A number of dangers are inherent in this strategy:

■ you may find it exceptionally difficult to raise your prices without demonstrating an improvement in the product in compensation.

■ you may find that new customers do not remain faithful to you when you increase the price but return to their original supplier.

■ you may trigger off a price war with your competitors.

The likeliest use of the strategy occurs when you are introducing a new product to the market, and the competition is weak. In this case, you can establish a large market share without attracting strong competition because of the large profits to be made.

Few small firms will have the financial and managerial resources available to achieve this strategy of establishing a large market share successfully; it is really too risky to be considered. Instead, they should look more closely at devoting the available resources to promotion or advertising.

Facing severe price competition

Low prices or a price-cutting war is an advantage to very few people: you do not want it, other small competing firms do not want it; in the long run, customers do not want it, if it means a reduced number of suppliers and less choice. It may only be in the long-term interest of a large company, if that is your main competitor. So whatever you do, try to avoid triggering it off.

If one of your competitors cuts prices, what should you do? Try to avoid the instant reaction of following prices downwards. Instead, try to concentrate your customers' minds on the non-price benefits (see p. 177) of doing business with you. If you have carried out some market research, you will know which are the non-price factors that buyers rate most highly, and these can be emphasized.

However, if you operate in a market that is very price-sensitive and does not differentiate between products, there is little choice but to match the price cuts. In this case, your survival will depend on savage reduction in your costs.

Selling at more than one price

If you have a range of different customers, you may be able to sell your product at a higher price to some of them and a lower price to others (called 'price discrimination'). For example, a solicitor or accountant might have one rate for individuals and another for corporate customers; an entertainment provider might have a reduced rate for, say, children, students and elderly people; a farmer might have different prices for sales direct to the public, sales to distributors, and sales to firms that are going to further process the product; a supermarket in a large town where there are many competitors might charge less than one in a rural area with far less competition; you might have to charge less for overseas sales than for sales in the UK.

Price discrimination is possible where you can divide your likely customers into distinct groups that are willing to pay different amounts. Yours must also be the sort of product or service that cannot be readily resold. This is more often the case with services. For example, if you are a landscape gardener, there is no real way for one customer to purchase the work you have done for another. In general, unless you have a monopoly over the supply of your product (which is unusual for a small business), you can discriminate on price only if other suppliers are doing the same – otherwise, by charging a higher price, you will simply lose customers to your competitors.

Successful price discrimation should boost your revenue above the level you would have had charging a single price to all customers. This is because setting a single price would lose customers unwilling to pay that much and give an unnecessary discount to others who were willing to pay more.

Pricing with more than one product

If you have more than one product, the sales could be interlinked if they are:

■ competing with each other; or

■ complementary to each other.

You need to ensure that your pricing policy is consistent across the range of your products. With competing products, the prices need to make sense. There needs to be a recognizable gap in the prices if one is a high-quality product while the other is of lower quality.

The pricing considerations are different if your products are complementary, that is, if you sell one, you are likely to sell the other. Once your customer is hooked, there will be lots of scope for charging high prices on a complementary item, as long as it is not so blatant that it puts off buyers from the starting product.

Summary

1 There is a range of prices that you can charge.
2 The lowest price is set by the contribution to overheads that it makes. Never go below this price. Only accept this price if you have spare capacity and there is no prospect of selling your product or time at a higher rate. If you have little or no spare capacity, choose the sale that gives you the biggest contribution.
3 Do not use costs as the basis for setting your prices, at least not without first trying to price the product according to what customers will pay.
4 If you go for the highest price possible in the market, you will restrict the amount you can sell. It will not give you the maximum possible level of profits. However, a specialist niche of this type can be attractive to a small business.

5 When it comes to setting a price, you have to compare your product
with others, establish how responsive sales are to a change in prices,
work out your strategy if it is a new product or coming to the end of its
life, analyse what price conveys to your customers and decide what position your product is aiming for in the market. Use the guide on p. 180.

6 The market leader has several advantages; the main ones are that it
means you can achieve more sales at a higher price than the competition.

7 Justify a higher price by stressing non-price benefits, such as quality,
reliability and delivery.

8 Avoid pitching your price too low through fear or misunderstanding of
what buyers are interested in.

9 A strategy of increasing market share through low prices is dangerous
for a small business.

10 If you are facing severe price competition, try to distract attention from
price by emphasizing the product benefits.

11 If your customers can be divided into distinct groups, you may be able
to increase revenue by charging several different prices.

Other chapters to read

2 Who will buy? (p. 13); **12** The right name (p. 128); **13** Getting the
message across (p. 136); **14** Getting new customers (p. 149); **15** Building
customer relationships (p. 163); **25** Staying afloat (p. 305); **26** Moving
ahead (p. 322).

17

Choosing your workplace

One of the jokes that can be made about people starting small businesses is that the first thing they want to do is to search for premises. It is an understandable desire, as premises are tangible proof of the creation of an enterprise. However, today it is possible to run a business, even with several people, without ever having separate business premises.

The concept of 'the virtual business' is no longer a joke. Given the communications now available – e-mail, broadband, fax, phone and mobile phone – it would now be possible for several people to group together, operating from their respective homes, and to create a business, communicating regularly and at length. You could also use freelancers and subcontractors, again operating from their homes, rather than employees.

At a stroke, a 'virtual business' removes the burden of two major overheads, rent and employees, and many enterprises are discovering the benefits that this brings. You could adopt this strategy as an initial phase until the business is more established, or as a permanent way of operation.

If you decide that your business cannot operate without premises, it is a very important step to take. Finding the right premises at just the right location for just the right price can prove to be extraordinarily difficult.

Unless you have decided to retail only through the Internet, a large part of the setting-up process for a retail business will be devoted to the search for a good location. And you cannot afford to compromise and take premises that with a bit of luck will be OK. You have to be satisfied that the premises meet all your criteria; if they do not, carry on the search until you find the right site.

What is in this chapter?

■ where is your business to be located? (p. 183).

■ working from home (p. 186).

■ what other sort of premises? (p. 187).

■ searching for premises (p. 188).

■ investigating and negotiating (p. 190).

Where is your business to be located?

An important first exercise would be to start with a blank piece of paper and think about location from first principles. What is the ideal location for the type of business you have in mind? At a later stage, you can introduce the constraints placed on location, such as home and family. You should know the ideal location so you can estimate the effect of concessions you are making to these outside non-business constraints. There may be further constraints, such as the lack of finance, which may cause you to compromise.

Communications

How dependent is the success of your business on communications: road, rail, air, bus? This could be important if:

■ you deliver your product.

■ your business is service-based to particular areas of the population.

■ you sell your product direct, using salespeople.

■ your business is dependent on import and export.

In these and other categories of business, an ideal location would allow easy access to the relevant parts of the country. For example, if import/export is your trade, a location within reach of a major airport could be an advantage. Or, if you sell direct to the whole country, you need access to motorways.

Labour

If your business is dependent on the use of certain skills, you may find that one part of the country is more abundantly endowed with potential employees who have already acquired those skills than other parts. On the other hand, skills may be irrelevant; what you may need is a ready pool of unskilled labour, in which case some areas have higher unemployment than others.

Centres of population

Your business may need to be located near particular centres of population. If you are trying to sell your product in large volume, being in a large centre of population may be an advantage. Or you may want to choose an area with a specific structure of population if your product or service is sold only to particular sectors. For example, if you plan to open a bookshop, you need a town or population area of a certain size. You also need a population well endowed with the particular characteristics of those who buy books. Your market research will help you to identify what those characteristics are.

Suppliers

Your business may depend on supplies of a particular raw material or some other product. Costs would be lessened if your business was located near the source of supply. This could be either the main distributor of the item or where the item is grown or produced.

Government and local authority assistance

Your business may be location-independent. Thus you can look at some of the deals that the government and local authorities produce to stimulate the founding of new businesses in specific regions.

The government has designated some poorer regions of the UK as assisted areas. These are parts of Cornwall, West Wales and the Valleys and the Highlands and Islands of Scotland and the whole of Northern Ireland. If you locate your business in one of these, you may be eligible for grants. You can get a list of assisted areas from your local Business Link*.

The government has also created 2,000 enterprise areas. If you locate your business in one of these, you may be eligible for grants or loans from, for example, a community development finance initiative. A new Business Premises Renovation Allowance has been introduced from 11 April 2007. Under this scheme, you can get tax relief in the year you incur the expenditure for the full cost of renovating or converting business premises in an assisted area to bring them back into commercial use where they have been vacant for a year or more.

Since 2006, if you locate in a Neighbourhood Renewal Fund area, you may be eligible for grants or other support through a new Local Enterprise Growth Initiative (LEGI). Funding for this is being provided by central government, but local authorities decide how to use the money in their area. There are 88 neighbourhood renewal fund areas, though not all will be included in the LEGI programme. For a list of these areas, see *www. neighbourhood.gov.uk*.

England is divided into nine regions, each with its own Regional Development Agency* (RDA). The RDAs for each of the other countries of the UK are Invest NI*, Scottish Enterprise*, Highlands and Islands Enterprise* and the Welsh Assembly Department of Enterprise, Innovation and Networks*. The RDAs coordinate economic development and regeneration in their region. Many of them have adopted a 'cluster concept' which means they focus on a specific industry – often one which has historical links to the area. The aim is to bring together businesses relating to the chosen industry to foster growth and cooperation. For example, the relevant RDAs are currently promoting Manchester, Newcastle, York, Bristol, Nottingham and Birmingham as 'science cities'. Locating in an RDA area that supports your particular industry could give you access to funding, a skilled workforce and suitable premises.

To find out what help is available regionally, contact your local Business Link* or use the interactive search tool on the Business Link web site*. If you have a specific area in mind already, contact the Business Link*, local authority for that area and the regional government office* to check out what help might be on offer. Don't use a firm specializing in telling you about grants – some of them are cowboys, and you could end up paying a few hundred pounds or more for information you can get free from your local Business Link*.

The final choice of location

It would be unrealistic to assume that domestic constraints are not important in locating a business. The extra benefits gained from moving to another area may simply not outweigh the domestic upheaval and cost of moving house when you want to start your business.

If you decide not to move your home, it makes sense for your offices to be close to your home, as long as other business considerations do not apply. If it would not adversely affect your business to be near your home, it can be an advantage as it cuts down on your wasted travelling time from home to office when you probably need all your time for business problems.

Working from home

Many small businesses will start off in the back bedroom. Some, especially if they are part-time businesses, may stay there permanently. Working from home has several advantages: it is free, it involves no travelling, the work can be combined with any domestic tasks to be done, there are no fares or expensive lunches to be bought, you can wear what you like, and it protects your house from burglars.

However, working from home involves an extraordinary amount of self-discipline. It is all too easy to find some domestic job that needs doing. It can also be frustrating to have your work interrupted by callers or other members of the family. And your work never goes away; you cannot leave it behind when you walk out of the office door. This can lead to extra worry.

Ultimately, you may also find it lonely, and you may find the lack of stimulation from fellow workers and colleagues very dispiriting. And another disadvantage of using your home as working premises is the poor impression it could create on customers if they need to visit you.

Good organization is the key to being able to work successfully at home. Your work space needs to be separate from the rest of the house; a room is ideal, but a corner set aside for work is better than nothing.

You should also try to be strict about the time set aside for work. Try to start at a definite time each day. Persuade friends that you are serious about your work and you will be hard at it between certain times. To solve the problems of loneliness and loss of stimulation, try to build a network of others working from home.

The obstacles to turning your home into a successful workplace could include the possible need to get planning permission. This may occur if your business alters the residential character of your home. This might be the case if you convert part (a garage, say) into a workshop, your business is noisy or involves hazardous materials, customers will visit your home or you will have employees working there. But provided your business is unobtrusive, you probably will not need permission. If in doubt, contact the planning officer* at your local authority.

Other possible obstacles include:

- the existence of restrictive covenants on the land (ask your solicitor*).
- the existence of a mortgage (check with building society or bank).
- restrictions on insurance (check with insurance broker* or company).

■ problems with the environmental health department if your business is food production, for example.

Working from a home that you own may mean that some capital gains tax will be due when you sell it (p. 367). Check with your accountant*. But you should be able to organize things so that this does not happen. You might be liable for business rates on the part of your home used for business (and the band your home is in for council tax might then be reduced) but not if your business does not alter the essentially residential character of your home (p. 368). Contact the Valuation Office Agency* for guidance. You will also need to consider insurance for an office you run from home. An increasing number of insurers will let you cover business equipment as an extension to your normal house contents insurance. But, more usually, you need to take out separate insurance to get additional cover, for example for business interruption (see Chapter 22).

What other sort of premises?

After settling on a location, your search can home in on the premises you need. There are two aspects. First, you need a tighter specification of location, for example town, district, neighbourhood or even street. This very tight specification mainly applies to retail business. Most of the considerations you need to take into account are explained on p. 87. The second aspect is the type of premises. The factors that influence your choice include:

■ *appearance*: if customers and suppliers are likely to come to your offices, appearance can affect your credibility and your image.

■ *parking or public transport*: if you have staff or visiting customers and suppliers, you'll want either good transport or parking. The planning officer* (see p. 192) may need to be satisfied that you have adequate parking, unless there are good public transport links.

■ *cost*: you obviously want to keep your costs as low as you can, consistent, that is, with achieving your business objectives. Keep an eye on business rates.

■ *size and layout*: your business activity may impose constraints on the amount and exact physical layout needed.

■ *physical environment needed for maximum work efficiency*: cold, noise, dirt and dark can all mean people do not operate at their best.

The type of business may well dictate your choice of premises between office, factory, workshop or warehouse, for example. But a number of specialized options are open to small businesses.

Managed workshops and small business centres

In many places, there are centres designed especially for small businesses. These provide small offices, workshops or factory space. There may well be an element of joint services thrown in, for example a telephone answering service or secretarial facilities. There could even be an advisory team to help you with initial management problems.

Sharing accommodation in this way with other small businesses has its attractions; there can be mutual support and business introductions, for example. You may also be able to run a more efficient business because of the shared facilities than from an office on your own.

Some workshop groups are organized as 'business incubators' designed to foster rapid growth through an entrepreneurial and learning environment, high profile and access to mentors. Contact UK Business Incubation*.

Science parks

Finding premises in a science park has its attractions for high-tech businesses. Most science parks are attached to universities. The theory is that by grouping innovative businesses together and in close proximity to the research facilities of the university, this will provide a breeding ground for new ideas. Whether this happens or not, your business may be able to project a high-tech image as a result of being located in a park. For information, contact the UK Science Park Association*.

Searching for premises

There are two aspects to searching for premises. First, you have to find out about premises that are vacant. Second, you have to decide whether any of the premises you see meet your needs.

There are several places to look to find vacant premises:

- local newspapers or web sites, such as *www.startinbusiness.co.uk*.
- estate agents. You will find that not all estate agents handle commercial property. The estate agent dealing with a particular property may not be local at all but could be based many miles away.

■ contact the local authority*. Many of them keep lists or registers of vacant industrial or commercial property within their boundaries. Some have disused public buildings for sale. Indeed, it can be worthwhile having a discussion with the local authority, for example the industrial development officer, as there may be special schemes to help you within certain areas of the authority.

■ local Business Link*, local enterprise agency* or equivalent (see Chapter 3).

Once you have gathered together information about premises for renting or buying in the area, the next step (before you go to see any of them) is to draw up a checklist of the priority points your premises need:

1 *Space* How many sq. ft do you need? For offices, allow roughly 100 sq. ft per employee.
Office ....
Storage ....
Factory ....
Retail ....

2 *Working environment* What is the importance of these factors?
Appearance for customers and suppliers ....
Light ....
Noise ....
Cleanliness ....
Smells ....
Fire hazards ....
Neighbours (type of work) ....

3 *Ease of access* Do the premises need?
Good access for pedestrians ....
To be near a bus stop or railway station ....
Good parking facilities ....
Delivery facilities ....

4 *Services and facilities* Would you like already installed?
Partitions/fittings ....
Telephone/ISDN line ....
Burglar alarms ....
Central heating ....
Lighting/electricity points ....
Air conditioning/ventilation ....
Cooking/refrigeration ....
Computer network ....

5 *What about cost?*

Rent per sq. ft ....

Rates per sq. ft ....

Maintenance ....

Running costs ....

Rent reviews ....

Premium for getting in ....

Rent-free period ....

Decoration ....

Fittings needed ....

Phones, electricity, security, etc. ....

Length of lease ....

When you have worked out a shortlist of properties that you want to see, it can be useful to draw a quick sketch-plan of the premises. At your leisure, you can mark where the various parts of the business will be put and get some idea of how comfortably your particular business fits into those premises.

Investigating and negotiating

Before you sign anything, there are several steps to take to investigate the premises further. These steps are to estimate costs, to check the structure of property (if it is freehold or a repairing lease), to investigate the legal side of things, and to look at local authority requirements.

To estimate costs

There are a few things to investigate before estimating costs. First, do not rely on the measurements given by the estate agent or landlord. Measure the premises yourself. There is a chance that the area is less than said, which could mean lower rent for you if you have been quoted a rent per sq. ft.

Second, it would be a good idea to look at the premises a number of times on different days and at different times of the day. This should allow you to get a better idea of decoration, heating, lighting or noise insulation needed.

Third, make sure you estimate or allow for all the running costs as well as alterations and improvements you would need to make.

It is always worthwhile trying to negotiate a lower rent and, in particular, asking for a rent-free period of three, six or twelve months if there is a lot of vacant property around, as for example in a recession.

To check the structure of property

Many leases make the tenant responsible for the repairs and maintenance of the premises. Get a survey from a member of the Royal Institution of Chartered Surveyors*. You can also use a survey to negotiate that the landlord pays for certain improvements before you take the premises.

To investigate the legal side of things

Your solicitor* should be asked to undertake a perusal of the lease. The sort of points to look out for are:

- can the premises be used for the type of business you have in mind?
- how long is the lease? Commonly, it is between three and twenty years.
- will you have the right to get a new lease when this one runs out?
- are the premises listed? This can restrict the way you adapt and extend them to suit your business needs.
- are there rent reviews, and when are they?
- can you sublet part or all of the premises?
- who is responsible for the repairs and the insurance?
- is the lease actually owned by the person trying to sell it?
- are the premises likely to be affected by any road or town improvements or alterations?
- who is paying for the landlord's legal costs? It is general practice for you to pay them, but it is always subject to negotiation. At any rate, agree beforehand that you will only pay a reasonable amount.
- is it possible to rent the premises on a weekly agreement, rather than sign a long lease? This gives you flexibility, but you lose security. An informal arrangement like this may be possible at times when there is a glut of vacant property.
- does the landlord want you to give a personal guarantee? Your solicitor should spell out to you the implications of doing so and help you to negotiate to try to avoid this.

To look at local authority requirements

A simple step you can make for yourself is to call the planning and building control officer to find out what is the current approved use for the premises. If your intended use is the same, you may need to do nothing more. If a change of use is required, your solicitor* should be able to help. The planning officer can also advise you if your premises have listed building status.

Depending on the nature of your business, you may need to consult:

■ planning and building control officers.

■ environmental health officers.

■ fire officers.

■ the Health and Safety Executive.

Summary

1 Could your business be a 'virtual business'? Improved communications means that a business could be started by several of you, each working from home.

2 Look at location with an open mind. Would your business be off to a better start moving to a different part of the country? Locations with assisted area status can offer considerable benefits and some RDAs specialize in supporting businesses in particular sectors.

3 As well as conventional premises, small businesses can also look at shared workshops and offices, and setting up in a science park.

4 Before you inspect any premises, draw up a list of what you think are your business needs.

Other chapters to read

8 Less than 100 per cent (p. 74); **18** Information technology – and other equipment (p. 193).

18

Information technology – and other equipment

Fifteen years ago, small businesses could get by without investing heavily in information technology (IT). Since then, two changes have occurred. First, the price of all IT equipment has plummeted, so for a small outlay a small business can become efficiently and comprehensively equipped with fast computers, clever software and communications with the outside world. Second, the way of doing business has changed dramatically. Face-to-face selling and contact and networking at meetings or at the golf club were the main means of arranging business deals. These are still important today, but a whole new way of doing business has emerged. Communications are now by e-mail, by phone or on the Internet. Such a sea-change in culture is a major boost for small businesses. Using information technology wisely allows small businesses a much greater reach to customers and suppliers and allows a business to put across the appearance of efficiency and control, attributes normally associated with larger companies.

Small businesses now need an IT strategy. Investment in IT should be a priority, but there are two particular types of business where this should be given even greater emphasis.

You can now run a 'virtual' business from wherever you are based, whether it be in a remote part of the country, a farm in Sussex or a loft in an inner city area. Using IT allows you and other members of your team to remain in locations where you want to live, each of you using your own home as your particular base, and yet build a business together.

The second category where IT is especially important is for growth businesses. Growth businesses invest heavily in IT because they are constantly searching for ways to carry out their work more efficiently, to give faster and better service to customers, to rid their businesses of the endless paper trail, and to keep the overhead burden caused by taking on employees to a minimum.

What is in this chapter?

- choosing information technology (p. 194).

- choosing other equipment (communications, furniture, cars) (p. 196).

- how to pay for equipment (p. 198).

Choosing information technology

The first question you need to ask is what you want a computer to do in your business. Quite apart from specialist functions such as computer-aided design, a range of general business tasks can be carried out, such as:

- *word processing*: a computer can be invaluable if in your business you send out a lot of routine letters, such as sales letters, quotes or mail shots. A computer with a word-processing program can be time-saving and produce a high-quality service.

- *accounts*: there are a number of computerized accounting packages, including some simple software designed especially for small businesses.

- *financial control and planning*: the programs range from cash management to sophisticated systems for working out forecasts and updating them at regular intervals. A software program can considerably simplify the task of forming and updating cash flow and profit-and-loss forecasts and helping you to manage your cash. Some of the banks now give business planning software and accounting software away free as part of an introductory package.

- *database-type work*: if you have a large list of potential customers and send out mail shots or want to record information about them, using database software can improve your efficiency dramatically.

With the move in sales methods towards direct selling, often by mail or telephone, the use of databases becomes more and more important. And if you are adopting a strategy of building a group of customers with like needs and interests and developing products to meet their requirements, database software is the only answer.

Choose your database package with care and if necessary use an IT expert to set it up correctly for you before you start building your business. Altering your database structure after you have been in business a while is expensive and problematic.

You must comply with the requirements of the Data Protection Act – see p. 167. If you are going to hold personal data, you may need to register as a data controller with the Information Commissioner*.

■ *stock control*: this can be important for retail outfits. Some computer systems link up to the cash till, so that levels of stock and need for re-ordering are worked out automatically.

■ *information gathering*: if yours is a research-based business, you can now access a huge amount of information via the Internet. And all businesses may find it useful to check or gather information from, for example, government web sites, trade bodies and Business Link*.

■ *selling*: the Internet may be a suitable medium for selling your product, in which case you will need a web site.

A computer system is made up of hardware and software. The hardware is the computer and peripherals such as printer, modem, router and scanner. These are now mass-market products, and you can easily shop around to get the cheapest deal. If you have more than one computer, you will probably want to network them to improve efficiency and allow you to share data between computers and to share printers. The software is what makes the computer carry out various tasks. There are two sorts of software: operating software, which makes the computer go; and application software, which does the specific job, for example cash management, word processing or e-mail. This software can come as a 'package' with your hardware. Don't even consider having software written specially for you, although you can get simple adaptations to the packaged software by using what are called 'scripts', 'macros' or 'templates'.

Both aspects of a computer system are important, although with the development of cheaper and better hardware, choosing the software becomes the prime task. You can buy computer systems from High Street stores, computer superstores, or computer dealers who specialize in business computers and software.

In conclusion, it's crucial to have a fast computer. Buy one off the shelf that comes with ready-made packages, such as word processing, spreadsheet, accounts package, database software, e-mail and access to the Internet. But if you know particular aspects are more important to you, choose the specific software package and install it yourself.

You will also need to select a printer, and you can choose either a laser printer (the best quality) or a good ink-jet. If you design your letterhead with care, for example in black only, you can print it yourself. Even if your letterhead is in colour, unless you want a large quantity, you can get cheapish colour printers to print in-house.

If there is more than one of you in the business, you need to set up a network with a server. A network allows you to switch documents from one machine to another without making paper copies, and it allows more than one of you to work in the same application software at the same time.

Get advice from an IT consultant on the best way to set this up so it works properly. Don't use gifted amateurs or friends. Ask your Business Link* adviser to recommend an IT consultant.

Choosing other equipment

The right communications

Computers these days come with an internal modem as standard. This enables you to link to the Internet and send and receive e-mails and faxes through your ordinary phone line.

E-mail and faxes can be read on screen, printed out, saved wherever you choose on your system and even dropped into other files you are working on, such as a database or a word-processed report. E-mail, in particular, is very flexible, allowing you to send and receive whole files, not just simple messages. A modem also opens up the world of the Internet to you, giving you the ability to explore external databases and gather information from governments, libraries, universities, companies and others. It is now possible to get on to the Internet for the cost of a local call from virtually anywhere in the UK, so 'surfing the Net' need not be costly.

Instead of connecting to the outside world through a modem, opt for a broadband (ADSL) connection if you can. Broadband can be used to give you an 'always-on' connection for a flat monthly fee. It can work out cheaper than a modem if you are a heavy Internet user. Even if you are a lighter user, it can be worthwhile, because digital connections are fast and high-quality. Broadband is now widely available even if you live in a rural area.

Phone systems are also important. Even if you are working in the home, and there is only one of you, consider a separate business line. But an advantage of a broadband Internet link is that you can use your phone simultaneously.

On your phone system if you are working from home, you may want all the services such as call diversion, call waiting and voicemail. These allow you to present a more professional image to the outside world. Once your business is beyond the one-person stage, spend some time researching to find a telephone system that meets your requirements, as an inadequate system leads to inefficient working.

For receiving faxes, consider a plain-paper fax that can double as a photocopier if your only need is for the odd one or two pages to be copied (if you'll need to copy a lot, get a dedicated photocopier). Alternatively, many printers now double up as a copier (and also scanner). If you regularly need large amounts of copying, consider buying your own photocopier. You can set up your computer to send and receive faxes. This will not suit everyone. On some systems, your work session on the computer is interrupted if a very large fax is coming in. And sending handwritten comments on a document can be more cumbersome because you'll need to scan in the document first.

The right furniture

Choosing the right furniture for your business depends essentially on the type of business. Cheap, second-hand desks and chairs may not be good business sense. If you think it possible that customers or suppliers will visit your premises at regular intervals, it is crucial to select furniture that projects the image you have planned for your business.

The right car

A car can arouse great emotions. It is one of those peculiar purchases where it can be difficult to disentangle desires from needs. The car you drive somehow projects something about your own personality; it is often regarded as an extension of it. Nevertheless, caution is needed before personal desires get confused with business needs.

It is often argued by business owners that a prestige car is needed to project an image of credibility, for exactly the same reasons outlined above for furniture. But a cool, hard look is needed at that claim. Will customers and suppliers really see you driving into their car parks? To project the image that is needed, is the souped-up version essential? Will not the same effect be created by the slightly cheaper version? The argument that one car will cost only £50 more a month to lease than another is weak. You need to look at the cost over a longer period of time, say two years, or however long you intend to keep the vehicle. It would be a mistake to swing too far in the opposite direction and choose a second-hand car that is rusting or requires excessive maintenance.

If you run your business as a company, you will either have a company car or be using your private car on business. Either way, the tax system encourages you to choose a fuel-efficient vehicle (see p. 362).

How to pay for equipment

There are four main ways you can pay for equipment – buy outright, hire purchase, leasing and contract hire.

Buying outright

This does not necessarily mean buying it with your own money; you could use a bank loan or overdraft to finance the purchase of the equipment. The advantage of buying outright is that you own the asset, which will be entered in your balance sheet. This will make your balance sheet stronger. Also, the tax system is very favourable for some types of equipment, allowing you to write off the whole cost in the year of purchase (see p. 362). From April 2008, all businesses will have an annual investment allowance that will allow you to fully write off the cost of plant and machinery each year up to a set amount (£50,000 in 2008–9). The disadvantage of outright purchase is that it uses up large lumps of cash, maybe when you are short of funds.

Hire purchase (or credit sale)

Ultimately, you will own the asset outright at the end of the hire period. This means that hire purchase confers some of the same advantages of buying outright. As with outright purchase, you can claim a capital allowance from the time you start using the equipment, and you will be able to take the equipment into your balance sheet as an asset, with what you owe as a liability on the other side.

Using hire purchase also means that you are not laying out such a large sum initially, compared with buying outright, which can be helpful for cash flow. However, the payments you make will consist of capital, as well as interest. You get tax relief only on the interest part of the payments. If you are a sole trader or small partnership, hire purchase deals up to £25,000 are within the scope of the Consumer Credit Act 1974 (as amended by the Consumer Credit Act 2006) but larger hire purchase deals, and deals of any size if you operate as a company, are not covered. The Act provides protection against unfair terms and access to the Financial Ombudsman service in case of dispute.

Leasing

If you lease equipment, you are not the owner of it, although you may be able to buy it at the end of the lease. The company that organizes the lease is the initial owner. The main advantage of leasing is that there is no capital outlay, so it can be a big help to cash flow.

In general, you do not claim the capital allowance for the equipment; the company organizing it claims the allowance. However, all the payment you make is treated as an expense, so you get full tax relief on it.

There are different sorts of lease. If the lease is a closed-ended one, it means there will be a fixed period of one to five years. At the end of the agreed period, there may be an option to buy or to take on a further lease for a nominal rent. An open-ended one means you can end it when you like after the expiry of an agreed minimum period.

Contract hire

This is a form of leasing, mostly used for financing a fleet of vehicles. In this case, what is in the contract is not a specific vehicle or vehicles but the use of an agreed number of the specified type. The length of the agreement is usually shorter than the estimated life of the equipment. Use of the vehicles can be provided with or without the maintenance. You may be able to arrange to buy the vehicle at the end of the agreement.

Summary

1 A good computer and Internet connection, giving you access to e-mail and the World Wide Web, are crucial.
2 An IT strategy needs to be developed if your business is to grow.
3 Choosing the right communications equipment can be important for the efficiency of your business.
4 The furniture and fitting out of your premises can have an impact on your credibility with customers and suppliers.

5 Your car may affect the image of your business less than you believe.

6 You can pay for equipment by buying, hire purchase, leasing or contract hire.

Other chapters to read

8 Less than 100 per cent (p. 74); **17** Choosing your workplace (p. 182); **29** Tax (p. 350).

19

Professional back-up

Luck can make a lot of difference to the success or failure of an enterprise, but you cannot sit around waiting for luck to land on your doorstep. You must take all the steps you can to ensure success. Weaknesses in specific skills must be covered; you may be able to obtain advice and guidance from your local Business Link* or an enterprise agency. But there may still be some skills for which you must seek outside professional help.

The time to seek out and engage professional advisers will be fairly early in the planning stage. Thus their expert advice can be taken before your plans are firmly formulated. If the adviser is good, this should help you to avoid making the sort of expensive errors and misjudgements that could mean your business begins with a permanent disadvantage.

The sort of adviser that could be helpful to you includes:

- accountant and book-keeper (p. 202).
- bank (p. 203).
- solicitor (p. 205).
- surveyor, estate agent (p. 206).
- designer and web designer (p. 207).
- financial adviser (p. 208).
- IT and web specialists (p. 209).

Accountant and book-keeper

The advice that accountants may be able to give ranges from the basic services, such as book-keeping, to the more sophisticated, such as tax planning or raising funds. Not every accountant will offer every sort of advice. For example, a big firm of accountants is unlikely to undertake weekly book-keeping functions; an accountant working alone may not have the expertise to help with raising funds.

Some of the areas of advice are:

- *accounts*: doing the book-keeping, setting up accounting systems, advising on computerized accounting packages, preparing your annual accounts, auditing for a limited company.
- *finance*: managing cash, helping to raise finance and to negotiate with the bank manager, raising venture capital.
- *business purchase*: investigating possible acquisitions, analysing franchise opportunities, negotiating purchase prices.
- *tax*: preparing income tax, corporation tax and VAT returns, carrying out PAYE and National Insurance requirements for employers, personal and business tax planning, advice on raising funds under the enterprise investment scheme.
- *general business advice*: preparing business plans, budgets and forecasts and advising on the form of your business, that is, whether you should be a sole trader, in partnership or form a limited company.
- *preparation of prospectus*: to raise money from the public.

Quite a lot of accountants, particularly the large firms, also have management consultancy divisions, which can advise on the setting up of internal systems, computerization and so on.

How to choose

The term 'accountant' does not necessarily mean that the person so described has any formal accountancy qualification. If you want to employ someone who is a member of a recognized body, you should look out to see if there are letters after the name. The main organizations that will be of interest to you as a small business are:

- the Institute of Chartered Accountants in England and Wales* and the Institute of Chartered Accountants in Ireland*, whose members put

ACA or FCA after their name, and the Institute of Chartered
Accountants of Scotland*, whose members put CA after their name.

■ the Association of Chartered Certified Accountants*, whose members
put ACCA or FCCA after their name.

What you gain by using a member of one of these bodies is the knowledge
that a required course of training has been followed and certain exams
passed. In addition, if you want to appoint an auditor, you must appoint
someone who is a member of one of these bodies, which have been recognized by the DTI as auditing bodies.

If you need to find someone who will help with your book-keeping and
preparation of your tax returns, and your business is fairly small-scale,
employing fully qualified accountants may be the equivalent of cracking a
nut with a sledgehammer. You may be able to find someone else quite competent to carry out the limited range of jobs you have in mind, but
obviously at a much cheaper rate.

The only satisfactory way of choosing an accountant is by recommendation
and taking up references. Ask your bank manager. Colleagues and friends
who use the services of accountants are also possible sources of recommendation. References should always be taken up.

There is a case to be made for opting for one of the bigger firms of accountants if you want to raise money from outside organizations or the public.
Investors may look at the proposal with more confidence if your financial
advisers are well known, rather than from a small firm of accountants
(however good at their job).

As with any business negotiation, there should be a discussion about the
scope of the work to be done and clear agreement on what this is and what
it will cost. Really you must satisfy yourself, before any work is begun, that
the accountant knows what you want and is capable of doing it.

If it is management consultancy that you are interested in, find out if the
consultancy is a member of the Institute of Business Consulting*. An
important point to check is that the consultant has experience of the problems of small businesses.

Bank

Banks obviously offer a wide range of financial facilities, such as current
accounts, provision of overdrafts, longer-term loans, leasing and factoring,

and import and export assistance. There is more detail about the provision of finance in Chapter 24. Most of the banks also have specialist services for small businesses and networks of small business centres or advisers. Some of the banks offer free banking for the first year or longer if you open a business account with them.

The role of adviser sits rather uneasily with the provision of finance. Some small businesses may hesitate to discuss business problems completely frankly in case it should affect the bank's judgement about extending an overdraft, for example. However, this worry may be illusory, as most bank managers or advisers should be competent enough to spot problems from the figures presented.

Following a review of business banking in 2002, banks have had to make a number of improvements to their services in favour of business customers. These include:

- either the payment of interest on current account balances (of at least base rate less 2½ per cent) or exemption from transaction charges on items paid into and drawn from the account. These price controls are currently being reviewed by the Office of Fair Trading* but are widely expected to be left in place.

- unbundling services so that, in particular, you can take out a bank loan without having to open a current account at the same bank.

- faster and easier transfer from one bank to another, including portable credit histories available on CD-ROM.

- making charges and interest more comprehensible with a view to enabling league tables of accounts to be published.

- investigating the feasibility of branch sharing so that from a single outlet you have a choice of banks.

Most banks have also agreed to abide by a voluntary code of good practice for business accounts. Ask your bank for a copy.

How to choose

The bank that holds your personal account may not be the automatic answer. There can be a strong case made for separating your business and personal affairs so that one cannot influence the other.

If your business is planned to be on a large scale, for example you are raising substantial funds and are looking for very fast growth such as profits of £200,000 to £300,000 within five years, it may make sense to put your account with one of the larger branches. This is particularly so if you can build up a relationship with the bank manager. The manager of a large branch will have more discretionary power; this means that fewer decisions will need to be referred upwards to regional decision-makers within the bank, thus losing the personal touch.

There is probably no advantage in opting for a larger branch if you are likely to be working on your own or on a small scale. Convenience will be more important.

The British Bankers' Association* in conjunction with Moneyfacts* publishes comparative tables of business current accounts on its web site to help you to choose an account on the basis of transaction charges and interest paid.

Solicitor

Solicitors can be particularly useful during the formation of your business. The specialist advice they can give includes:

■ *business advice*: on the legal form of your business (that is, sole trader, partnership, limited company), on personal guarantees, steering you through the maze of employment law, helping with debt collection by advising on writs and winding-up orders.

■ *contracts*: conditions and terms of sale of your product, leases, franchise contracts, for example.

■ *legal entity*: forming companies and drawing up partnership agreements.

■ *preparation of prospectus*: to raise money from the public.

■ *product protection*: helping to obtain a patent or register a trade mark or an industrial design.

■ *protection of intellectual property*: increasingly important in this era of 'knowledge-based' businesses, copyright and design right protection.

Many solicitors belong to the Lawyers for Your Business* scheme. This offers a free initial consultation for those running young or growing businesses, plus a clear indication of the cost of further advice.

How to choose

Very similar considerations apply to the choice of solicitor as to that of your accountant. Solicitors specialize in different branches of the law, so you should ensure that the firm can give you the advice you need on specialized topics. If the specific partner you deal with cannot do this, another partner in the same firm may be able to do so, but it is your responsibility to question abilities closely to satisfy yourself that the advice will be soundly based. A wise precaution can be to take up references.

As with accountants, some businesses would be advised to choose a large firm because of the credibility the name would add to your quest for raising large sums of money.

For whatever you want doing, ask for an estimate of costs; if the answer is that it is not possible because the solicitor does not know how long the work will take, ask for the daily rate. But a solicitor who cannot give you an estimate is not impressive. Many solicitors offer a package price for jobs like forming a company.

The law requires solicitors' fees to be 'fair and reasonable'. When you receive the bill, if you do not understand how it is made up, your solicitor will have to get a certificate from the Law Society declaring the bill to be fair and reasonable if you demand it.

To find a solicitor in your area, you could contact the Law Society*, Law Society of Scotland* or Law Society of Northern Ireland*.

Surveyor, estate agent

You may at some stage want the help and advice of a surveyor or estate agent in your search for suitable premises. This may include:

■ structural surveys. This could be important if you are considering buying a freehold or signing a lease that includes the condition that you carry out repairs and maintenance.

■ finding and assessing suitable premises and negotiating with the landlords or vendors.

■ advice on whether planning permission or the landlord's consent for change of use is required and helping to make the application for you.

How to choose

For advice on structure, repairs and maintenance use a qualified surveyor, that is, a member of the Royal Institution of Chartered Surveyors*.

Designer and web designer

Design can be a crucial element in the success of a business. It may not appear as obvious as the need for accounting or legal expertise, yet it is. Designers can give help and advice on the visual elements of your business and product. There are specialists in:

▦ setting the image of your business or corporate identity (p. 128).

▦ fitting out premises, where this is important for customers or suppliers (p. 197).

▦ designing what your product looks like or product positioning (p. 16).

▦ designing your web site (p. 147).

▦ selecting what your employees wear and what your vans look like (livery specialists).

▦ using letterheads, logos, brochures and leaflets (pp. 131, 138).

▦ packaging.

Using a design shop can be a more cost-effective alternative than an advertising agency for a small business, especially as you are likely to adopt other means of getting your message across than straight advertisements.

You may find that some printers have designers working with them, and this could be the most cost-effective of all. However, cheapness is not the best option if you fail to achieve your objectives because of the poor quality of advice. You must still assess how good the advice is.

Before you approach a designer, you should have a clear idea of what you want, although be prepared to listen to suggestions. You should ask the designer to show you a wide range of ideas in what is called 'scamp' form, which is a very cheap way of letting you see what sort of impression the idea will give. Settle on two or three ideas that you think are consistent with your product or business and ask the designer to work in more detail on these.

How to choose

The best way of finding a designer whose advice you value is to ask friends and colleagues for recommendations. Another approach is to keep an eye open for work you admire that other businesses have, for example a logo you think good or an effective premises fitting. Most businesses will be flattered if you ask who helped design it. Whichever way you choose of finding some names of designers, ask for references and see examples of the work done.

Financial adviser

As well as advising on the financing of businesses, these advisers can act as an intermediary between those wanting funds and those with money to invest, such as venture capital funds or business angels (private individuals with the funds and the willingness to invest in private companies).

They may also be able to give advice on raising money and floating on the Alternative Investment Market or AIM (the junior market for young and small companies of the London Stock Exchange*). There is also a trading facility called PLUS (formerly Ofex), which your adviser might be able to introduce you to.

Financial advisers will look into a business plan and proposal, and their sponsorship of it should carry some weight with investors, but this applies only if their reputation is sound. Many large firms of accountants, stockbrokers and merchant banks have specialist corporate finance sections.

Financial advisers may be able to:

- advise on the organizational structure, in particular whether there are gaps in the top management and how the structure can be strengthened to attract investors.
- check your projections, advise on the strength of your business plan.
- advise on the amount of money and how to raise it.
- help to produce a prospectus that can be issued to the public or other investors.

How to choose

There are those who are very good and those who are awful, but, unfortunately, there is no clear-cut way of finding the name of a good financial adviser. Probably the best way is to ask other people how they raised funds and if they would recommend the person who helped. Magazines that are aimed at those running small businesses may have articles about who has raised money and how much. Contact the managing director of the firm that raised the funds and ask for a recommendation. However you get the name, always ask for references.

A financial adviser may charge a flat fee or a fee dependent upon the sum raised, say, between 2½ and 20 per cent of the money raised. But there may also be demands for shares or options on shares and directorships.

IT and web specialists

It's crucial with a small business to incorporate what you need from IT to allow you to operate your business as efficiently as possible, thus allowing you to keep your head count on the low side. An IT specialist can offer the following advice:

■ advice on hardware, software, setting up networks.

■ accounting and spreadsheet packages.

■ databases and how to set them up to gather as much data as possible from your business.

■ web sites and how to incorporate them into your business model.

How to choose

You can ask your Business Link* to recommend a specialist. Or you could ask among your local business networks or look among trade magazines (always take up references).

Summary

1 You can improve your chances of success by using professional advisers with their expert knowledge. Select your advisers at an early stage in your business planning.
2 Agree with your advisers at the outset what work they will do for you. Make sure you both understand and agree the scope of the work.
3 Take up references and ask for estimates of costs before the work begins.

Other chapters to read

3 A spot of coaching (p. 27); **22** Insurance (p. 262); **24** Raising the money (p. 290).

20

Getting the right staff

Deciding when to take on an employee is a delicate balancing act. On the one hand, if you increase your staffing levels, you might not be able to cover increased costs straight away. On the other hand, extra manpower could free you to spend more time on other activities, such as marketing or planning, which should, in the end, mean increased profits.

A useful rule of thumb for choosing the best time to increase your staff is to ask yourself if you can generate enough extra sales to cover the cost of taking on that extra employee. If you will not be able to increase your sales straight away, you could still employ someone; but, in this case, you will need to be able to keep your business going until you have been able to build your sales up to the new level you need. It all sounds straightforward, but in practice it is very tricky. It is like being on a seesaw. One step in the wrong direction can tip the balance against you.

If you are clever enough, or lucky enough, to get your timing right, you will not want to throw away your advantage by employing the wrong person. The whole process can take several months, so finding you have made a mistake and having to recruit again can throw your business off its planned course. Nor should you underestimate the emotional problems of getting rid of an unsuitable employee, which can unnerve the toughest of businessmen or businesswomen and unsettle other employees.

What is in this chapter?

This chapter looks at how to recruit. It should help you to answer these three questions:

1 Do I know what I'm looking for?

2 Will I recognize it when I see it?

3 Can I make sure that, if I offer the job, it will be accepted?

There are sections on the job that needs doing (p. 211), the employee you want (p. 213), getting the right person to apply (p. 216) and interviewing (p. 221). The cost of employing staff is covered on p. 225.

The job that needs doing

Before you plunge into adding that extra employee, look carefully at the work to be done. It is very important to sort out in your own mind what the job entails. Once you have done this you can define the person you need. If you fail to do this preparatory work, you might find yourself employing someone who is not capable of doing the work. This list of topics might help you to organize your thoughts about the job:

■ *level of skill*: when you decided you needed an extra pair of hands, was it because you needed work done that you did not feel competent to carry out yourself? Does the work require a special skill?

■ *training*: if you have the skill to do the job, but not the time, would it take a lot of training to employ someone without that particular skill and teach them on the job? Would you have the time to carry out that training?

■ *length of time*: do you estimate that this extra work will need doing for a long period of time? Or is it a temporary bulge? Watch out for mistaking a backlog of work that can be cleared up quickly for a permanent increase in activity.

■ *how much extra work*: can you quantify how much time will need to be spent by someone to carry out the work? Is it a full working week? Do not assume that if you find the work difficult and time-consuming, because it is outside your range of skills, a skilled employee will take as long.

■ *experience*: do you think the job requires a lot of experience? Would the employee need to be able to make independent judgements? Or is it intended that the work will be closely directed by yourself or another?

■ *responsibility*: how much responsibility will the employee have? Will the employee be required to man the office alone? If the job is selling, will the person be required to go out selling unsupervised? Will the employee handle money? Or be responsible for other staff? To whom will the employee be responsible?

- *tasks*: list the things that need to be done by your new employee. Work out for whom the tasks will be done and the importance of the tasks.

- *authority*: work out what your new employee can do without asking you or someone else for permission – for example, making appointments, spending money up to a certain limit.

- *contacts*: will your new employee need to deal directly with the general public or your customers? Will the contact be face to face, on the telephone or by letter? If the contact is by e-mail/Internet, you need to make clear the authority of your employee and how far he/she may be able to bind your business.

- *special circumstances*: does the job involve working during unsocial hours? Will your new member of staff need to do much travelling away from home? Will the working conditions be unpleasant or dangerous?

- *future developments*: consider how the job might develop and expand in the future. You need to assess a job hunter for this potential too.

Setting out your thoughts in this way may seem like overkill if the job is relatively simple. But hiring and firing a succession of unsatisfactory people will be more time-consuming and disruptive to your business than spending an hour or so defining the job; and marshalling your thoughts in this way will also help you to decide whether there really is a job that needs doing.

Another way of examining your needs would be to fill in a job description form. Try using the simple one below:

Example: job description

Job title: ....

Purpose of job: ....

Whom the employee works for: ....

Who works for the employee: ....

Main tasks: ....

1. ....

2. ....

3. (and so on) ....

What authority the employee has: ....

1. ....

2. ....

3. (and so on) ....

Duties: ....

1. ....

2. ....

3. (and so on) ....

Contacts: ....

Internal: ....

External: ....

Possible development of the job: ....

The employee you want

Your next task is to match the employee to the job. Decide if you need someone full-time or part-time. Think about what experience, qualifications and personal abilities are needed to do the job.

Full-time employees?

Conventionally, most employees are permanent, full-time and salaried, but this may not suit your business. Do not ignore other ways of getting the job done. Look closely at help from your family, contract or temporary staff, part-time staff, commission-only salespeople or agents, and/or fixed-term contracts.

Your family

Do not overlook the possibility of your spouse or civil partner or a relative helping out. Employing your family may not be the permanent solution you seek, but it may help to tide you over until you are confident that taking on an extra employee is justified.

Freelance staff

For quite a number of jobs it is possible to get people who are happy to work on a freelance basis. This means you will pay an agreed fee but have no responsibility for National Insurance contributions, sickness payments or holiday pay. And if the extra work comes to an end, you need feel no responsibility towards finding more work for a contractor, as long as you made it clear that the work was temporary or was a contract for a particular piece of work or period of time, but less than a year.

A further advantage of using freelance staff is that it can be a good opportunity for you and the person to size each other up and see if you could work together before you offer a permanent job.

There are two main disadvantages of solving your extra workload in this way. First, it can cost you more than taking on permanent staff to get the particular piece of work done. If the job involves a skill that is widely demanded and in short supply, a self-employed contractor's rate is likely to be correspondingly high. And if you are using a temp, you will have to pay a fee if an employment agency introduces the temp. Second, while some contractors or temps may be keen and enthusiastic, others may be less so.

Your legal obligations to temporary freelance workers or to people who contract out their services is rather hazy. You may also find that someone you regard as a freelance is considered an employee by the HMRC and the Department for Work and Pensions (DWP). Seek advice so you do not get this wrong.

You could also consider whether you may be able to receive some temporary help by using one of the government's schemes, such as the New Deal. This will give you help towards the cost of taking on a new employee – a subsidy of up to £60 a week for six months per employee aged 18 to 24 and up to £750 towards training them. The subsidies are higher (up to £75 a week) where someone is aged 25 or more. If you think you have a suitable New Deal vacancy, contact your local Jobcentre Plus*. You are more likely to find a candidate if your business is located in an area of high unemployment.

Part-time staff

If the work you want doing does not add up to a full working week, consider getting someone in on a part-time basis. Your duty as an employer is pretty much the same whether your staff are full- or part-time – see Chapter 21.

Commission-only salespeople or agents

Do not automatically think in terms of a salaried employee if you are looking to boost your selling effort. You may be able to find someone competent who would prefer to be paid by getting a commission on each item sold. Again this will cut your risks – no sales means no pay. However, the commission you will pay will be greater per item than to a salaried employee who also gets commission on sales.

Fixed-term contracts

You may need people to carry out specific projects that cannot be undertaken by your full-time employees.

Whatever category you decide to utilize, you need to ensure that where appropriate the national minimum wage is being paid (see p. 236). It is illegal to treat fixed-term employees less favourably than permanent employees. For example, they must be employed on the same terms, in most cases offered the same training opportunities, and so on. You may need to seek further advice concerning this.

Who is right for the job?

Try to develop an idea of the sort of person who will perform well in the job and in your business. Use the groups of characteristics listed below to help you to sort out what is important for the job and what is not. You can use this to help you to specify the person you need for the job and to help you to collect your thoughts while interviewing.

Here are some useful ways of grouping characteristics:

- *physical make-up*: this covers the employee's health, physique, appearance, manner and speech (take care that you do not inadvertently discriminate on sex, race, disability, religious beliefs, sexual orientation or age).
- *achievements*: what education, qualifications and experience do you expect?
- *general intelligence*: this is rather difficult to judge if you are not a psychologist, but what sort of reasoning ability should the person have? How quickly do they understand what you are saying?
- *special aptitudes*: what particular skills do you need, for example mechanical, verbal, numerical or manual skills?
- *interests*: what are the person's hobbies and leisure activities? Are there any particular hobbies that would be more or less suitable for the person who is needed to do this job? Check how much time is spent on interests. Is this likely to conflict with the job?

■ *circumstances*: include only those factors that are essential to the job.

■ *personal characteristics*: this covers the slightly tricky area of whether the person has the right personality to cope with that particular type of job. Avoid focusing on characteristics that can be met only by certain sections of the population.

It would be a good idea to pick out of the list those characteristics that you think are very important and those that would be an advantage but are not crucial for this particular job. It is always tempting to demand very high qualifications, experience and so on, but it is wiser to be fairly flexible in your requirements and not overstate what is needed to carry out the job satisfactorily. In any case, you should always remember that employing someone who is over-qualified for a job may lead to a rapid staff turnover, as the employee may soon get bored.

As well as picking out those characteristics that you need or hope to find, it is equally important to sort out those that would be a definite disadvantage to someone carrying out the job.

Getting the right person to apply

Once you have completed the essential preparation and so got a clear idea of what job you need doing and what sort of person you would like to fill the job, your problem now becomes: how can I find the person I want?

The main ways you can tell job hunters about the job on offer are:

■ by advertising direct, on the Internet or in newspapers or magazines.

■ through recruitment agencies and consultants.

■ through friends, existing employees and business contacts.

■ by recruiting direct from colleges.

Use more than one method to fill a job as it will widen the field.

Advertising direct

You can get in touch with the local Jobcentre Plus*, if the vacancy is suitable. Failing this, you can advertise direct in the appropriate newspapers, magazines or web sites. This could be tricky if writing is not your strong suit. However, there are certain guidelines you can follow to help you.

Remember that the purpose of the ad is to attract someone who will be able to do the job very well and who will settle down happily in your business.

You have to tell job hunters enough about the job to stimulate their interest and make them feel it is worth having a closer look; equally, you want to use the ad as a starting point of the selection process. So you want to make it clear to those applicants who would be suitable that they should apply and to those applicants who would not be suitable that they should not. Finally, the ad should be interesting enough to attract attention compared with what else is on offer in that newspaper or magazine the same day.

From research that has been done on what attracts people to join a company, some of the more important points are listed below in order of priority:

■ the prospects for interesting and creative work.

■ the prospects for promotion and pay.

■ the quality and reputation of the company's products or services.

■ the opportunity to use 'brains'.

■ the security of the job.

■ the company's past financial record.

■ a congenial working environment.

How does your business and the job you are offering rate against these points? In your ad, draw attention to your strong points. Most small and new businesses would score highly on giving lots of scope for interesting and creative work and the opportunity to use 'brains'. In particular, an employee would be given the opportunity to be part of the whole business and not just in one department. However, if it is a new business, there may be little reputation built up for its products, and its financial record may be short.

When it comes to writing the ad, the style could be important in attracting job hunters' interest. Be informal and friendly – but not too friendly. Use 'you' and 'your' when you are speaking about the person needed and 'we' and 'our' when talking about your business, but avoid over-chatty comments and stick to the facts.

Checklist: what should be in the ad

■ *company name*: put in the name and logo, if you have one.

■ *job title*: use a title or description that will mean something to a stranger.

■ *pay*: state what salary can be expected. Job hunters interpret phrases like 'salary negotiable' as meaning a low salary.

■ *place*: state where the job is. If you are not offering moving expenses, this is very important. In any case, people like to know what the environment of the job is.

■ *the work*: describe the work to be done and say what authority the job has.

■ *the company*: state what your company does and what size it is. Avoid clichés about dynamism, fast-growing and so on; all companies use them.

■ *the person*: state your requirements, such as experience needed, qualifications and other qualities.

■ *how to apply*: name the person to write to, not just the job title. Tell the job hunter how you want them to give details of experience and qualifications – for example, send in brief CV, write for application form.

■ *when to apply*: give a closing date for applications, if possible allowing two to three weeks from the appearance of the ad.

■ *the law*: check that your ad is not breaking the sex, race, disability, religious belief or sexual orientation discrimination laws or the new age discrimination laws which came into effect from 1 October 2006 (see Chapter 21). And make sure the information is accurate, as the ad may form part of the contract between you and your new employee.

How to apply

Asking for too much information from job hunters can deter people from applying, and you should remember that your business is competing with all others for the best talents. Keep your demands to a minimum. Asking applicants to write in has the advantage of letting you see what their written work is like, but you do need to allow people to contact you by phone if they are unable to write (due to disability).

If you do give a telephone number that job applicants can ring, make sure it is always manned – and by someone who knows what they are talking about. You can use the telephone to sift out people, as well as to give them information. This can be done by preparing a shortlist of key questions that you can ask over the phone. Keep a written record of why you have filtered people out so that you can explain the reasons if ever challenged.

An application form has the advantage of allowing you to compare information presented in an identical format. But specify an alternative method if individuals are unable to complete the application form. In any case, drawing one up would take you some time and may not be worthwhile, unless you are considering employing many people.

Where to put the ad

It depends on the job. Different newspapers, magazines and web sites will give you the response you need for different jobs. There are trade magazines that may have cornered the market for job ads in a particular specialization, for example computing. For jobs that are not so specialized, local newspapers may provide a good response, for example for clerical staff. A magazine called *British Rate and Data* (BRAD)* lists newspapers and magazines and gives details of the cost of advertising and a profile of the readership. Your local library should be able to tell you where to see a copy.

Increasingly, jobs are advertised on the Web. Some newspapers also offer you a web position as well as an ad in the newspaper. But there are an increasing number of web sites devoted solely to advertising jobs.

The best market research about where job hunters look for jobs may be to ask people who work in that field where they would look for a new job.

The cost of advertising

The bigger the circulation of the newspaper or magazine or the number of hits on a web site, the more they charge for advertising. You have to weigh up the cost against the benefit of getting the size of response you need. Sometimes if the response is too high, it can overwhelm you.

Recruitment agencies and consultants

If you do not have the time to handle the advertising and to sift through all the applications, you can use an agency. Obviously, you have to pay for this, so you must be sure it is worth the extra cost; and do not forget that you will have to spend time in selecting the right agency, so the time saving may not be as great as you think. Nor can you afford to skip any of the preparatory stages; you will still have to decide what the job is and what sort of person you want so that the agency can do its job.

There are several different types of agency:

▩ Jobcentre Plus*.

- private employment bureaux (Adecco, Brook Street, Office Angels or Reed, for example).
- selection consultants.
- search consultants (or headhunters).
- web sites.

Using Jobcentre Plus is free and can be a useful source of applicants for manual and clerical jobs, but do not expect too much from the screening process. The private employment agencies charge varying amounts ranging from 6 to 20 per cent of first year's earnings, depending on the agency and type of job to be filled.

You can get a list of members of the Recruitment and Employment Confederation (REC)* to help you to pick out an agency. You should also look in trade magazines to see which agencies advertise which types of job.

Friends, existing employees and business contacts

If you do get a strong recommendation from someone, do not rely on the friend's advice. Ask your prospective employee for a *curriculum vitae* (CV) and give them a copy of the job description (p. 212) and the advertisement you would have used. Observe all the necessary precautions by conducting a full and careful interview (see more about all this below).

This method of finding your new employee is not to be ignored, as it has several advantages. First, it is cheap. Second, if it is through a friend, you will start off knowing something about the abilities of the new person. Third, a new employee recruited in this way may find it easier to settle down in your organization.

The main disadvantage arises if the appointment proves unsuccessful; this can be embarrassing if the contact was made through a friend and disruptive to a previously harmonious working relationship if the recommendation came from an existing employee. You also need to be careful that you do not miss out on possible good applicants because they are not known to you.

Recruiting direct

If you are looking for someone who does not need experience in your particular field or skill, you could try going direct to further education colleges. The sorts of skills you might be able to recruit direct in this way include secretarial, hotel and catering, and retail management.

If the type of job you have in mind could be done by a young school-leaver to whom you could give on-the-job training, consider whether you could use the apprenticeship scheme for people aged 16 to 24. Contact the Learning and Skills Council* for information.

Interviewing

An interview has two purposes:

1 It helps you to choose your new employee.
2 It helps your new employee to choose you.

It is important to remember that you should structure the interview process to enable you to find out what the applicant is really like and to allow the job hunter to find out about you and your company and decide that this is the job he or she wants.

Before you get to the interview stage you will have to sift the applications and decide who to select for a closer look.

Who should you see?

If your ad was successful, the sifting process will not be a case of eliminating totally unsuitable candidates; rather it will be to rank the applications according to how closely they match your ideal. If you are tempted to see someone who does not fit the bill but looks interesting, think twice. It means either that the requirements you set for the job were not the right ones or that you will be wasting your time on an unnecessary interview.

Once you have ranked them, choose to see the top five, say. If you do not find anyone in that group, you could try the next five. After that second-ranking group, if you still have not found the ideal person you may have to accept that your ad has been unsuccessful. You will need to reconsider how to find the person you want. Keep a written record of interviews so that you can return to consider a candidate later if necessary and justify why he or she has not been selected.

Setting tests

Setting a test can be a very useful way of checking how a prospective employee will tackle a task in a pressure environment and what level of skills has been attained. The task set must be relevant to the job proposed to provide you with any useful information. The results of the test can be discussed and analysed in the interview.

Getting ready for the interview

There are two stages. First, you must gather together the essential information you will need to give the job applicant. This can be conveyed in written form or orally, in which case you need the facts at your fingertips if you are to sound organized and efficient to the job hunter.

The questions you might be asked could be about:

- *holidays*: you need to be able to say how many weeks, when they can be taken and any restrictions you intend to impose.
- *illness*: explain what will happen if your employee is away from work because of illness.
- *starting date of the job*: if this has been decided.
- *hours of work*.
- *salary matters*: such as when they are paid, any rules on overtime, bonuses or commission, if applicable.

The second stage of preparation is to work out what key questions you want to ask. One type of question would give you comparable information about the people you see. This could be a test question, such as describing a typical event in your business and asking what each person would do in those circumstances.

The second type of question is to help you to pinpoint each candidate's strengths and weaknesses. The only way this can be done is by good preparation, reading the candidate's CV or whatever. There is no short cut. What you should look for is anything that seems odd or is not a smooth progression. Watch out for any unexplained gaps in the person's story; this may give you hints about poor health, or unsatisfactory jobs or character. Notice very frequent job changes, as this could raise questions in your mind about job success, as could a failure to match in employment the level of achievement suggested by educational qualifications.

Useful interview questions

1 What is the best part and worst part of your present job, and why?
2 What bit of your work do you find difficult and what bit the easiest?
3 How do you rate your present boss?

4 Describe your ideal boss.

5 What do you consider to be your greatest success and why?

6 What do you consider to be your greatest failure and why?

7 When were you last angry at work? What caused the anger? What form did your anger take?

8 What is most important to you about the job you are looking for?

9 What will your family and friends think of your new job?

10 What are your greatest strengths?

11 What are your weaknesses?

12 What worries you most about the job?

13 What excites you most about the job?

These are all examples of the kind of open question that should prompt the candidates to reveal a bit more about themselves; use whichever seems most appropriate. As well as these questions, there are more straightforward ones about the present job, the career, education and so on that need to be asked.

Holding the interview

Some thought needs to be given beforehand to where the interview should be held and who should be present. The person you are interviewing will feel more relaxed if the interview is private and uninterrupted, so try to find somewhere where the interview will not be overlooked or overheard. If you are not going to be the new employee's boss, perhaps the person who is should sit in on the interview. If this is not possible, arrange for the new person's superior to see the candidate separately, if necessary on another day, before deciding to offer the job.

What should happen in the interview?

Roughly, a useful interview could run along the following lines:

1 Spend a few minutes putting the applicant at ease, for example by talking about his or her interests.

2 Ask open questions, which the person you are interviewing will have to answer with more than a yes or no. The questions you ask should allow you to get some idea of whether the person could do the job well.

3 Also ask closed questions designed to test a candidate's knowledge and skill, specific questions such as 'On what date ...?' and hypothetical questions, 'If you were ...'

4 Try using silence sometimes as a way of getting the person to expand. For example, once the person has finished explaining something, do not always leap in with another question but remain silent. Sometimes, the person being interviewed will be prompted to be more revealing.

5 Keep in control of the interview while doing little talking, perhaps less than a third of the total time.

6 Concentrate on listening and observing your applicant. This helps you to judge the replies and to pinpoint areas where you need to probe more. You should also reflect on what the person has said and feed it back to them.

7 Be flexible; do not stick rigidly to a planned script. Try to develop what your interviewee has said.

8 Take notes. They do not need to be very comprehensive but sufficient to jog your memory when assessing the interview afterwards (bear in mind that the applicant has the right to see your notes – see below).

9 Give a little detail about the job and how it fits in your business. You can miss out this and the next stage if you have already concluded that the person is not suitable and thus save wasting time. It is important not to do this stage before asking the questions. If you do, you may have fed the person with sufficient information so that he or she knows how to answer your questions.

10 Ask the job applicant if there are any questions, or if he or she wishes to tell you anything else about suitability for the job that has not been brought out by the questions.

11 If the person seems promising, spend some time making sure that the job would be accepted if it was offered. After all, the person is selecting a new job in the hope that it will last for a while and will want to be confident that your job really is the best choice.

After the interview

Summarize the interview in writing straight afterwards while your memory is fresh. The aim of the summary will be to allow you to look back when you are choosing between the candidates, and to judge how closely each person matched up to the job you want done. In particular, you will want to remember later the person's strengths and weaknesses. And you may be challenged as to why you recruited a candidate and would need a written record to defend any discrimination allegations. Under the Data Protection Act 1998, a candidate has on request a right to see any interview notes you hold.

There are some other important actions to be taken before someone joins your staff. First, always take up references. It can be much better to speak to a referee direct on the phone than to interpret what the written word may be hiding; people can be much more unguarded 'off the record'. Always ask the direct question, 'Would you re-employ this person?' Second, if the job is an important one, consider having a medical done. It might throw up a problem that you would want to know about before hiring. Third, if the job involves driving, always ask to see the driving licence; do not be fobbed off by excuses.

Making the offer

Always make sure your written offer letter is conditional upon satisfactory references and medical, if applicable. Remember that this letter (and the ad) forms part of an employee's contract of employment (p. 234).

When the new employee joins

A new employee will feel more positive when starting a new job if presented with a planned induction and training period. It is well worth the extra effort on your part to prepare this in advance.

If it all goes wrong

Sometimes you can make mistakes. If it is a really bad one, you will need to know how to deal with it. In Chapter 21, there are details about the law on dismissing staff.

It could be worthwhile to interview a job leaver to see why it did not work out from the employee's viewpoint. You can learn from your mistakes and make a better choice next time.

The cost

The costs can be divided into two groups:

1 One-off costs of employment, such as advertising. There is also the time you spend interviewing or sifting through applications and the time and possible expenditure spent on training a new employee.
2 Continuing costs of employment, such as salary, employer's National Insurance (NI) contributions, fringe benefits you offer and extra office equipment. There will also be the extra costs created by the person carrying out the job, such as more stationery, petrol or telephone use.

What is your break-even point?

Your break-even point is the point at which your business is making the right amount of sales to give you enough profit to cover your overheads, which include rent and rates, heating and lighting. Sometimes employee costs are overheads and sometimes they are not. It all depends on what they do. If what the employee does is related to the level of sales, their costs will be called direct and are not part of overheads. Examples would include staff whose time is paid for by customers, or employees who are directly involved in making a product. But if the employee's job is something like accounting, marketing or general clerical duties, their costs will be included in overheads. In your business there may be a grey area in which it is difficult to decide whether the employee's costs are direct or not.

The purpose of finding your new break-even point is to work out how many extra sales you need to make to cover the cost of your new employee. You can see how to work out the break-even point in more detail in Chapter 25.

Finding your break-even point

First, you have to find what your gross profit margin is. This is your gross profit as a percentage of sales. You work out gross profit by deducting the amount of your direct costs from the value of your sales. Direct costs will be the purchases you need to make to supply your service or product and the costs of any labour directly associated with your sales.

Once you have worked out your gross profit margin, your second step is to work out the amount of your overheads (for example, rent, rates, heating, lighting, telephone costs, professional fees or labour costs, such as secretarial or book-keeping).

To find your break-even point, your third step is to divide the amount of your overheads by the gross profit margin. This will give the level of sales you need to make to cover your overheads.

Example

Jeremy Jones needs someone to act as a secretary and book-keeper. He used the checklist on the right to work out the extra cost involved. The calculation is quite simple and looks like this for the full year:

Salary	£14,000
Employer's NICs	£1,123
Extra use of telephone, etc.	£559
Total	£15,682

Jeremy now works out how it will change his break-even point:

He has estimated sales of £40,000 for this year with direct costs of £20,000. This gives a gross profit of:

£40,000 − 20,000 = £20,000

And his gross profit margin is:

$$\frac{£20,000}{£40,000} \times 100 = 50\%$$

His overheads, without taking on an assistant, come to an estimated £5,000 and after would come to £20,682 (£5,000 + £15,682).

Jeremy finds his break-even point before he employs someone. This he gets from the following equation:

$$\frac{overheads}{gross\ profit\ margin} \times 100 = \frac{£5,000}{50} \times 100 = £10,000$$

of sales to cover his overheads. If he employed an assistant, the break-even point would become:

$$\frac{£20,682}{50} \times 100 = £41,364$$

Jeremy needs sales of £41,364 − £10,000 = £31,364 to cover the extra overhead created by employing his new assistant. As he has estimated his sales at £40,000 (compared with the £41,364 he needs), he decides not to go ahead with employing an assistant at this time.

Checklist: work out the extra cost of employment

	this year	full year
	£	£
Salary or wages (including holiday pay)	. . .	. . .
Estimated commission, bonuses, overtime payments	. . .	. . .
Employer's NI contributions (see p.240)	. . .	. . .
Other possible costs or benefits:		
▨ employer's pension contributions	. . .	. . .
▨ use of car	. . .	. . .
▨ payment of subscriptions to professional societies	. . .	. . .
▨ cost of sick pay insurance	. . .	. . .
▨ others	. . .	. . .
	. . .	. . .
	. . .	. . .
	. . .	. . .

▶

	this year	full year
	£	£
Additional office space required	...	...
Additional equipment needed	...	...
Extra use of telephone, stationery, heating, lighting and so on	...	...
Total	...	...

Notes

1 Most small businesses will not be providing many fringe benefits, but you may need to consider doing so if you want to employ an experienced and skilled member of staff, for example an accountant or salesperson.

2 You will need to break down these costs into monthly expenditure (p. 269).

3 This breakdown of costs assumes that you rent, lease or hire any additional equipment, rather than buying it outright. For help in deciding which is the right way for you, see p. 198.

Summary

1 Work out the costs of employing an extra person and watch the effect on your break-even point.

2 Make sure there is a job to be done.

3 Look to see if the work can be carried out in a non-permanent way, for example temporary staff, contract or freelance worker.

4 Draw up a job description, no matter how simple or low-level the job seems.

5 Get a mental picture of the person for the job. Do not overstate your requirements. Pick out the characteristics that would be a disadvantage in doing the job well.

6 You can save money by drafting your own ad. Use our checklist to make sure you include the necessary information.

7 Prepare thoroughly for interviews.

8 Ask open questions to get the job applicant to talk. Keep notes.

9 Don't forget to insist on a medical, if necessary; check all references and see the driving licence, if driving is part of the work.

10 Work out an induction and training programme. Do not put all the effort into finding the right person for the job and then, by not training them properly, end up with employees unable to function effectively and productively in your business.

Other chapters to read

21 Your rights and duties as an employer (p. 229); 25 Staying afloat (p. 305).

Your rights and duties as an employer

The idea of employment law can conjure up images of the Gorgon. You, as an employer, turned to stone when faced with the legal pitfalls of employment. The myth remains that you cannot sack anyone. Well, it is not true.

By and large, you can employ whoever you want. You can set up your own criteria about who you want to employ, but there should be good reasons for it – not solely because of sex, race, disability, marital status and so on. You can normally dismiss unsatisfactory employees. But the law sets out that it should be done fairly. If you do not do so fairly, then you may have to be prepared to pay compensation. Moreover, there are rules about how you treat employees while they work for you. If disgruntled employees leave, they may claim your actions amounted to constructive dismissal, which could again result in you facing a bill for compensation. So it makes sense to have a good working knowledge of employment law.

This chapter should give you some guidelines about how to:

- take on an employee (p. 232).
- pay staff (p. 236).
- provide a safe and healthy working environment (p. 243).
- avoid discrimination (p. 245).
- treat an employee if pregnant or a parent (p. 251).
- dismiss them if unsatisfactory (saying goodbye) (p. 256).

If you need more advice and guidance, contact the Advisory, Conciliation and Arbitration Service (ACAS)* or see the Directgov web site (*www.direct.gov.uk/ employee*). If your worry is sex discrimination, the Equal Opportunities

Commission* would be able to help, and the Commission for Racial Equality* can give guidance on racial discrimination. The Disability Rights Commission* covers disability issues. Under the Equality Bill 2006, these three existing commissions will be completely replaced by a new Equality and Human Rights Commission by 31 March 2009 at the latest. This new body will be responsible for all types of anti-discrimination, including new areas such as age discrimination. All the existing bodies mentioned produce a range of free guides to the various areas of employment law. Some are listed in this chapter. They can be obtained from the body concerned or Jobcentre Plus*.

Employment law is very complex. It is also changed frequently. However, in order to help business to keep track, the government introduces most changes to laws affecting businesses (including employment law) from either of two common commencement dates each year: 6 April (coinciding with the start of the tax year) or 1 October. Through the Business Link* web site, you can arrange to have regulatory updates e-mailed to you. This chapter can do no more than give general guidelines, and the coverage cannot be considered comprehensive.

Bird's eye view of your rights and duties

In general terms, apart from what is in the employment contract, what can you expect from your employees, and what can they expect from you?

Your rights

1 Employees should be honest, obedient and not act against your interests.
2 They should not disclose confidential information about your business.
3 They should take care of your property.
4 Any patents, discoveries or inventions made during working hours generally belong to you.
5 Your employees should be competent, and work carefully and industriously.

Your duties

1 You should behave reasonably in employment matters.
2 You should practise good industrial relations and provide, for example, a written statement of terms of employment, including disciplinary procedures and grievance procedures.
3 You should pay your employees when you agreed to do so.
4 You should take reasonable care to ensure the safety and health of your employees.

As well as these general rights and duties, your employees acquire certain rights by law – see the *Legal life-cycle of an employee* (below), which applies to full- and part-time workers.

What is in the rest of this chapter?

The rest of this chapter fills out the details. But it cannot cover every single employment possibility.

Legal life-cycle of an employee

How long employed	What you must do
New starter	**1** Do not dismiss for automatic unfair reasons such as maternity, health and safety, or asserting a statutory right such as the right to written terms and conditions. There are many statutory rights, and these are increasing with new legislation – seek advice.
	2 Do not discriminate on racial grounds or, since 1 October 2006, on the grounds of age (p. 247).
	3 Do not discriminate on grounds of sex (p. 246) or against married people.
	4 Pay equal pay to men and women (p. 239).
	5 Do not discriminate because of trade union membership (p. 250).
	6 Do not treat part-time employees less favourably.
	7 Pay statutory sick pay (SSP) when required (p. 238).
	8 Give maternity leave when required (p. 253).
	9 Make sure you pay the the national minimum wage (p. 236).
	10 Provide access to a stakeholder pension scheme (unless exempt) (p. 399). (From a future date, likely to be 2012, it is proposed that you will have to contribute to a pension scheme for each employee unless they opt out.)
	11 Do not discriminate against disabled people (p. 247).
	12 Do not discriminate on basis of sexual orientation, religious or similar belief (p. 248).
	13 Give an itemized statement with pay (p. 237).
	14 Give paid time off for ante-natal care (p. 251).
	15 Consult recognized trade union about redundancy (p. 260).

16 Do not dismiss unfairly because of pregnancy (p. 251).

17 Give written reason if dismissing because of pregnancy.

18 Do not insist an employee works more than 48 hours a week and give 20 minutes' rest break after six hours of work (p. 242).

19 Give four weeks' paid holiday (p. 238).

One month or more

20 Give the minimum notice periods required by law (p. 260).

21 Pay guaranteed pay if you have no work (p. 239).

Within two months

22 Give a written statement of the main terms and conditions (p. 234).

Six months or more

23 Give paternity leave and adoption leave if requested by new parents (p. 251).

24 Pay statutory maternity pay (SMP), statutory paternity pay (SPP) and statutory adoption pay (SAP) to employees who qualify (pp. 253, 254).

25 Seriously consider requests by parents for flexible working (p. 255).

One year or more

26 Give written reasons for dismissal (other than pregnancy), if requested.

27 Do not dismiss unfairly (p. 256).

28 Give paid time off work to look for work in redundancy.

29 Give job to employee back from maternity leave, unless original/alternative unavailable (p. 254).

Two years or more **30** Pay redundancy money (p. 260).

Taking on an employee

The most important part of employing someone is to select the right person for the right job in the first place. The techniques of job description, advertising the job, selecting for interview and interviewing are covered in Chapter 20. However, there are certain legal points to look out for to ensure that you and your employee get off to a happy start.

What you must do

1 Do not discriminate because of sex, marital status, disability or race in ads, interview and job descriptions. You must also avoid discrimination on the grounds of sexual orientation, religious or similar beliefs and age.

2 Tell your tax office when you take on an employee.

3 Give your employee a written statement within two months of starting work.

Starter rules

You should be careful that sex, racial or other sorts of discrimination do not creep into ads or interviews. Avoid using job titles that imply one sex or the other – 'foreman', for example. If you use this sort of job title, include in the ad a note that you welcome applications from both sexes. Avoid using 'he' or 'she' to describe a job applicant in an ad as it suggests you want applications from men only, if you use 'he', or women only, if you use 'she'. And be careful that illustrations don't give the impression that the job is a man's or woman's. In an interview avoid asking women about their husband, their marriage or family responsibilities or whether or not they intend to have a family.

Since 1 October 2006, you must also take care not to discriminate, either directly or indirectly, in ads and interviews on the grounds of age unless there is a justifiable reason for recruiting someone within a particular age range. This means, for example, making sure you place ads in publications that are likely to be read by a spread of people of different ages. Note that advertising for a younger person simply because you think they would be cheaper then an older worker will not count as a justifiable reason. If you advertise for graduates, you need to make clear that graduates of any age are welcome not just people in their twenties. Advertising for people with a minimum number of years' experience would exclude younger applicants, so you need to be certain you have objective grounds to justify the experience requirement. In interviews, avoid age-related questions, such as how the person would feel managing older or younger workers.

The job should be described accurately in the ad and in the letter offering the job. These two can form part of the contract of employment. When you do take on an employee, you should tell your tax office. Remember to get your new employee's P45; if your employee does not have one, fill in a P46. By the time your employee has been with you for two months, you must have given them a written statement of the conditions and terms of the job (see below).

It would be wise to take note of the actual day on which your employee starts. The date can determine whether you may be able to dismiss your employee fairly or not, if things do not work out. Remember that dismissal because of sex, marital status, disability, race, age or for automatic unfair reasons require no qualifying period and will be unfair from day one.

What is the contract of employment?

The words 'contract of employment' conjure up thoughts of a written document. But the terms of your employee's contract of employment can be made up of anything you write or indeed say. It can include what you say in the ad, in the interview, in the offer letter, when your employee starts work and any subsequent chat you have about the terms and conditions of the job.

The basic contract is offer of employment, acceptance of employment and agreed amount of payment; these can be oral or written. Anything else makes up the terms. It is far better to have the terms in writing, which are then signed by both the employee and the employer. There is a legal requirement to provide a written statement of terms within eight weeks of the start of employment.

What you have to put in the written statement

The statement should include your name and your employee's name. You have to say when your employee's present job began and when your employee's period of continuous employment began.

You also have to give information on various terms and conditions. The terms and conditions are:

- the scale or rate of pay, including how it is worked out.
- at what intervals payments will be made (weekly, monthly, etc.).
- hours of work, including normal working hours.
- holidays, including public holidays, and holiday pay, including how it is worked out.
- place of work.
- your employee's job title or a brief outline of the work.

As well as the statement, you must give further information on:

- sickness or injury and sick pay.
- pensions and pension scheme.
- length of notice to be given by you and your employee.

▪ if the contract is 'temporary', an indication of the expected duration.

▪ details of any collective agreement affecting the job.

There has to be a written note giving information about new disciplinary rights and procedures that came into effect from 1 October 2004 (see p. 256). Finally, you also have to state whether a contracting-out certificate under the Social Security Pensions Act 1975 is in force that applies to your employee – see p. 397 for the significance to you of being 'contracted out'.

Who gets a written statement?

Most employees do, unless:

▪ you have already given your employee a written contract of employment that includes all the above items.

▪ the employment is for less than a month.

▪ your employee will be working mainly outside Great Britain.

Booklets

▪ Equal Opportunities Commission (EOC), *Code of practice on equal pay.*

EOC, *Recruiting staff.*

▪ Commission for Racial Equality (CRE), *Statutory code of practice on racial equality in employment.*

CRE, *Equal opportunities is your business too.*

CRE, *Racial equality and the smaller business, A practical guide.*

▪ Department for Business, Enterprise and Regulatory Reform (DBERR), *Written statement of employment particulars* 06/543.

DBERR, *Example form of a written statement of employment particulars* 06/534.

▪ Advisory, Conciliation and Arbitration Service (ACAS), *Employment guides for small firms* ST104.

ACAS, *Recruitment and selection* SO6.

ACAS, *Contracts of employment* SO2.

▪ Disability Rights Commission (DRC), *Getting into work – my rights* EMP13.

Pay and working hours

There are quite a lot of rules about how you can pay, how much you have to pay and what you have to give with pay.

What you must do

1 Act as collector of income tax and National Insurance contributions for the government using the PAYE system (p. 240). You may also have to deduct student loan repayments to pass to the HMRC. On the rare occasion it happens, you may also have to act to enforce a court order, by deducting sums from an employee's earnings under what is called an attachment of earnings. This may occur, for example, for paying maintenance under a Child Support Agency ruling or for paying a fine.

2 In most cases, do not deduct anything from your employees' pay unless it has been agreed in writing that you can do so, for example in the contract of employment.

3 Pay statutory sick pay, statutory maternity pay, statutory paternity pay and statutory adoption pay if due.

4 Give equal pay to employees carrying out broadly similar work or work of equal value.

How much do you have to pay?

In many cases, deciding how much and how often you pay your employee will be negotiated between you and your employee. Whatever is decided will be part of your employee's contract of employment. You can also negotiate the question of bonuses, commission, overtime, holiday pay and sick pay.

If your business was formerly covered by a Wages Council (now abolished), any employees previously covered by a wages order will retain those rights. You will have to vary their contracts to change this, and this can be a tricky procedure, so take advice.

A statutory national minimum wage was introduced from 1 April 1999. You must pay employees at least:

Age of employee	Year starting 1 October	
	2006	*2007*
22 or more	£5.35	£5.52
18 to 21	£4.45	£4.60
16 or 17	£3.30	£3.40

What you can, or have to, deduct from pay

You cannot deduct anything from your employee's pay unless it has been laid down by law or unless it has the written agreement of your employee.

However, you can make some deductions if your employee has agreed in writing. For example, you can deduct a sum of money and hand it over to someone else, such as dues to a union or donations to a charity under a payroll giving scheme or contributions to a pension plan.

What you have to give your employee with the pay

You must give your employees a detailed written pay statement when or before they are paid. What must be written in the statement is laid down by law:

■ the amount of your employee's salary before any deductions are made.

■ if you deduct any sums of money, which can vary from pay day to pay day, you must say what the amount of each deduction is and what it is for.

■ if you deduct any sums of money that remain the same on each pay day, you can do one of two things. Either you can say how much each deduction is and what it is for on each pay slip. Or, on the pay slip, you can say what the total of these fixed deductions is and separately from the pay slip give a statement of what the sums of money are used for.

This separate written statement must be handed out at twelve-monthly intervals. It must say how much, when and why any deductions are made, and you must hand it to your employee before or when they are made. If these fixed deductions are changed, you have to give your employee written notice or an amended written statement.

■ the amount of your employee's pay after all deductions.

If your employee is paid by more than one method, your pay slip should show how much is paid in each way, half in cash and half by bank transfer, for example. And remember that employees are entitled to see pay records to confirm that you are complying with the national minimum wage. So you must keep records for these purposes.

Do you have to give holiday pay?

All employees are entitled to four weeks statutory paid holiday leave a year. They have this right from the first day of work. Leave accrues at a rate of one-twelfth of the annual entitlement for every month worked rounded to the nearest half-day. This statutory holiday entitlement is not in addition to bank holidays – and can include them. You therefore need to make the position clear in the written statement of terms, which can be more generous than the statutory minimum if you like. The holiday entitlement is calculated *pro rata* for part-time employees. A court case in March 2006 determined that it is illegal to roll up holiday pay and give it as extra wages instead of allowing paid time off.

Do you have to give sick pay?

Yes and no. If you have agreed to give your employee pay while ill, you must do so as it is part of the employment contract. How much pay and for how long should be set out by you in the written statement of employment given to your employee within two months of starting the job (p. 234).

If you have not agreed to pay your employee while ill, then your only obligation is to give statutory sick pay. Employers are required by law to pay SSP to their employees during sickness if the qualifying conditions are met. The weekly rate for 2007–8 is £72.55 for employees with average weekly earnings of £87 or more. All employers are eligible to reclaim the SSP paid out in any month where it comes to more than 13 per cent of the total National Insurance contributions (both employer and employee) paid.

Employees will qualify for SSP if they are aged 16 and over and are sick for at least four days in a row. This is known as a period of incapacity for work (PIW). All days count towards sickness, including weekends and public holidays, but you only pay SSP after the qualifying days. These are normally the days your employee does not work. No SSP is payable for the first three days of sickness in a PIW – these are known as waiting days.

For absences of four to seven days it is usual to ask your employee to sign a self-certificate form (your own or form SC1 or SC2, available free from Social Security offices). For absences of more than seven days, it is usual to ask for a medical certificate. You cannot insist on a medical certificate for absences of less than seven days.

Your employee is not entitled to SSP if his or her average weekly earnings before sickness were less than the lower earnings limit for National Insurance contributions (£87 from 6 April 2007).

For more information about the SSP scheme, see HMRC* guide E14 *What to do if your employee is sick.*

If you have no work for an employee, do you have to pay?

Generally speaking, pay is negotiated between you and your employees, without any government intervention. Whether employees are paid when there is no work or they are unable to work will be decided by negotiation. However, in most cases you will pay your employees' salary or wages regardless of how much work you have and regardless of whether something happens, such as a power strike, that means your employee cannot do the work required.

But if your employee is paid by the hour or on piece rate, you do not have to pay:

■ unless you have agreed to do so in the contract of employment; or

■ unless you have to make what is known as a guarantee payment.

You may have to make this payment, once your employee has worked for you continuously for a month, for any complete days when he or she is not provided with work throughout a day during which there would normally be work. Guarantee payments can apply to all workers, not just hourly and piece-rate workers. You have to pay £19.60 a day for workless days (from 1 February 2007) unless they earn less than that a day.

This payment may be made up to five times in a three-month period. The limit on the payment is reviewed, but not necessarily changed, each year.

Note that you can make a provision within the written statement of terms for lay off or short-time working.

Equal pay

You cannot pay one employee more than another because one is a man and the other a woman. For example, simply to say that a man is stronger is no defence to justify higher wages. If your employees are doing the same or broadly similar work or work of equal value, you should pay the same rate to each and give each the same terms of employment. 'Broadly similar' means that the differences between the two jobs are not of practical importance.

You can pay one employee more than another if there is a genuine non-sex-based reason for it. An example would be if one of your employees had been with you for many years and you had a scheme to pay employees a higher rate after a number of years.

Anti-age discrimination regulations came into force from 1 October 2006. In some circumstances you will still be able to pay workers of different ages different levels of pay. These include differentials that depend on length of service of five years of less, and differences that recognize loyalty and experience or whose purpose is to motivate staff.

How to operate the PAYE system

You have to act as a tax collector for the government. The government department that deals with tax is Her Majesty's Revenue & Customs (HMRC). On each pay day you have to deduct the correct amount of tax and National Insurance contributions from your employee's pay and you have to send it to the tax collector. Here are the steps to take when you employ someone:

1 Tell your tax office. If it is your first employee, tell your own tax inspector. You will be told which is your PAYE tax office as an employer, which could be different from the office that handles your individual tax affairs.
2 Work out the tax and National Insurance contributions you have to deduct each pay day. Your PAYE tax office will send you the tax and NI tables you need to calculate this.
3 Fill in the deductions working sheet you have been sent by the tax office. Do this for each pay day.
4 Within 14 days of the end of each month, send the tax and NI contributions to the accounts office. You will have been given pay slips to send in with the money. Alternatively, you can register to deal with PAYE over the Internet – contact the HMRC e-filing helpdesk*.
5 At the end of each tax year (5 April), you will receive a return form from HMRC asking for details of the pay and benefits of each employee. You must send in these details by the date on the form – if you don't, you'll be fined. You can use your deductions working sheet to complete the return. As you fill in the return, two extra copies of it are automatically produced. You give one of those copies to your employee as form P60 no later than 31 May. The other two copies you send to the tax office, together with a statement summarizing the returns for all your employees. End-of-year returns for the 2009–10 tax year onwards must be filed over the Internet if you are a small employer – defined as having fewer than 50 employees. (Larger employers must already file by

Internet.) If you choose to switch to Internet filing earlier than this, you qualify for tax-free incentive payments which can either be set against a subsequent PAYE bill or paid out to you. The incentives are:

End of year returns for tax year	Amount of incentive
2007–8	£100
2008–9	£75

You will not have to do this if your employee earns less than a certain amount – in the 2007–8 tax year, the PAYE threshold is £100 a week or £435 a month. But even if your employee earns less, you still have to tell your tax office.

Your employee should give you a P45 on the first day of the job; if not, you should fill in P46. You should fill in a P45 when an employee leaves. You send the top part of it to your tax office (or via the Internet) and give the rest (parts 2 and 3) to your employee.

For guidance on your tax and National Insurance duties as an employer, contact the relevant HMRC employers' helpline*.

Fringe benefits as pay

Fringe benefits, such as a pension scheme, childcare vouchers or cheap meals, can be worth more to an employee than a salary rise. How much of your employee's pay package is made up of salary and how much of fringe benefits is generally a matter of negotiation. However, as part of a package of measures aimed at increasing future retirement incomes, it has been proposed that from 2012 all employers will have to pay a minimum 3 per cent of pay into a pension scheme for each employee (unless the employee opts out). It is expected that there will be a transitional period during which small employers will be given cash help meeting this cost. The proposals are still at an early stage and full details will not be available for some time.

Your employee may have to pay income tax but usually no NI contributions on the taxable value of the benefit. However, you have to pay employer's NI contributions (called Class 1A contributions) on most of the benefits you give your employee. There are some exceptions, such as money you pay into a pension scheme or plan on behalf of the employee.

You have to send in a form P11D each year to HMRC by the date on the notice requesting information, which gives information about fringe benefits and expenses. The form needs to be filled in for:

■ employees earning at the rate of £8,500 a year or over, including the taxable value of fringe benefits and expenses. So you might have to fill in a form for employees whose salary is much less than £8,500, if they also have a lot of perks; and

■ any directors, unless the director earns less than £8,500, including perks, works full-time for you and has 5 per cent or less of the shares, including what his or her family and friends own.

Working time regulations

The following rules apply:

■ if working more than six hours a day, employees are entitled to a minimum 20-minute break away from their work station if possible.

■ for most employees, working hours must be limited to an average of no more than 48 hours a week over a reference period. The normal reference period would be a period of 17 weeks, although it can be extended in certain circumstances to 52 weeks. An employee can agree to work longer than this, but it must be in writing and the employee must be able to give notice to withdraw agreement (on a maximum of three months' notice) – this exemption from the 48-hour limit is called the 'opt-out'. The UK is the only country in Europe that uses the opt-out and, at the time of writing, the European Parliament was negotiating with the UK to build in some extra safeguards. These could include giving employees the right to change their mind once a year about working longer hours, and possibly an overall cap on the length of working week of, say, 65 hours.

■ employees are entitled to one rest day in every seven or two days in fourteen.

■ a working day should be no longer than 13 hours, although it depends on how it is dealt with and what break there is between that shift and the next. There must be an uninterrupted break of eleven consecutive hours in each 24-hour period (although this can straddle two days).

There are also regulations concerning night workers.

Booklets

■ HMRC, *Employer's further guide to PAYE and National Insurance contributions* CWG2.

HMRC, *Day-to-day payroll* E13.

HMRC, *What to do if your employee is sick* E14.

HMRC, *Employer's guide to the collection of student loans* E17.

■ EOC, *Are you providing equal pay?*

EOC, *Equal pay, fair pay.*

EOC, *Code of practice on equal pay.*

■ DBERR, *A detailed guide to the national minimum wage* 04/1253.

DBERR, *Pay statements: what they must itemise* 06/538.

DBERR, *Individual rights and responsibilities of employees* 06/1833.

DBERR, *Limits on payments and awards* 07/512.

DBERR, *Guarantee payments* 06/536.

■ ACAS, *Paying employees* S10.

ACAS, *Holidays and holiday pay* AL03.

ACAS, *Employing older workers* AL09.

Safe and healthy working environment

You have to provide a reasonable standard of health and safety not only for your employees but also for visiting workers, other visitors and members of the general public who may be affected by what you do. This applies to the safety of the premises as well as to any risks arising from the work itself.

Note that an inspector has the right to enter your workplace to examine it and enforce legal requirements.

What you must do

Once you have employees there are additional rules. Broadly:

1 Tell whichever organization is responsible for health and safety at work for your business what your business name and address are. If you have an office, shop, warehouse, restaurant or funeral parlour, for example, your local authority* will be responsible. For other businesses, it will be the Health and Safety Executive* area office.

2 Get employer's liability insurance and display the certificate at each place of work.

3 Bring your written statement on your policy for health and safety at work (if you have five or more employees) to your employees' notice or create one and make any breach the subject of the disciplinary procedure.

4 Display the health and safety law poster or hand out the equivalent leaflet.

5 Make an assessment of the fire risks of your workplace – and keep a written record if you have five or more employees.

6 Train and appoint a first-aid officer or someone who is responsible for your policy.

Insurance

You must have employer's liability insurance to cover you for any physical injury or disease your employees suffer as a result of their work (p. 263). The latest certificate must be displayed.

Safe working environment

You must see that the place where your employees work, and the entrance and exit to it, are reasonably safe. Making a safe place of work includes things like fire exits and extinguishers, electrical fittings, storing material, machinery, hygiene, first aid; the list is very wide and covers all aspects of work.

You also have to take steps to provide a system of working for your employees that will give adequate safety. This includes making sure your employees are given adequate information and are trained well enough to carry out the work safely. And you also need to check that the system of working is actually being carried out.

You must provide equipment, materials and clothing that enable your employees to work in reasonable safety. You could be held responsible if there is a defect in the things you give to your employee that causes an accident.

If there is a risk of injury from criminals or others, you must take steps to protect your employees.

Competent workers

If you know one of your employees is incompetent, and if one of your other employees is injured as a result of that incompetence, you could be held liable. And even if you do not believe your employee to be inefficient, but your employee behaves negligently while carrying out your work, and another employee or a member of the general public is injured, you can be held liable.

If one of your employees breaks a safety rule that you have publicized, you can fairly sack that employee. However, you must have made clear beforehand that breaking the rules would result in sacking, so include this in your disciplinary code. The reverse side of the coin is that if you do not take reasonable steps for the safety of your employees, an employee could resign and claim constructive dismissal (p. 260).

Paperwork

If you have five or more employees, you must have a written statement on your policy for health and safety at work and how that policy is to be carried out. This statement should be displayed so that employees can see it.

Regardless of the number of employees, you must also either display the health and safety law poster at work or hand out the appropriate leaflet. You can get these from your local HSE office.

If you have ten or more employees, you must keep an accident book to record work accidents. If you have a 'factory', you have to keep a book like this regardless of the number of employees. And for all businesses certain accidents must be notified to the authority that regulates your business for health and safety.

You must make an assessment of the risks relating to your work premises and identify any safety measures you need to take. If you have five or more employees, you need to keep a written record of this.

Booklets

■ Health and Safety Executive (HSE), *Health and safety regulation: a short guide.*

Discrimination: what to watch out for

In general, you cannot discriminate on grounds of sex, disability or race, marital status, union membership, sexual orientation, religious or similar beliefs or age.

At present, there are three main bodies that deal with discrimination issues – the Equal Opportunities Commission (EOC)*, the Commission for Racial Equality (CRE)* and the Disability Rights Commission (DRC)*. However, legislation has been passed to replace these three commissions with a new

Equality and Human Rights Commission by 31 March 2009 at the latest. This new body will be responsible for all types of anti-discrimination, including new areas such as age discrimination. As well as contacting the EOC, CRE and DRC, you can get guidance on how equality legislation applies to your business by contacting Equality Direct*.

What you must do

1 Do not discriminate on grounds of sex, race, marriage, disability, sexual orientation, religious or similar belief or age.
2 Do not refuse to allow your employees to join a trade union or dismiss them for trade union activity.

Sex and marriage

Discrimination means less favourable treatment of a man or woman on the grounds of sex or because they are married. It covers pay and conditions of the job, as well as opportunities for promotion, for example. You cannot discriminate:

- in advertising or interviews for the job.
- in the terms in which the job is offered.
- in deciding who is offered the job.
- in opportunities for promotion, transfer or training.
- in benefits to employees.
- in dismissals.

You need to be particularly careful that you do not introduce requirements for a job or promotion that are likely to be met by one sex more than the other. For example, if you insist that the person for the job needs to be six feet tall, you will be discriminating against women. The same could apply if you insist on some technical qualification more likely to be held by men than women. But you can insist on height, technical or other qualifications if you can show that these are genuinely necessary for the job.

Under new regulations, discrimination based on sexual orientation is outlawed. This covers orientation towards people of the same sex, opposite sex or both but does not extend to sexual practices or preferences. The discrimination may relate to someone's actual orientation or their perceived orientation – so harassment of a worker because he or she was thought to be homosexual would still be illegal, even if the person was not in fact homosexual.

Disability

Disabled employees have the right not to be discriminated against either in the recruitment procedures you use or during the course of their employment (for example, they must be treated equally when it comes to opportunities, training, promotion, and so on). As an employer, you are under a duty to take reasonable steps to remove physical barriers and to adjust your working practices so that any disabled employees can exercise these rights.

Employers with fewer than fifteen employees used to be exempt from the requirements. However, since 1 October 2004 this exemption has ceased. 'Employee' includes both full- and part-time workers, apprentices, contract workers working for you and workers you contract out to others.

The Disability Rights Commission (a public body formed to pursue people's rights under the Disability Discrimination Act 1995) has drafted a code of practice clarifying the duties of employers under the disability discrimination legislation.

Race

Racial discrimination means treating one person less favourably than another on racial grounds, which includes colour, race, nationality or ethnic or national origins. As with sex discrimination, racial discrimination also applies if you make a requirement for a job that one racial group would find more difficult to meet than another group (unless this is a lawful requirement for the job). This is known as indirect discrimination and is unlawful. An example of this would be to insist on certain clothing being worn or to ask for a high standard of English when it is not necessary to do the job. And you cannot discriminate against a black employee because of how customers might react (for example, someone working in a pub).

You cannot discriminate:

- in advertising or interviews for the job.
- in the terms in which the job is offered.
- in deciding who is offered the job.
- in opportunities for promotion, transfer or training.
- in benefits to employees.
- in dismissals.

If one of your employees takes you to a tribunal claiming racial discrimination, it is unlawful for you to victimize the employee. It is also unlawful to instruct or put pressure on others to discriminate on racial grounds.

Religious and similar beliefs

Since 2 December 2003, it has been illegal to discriminate on the grounds of someone's religion or similar beliefs. Until a body of case law has developed, what counts as discrimination is something of a grey area. In the first case to be decided under the new law, a bus cleaner was awarded £10,000 compensation after being sacked for taking extended leave to make a pilgrimage to Mecca. Other areas that could possibly give rise to discrimination claims might include dress code and canteen menus.

Beliefs similar to religious beliefs have not been defined in the regulations, and it will ultimately be for tribunals to decide whether particular beliefs come within the scope of these rules. A tribunal might consider, say, whether the beliefs involve collective worship, way of life or view of the world.

As with sex and race discrimination, these new rules will apply to recruitment, promotion, transfer, training, benefits and dismissals and cover both direct and indirect forms of discrimination.

The government has already announced that, when the age discrimination legislation takes effect, employers will be allowed to set a default retirement age of 65. Employees will have the right to request working beyond this age, and you will have to consider any such requests. However, you will be able to turn down a request or set an earlier default retirement age if you can show objective grounds for doing so.

The new legislation will tackle all types of age discrimination, whether against young people or older employees.

Age

Anti-age discrimination regulations came into effect from 1 October 2006. These ban discrimination, harassment and victimization on the grounds of age when recruiting, training and employing people. The regulations apply to all workplaces and affect the way you treat all employees, not just older workers.

A job applicant or employee who feels they have been the target of age discrimination can take their case to an employment tribunal which can award compensation of an unlimited amount. Along with the person doing the discriminating, harassment or victimization, you as employer can also be found liable for the actions of your employees. Therefore, it makes sense to have an equality policy at work which includes age, and to make sure that your workforce is aware of and trained in the practice of the policy.

See p. 233 for how the new regulations can affect your approach to recruitment and interviewing. Other areas affected by the legislation include providing training, pay and benefits (see p. 239), redundancy (see p. 260) and retirement (see below).

There are some circumstances in which you are allowed lawfully to discriminate on the grounds of age. These are:

- *where you can objectively justify the discrimination*: this means having a legitimate aim for discriminating, good grounds for thinking that the discrimination will achieve the aim and no better alternative.

- *length of service*: you are allowed to offer additional rights or benefits to employees who have completed a minimum period of service of five years or fewer. For longer periods, extra rights and benefits are permissible provided that they aim to reward experience or loyalty or keep staff motivated, and you can prove that the discrimination is effective. Proof might take the form of, say, monitoring staff performance or the results of staff surveys.

- *minimum wage*: the national minimum wage (see p. 236) is exempted from the regulations. Similarly, you are allowed to pay more than the national minimum wage to employees of different ages provided you follow the same pattern – in other words with lower amounts for younger workers and using the same age bands (16 and 17, 18 to 21, 22 and over).

- *statutory authority*: this enables you to comply with the law where, for example, it sets a minimum age for holding a licence.

- *redundancy*: see p. 260.

- *life cover*: if an employee retires early due to ill health, you are allowed to continue providing them with life cover up to their normal retirement age.

- *genuine occupational requirement*: this might apply where, for example, a theatre needs a young actor to play a particular role.

The regulations also affect retirement. In most cases, normal retirement age will be the national default age of 65. Generally, it will be illegal to force an employee to retire earlier than this. But you can set a lower normal retirement age if there are objective reasons for doing so. You must notify an employee of their approaching retirement date within six months. The employee then has the right to ask to stay on. You are required to consider the request but you can turn it down and you do not have to give your reasons for doing so.

Trade unions

A tribunal will find the dismissal unfair if you sack an employee for:

- belonging to an independent trade union (that is, a union that is not controlled by an employer) or for not being a member of a trade union.

- taking part in trade union activities (for example, meetings) at the appropriate time, which is normally outside working hours or inside working hours with the agreement of the management. Industrial action does not count as a union activity.

Employees can also complain to an employment tribunal if you penalize them, but do not dismiss, or if you make them redundant for any of the above actions.

Criminal offences

In some cases, people who have been convicted of an offence do not have to tell you about it. If you ask, they can lie about it quite legally. The people who can do this are usually those who have had sentences of thirty months or less. They can keep quiet about their convictions after a specified time, which varies, but it is not more than ten years and not less than six months, and it also depends on the type of conviction.

If you employ someone who is entitled to keep quiet about their convictions and you subsequently discover their past, you cannot fairly dismiss the employee.

However, if your employee is required to drive a vehicle during work, you would need to insist on knowing about any driving conviction or disqualification. Your insurance cover would be affected by this.

Health and disablement

You can refuse to employ someone if you are unhappy about their state of health. If one of your employees has been absent from work due to sickness, you may be entitled to dismiss on these grounds, providing a proper procedure is involved and subject to the length of time the employee has been absent. This involves consulting with the employee concerned, obtaining up-to-date medical evidence and considering any suitable alternatives for the employee before dismissal.

It is illegal to treat someone less favourably than other employees because they are disabled – for example, by offering them lesser benefits or fewer opportunities for promotion or training.

Booklets

■ EOC, *Equal opportunities is your business too.*

■ ACAS, *Religion or belief in the workplace* EEL01.

ACAS, *Sexual orientation and the workplace* EEL02.

ACAS, *Age and the workplace* EEL03.

■ Disability Rights Commission (DRC), *Disability, health and employment: a short guide for small and medium-sized employers* EMP4.

DRC, *Health and safety* EMP8.

Maternity and parental leave

Pregnant employees, married or unmarried, have several rights, such as the right not to be dismissed unfairly, the right to maternity leave and the right to return to work – but there are many conditions and exceptions, which can only be glossed over in this section.

From 6 April 2003, working parents acquired a range of new rights. These include paid leave for new fathers and parents who are adopting a child, plus the right of parents with young or disabled children to request flexible working.

Maternity leave and pay have been improved for women expecting their babies from April 2007 onwards. Regardless of how long the woman has worked for you, she is entitled to up to 52 weeks' maternity leave (previously only 26 if she had worked for you for less than 26 weeks) and, if she has been with you for at least 26 weeks, may claim statutory maternity pay for 39 weeks of her leave (previously 26 weeks). Similarly, maternity allowance is now payable for 39 weeks.

The government is committed to extending paid maternity leave to the full 52 weeks by the end of the current Parliament (which could run to May

2010) and aims, at some stage, to introduce further measures which would allow some paid maternity leave to be transferred from the mother to the father.

From April 2007, the right to request flexible working (see 255) has been extended to employees who are caring for an adult, as well as those caring for a young child.

What you must do

1 Give reasonable paid time off work so that your employee can have ante-natal care.
2 Do not dismiss your employee because she is pregnant.
3 Give your employee statutory maternity pay – SMP (see p. 253).
4 Give your employee her job back – see opposite.
5 Give new fathers up to two weeks' leave and statutory paternity pay.
6 Give parents who are adopting time off and statutory adoption pay.
7 Seriously consider requests from working parents for a change in their hours or work pattern.

Dismissing while pregnant

A woman will automatically be held to be unfairly dismissed if (among others) the reason for dismissal is that she is pregnant or for any reason connected with her pregnancy.

An Employment Appeal Tribunal has also found that it can be sex discrimination to dismiss a woman because of pregnancy if you would not dismiss a man who would need similar time off for an operation.

If a pregnant employee cannot do a particular job or it would be illegal for her, then the employer is entitled to offer her a different job that she can perform where appropriate. An employee is entitled to receive no less favourable terms than that of her previous position. If there is no other position, then she may be entitled to be suspended on pay, but she cannot be fairly dismissed in these circumstances unless the dismissal can fit one of the legal categories and has no relation to pregnancy.

Maternity leave

Regardless of how short a time she may have worked for you, your employee is entitled to 52 weeks' maternity leave. Thirty-nine weeks of this will normally be paid leave.

The employee must normally tell you by the end of the fifteenth week before the expected week of childbirth (EWC) that she intends to take leave. She can then take the full 52 weeks without giving you any further notice. However, if she wants to come back to work early, she must give you eight weeks' notice of her intention.

If your employee is off work sick during the four weeks before the start of the EWC, her leave will be deemed to have started automatically. Otherwise, it starts when the employee chooses, provided this is no earlier than the beginning of the eleventh week before the baby is due.

During her leave, the employee's pension and other employment rights may be protected, though this depends on the terms of the contract. She has the right to return to work at the end of her leave – normally to the same job she had before her leave started.

Maternity pay

You must normally pay statutory maternity pay (SMP) to an employee during the first 39 weeks of her maternity leave even if she is not going to return to you after the birth of her child. You pay SMP if your employee:

- has stopped working for you.
- is still pregnant at the eleventh week before her baby is expected.
- has average weekly earnings of at least £87 a week for 2007–8.
- has been continuously employed by you for six months or more by the end of the fifteenth week before the baby is due.

The amount of SMP is 90 per cent of average earnings for the first six weeks of the period. Thereafter, it is £112.75 a week in 2007–8 (or 90 per cent of weekly average earnings if this average is less).

You can claim back some or all of the SMP that you pay out. You get the relief by deducting it from the tax, National Insurance contributions and other PAYE deductions you would otherwise hand over to HMRC. If the amount you must pay out to employees exceeds the PAYE deductions you've collected, apply to HMRC for advance funding. You can recover the SMP you pay out in full if the employer's and employees' National Insurance contributions you collect come to no more than a set amount, which is £45,000 in 2007–8. If the National Insurance comes to more, you can claim back 92 per cent of the sum you pay out (and have to fund the remaining 8 per cent yourself).

Right to return to work

Your employee has the right to return to work if she has worked for you continuously for one year at the beginning of the eleventh week before the baby is due. (There is at present an exemption for employers with less than five employees to refuse the right to return.) Your employee may lose the right to return to work if:

- her job no longer exists because of redundancy and there is no suitable alternative job (in which case redundancy pay may be due).

- it is not practicable for her to return to her job and you have offered suitable alternative work, which she refuses.

Employees used to have to notify their employers if they were going to exercise their right to return to work. Under rules that came into force in December 1999, it is now assumed that the woman will return to work at the end of her maternity leave. No earlier than 21 days before the end of her 18-week ordinary (statutory) maternity leave, you can ask your employee to confirm that she will be returning to work, and she is obliged to respond.

Since 6 April 2003, you are required to consider all requests for flexible working from parents of young children (see p. 255).

Booklets

- DBERR, *Pregnancy and work* 06/1886.
- HMRC, *Pay and time off work for parents* E15.

Parental leave and time off for dependants

Since 15 December 1999, employees who have worked for you continuously for a year or more have the right to take up to 13 weeks' unpaid parental leave to care for their child during their first five years of life. In addition, since 6 April 2003, fathers have the right to take at least two weeks' paternity leave following the birth or adoption of a child and are entitled to claim statutory paternity pay (SPP) for up to two weeks. Also from 2003, people adopting a child are able to take up to 26 weeks' leave and claim statutory adoption pay (SAP). Employers are responsible for paying SPP and SAP and are entitled to at least partial reimbursement, in a similar way to statutory maternity pay (see p. 253). If the amount you must pay out in these benefits comes to more than the PAYE deductions you hand over to HMRC, you may be able to apply for advance funding from HMRC.

Employees with at least a year's service have the right to take reasonable or unpaid leave to attend to domestic incidents/emergencies/family crises. This covers, for example, sickness, injury, a death in the family, a partner giving birth or a serious incident at school. The legislation does not include any default rules about how this right should be put into practice. So, unless you draw up your own policy and make it part of the terms of employment, there is no requirement for your employee to tell you they are taking this leave or to inform you of how long they expect to be away. You will need to make clear whether this will be paid or unpaid and how you will deal with this in practice.

Flexible working

From 6 April 2003, parents of a child under the age of 6 (or under 18 in the case of a disabled child) have the right to ask to switch to flexible working in order to care for the child. From 6 April 2007, this right has been extended to employees caring for a spouse, civil partner or relative who lives at the same address and who is in need of care. The request may relate to the hours they work, the times they are required to work and where they work (e.g. from home or an office). You, the employer, must consider the request. However, you can refuse if you have good commercial reasons for doing so. These might be:

- the burden of additional costs.
- detrimental effect on meeting consumer demand.
- inability to reorganize work among existing staff.
- inability to recruit additional staff.
- detrimental impact on quality.
- detrimental impact on performance.
- insufficiency of work during the periods the employee proposes to work.
- planned structural changes.

An employee will have the right to take you to an employment tribunal if you refuse to consider a request for flexible working or you have refused the request on the basis of incorrect facts. But the tribunal will not be able to consider the merits of the commercial reasons you have given for refusal. If the tribunal finds in favour of the employee, it will be able to order you to pay compensation.

Booklets

- DBERR, *Parental leave* 06/566.

  DBERR, *Time off for dependants* 99/1186.

  DBERR, *Paternity leave and pay* 06/547.

  DBERR, *Adoptive parents – rights to leave and pay* 03/1717.

  DBERR, *Flexible working – the right to request and the duty to consider* 06/2158.

Saying goodbye to an employee

In most circumstances, you have got one year to assess employees (make sure you have a probationary period), and during that time you can dismiss them without any fear of being taken to an employment tribunal and accused of unfair dismissal. However, you will automatically be guilty of unfair dismissal, regardless of the length of time the employee has worked for you, if you sack him or her or if the reason for the dismissal is:

- trade union membership or activity.

- not being a member of a trade union.

- acting as a representative for negotiations about redundancy, and so on.

- being pregnant or taking maternity leave.

- taking action on health and safety grounds.

- trying to enforce a statutory employment right (such as requesting a written statement or refusing to allow an employee to bring a work colleague or trade union representative to any disciplinary grievance hearing).

- refusing to do shop or betting work on a Sunday.

- acting in his or her role as a pension scheme trustee.

- reasons relating to the national minimum wage.

- reasons relating to the working time regulations.

- reasons relating to the transfer of employment rights from one employer to another.

- 'whistle blowing', where protection is given by the Public Interest Disclosure Act 1998.

And if you dismiss an employee who would qualify for paid suspension on medical grounds, you could be guilty of unfair dismissal if the employee had been with you for a month or more.

However, be careful in how you dismiss an employee who has been with you for less than one year in case he or she can claim breach of contract. The statutory minimum notice can be added to the dismissal date for the purpose of the calculation.

You are normally automatically guilty of unfair dismissal if you fail to follow a specified three-step procedure. This procedure is mandatory in nearly all cases. If you fail to follow it, a tribunal will order you to pay a minimum of four weeks' pay in compensation to the employee, and any additional compensation will be increased by between 10 and 50 per cent.

Since 1 October 2006, employees aged 65 and over have become newly eligible to claim unfair dismissal.

What you must do

1 Follow the three-step procedure: put it in writing; meet and discuss; appeal.
2 Behave in a reasonable way when dismissing an employee.
3 Give your employee the right notice.

How you can sack an employee

There are five reasons that may mean a dismissal is fair, although you will also have to demonstrate that you have followed the three-step procedure and been reasonable in the circumstances. The reasons are:

1 *Being incapable of doing the job*: this covers skill, competence, qualifications, health and any other mental or physical quality relevant to the job. Note that you do not have to prove to an employment tribunal that an employee is incompetent, merely that you believed it to be so and that you have acted reasonably. But you must make sure that your employee is aware of the requirements of the job and why and how they are not being met.
2 *Misconduct*: for example theft, insolence, horseplay, persistent bad time-keeping, laziness.
3 *Redundancy* (see p. 260).
4 *Legal reasons*: for example, if a van driver could no longer carry out his or her duties because of losing his or her driving licence.

5 *Some other substantial reason*: for example, if it is not financially viable for the firm to continue to employ an employee.

As you can see, it is possible to dismiss an employee if you are dissatisfied. But it is very important to follow the correct procedure and to act in a reasonable way. It can save you an awful lot of time and money if you do because you can demonstrate to an employment tribunal that you have acted correctly and fairly.

Dismissal is the final step in a disciplinary procedure. The mandatory three-step procedure applies both to dismissal and also to most disciplinary action that falls short of dismissal. The three steps are set out below. Following them on their own is not enough. You must also act fairly and reasonably at all times and in the context of the circumstances of the case, and this will usually be judged by reference to the ACAS* *Disciplinary and grievance procedures* CP01 (price £2.95).

The standard three-step dismissal and disciplinary procedure

Step 1 *Put it in writing*	You must write down what the employee has done that may result in their dismissal or disciplinary action and send a copy to the employee.
Step 2 *Meet and discuss*	You must invite the employee to a meeting at a reasonable time and place in order to discuss the matter. The employee is entitled to be accompanied by a colleague or trade union representative if they choose. Following the meeting, you must tell the employee what you have decided and offer your employee the right to appeal against your decision.
Step 3 *Appeal*	If the employee wants to appeal, they must tell you. You must then invite the employee to a further meeting to hear the appeal. Where possible, a more senior manager should attend this meeting. The employee is entitled to be accompanied by a colleague or trade union representative if they choose. After the meeting, give the employee your final decision.

Step-by-step guide

1 When you first become dissatisfied with an employee, tell the employee so in writing (step 1 of the standard procedure).
2 Meet the employee to discuss the problem and to explore constructively how things might be improved (step 2 of the standard procedure).

3 Consider whether the matter can be resolved informally, for example through training for the employee or extra supervision of their work. Inform the employee of how you expect them to improve, over what time period and when their progress will be reviewed.

4 If an informal solution is not possible, take formal action. You should normally follow these stages: first written warning, final written warning. Inform your employee that they have the right to appeal against your decision (step 2 of the standard procedure). Written warnings must set out the nature of the problem, the improvement or change you require and the consequences for the employee of failing to comply. At each stage, you should meet again with the employee to give them a chance to present their case. A written warning should be disregarded after a specified period without further action (say, six months, or twelve for a final warning).

5 If the employee requests an appeal, arrange a meeting to hear the appeal. Tell the employee your decision (step 3 of the standard procedure).

6 Repeat steps 2 to 5 above as necessary.

7 If the problem persists, you may decide to dismiss the employee or possibly offer them an alternative job. Make sure you give the correct notice (see opposite). You must again follow the standard three-step procedure, so give your reasons for dismissal/transfer/demotion in writing, meet with the employee and give them the opportunity to appeal.

Sacking someone on the spot

It can be done, and exceptionally a tribunal may judge it to be a fair dismissal provided the circumstances were extreme (for example, gross misconduct, such as dishonesty) and you have followed a modified statutory procedure. Under the modified procedure, you must immediately after the dismissal give the former employee in writing an explanation of your reasons for the dismissal, including the evidence for your decision, and inform the employee that they have the right to appeal. If they take up this right, you must meet with them to hear the appeal and give the employee your final decision following the meeting.

However, in most cases, you reduce the risk of problems if instead you follow the full three-step procedure. Consider suspending the employee on full pay (which does not count as a disciplinary measure) while you investigate and go through the standard three-step procedure.

Can it be unfair dismissal if your employee resigns?

It may seem a paradox, but the answer is yes. It can be unfair, if it is a constructive dismissal. So watch out. If you increase working hours without extra pay, cut your employee's fringe benefits or accuse an employee of something, such as theft, without investigating it properly, it may count as constructive dismissal.

Making an employee redundant

You can make an employee redundant if you are cutting down generally on the number of employees or if your need for a particular skill in your business ceases or diminishes. But you must make the redundancy fair; do not choose married women, trade unionists, part-timers or people over a certain age, for example, as reasons for redundancy. And you must consult the recognized trade union (if appropriate) about the proposed redundancy.

If an employee has been with you for two years, you will have to pay redundancy pay. The amount depends upon the age of the employee and varies between ½ and 1½ weeks' pay for each year the employee has worked for you. There is a limit on the amount of a week's pay.

Since 1 October 2006, generally you will breach the new anti-age discrimination regulations if you select employees for redundancy on the grounds of age. This means, for example, that generally you cannot operate a last-in-first-out policy (which could discriminate against younger employees) or a policy of making those with the longest service redundant (which would tend to discriminate against older workers). However, age-related redundancies are allowed if you can objectively justify them. Note that since 1 October 2006, workers aged 65 or over are entitled to redundancy rights.

The statutory redundancy pay scheme, which pays larger amounts to older workers, is exempt from the age discrimination regulations on the basis that it is harder for older workers to find similar employment elsewhere and so the larger compensation is objectively justified. If you offer more generous redundancy terms, generally your scheme will also be acceptable under the regulations if it is based on the statutory scheme (for example, based on higher pay than the statutory scheme or paying out a higher multiple for each year).

How much notice do you have to give?

You must give your employee:

■ one week's notice if your employee has been with you for one month but less than two years.

■ two weeks' notice if your employee has been with you for two years.

■ an extra week's notice for each extra year your employee has been with you, up to a maximum of twelve weeks' notice.

If your employee's contract specifies a longer notice period, the longer period applies.

These minimum notice periods do not apply to the notice given to you by your employee, who by law has to give only one week's notice if employed by you for a month or more. So, if you want to make sure your employee has to give more notice, you must put it in the contract of employment.

What to do when an employee leaves

You must fill in form P45. Send part 1 to the tax office and hand parts 2 and 3 to your employee. If an employee dies, you should also fill in form P45 and send all three parts to the tax office.

Booklets

■ DBERR, *Rights to notice and reasons for dismissal* 07/534.

DBERR, *Dismissal: fair and unfair* 07/829.

DBERR, *Unfairly dismissed?* 07/828.

DBERR, *Limits on payments and awards* 07/512.

■ ACAS, *Disciplinary and grievance procedures* CP01 (price £2.95).

Summary

1 Do not be too frightened of employment law. On the whole, you can employ who you want and sack them if they prove to be incompetent.
2 Behave reasonably towards your employees, giving them a chance to explain their actions. If you do this, you can cut down the chances of being found guilty of unfair dismissal in an employment tribunal.
3 Use all the agencies who are set up to advise in this very complex area.
4 Seek legal advice. Getting it wrong can be expensive and time-consuming.

Other chapters to read

20 Getting the right staff (p. 210); **28** Keeping the record straight (p. 340).

22

Insurance

Deciding what insurance you should have must rate as one of the least exciting decisions you have to make for your business. Paying out money to cover you against hazards, which you fervently hope will not happen, ranks fairly low in satisfaction. But it should rank quite high in priority. Failing to get the right insurance might mean the collapse and end of your business.

There are two different categories of business insurance:

1 Insurance you must have by law.
2 Insurance you could consider to cover risks and disasters.

Buying the insurance

Not only do you want the right sort of insurance, you want it at the right price and with the right company. The obvious place to start your search for your business insurance is with an insurance broker. A broker can, in theory, deal with the full range of insurance companies and should be able to find the lowest quote for you. Note that the cost of the insurance may vary depending on the location of the business; at the extreme, you may find it difficult or expensive to buy insurance for some areas.

There are different types of insurance intermediary. Those using the name 'broker' are usually independent and can arrange insurance for you with any company in the market. Other intermediaries – for example, those calling themselves 'consultants' – could be independent but more often will be acting as agents for just one or a handful of companies. It's important to check this before you do business.

Insurance companies, brokers and other intermediaries are regulated by the Financial Services Authority (FSA)*. It is illegal for a firm to trade without being authorized by the FSA and, provided you deal with an authorized firm, you are protected by complaints procedures and a compensation scheme if anything goes wrong. Firms are also required to comply with rules about how they conduct business, which includes finding out enough about your needs and circumstances to recommend only a suitable policy and drawing your attention to any unusual or onerous terms in the contract. Under the FSA rules, you must be given a document headed 'Key Facts', which summarizes all the main features of the policy in an easy-to-understand way that can be used easily to compare one policy with another.

You can check whether a firm is authorized by the FSA by using the FSA Register*. You can get a list of brokers in your area from the British Insurance Brokers Association (BIBA)*, a trade body that also sets standards of practice for its members. If you prefer to deal online, using a search engine (see p. 22) will give you a long list of online companies and brokers.

Insurance you must have

1. Employer's liability

You must have insurance to pay out for your legal liability if one of your employees is injured or ill as a result of working for you and you have been negligent. The amount of cover (the amount of money the insurance company will pay out if you claim) is generally unlimited but must be at least £5 million. The law also requires you to exhibit a certificate of employer's liability insurance at each place of work.

Premiums for employer's liability insurance have soared in the past few years. There is anecdotal evidence that some employers, no longer able to afford cover, are making do without it. Don't be tempted to follow this course. It is illegal to carry on a business in which you employ people if you do not have this cover, and you could be personally financially ruined if an employee has an accident at work and claims against you.

You do not need employer's liability insurance if you are not a limited company and the only people you employ are close family members (your spouse, civil partner, children, parents, grandparents, brothers or sisters). Since 28 February 2005, you no longer need this insurance if you operate as a limited company, you own at least 50 per cent of the shares and you are the only employee.

2. Motor insurance

You must insure your liability to others, known as third party liability, which occurs because of a car crash or other motor vehicle accident. This includes death or injury to anybody (but not your employees while working, as they are covered by employer's liability insurance, see above) and damage to third party property including other vehicles.

A further addition to third party cover that could be worth your while is fire and theft cover. Finally, if you want to get cover for accidental damage to your vehicles, regardless of who is to blame for the accident, you want a comprehensive insurance policy.

If you have a car or other vehicle for your own private and social use, and you want to use it for your business, you should tell your insurance company. You may need to pay an extra sum to get it covered for business.

Be clear about what the car is going to be used for when you fill in what is known as the proposal form (the form you fill in to apply for the insurance). You will probably have to pay extra money if the car is used for some purposes, such as by a sales rep. Failure to tell the insurance company may mean that it will not pay out if you make a claim.

3. Insurance needed by contracts

Check all the contracts you have (for example, under a lease or hire purchase agreement) to see what insurance you are committed to get.

4. Engineering equipment

By law, certain equipment, such as pressure vessels and lifting tackle, has to be inspected and passed as safe at regular intervals. You can combine the maintenance with an insurance policy to cover you against the risk of explosion, accidental damage and breakdown.

Other insurance you can get

1. Insurance against fire and other perils

This covers destruction or damage to your buildings and contents through fire. You can also be covered for other risks, such as lightning, explosion, aircraft, storm, flood, riot and malicious damage. Standard business property insurance normally specifically excludes loss or damage caused by terrorism, but you can buy back this cover for an extra premium. If you work from your own home, you will still need to get your own insurance policy and there are some special schemes available – consult an insurance broker*.

Worth getting? *Yes.*

2. Insurance for loss of profits

This covers you if your business is disrupted by fire or some other insured peril. It can pay out money to pay your employees, maintain your profits and pay for the extra cost of your fill-in working premises. These 'business interruption' policies normally only cover incidents where the interruption stems from damage to your business premises. However, you can separately buy 'contingent business interruption' insurance to provide cover where the disruption to your business is from some other cause, such as an epidemic, transport disaster or a strike at your suppliers or customers. (You cannot buy cover against a strike by your own workers.)

Worth getting? *Depends* on your business. In most cases, yes to standard business interruption insurance; but if your business is small with few employees, and you could easily find somewhere to work, for example your home, you may not consider it necessary. Note that using your home could cause problems with insurance, so check with your insurance company. Rather than insure for full loss of profits, you could consider insuring for the cost of finding somewhere else to carry on working. In the case of contingent business insurance: probably not worth getting unless your business is particularly vulnerable. You might consider other ways to manage risks, for example, diversifying your supply chain or customer base to lessen the impact of third-party strike action.

3. Insurance against theft

This covers you for loss or damage to the contents of your premises. Theft for insurance purposes means that someone has forced an entry to or exit from your workplace, so if you want to be covered against theft by your employees or visitors, you'll have to pay extra and get fidelity insurance.

Worth getting? *Yes.*

4. Loss of money

Cash and near-cash, such as cheques and stamps, can be insured against theft from your premises or from the homes of directors or employees of your company or in transit.

Worth getting? *Yes*, if your takings are in cash. Otherwise, no.

5. Goods in transit

This insurance covers loss of or damage to your goods in your own vehicles, or other means of delivery, such as post or road haulier.

Worth getting? *Probably*, unless you don't sell in this way.

6. Credit insurance

This protects you against your customers failing to pay. You probably will not be able to get this insurance until you have been in business for some time.

Worth getting? *Probably not*, if you deal mainly in cash or payment on delivery. For selling on credit, by the time you can get this insurance, you will be able to work out for yourself how likely a problem bad debts will be. It is probably better to operate good credit control (p. 314) or use a factoring service (p. 318). However, if you have only one large or a couple of big customers, you should have credit insurance.

7. Public liability and product liability

This will cover your liability to visitors and members of the public if your business causes injury or illness to them or damages their property. Product liability insurance covers you for these risks, which occur as a result of the goods you are producing, selling or repairing up to a limit each year.

You need to make sure that the amount of cover is high enough. Damages in the courts have been as high as £1 million. You may need cover for more than this, especially if you do business in the USA.

Worth getting? *Yes*. With product liability, you may not need it if your products are very unlikely to cause damage or if yours is a service business.

8. Professional indemnity

If you are the sort of business where the end-product is expert advice, this insurance can cover you against claims from your clients for damage caused by your negligence or misconduct.

Worth getting? *Yes*. These sorts of claim are on the increase.

9. Legal expenses

This insurance would enable you to pay for legal assistance if you are involved in a contractual or employment dispute, plus some other legal procedures.

Worth getting? *Probably not*. Most legal disputes are generally in the employment field. It would be far better to concentrate on getting well organized in this area to cut the risk of being taken to a tribunal and charged with unfair dismissal or breach of contract, for example.

10. Keyman insurance

If your business is heavily dependent on one or a few people for its future success, you can get keyman life insurance, for example for a sum of £250,000 to be paid to your business in the event of one of those people dying or being ill for a considerable period. To get cover, you must be able to prove the person's death would cost your firm money.

Worth getting? *Yes*.

11. Other insurance

There are some other types of insurance that you should consider, depending on your business. These include:

- glass breakage, which is important for shops.
- cover for frozen food.
- computers and computer records.
- fidelity insurance, which covers you against fraud or dishonesty by your employees.
- business machines and equipment.
- agricultural and fish-farming operations.
- directors' and officers' liability.

Insurance for you and your family

If you and your family are not covered by insurance for various personal mishaps, you may find it difficult to carry on your business, so do not neglect your personal needs. Almost everyone should have life insurance, income protection insurance and a pension plan.

Make sure that you and your spouse/partner have enough life insurance to protect you in the event of your early deaths. For this purpose, do not go for the sort of life insurance that is really an investment but go for term insurance, family income benefit, mortgage protection, and so on.

Income protection insurance would pay out an income if you were too ill to work and could pay for a temporary manager. You should consider this carefully. And do not forget pensions, which are covered in detail on p. 396.

Summary

1 Do not delay in taking out the insurance you need.
2 Use a registered insurance broker to act for you.
3 Shop around. Seek advice from more than one broker and ask for several quotes for each insurance you need.
4 Do not neglect personal insurance requirements. Life insurance for your family, income protection insurance and pensions should be looked at carefully to determine the level you need. Use an independent financial adviser* who is authorized to advise you on these topics.

Other chapter to read

31 Pensions and retirement (p. 396).

23

Forecasting

Forecasts are the kernel of your business. They are the basis on which you raise money, negotiate premises and order raw materials. These are only a few of the decisions that need to be made in advance with only your forecasts as guidance on how much is needed. Making a wildly inaccurate forecast can, for example, lead to raising insufficient funds. When the business fails to meet expectations and begins to run short of money, it may prove impossible to raise further funds. Lenders are very wary of handing out more when forecasting has proved to be mistaken. The result could be liquidation, or bankruptcy if you are a partner or sole trader, and the end of your dreams.

However, making no forecasts at all is even sillier. You would have no guidance on when to take certain basic business decisions.

Given the importance of attaining a reasonable estimate of future sales, costs and cash balances, it follows that making the forecasts is a process that should not be hurried or treated casually (and can usually be carried out with the help of a computer program). You must constantly strive to seek information on which forecasts can be based; you must constantly curb your over-optimism, which can lead to estimated sales figures that are too high and estimated cost figures that are too low. Question your first forecasts for the realism of their assumptions before accepting any figure as a part of the final forecasts.

Nevertheless, it is realistic to accept that some of the figures will be nothing more than a best guess given the current state of information available to you. However, your figures should have some grounding in fact, so when you present your case to your bank manager or other source of finance you can support the figure when challenged.

It is important to make the forecasts in your plan realistic so that if your business idea does not hold water, you can discover this at the planning stage. You do not want to discover two years down the track that your business will not work, after you have committed money, time and effort. Do not underestimate the mental anguish and financial problems that can be caused by a struggling business (p. 335).

What is in this chapter?

There are three forecasts you need to make:

- cash flow (p. 270).
- profit and loss (p. 276).
- balance sheet (p. 280).

Finally, on p. 284–88, there are some example forecasts.

Cash flow forecast

The first point to note is that cash and profit are not the same thing at all, so the two forecasts may be quite different.

A cash flow forecast is a record of when you think you will receive cash in your business and have to pay it out. In your business plan, you should include monthly cash flow forecasting for at least one, preferably two years ahead. Depending on the size of your business, you may need to include yearly cash flow forecasts for a further three years.

On p. 272, there is a blank cash flow form, which shows the typical headings and layout of a forecast. Obviously, the headings will vary with the nature of the business. See p. 284 for an example forecast.

Detailed calculations for cash flow forecast

Do the cash flow forecast for your chosen accounting year. If, for example, you choose to end your accounting year at the end of April, your cash flow forecast will run from 1 May to 30 April.

It is important to make realistic assumptions about when you will receive the cash, or when you will have to pay it out. The purpose of the forecast is to throw up when your need for cash is at its greatest, so you can demonstrate what your funding requirements are.

1. Opening bank balance

This shows how much is actually in your business bank account at the start of each period. If you owe your bank money (have an overdraft), show this by putting the figure in brackets. If your forecast is made before you start trading, the opening bank balance is likely to be nil.

Your opening bank balance for one period will be the closing bank balance for the previous period.

2. Cash from sales

In here would go any cash you expect to receive when you sell your product, not in payment of an invoice you send out. If your business is a shop, most of your sales will be cash ones, so this would be the biggest element of your cash receipts. If you are registered for VAT, enter the figure you expect to receive, including VAT.

3. Cash from debtors

If you sell your product and do not receive payment at once, but instead send out invoices, you would enter here when you expect to receive the cash. Someone who owes you money (for example, has not yet paid your invoice) is a debtor. You should aim to get your invoices paid as quickly as possible, but most of your customers will expect to delay payment by at least one month (see Chapter 25 for how to get your debtors to pay).

If you are registered for VAT, enter the figure you expect to receive, including VAT.

4. VAT (net receipts)

If you are not registered for VAT, ignore this section (see p. 383 for details of whether you should not be registered). If you are registered for VAT, you will only expect to receive cash from the VAT system if for some reason your purchases, on which you can claim back VAT, are greater than your sales on which you have charged VAT.

This might happen as a rare occurrence if you have spent a lot of money while starting up, before your sales have got going. Another possible reason could occur if your sales are seasonal but your purchases are not. It could also happen if your sales are zero-rated, in which case you do not have to charge VAT on your sales, but you can claim it back on purchases (p. 388).

Monthly cash flow forecast

(for the period 1 January 2008 to 31 December 2008)

		Jan.	Feb.	–	Nov.	Dec.	Total
1	Opening bank balance (A)	. . .	. . .	–	. . .	. . .	. . .
Receipts							
2	Cash from sales	. . .	. . .	–	. . .	. . .	. . .
3	Cash from debtors	. . .	. . .	–	. . .	. . .	. . .
4	VAT (net receipts)	. . .	. . .	–	. . .	. . .	. . .
5	Other receipts	. . .	. . .	–	. . .	. . .	. . .
6	Sale of assets	. . .	. . .	–	. . .	. . .	. . .
7	Capital	. . .	. . .	–	. . .	. . .	. . .
	TOTAL RECEIPTS (B)	. . .	. . .	–	. . .	. . .	. . .
Payments							
8	Payment to suppliers	. . .	. . .	–	. . .	. . .	. . .
9	Cash purchases	. . .	. . .	–	. . .	. . .	. . .
10	Wages/drawings	. . .	. . .	–	. . .	. . .	. . .
11	PAYE/NIC	. . .	. . .	–	. . .	. . .	. . .
12	VAT (net payments)	. . .	. . .	–	. . .	. . .	. . .
13	Tax payments	. . .	. . .	–	. . .	. . .	. . .
14	Rent	. . .	. . .	–	. . .	. . .	. . .
15	Uniform business rate	. . .	. . .	–	. . .	. . .	. . .
16	Heating/lighting	. . .	. . .	–	. . .	. . .	. . .
17	Telephone	. . .	. . .	–	. . .	. . .	. . .
18	Professional fees	. . .	. . .	–	. . .	. . .	. . .
19	General expenses	. . .	. . .	–	. . .	. . .	. . .
10	Capital expenditure	. . .	. . .	–	. . .	. . .	. . .
21	Bank interest	. . .	. . .	–	. . .	. . .	. . .
22	Other payments	. . .	. . .	–	. . .	. . .	. . .
	TOTAL PAYMENTS (C)	. . .	. . .	–	. . .	. . .	. . .
23	CLOSING BANK BALANCE (A) + (B) – (C)	. . .	. . .	–	. . .	. . .	. . .

You may make your returns for VAT on a quarterly basis, so allow for this in your cash flow.

5. Other receipts

Put here any miscellaneous receipts of income that you expect to occur.

6. Sale of assets

This section is for you to record the proceeds you expect to get from selling any assets, for example a car or office equipment.

7. Capital

Put the amount of money you are going to invest and make sure you put it in the month you expect to invest it. If anyone else is expected to invest or to lend you money (not including an overdraft with the bank), slot it in here.

8. Payment to suppliers

Put in here when you expect you will have to pay suppliers for their services or materials. The longer you delay paying suppliers' invoices, the better it can be for your cash flow. This beneficial effect has to be balanced by any ill will created by late payment. A realistic assumption for your cash flow forecast will be that you will not have to pay your suppliers' invoices until one month after you receive them. Whether you are registered for VAT or not, enter the amount including any VAT you will be paying to your suppliers.

9. Cash purchases

If you have to pay cash on the spot for purchases from suppliers, estimate the amount (including any VAT) and time in this section.

10. Wages/drawings

Put here the amount after deducting tax and National Insurance contributions under the PAYE system for wages.

11. PAYE/NIC

Total the amount of tax under the PAYE system and the amount of National Insurance contributions you will deduct from your employees each month, as well as the amount of the employer's contribution. You have to send this money in to the tax collector within two weeks of the end of the month (but if your PAYE and NIC payments are £1,500 a month or less, you can make quarterly payments, which will help your cash flow).

If your business is a limited company and you pay yourself a salary as a director, your personal tax and National Insurance contributions will be collected in this way.

If you are a sole trader or partner, your personal tax on what you pay yourself will not be collected in this way. Instead, you will pay tax, and Class 4 National Insurance contributions if you pay them, in two or three lumps, in January, July and any remaining balance the following January. Enter the amount in the section **Tax payments**. However, your Class 2 National Insurance contributions will be collected each month, and you should reflect the amount here under **PAYE/NIC**. For more about your personal tax and National Insurance contributions as a sole trader or partner, see p. 355.

12. VAT (net payment)

If you are not registered for VAT, do not enter anything here. If you are registered for VAT, you should estimate the amount of tax you will be paying over to the VAT collector each quarter or other period (see Chapter 30).

13. Tax payments

If you run a limited company, enter the amount of tax you estimate you will pay on your company's profits and when you will pay it. Corporation tax, that is, tax on your company's profits, is payable nine months after the end of your accounting year – ask your accountant* for more information.

If you are a sole trader or partner, your tax and any Class 4 National Insurance contributions payable will be paid in three lumps – on 31 January, 31 July and the balance or a repayment on the following 31 January. For how to work out the amount of tax you will be paying, see Chapter 29.

14. Rent

Enter the rent you will pay in each month or quarter.

15. Business rate

Enter the amount of the business rate and when you will have to pay it – see p. 368. Do not forget you can opt to pay your rates monthly over a ten-month period. This can improve your cash flow.

16. Heating/lighting

These bills will be paid each quarter in arrears or monthly by direct debit. Remember to cater for heavy winter usage.

17. Telephone

The phone bill will be paid quarterly or monthly in arrears.

18. Professional fees

Payment of these bills will be fairly erratic; you must make your best guess, but try to obtain an estimate.

19. General expenses

Enter an estimate for those continuing and recurring, but small, expenses. These could include postage, fares, newspapers, or whatever is required in your business. If your business is a mailing service, for example, you should have a separate heading for postage. What exactly goes in here will have to be decided by you.

20. Capital expenditure

If you are going to buy any pieces of equipment, such as a car, computer or machinery, enter the amount, including VAT, and when you estimate you will have to pay for it. If you are paying cash, put in the full amount. If you are going to buy on hire purchase or using a loan, you will enter the amount of the deposit and the monthly payments separately and in the correct months. Leasing payments will be monthly.

21. Bank interest and charges

If you have an overdraft or bank loan, estimate the amount and frequency of the interest charged. Get a quote from the bank manager.

22. Other payments

What goes in here depends on the nature of your business. It could include insurance, but if this is of reasonable size, you should have a separate entry.

23. Closing bank balance

Work out the closing bank balance for the period by adding the opening bank balance to the total receipts and taking away the figure for total payments. The closing bank balance becomes the opening bank balance at the start of the next period.

Profit and loss forecast

A profit forecast should show what level of profit you expect your business to produce at the end of the period, according to the accounting records you keep. Your accounts will not be drawn up on a cash basis, so many of the figures in your profit forecast will be different from those in the cash flow forecast. Below there is an explanation of how and why the figures will differ.

Detailed calculations for profit and loss forecast

1. Sales

The figure you put in here is the sum of the invoices you expect to send out during the accounting period. It is not necessarily the sum of the cash you receive during the period (unless your business is a shop that makes only cash sales, for example). You could also describe the sales figure as the cash you receive during the period plus what you are owed at the end of the period less what you were owed at the end of the previous period.

If you are registered for VAT, you do not include the amount of VAT you charge on your sales, unlike in your cash flow forecast.

If your business is likely to be seasonal, or if you know of events coming up that might temporarily increase or decrease your sales figures, show this monthly effect. A reader of your business plan will not be impressed by a monthly figure that is level or shows a very steady rate of increase unless you can demonstrate that this is a realistic assumption.

When forecasting sales, you need to consider two factors: the number of units you can sell and the price you can get for these units.

2. Cost of sales: purchases

You are estimating for this section those costs that you would expect to vary with the level of your sales; if your sales go up, the level of direct costs goes up, and vice versa. In real life, things are not quite so cut and dried and often the distinction between direct costs and overheads is blurred. The important point is for you to have a clear idea about which you regard as overheads.

Purchases could be the raw materials you buy from your suppliers to manufacture your products. Or, if you are not a manufacturing business, they would be the items that you purchase to sell on to your customers, having added on your profit margin.

Monthly profit and loss forecast

(for the period 1 January 2008 to 31 December 2008)

		Jan.	Feb.	–	Nov.	Dec.	Total
1	SALES (A) less cost of sales	. . .	. . .	–	. . .	. . .	. . .
2	Purchases	. . .	. . .	–	. . .	. . .	. . .
3	Labour	. . .	. . .	–	. . .	. . .	. . .
4	Other direct costs	. . .	. . .	–	. . .	. . .	. . .
	TOTAL (B)	. . .	. . .	–	. . .	. . .	. . .
	GROSS PROFIT (C) Take (B) from (A) less overheads	. . .	. . .	–	. . .	. . .	. . .
5	Rent and rates	. . .	. . .	–	. . .	. . .	. . .
6	Heating/lighting	. . .	. . .	–	. . .	. . .	. . .
7	Telephone	. . .	. . .	–	. . .	. . .	. . .
8	Professional fees	. . .	. . .	–	. . .	. . .	. . .
9	Depreciation	. . .	. . .	–	. . .	. . .	. . .
10	Employee costs	. . .	. . .	–	. . .	. . .	. . .
11	Other overhead	. . .	. . .	–	. . .	. . .	. . .
	expenses						
12	Drawings	. . .	. . .	–	. . .	. . .	. . .
13	Interest	. . .	. . .	–	. . .	. . .	. . .
	TOTAL (D)	. . .	. . .	–	. . .	. . .	. . .
14	Plus miscellaneous income (E)	. . .	. . .	–	. . .	. . .	. . .
15	NET PROFIT (F) BALANCE (C) + (E) − (D)	. . .	. . .	–	. . .	. . .	. . .

The figure you put in your profit and loss account will be different from the cash flow figures for payments to suppliers and cash purchases. For the profit calculation, you need the sum of the invoices you receive in the period for materials.

Another way of working out the purchase figure for this forecast is to say it is what you pay for supplies in the period plus what you owe at the end of the period less what you owed at the start of the period.

If you are registered for VAT, you do not include the figure for VAT that you are charged by your supplier for your profit forecast. If you are not registered for VAT, you do include the figure for VAT.

Points to look out for when you are forecasting costs include:

- make sure that the level of costs corresponds to the amount of sales you expect to make.
- allow for any changes in the prices of raw materials that you can reasonably expect to occur in the period.

3. Cost of sales: labour

Here include the cost of your employees who are directly involved with manufacturing your product. As with purchases, the distinction between staff who are directly involved with production and those who count as overheads can be blurred. On the whole, if you do not think that employees' wages are directly related to the amount of work you have, it may be more satisfactory to include employee costs in overheads.

Remember to include all your employee costs; this implies gross salary, your National Insurance contributions as an employer plus any other costs.

The figures may diverge slightly from those in the cash flow forecast, as PAYE and NI contributions are due the following month. Differences will show up only when you first take on an employee or their salary rises.

4. Cost of sales: other direct costs

Estimate here any other direct costs that you foresee.

5. Overheads: rent and rates

In the profit forecast, the total for rates should be spread evenly over the whole year. With rent, you should enter the cost for each period, which may not coincide with the timing of the payments.

6. Overheads: heating/lighting

You need an estimate for the cost of heating and lighting that you will use in each period. Usually you're billed quarterly. This is the case even if you have chosen to pay monthly by direct debit, in which case the quarterly bill is set against the sum of your monthly payments.

7. Overheads: telephone

The treatment of the phone is similar to that for heating and lighting.

8. Overheads: professional fees

The figure to include here is what it costs you in legal and accounting fees. You should include the cost in the period in which the work is done for you, even if you do not receive the bill until the next period.

9. Overheads: depreciation

Depreciation is what you deduct from the value of an asset to reflect the fact that it is wearing out. This is an item that does not appear in the cash flow forecast. You work it out by taking the value of capital equipment at the start of each period and estimating a figure for its depreciation during the period. Typically, cars and office equipment are written off over three, four or five years.

Note that you do not put in the profit forecast what you pay for capital equipment, which does appear in the cash flow forecast.

10. Overheads: employee costs

This should be your estimate of employee costs that are not directly related to the volume of your sales, see p. 226.

11. Overheads: other overhead expenses

Include overhead expenses not slotted in elsewhere.

12. Overheads: drawings

What you pay yourself.

13. Overheads: interest

Estimate the interest on loans and overdrafts during the year.

14. Miscellaneous income

Put here an estimate of the other income you might receive, not as a result of the sales of your products. For example, if you have money invested, it might include interest.

15. Working out the net profit figure

You can work out a gross profit figure (C) by deducting the figure for direct costs (B) from the sales figure (A). On p. 306 you will see how you can use the gross profit figure to work out the break-even point for your business.

Once you have arrived at an estimate for gross profit, deduct the figure for overheads (D) and add on the amount of any miscellaneous income (E) to give your forecast net profit level (F).

Balance sheet forecast

A balance sheet for your business will show what you owe and what you are owed on one particular day. A forecast one will show your estimate of that picture at the end of the period.

There is more about accounting records needed to produce the right information for a balance sheet once you are in business in Chapter 28. Your accountant should be willing to help if you find it difficult to produce a balance sheet yourself. If your business is likely to be fairly small-scale and you are only approaching your bank manager, and for a fairly modest sum, a forecast balance sheet may not be necessary.

In this section there are brief guidelines on how to work out what the balance sheet might be at the end of the period, once the forecast cash flow and profit and loss account are drawn up. And on p. 288 there is a blank balance sheet forecast for you to complete.

Detailed calculation for balance sheet forecast

One important check on your balance sheet figures is to note that the figure for total assets should equal the figure for capital and liabilities together.

1. Fixed assets

These figures are fairly straightforward to work out. You know from your cash flow forecast when you plan to buy particular bits of equipment. Include all equipment that you have received before the end of the period, even if you have not paid for it. A fixed asset is something of a permanent nature, likely to remain in use in your business for some time.

The value you put in here is not just what you paid for the equipment; you also have to allow for the fact that it will have depreciated since the period started. You can obtain the figure for depreciation from your profit forecast. Deduct these figures from the appropriate cost of each piece of equipment, or written-down value at the start of the period, and enter the figures here.

Example

Richard Petworth is working out the depreciation for the office furniture he has bought for his business. There are a number of different ways of calculating this, but for office furniture he thinks he will write off the value in equal lumps over five years; this is called straight-line depreciation.

The furniture cost Richard £2,000. This means he writes off £400 from the value of it each accounting year. The written-down value at the end of the first accounting year is £1,600.

2. Current assets

The main current assets you are likely to have in your business are:

■ cash.

■ debtors (that is, what your customers owe you).

■ stock (that is, products you have in store, either raw materials to make your product, half-finished products or unsold finished products).

Take the figure for cash straight from your cash flow forecast.

You can derive the figure for debtors from the cash flow and profit forecasts. You will have made some assumption about number of units sold in each month and how quickly you will be paid your cash. From this you can calculate how much you would be owed for sales by your customers at the end of each period. Remember to include VAT if you are registered.

The figure for stock can also be derived from the other two forecasts. Count as stock all goods received from your suppliers to be used in your product but not yet used in products sold, even if you have not yet paid your suppliers' bills. These should be shown at their 'cost' to you.

3. Capital

Put here the capital you used to start your business. The figure for profit and loss you take from your profit forecast. It is the cumulative figure at the end of the period. If you forecast a loss, put it in brackets and it will be deducted from your capital.

Example

Betty Crop and Roger Cartwright are planning to start a knitwear business on 1 January. Their aim is to design knitwear and sell in small quantities (five to ten) to boutiques. Later they hope to produce in bigger quantities selling to department stores. The knitwear will be produced by outworkers.

The final price of the knitwear in the shops will be £90–£120, but Betty and Roger will receive £50–£60. The average cost of the raw materials will be £12 and they will pay each outworker £10 for each garment, on average. They have to take into account seasonal changes in sales, although they will design a range of cotton knitwear for the summer.

They will have to buy raw materials in advance on thirty days' credit and pay each outworker on completion of each garment. They will sell to the boutiques on thirty days' credit, but realistically will allow for an average sixty days' credit in their cash flow forecast.

At first they will work from home, but later in the year would like 500-sq. ft offices – they hope to get light industrial premises at £7 a sq. ft on the outskirts of London. When they have premises they would like to employ someone for clerical work and organizing the outworkers, leaving themselves free to design and sell.

Given their forecast level of sales, Betty and Roger do not need to register for VAT. They produce cash flow (p. 284) and profit and loss forecasts (p. 286) to see how the business will shape up.

Conclusions

Betty and Roger should take advice before going ahead with their business; their idea is not viable as it is currently presented, especially with the increase in overheads (rent for premises and assistant's wages) in the second half of the year. They would certainly need to put in more money, but even then, unless they can increase their sales figures, the long-term prospects must be fairly negative.

4. Liabilities

Loans from the bank or another lender that are not due to be repaid within one year are medium- or long-term liabilities. Current liabilities are mainly:

- overdraft.
- tax payable, including VAT.
- creditors (that is, what you owe your suppliers at the end of the period).

The figure for overdraft can be taken from your cash flow forecast.

If you have made a profit in the period, you will need to estimate what tax will be payable. You may also have to include a figure for what you owe HMRC in VAT (if you are owed VAT, you should have an entry in the current assets section for this).

In the same way as you worked out debtors, so creditors can be estimated using the two other forecasts. It is the value of the amount of goods you have that you have not yet paid for.

Cash flow forecast

(for 1 January 2008 to 31 December 2008)

	Jan.	Feb.	Mar.	Apr.	May	June
Opening balance	–	£7,820	£5,970	£6,330	£7,060	£6,880
Sales	–	–	1,900	1,900	1,350	1,350
Capital	10,000	–	–	–	–	–
Total: *Cash receipts*	£10,000	–	£1,900	£1,900	£1,350	£1,350
Raw materials	380	380	270	270	110	760
Outworkers	350	350	250	250	100	700
Capital equipment	600	–	–	–	–	350
Stationery/labels	200	–	200	–	200	–
Heating/lighting	–	70	70	–	70	70
Phone	–	300	–	–	300	–
Bank	–	–	–	–	–	–
Rent and rates	–	–	–	–	–	875
Assistant	–	–	–	–	–	–
Car expenses	50	150	150	50	150	50
Drawings	600	600	600	600	600	600
Total: *Cash payments*	£2,180	£1,850	£1,540	£1,170	£1,530	£3,405
Closing balance	£7,820	£5,970	£6,330	£7,060	£6,880	£4,825

	Jul.	Aug.	Sep.	Oct.	Nov.	Dec.	Totals
Opening balance	£4,825	£2,580	£249	£(3,443)	£(5,724)	£(2,541)	
Sales	550	550	550	550	6,500	7,350	22,550
Capital	–	–	–	–	–	–	10,000
Total: *Cash receipts*	£550	£550	£550	£550	£6,500	£7,350	£32,550
Raw materials	760	760	870	870	870	760	7,060
Outworkers	700	700	800	800	800	700	6,500
Capital equipment	–	–	–	–	–	–	950
Stationery/labels	200	–	200	–	200	–	1,200
Heating/lighting	–	–	400	–	–	400	1,080
Phone	–	300	–	–	300	–	1,200
Bank	5	21	47	61	47	34	215
Rent and rates	50	50	875	50	50	875	2,825
Assistant	400	400	400	400	400	400	2,400
Car expenses	80	50	50	50	50	50	930
Drawings	600	600	600	600	600	600	7,200
Total: *Cash payments*	£2,795	£2,881	£4,242	£2,831	£3,317	£3,819	£31,560
Closing balance	£2,580	£249	£(3,443)	£(5,724)	£(2,541)	£990	

Profit and loss forecast

(for 1 January 2008 to 31 December 2008)

	Jan.	Feb.	Mar.	Apr.	May	June
Sales	£1,900	£1,900	£1,350	£1,350	£550	£550
less Direct costs						
Raw materials	380	270	270	110	760	760
Labour	350	350	250	250	100	700
Total direct costs	730	620	520	360	860	1,460
Gross profit	£1,170	£1,280	£830	£990	£(310)	£(910)
less Overheads						
Rent and rates	–	–	–	–	–	380
Heating/lighting	56	56	56	56	56	56
Telephone	100	100	100	100	100	100
Stationery/labels	50	50	50	50	50	50
Administrative staff	–	–	–	–	–	–
Bank	–	–	–	–	–	–
Depreciation	68	68	68	68	68	73
Car expenses	78	78	78	78	78	78
Total overheads	352	352	352	352	352	737
Net profit	£818	£928	£478	£638	£(662)	£(1,647)

	Jul.	*Aug.*	*Sep.*	*Oct.*	*Nov.*	*Dec.*	*Totals*
Sales	£550	£550	£6,500	£7,350	£7,350	£5,400	£35,300
less *Direct costs*							
Raw materials	760	870	870	870	760	940	7,620
Labour	700	700	800	800	800	700	6,500
Total direct costs	1,460	1,570	1,670	1,670	1,560	1,640	14,120
Gross profit	£(910)	£(1,020)	£4,830	£5,680	£5,790	£3,760	£21,180
less *Overheads*							
Rent and rates	380	380	380	380	380	380	2,660
Heating/lighting	134	134	134	134	134	134	1,140
Telephone	100	100	100	100	100	100	1,200
Stationery/labels	50	50	50	50	50	50	600
Administrative staff	400	400	400	400	400	400	2,400
Bank	5	21	47	61	47	34	215
Depreciation	73	73	73	73	73	73	851
Car expenses	78	78	78	78	78	78	936
Total overheads	1,220	1,236	1,262	1,276	1,262	1,249	10,002
Net profit	£(2,130)	£(2,256)	£3,568	£4,404	£4,528	£2,511	£11,178

Balance sheet forecast

(on 31 December 2007)

ASSETS

1 Fixed assets

Freehold property	£......	
Leasehold property	£......	
Office equipment	£......	
Vehicles	£......	
Plant/machinery	£......	
Other equipment	£......	
Total fixed assets (A)		£......

2 Current assets

Cash in hand and at bank	£......	
Stock	£......	
Debtors	£......	
Total current assets (B)		£......
Total assets (A) + (B)		£......

Capital and liabilities

3 Capital

Shareholders'/proprietor's capital	£......	
Profit and loss	£......	
Total capital (C)		£......

4 Medium-term liabilities

Loans	£......

5 Current liabilities

Overdraft	£......	
Tax payable	£......	
Creditors	£......	
Total liabilities (D)		£......
Total capital and liabilities (C) + (D)	£......	

Summary

1 Forecasts are very important if you make commitments on the basis that the figures are reasonably accurate.
2 Make the forecasts conservative.
3 A cash flow forecast is not the same as a profit and loss forecast.
4 If you find it difficult to produce the forecasts, ask for help, for example from a Business Link* or an accountant*.
5 The treatment of VAT and depreciation need special attention.
6 Once you have the forecasts, use them to assess how viable your business will be and whether you will be able to make a living from it.

Other chapters to read

6 The business plan (p. 63); 24 Raising the money (p. 290); 28 Keeping the record straight (p. 340).

24

Raising the money

Raising money needs careful planning, like a military campaign. You should regard it as the biggest sale you are ever likely to make. You need to get your act together to present your case. You need to know how much money you want, who to approach, how long you want the money for, and what security you can offer backers. You also need to know the business plan, the financial figures and the marketplace inside out.

But that is not all. You should expect indifference, lack of interest, disbelief and doubt. You have to convince, persuade and excite sober, serious business people about the prospects for your business. This cannot be achieved by overstatement or rash predictions about success. Demonstrations of competence and skill are what is required.

Of course, a few strike lucky. There may be the odd story about bank managers agreeing overdrafts over the phone, or someone being able to pick and choose from a variety of backers who all want to put up the funds. But for most it is a hard, hard job.

What is in this chapter?

This chapter looks at:

- *money*: it explains how much you should consider raising (see opposite), what it is for (p. 292) and what type you want, for example loans or shares or both (p. 293).

- *lenders and investors*: it considers how much you and your family can provide (p. 295), what the government, local authorities, charities and so on can do (p. 297), what banks offer (p. 298), what can be obtained from private investors (p. 300) and what venture capital funds do (p. 300).

■ *the presentation*: how to do it (p. 303).

The money

How much money? What should you ask for?

Only when you have drawn up your business plan and done your cash flow and profit forecasts will you know how much money, if any, you need to raise. Take a few deep breaths before you rush round to make an appointment with your bank manager to see if you can get the overdraft you need. First, your bank is not always your first port of call, as you can see from later pages in this chapter. Second, you should take a further, closer, more critical look at the amount of money you think you will need.

Being optimistic, as anyone starting a business must be, you naturally believe you are going to make the sales you have projected on the timescale you estimated and keep the costs down to your forecast figures. But supposing things do not work quite as you hope. Going back to your lender and asking for more money within a short space of time does not inspire confidence, and you may find your second request rejected, if it is not part of your plan. And there you are with a new business to which you have committed time and money, which is now short of cash, and you are unlikely to find any way of raising more.

There is a body of opinion that says when you first approach your lender or investor, ask for twice as much money as you think you will need. At any rate, be very conservative and go for more money than you think you are going to use. Obviously, the business plans that you present need to tie up with your request for cash, so adjust them if need be, incorporating more conservative figures.

There are drawbacks. First, if your figures are too conservative, it may make your business proposition unviable altogether; if this happens, you do not need to worry about being forced to go back for more, your business will not even get off the ground in the first place, because you will not get the initial backing. The second obstacle to this approach is that it is the natural inclination of any investor to try to make you manage with less money than you say you need.

The sensible advice is steer a middle course: be pessimistic, while retaining a sensible business proposal.

At this stage, you know more than ever before about your proposed business and are likely to be very committed to it. But if the business does not look right, do not be afraid of ditching this plan and looking for a better one. You probably have only one chance of raising money for a business proposal, so do not choose a failure because it was your first idea.

For many people, this is the first point at which you are really learning what makes a business tick. One sign of a successful entrepreneur is that you can learn from your information and experience and can adapt. You want to go for calculated, but good, risks. If you have already started trading, your business course is set.

Large sums of money

There is another odd fact about raising money: different sums of money can be harder or easier to find, depending simply on their size. Surprisingly, it is sometimes said to be much easier to find very large sums of money for your business (£2 million plus) than sums in the £20,000 to £1 million range (these figures are an indication only; there are always exceptions). This quirk of business funding is of no interest to the vast bulk of people who want to become self-employed or start a business in a small way, but if your plans are on a larger scale, think about being bigger still.

This oddity occurs because there appear to be more people around who are willing to invest in either small businesses that are past the start-up stage (that is, not brand new) and into a big expansion phase or in new businesses that look capable of very fast growth in profits. To achieve either of these objectives, the amount of money invested needs to be substantial to stand any chance of success. Other preconditions for success, apart from large funds, are a very strong management team and a sound market. If you cannot demonstrate that both of these apply to you and your business, your chances of raising very large sums of money are virtually nil.

The money: what is it for?

From your forecasts, you should have an indication of when your need for extra cash arises, how long it lasts for and when you would be able to pay it back or give a good return on it. When starting up, you need money for:

- the 'once-in-a-business-lifetime' expenses of setting up. These include what you have to spend on your premises, on IT equipment and furniture, on legal and professional costs, and on initial marketing expenditure.

■ working capital. This is what you need to keep yourself going in the time gap between paying out cash for raw materials or stocks and getting in cash from the people you sell to. All businesses need working capital; the amount varies depending on the type of business, the credit terms you can negotiate from suppliers and the credit you extend to customers.

The longer you can get your suppliers to wait for their payment and the shorter the period you allow your customers to pay, the less working capital you need. Your working capital requirements will also be less if you do not need to hold big stocks of goods.

In practice, all these things are easier said than done and you need to work out a strategy for controlling your business that meets your need to keep down the money tied up with working capital, coupled with keeping your suppliers and customers happy. This is covered in more detail in Chapter 25.

If your business is up and running, you may need funds simply because it is growing and hence the amount of working capital necessary has gone up. Or you may have some specific expansion in mind.

The money: what type do you want?

Overdrafts

If your need for the money is likely to be fairly short term, an overdraft or some sort of short-term loan is your likeliest bet. Your need for finance in the short term could be to cover a temporary shortage of cash, or it could cover your start-up requirements if these are fairly small.

An overdraft is quick to arrange and relatively cheap, but there will be an upper limit above which you are not to go without the permission of the bank manager. The serious drawback with an overdraft is that the bank can demand instant repayment. While this does not happen very often, you can bet that if the bank does demand repayment or reduction of the overdraft, this will occur when you cannot do so.

If there are no assets, such as debtors, to be taken as security for the overdraft, it is likely that your bank manager will require that you give some personal assets or, less likely, a personal guarantee as security even if you have formed a limited company. One benefit of getting substantial funding is that as a result of the strong balance sheet, personal guarantees, although asked for, can sometimes be avoided.

As a self-employed person you are personally liable anyway, so no further guarantees are needed. In the extreme, this means that if you cannot repay an overdraft, your bank could take you personally to court to recover its money and your personal as well as business assets could be seized.

Note that banks may be wary of taking stocks as security for an overdraft. The manager may insist on property or debtors as the only acceptable security. Always negotiate about the level of security needed; it is in your interests to give up as little as possible.

Longer-term loans

If you know at the outset that you are unlikely to be able to repay the money you want to raise in the short term, a longer-term source of finance might be the answer (p. 297).

Selling shares

If you have formed a limited company, you may be willing to sell some of the shares in return for an investment in the business. If you do this, it means you will lose some of the potential gains you might get as a result of the shares increasing in value as the profits of the business grow. This is what an outside investor is looking for. The aim is generally to get a good return on the money invested through the shares increasing in value, rather than a stream of income from the business in the form of dividends.

An outside investor, such as a venture capital fund, will at some stage want to sell the shares to realize the profits. If you are hoping to raise money in this way, put in your plan that you intend to have your company floated on the stock market or the Alternative Investment Market (AIM), say, or that you would like to sell the company, as most venture capital funds want to be invested in a business for a fairly short period, typically three to seven years. Other potential outside investors include 'business angels' – many of these are people who have made money from their own businesses and are looking to invest both finance and expertise in other new or small businesses.

The value you can obtain for your shares, if you are a new company, is a very vexed question. Frankly, they are not worth very much yet, so you might find that you are having to sell a bigger proportion of the shares than you would like to raise the money you need. This can lead to problems about voting control. What the value of the shares is can lead to a lot of haggling.

Opting for this route to raise money needs professional help; you need, perhaps, accountants*, solicitors* and financial advisers*. Ask for references from these professionals to help you to steer clear of rank unprofessionals.

Taking partners

If you have started out as a sole trader but need to raise additional capital, you could do this by taking a partner. What share of the profits each partner gets in return for the capital put in is a subject to be negotiated. There also needs to be clarity about the management role each partner will have. For your own sake, you should do this before you form the partnership. A written partnership agreement is a must (p. 48). A limited liability partnership (p. 49) allows you to work out how you want to divide rewards without making it public, while giving the protection of limited liability.

Lenders and investors

You and your family

The first fact you must come to terms with is that if you do not invest in your business idea, you cannot expect anyone else to do so. As a rough rule of thumb, the absolute most you will probably be able to raise from outsiders is five times as much money as you are putting in yourself, but, needless to say, there are always exceptions. If you are planning a substantial business and looking to raise £1 million or more, say, you may find that investors will put up ten or twenty times as much as you. But normally, you can expect someone to match your own investment, or put up two or three times as much as you do as a maximum. But in the worst case, it could be nothing.

Example

Winston Carpenter has £10,000 to invest in his business. He works out from his forecasts and his business plan that he needs to raise more money. He is unlikely to be able to raise an extra £50,000 or more, but with a good presentation of his idea, he may persuade someone to lend or invest £20,000, say.

The rationale behind this insistence on how much you must invest yourself is that lenders, such as banks, and investors, such as venture capital funds, want you to be committed to your business, to make you work very hard and with great determination to be successful. If you have not risked the proportion of capital they would like, they may doubt your commit-ment. However, if you can point to the fact that even though it is a low proportion of the total invested in your business, the sum of money you are investing is still a sizeable proportion of your own personal assets, you could be convincing.

Where are you going to get your share of the money?

If you have money tucked away somewhere, or if you have a lump sum as a result of being made redundant, this is a relatively easy question to answer. Another common source of the money for your stake is to be given or lent it by someone in your family. But being financed by your family can lead to heartache if things start to go wrong. So do not enter on this course lightheartedly. Conversely, you are more likely to convince your family than anyone else.

Another possible way of raising your share of the funds is to use your per-sonal assets to act as security (for example, a second mortgage on your home) or by giving a personal guarantee. The drawback with this is that if your business fails, you have to find the money to carry on making your repayments, or you have to sell your home. You must give careful consider-ation before giving personal guarantees or using your home to raise money in this way for your business, and the bank may insist that you first take legal advice.

It would make sense to have some sort of agreed family plan for what would happen if your business failed. For example, you should discuss openly whether you are ready to sell your house and move to a smaller one should the security be called upon to repay your loan. If you cannot have some sort of strategy in your domestic life that is acceptable in return for the prospect of going it alone, you are likely to have family problems when the inevitable pressures mount on the business.

You can get tax relief on these loans. If you are a sole trader or partner, any interest you pay on a loan for business purposes is allowable as a deduction against tax in working out your taxable profits. If you take on a loan to invest or lend money to a close company (most family companies are) you can get tax relief at your highest rate of tax on the interest you pay. To be eligible for this tax relief, you must either own more than 5 per cent of the shares or own some shares and work for the greater part of your time for the company.

When should you put in your money?

The best advice is not necessarily to start your business straight away, investing your money and subsequently approaching other investors later when you need it. The wisest course may be to prepare your forecasts and your business plans and to approach possible sources of finance before you start your business and before you actually need the extra money. To plan ahead and get a commitment in advance can be crucial.

The reason why this could be the best approach is that investors have a couple of infuriating habits. The first is to ask what money you are going to put in when they put in their share. You may be able to point out that you invested £10,000, say, six months ago and since then have worked without drawing any salary, but investors are likely to be unimpressed. That is water under the bridge and may count for nothing as far as they are concerned. The second is for them to adopt an attitude of 'wait and see' how the business develops, while the cash is running out and you are under great pressure to raise more. In this way better deals can be struck for the investor. So do not necessarily rush out and use up your money, if you know you will need extra funds in due course; get your financial backing in advance.

Government, local authorities, charities, CDFIs

You may be able to get grants, allowances, cheap loans or prizes from a variety of sources, including central government and the European Union, the local authority for the area in which you are based or wish to locate, charities, such as the Prince's Trust (see p. 36) and, to stimulate regeneration in deprived areas, community development finance initiatives (CDFIs). Grants and other funding are often targeted at:

■ *specific types of spending*: for example research and development, property renovation or purchase of equipment.

■ *specific areas*: particularly deprived rural or urban areas – see Chapter 17.

■ *particular types of business*: say, farming or post offices. In areas of high unemployment, funding may be targeted at encouraging micro-businesses (very small firms, such as one-man plumbers or decorators) to start up.

■ *particular types of businessperson*: for example young people, women, people from ethnic minorities, the unemployed, older people.

All funding bodies receive far more requests than they can meet, so it is essential that you tailor each application to show how your project will meet the specified aims of the particular body.

Business Link*, Business Gateway*, Highlands and Islands Enterprise*, Business Eye*, LEAs* and LECs* have funding directories you can search to find out what grants and other sources are available in your area for your type of business and project. They can also help you to apply.

Government and European funding is often administered by your Regional Development Agency*. Local authorities are also often gateways to locally available funding. So you could also approach these bodies to see what grants are available in your area.

Banks

Your bank manager is an obvious port of call, but not always the best or the one you should make first of all. The advantage of going straight there is that if you have been a creditworthy customer with a good record, your manager should favour your application. And this is what should happen to the vast bulk of people with a good business proposition that is well presented and well researched.

But there are a couple of reasons why you should not head straight here or why you might expect not to secure the money you want. In the first place, your presentation of your plan will improve with the number of times you give it. If your bank manager really is your best possibility and you have not practised your presentation, you might blow the opportunity. It could pay you to approach another bank, simply to practise what you are going to say and be prepared for the questions that will be asked.

The second disadvantage may occur if you are looking to your bank to provide substantial funds. Each branch bank manager has a different discretionary lending limit; above the limit your application may need to be processed elsewhere, so you may lose part of the personal touch on which you were relying for a sympathetic hearing of your case.

The moral is shop around. Do not be put off by being turned down; try another bank or another branch that you think may be more used to business deals. Following a government review of business banking, banks must now make it much easier for you to carry your credit history from one bank to another, making it simpler for you to prove your creditworthiness. Banks must also 'unbundle' their products, so you can get a loan from a bank without being forced to move your current account to that bank. When shopping around, remember to ask what rate you will be charged; compare this with what other banks would charge. Banks can offer money in two ways:

1 Overdrafts (p. 293).
2 Loans.

Loans can be very flexible, and the exact terms vary from bank to bank. You can borrow money for periods of between two and thirty years. The rate of interest can be fixed, variable – a number of percentage points over the bank base rate – or in some cases at a monthly managed rate. Sometimes for larger loans (for example, £15,000 plus) you can negotiate a repayment holiday from repaying the capital you borrow. So for, say, one or two years, you pay only interest. You may also be able to arrange stepped repayments. The amount you can borrow can vary from £1,000 to £1 million. The type of loan you can get depends on the viability of your plan.

You can get a list of members that offer business loans from the Finance and Leasing Association*. The Internet can be a useful tool to help you to compare loans and see what's on offer, because some web sites – for example, *www.moneysupermarket.com* – have comparative tables of loans. Alternatively, use a broker to help you, but stick to members of the National Association of Commercial Finance Brokers*, who must follow a code of practice and have proper complaints procedures.

Small firms loan guarantee scheme

The Small Firms Loan Guarantee Scheme is designed to help relatively new small businesses that are unable to borrow in the normal way because they cannot offer adequate security for a loan. The scheme is currently open to businesses up to five years old and with an annual turnover up to £5.6 million if it is a manufacturing business.

You must be able to show that you have tried to get a conventional loan but failed because of lack of security. The Department for Business, Enterprise and Regulatory Reform (DBERR) then steps in to provide security by guaranteeing 75 per cent of the loan. In return, you pay a premium to the DBERR of 2 per cent a year of the outstanding loan.

Under the scheme, you can borrow amounts up to £250,000 and the loan can last up to ten years.

To use the scheme, you apply direct to one of the participating lenders, which include many of the major banks. You can get a list of participants from Business Link*. The lender will assess your application in the normal way, taking into account your business plan, what money you are yourself investing, other debts you have, and so on. Check the terms of the loan and try to negotiate on any arrangement fee. You may be required to take out life insurance to cover the loan.

Private investors

There is a growing body of private investors, often called 'high net-worth individuals', who are prepared to back business ventures. Sometimes, these people are called 'angels', that is they provide money for risky ventures.

The enterprise investment scheme and capital gains tax reinvestment relief give tax concessions to make it more attractive for private individuals to invest in unquoted companies. With deferral relief, it is possible to put off paying capital gains tax if a private investor sells some shares but reinvests the proceeds in the new shares of a private company.

British Business Angels Association

The British Business Angels Association* (BBAA) is a trade body for business angel networks which are organizations able to back entrepreneurs. The BBAA web site contains a list of members.

Another way to locate potential investors is through the Angel Bourse*. This is a specialist company that brings together investors seeking risk investments, companies seeking new funds and intermediaries working for them.

Small ads sections

There are often ads in newspapers with business to business sections, such as the *Guardian*, *The Times*, the *Financial Times* and the *Sunday Times*, from people wanting to invest in new enterprises. Alternatively, you could advertise for funds in the same way, although you have to watch out for various legal restrictions.

Venture capital funds

With a venture capital fund money is put up by pension funds, insurance companies, banks, investment trusts, industrial corporations, regional development agencies and private individuals. Some venture capital funds are set up as venture capital trusts (VCT), which offer tax concessions to investors and invests the fund in growing companies. Not all of the funds will provide money for people who are starting up; most only provide funds for businesses that are expanding. You can get information about VCTs from the British Venture Capital Association*.

Venture capital funds are looking for companies with very good management, operating in a market that is either very large or is growing fast. The funds want to invest in companies that could reach significant profits within three to four years. Many, but not all, want to be able to sell their investment in three to seven years and hope that the company will have grown enough in that time to be floated on the stock market or be sold to another company. This would allow the funds to sell their shares and turn their gains into cash.

If you approach a venture capital fund, the things to look out for are:

■ *quantity of shares*: the fund will normally want ordinary shares in return for the investment, as well as loan capital or preference shares, though there are exceptions. The percentage of shares varies from fund to fund; a few may want over 50 per cent, but it is unusual for a fund to want a majority stake in the company. The percentage of shares is not always affected by the amount of money you want to raise or by the voting structure.

■ *board director*: the fund will usually want to have one or two directors on your board, and you will have to bear the cost of this. You will normally be able to approve the choice of director. The fees for a non-executive director can be in the £15,000 to £25,000 range.

■ *due diligence*: this is the term for the investigation that a venture capital fund will want to undertake before investing in your company. This can include visiting your offices and other work location, taking up references from customers, potential customers and past employers, studying your accounts and selling systems, and having your product checked technically. The fund will want you to pay for this investigation; you can negotiate on this. How successful your negotiation will be depends on the level of interest shown by other funds.

■ *legal and professional fees*: there are yours and theirs. You will have to pay the legal costs for the funds on top of all your costs for raising finance. You will have legal and accounting fees, running into several thousands, plus the fee paid to a financial adviser, often based on a percentage of the money raised. In total, your share of the costs could run up to 10 per cent or more of the money you raise.

■ *syndication*: if you are trying to raise a very large sum of money, a venture capital fund may want a partner or two to provide the funds you wish. This may be because providing the amount of money you want could take up a fairly hefty chunk of the total money it has to invest, or it may just want to spread the risk. You may have to do a lot of the work yourself to bring together funds into a consortium to provide the money. This can prove very tricky and adds considerably to the amount of time it can take you to raise the money.

Recognizing that there is a shortage of venture capital for small businesses, the government has recently set up a number of schemes aimed at filling this gap, for example:

■ *Regional Venture Capital Funds (RVCFs)*: at least one fund has been established in each of the nine English regions. These funds access a mix of capital from the government, the European Investment Bank and private sector investors. The funds provide risk capital up to £250,000 (with the possibility of a further £250,000 follow-on investment) to new or existing small and medium-sized businesses that can show they have growth potential. On average, investments tend to be for around five years, but the longest would be ten years which is the maximum lifetime of the fund.

■ *Early Growth Funds*: these are a mixture of regional and national venture capital funds that can invest up to £100,000 in small businesses at an early stage in their growth. Usually, you will need matched funding from a private sector source at least equal to the amount invested by the fund.

■ *Enterprise Capital Funds*: These are venture capital funds designed to provide finance and mentoring to growing small- and medium-sized businesses. The government provides up to two-thirds of the venture capital with private investors supplying the rest. The funds have a fixed life after which the government takes out a set return and the rest is distributed to the private investors.

With all these schemes, to find out what is on offer and whether you might be eligible, contact Business Link*.

Other companies

The corporate venturing scheme was introduced to encourage established companies to invest in small, higher-risk trading companies. The investing company gets 20 per cent corporation tax relief on its investment in ordinary shares of the trading company, provided it holds on to the shares for at least three years. Deferral relief is given on gains where they are used to invest in another trading company under the scheme. And losses can be set against the investing company's income.

For your company to be eligible as the target investment, it must be unquoted at the time the investment is made (and with no firm intention to become listed). If, later on, you do become listed, your company does not cease to qualify. The investing company can take no more than a 30 per cent stake in your business.

The presentation: how to do it

There are a lot of useful tips on how to present your plan scattered through this chapter and Chapter 6. The step-by-step guide below draws all these tips together.

1 First impressions are all-important. The first thing prospective lenders and investors will see is your business plan. It must be well presented. It should look comprehensive without being over-detailed (if necessary, information can be put in appendices).

2 Practise your presentation of your plan. Do this by getting a colleague or friend to role-play or see if a counsellor at an enterprise agency will take you through it. If necessary, approach a source of finance that you regard as very low chance and use it to perfect your technique for those opportunities of which you are very hopeful.

3 The next step will be a face-to-face encounter. Look conventional; the people who have money to lend are middle-of-the-road types, so do not endanger your chances of getting the money by dressing in an odd way.

4 Get the facts at your fingertips. Your plan may look good, but if you sound unsure or muddled about the details, doubts about your management ability may be raised.

5 Be clear in your own mind what is interesting or exciting about your proposal. Do not get so bogged down by the details that you cannot bring out the really important points of your business idea.

6 Find out the names and positions of those who can invest. Try to get the real decision-makers, not their advisers or subordinates.

7 Listen carefully to the questions and make sure you answer what you have been asked.

8 If you are asked for further information, make sure it is as well researched and well presented as the rest of your plan and provide it quickly.

9 Do not be too defensive about your idea; assume beforehand that it will be critically assessed.

An online service, The Gauntlet (*www.the-gauntlet.com*), offers to test whether your ideas are ready for presentation to potential investors. It tests you and your business across 16 areas, providing you with a detailed report. The service costs £299. In some areas, The Gauntlet has agreements with local business organizations so that you can use the service for free. Check *www.the-gauntlet.com/clients/index.php* to see if you might qualify.

Summary

1 Treat negotiating for money with the same planning and thought as making a sale.

2 Be very certain that you ask for the right amount of money; it is very difficult to go round a second time to ask for more.

3 It can be difficult to raise less than £1 million.

4 Overdrafts are for the shorter term; long-term finance is provided by loans or selling shares, if you have a company.

5 As a rule of thumb, you will need to invest as much as an outside investor or perhaps half as much. Rare exceptions have managed to put in a much smaller proportion than an outside investor and still retain control.

6 Securing loans on your house or giving personal guarantees is a major step. Do not take it lightly or without discussing it with your family.

7 Money can be raised from banks, private individuals and companies, venture capital funds, charities or local authorities.

8 Make your presentation carefully. Follow the tips on p. 303.

Other chapters to read

6 The business plan (p. 63); **9** Off the peg (p. 80); **23** Forecasting (p. 269); **26** Moving ahead (p. 322).

25

Staying afloat

You are launched. You have premises, even if it is your own home. You have started selling and now must produce the goods. You may have raised money to help to finance the business. So what next? Staying afloat is the name of the game. Learning to live within the income your sales bring is a hard task, but one that has to be learned. A survey by Dun & Bradstreet found that the most common problem areas contributing towards failure are taking on contracts at too low a price, delays in receiving payments and being caught up in the cash flow problems of a larger company.

For some, it is easy: this could apply to you if your sort of business is consultancy, or design, or some other type of work where the overheads can be contained, at least until the time comes for expansion. For others, there is this point to strive towards before your business is truly afloat. This is known as the break-even point and is the point at which the contribution your sales bring is large enough to cover the overheads of your business, for example rent, rates, telephone and some employee costs.

When you see explanations of the break-even point in textbooks, it seems straightforward. Your business struggles towards the level of sales you find from the laid-down formula and once you have reached there, your business is ticking along nicely. In reality, break-even point is not like that at all. It has a most disconcerting habit of moving; as sales increase, so inevitably do the pressures on the business to get the job done. One way to ease the pressure is to increase the overheads and so the cycle continues. Trying to hit a moving target is notoriously difficult; and so is struggling to break even.

To stay afloat in the longer term requires more than being permanently at break-even; you need profits. These can be used to develop new products and markets as existing ones mature and decline.

These are the problems. What about the solution? Clearly, increasing the quantity and value of the sales are top priorities, as well as containing costs. But these take time. The business needs a breathing space to allow sales to develop. To allow yourself that leeway, you must control the business. And cash control assumes the major role in this. Your business will stay afloat (in the short term) if the money goes round; you hope you can keep it going long enough for sales to reach that moving target and get to break-even. You cannot do it for ever; at some stage, it will be clear that your business must raise more money or it will fail. If you are unable to get more funds, you do not want to reach the point of trading illegally, and you do not want your crash to take other small businesses with you. You have to recognize the warning signs (p. 336).

Any well-run business should be interested in cash control, whether struggling to break even or already well into profit. Making the cash go round more efficiently helps to increase your profits. Controlling cash is essentially a question of controlling debtors (that is, people who owe you money), creditors (that is, people to whom you owe money) and stock (including work in progress).

What is in this chapter?

- break-even point (p. 306).
- the plan to control the business (p. 310).
- cash (p. 311).
- your customers (p. 314).
- your suppliers (p. 319).

Break-even point

One management technique you should get to grips with is break-even point. This assumes extreme importance for the sort of business that makes losses initially; possibly, you may raise money to cover that loss-making period or find it yourself. What you are working towards is the point at which the contribution (strictly, gross margin) that you make from sales is sufficient to cover the overheads (also called indirect or fixed costs).

Overheads are the cost of setting up the structure of your business. For example, the cost of your premises does not rise and fall with the quantity of sales you are making. In the long run, you could move to cheaper premises, but this is a major upheaval. In the meantime, this overhead cost is fixed. The value of your sales needs to be built up to the level that contributes to the expense of the premises.

Other examples of overheads are insurance, the cost of equipment – such as cars and computers – heating and lighting, and the telephone. One vexed problem is whether employees are a fixed cost or not. For most businesses, they will be, certainly for a few months (see p. 226 for more about the cost effect of employing people).

How to work out your break-even point

To do this you need to know:

■ gross profit margin.

■ total cost of overheads.

If your product or service is the same item sold many times, you can work out the gross profit (or contribution) on each item sold. The gross profit on each item is the selling price less the direct cost of each item. Direct costs are those items that you only have to pay for because you make a product or provide a service, for example raw materials.

However, if the product can vary, work out the gross profit for one month's sales, say, and use this to find your gross profit margin.

The formula for break-even point of sales is:

$$\frac{\text{Overheads} \times 100}{\text{Price of product} - \text{direct cost of product}}$$

This gives you the number of items you must sell to cover the overhead costs, see Example 1 below.

or

$$\frac{\text{Overheads}}{\text{Gross profit margin}} \times 100$$

Gross profit margin is the gross profit divided by the value of sales times 100. This formula gives you the value of sales you must make to cover the overhead costs; see Example 2.

Example 1

Robert Atherton sells quantities of paper cleaning cloths. He buys them in large rolls, cuts them and distributes them as duster-size (twelve to each packet). He has worked out the direct cost of each packet of twelve as 10p and sells them for 26p. Thus, gross profit on each packet of twelve is 16p. His overheads are £6,000 in the year, £500 a month. His break-even sales of packets of twelve cloths each month are:

$$\frac{£500}{£0.16} = 3,125 \text{ packets}$$

Example 2

Jane Edwardes runs a web design company. Each web site depends on the customer's requirements and the cheapest is likely to be £5,000. For her business plan for the next twelve months, Jane has worked out the number of web sites she is likely to design. For the year, sales are estimated at £300,000 and the direct costs, that is, hardware, software and so on, are forecast to be £120,000.

Gross profit margin is:

$$\frac{£300,000 - £120,000}{£300,000} \times 100 = 60\%$$

The overheads of the business are estimated at £108,000 for the next year, that is, £9,000 a month.

The break-even level of sales for each month is:

$$\frac{£9,000}{60} \times 100 = £15,000$$

The diagrams opposite may help you to gain a better understanding of break-even. The level line shows the estimated level of overheads. The dotted line that starts at point O shows the amount of the direct costs for each level of sales. Total costs (line starts at A) are the sum of the direct costs and the overheads.

The continuous sloping line starting at O shows the value of sales at different levels of units sold. X is the break-even point. To the left of X, your business is making a loss; to the right, your business is making a profit.

Diagram 25.1 assumes that the level of overheads stays the same no matter what the level of sales you can make. Frankly, this is difficult to achieve in practice. Once you start doing more business, you may well find that your overheads will go up too. For example, you may find you need more secretarial help, given the increased amount of sales you are making. In

Diagram 25.2, you can see the effect on break-even point if there is an increase in overheads for the same business as below. Point X is now further to the right in Diagram 25.2 compared with Diagram 25.1. The break-even sales figure is now higher.

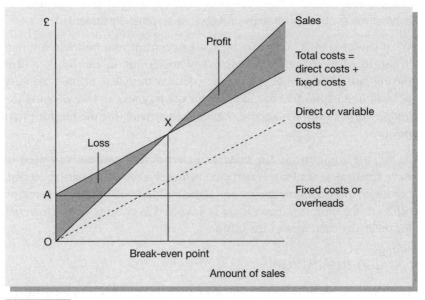

Diagram 25.1 Finding the break-even point of your business

Diagram 25.2 How an increase in fixed costs moves the break-even point upwards

The plan to control the business

When you produced your business plan before you started your business (p. 63), you incorporated some forecasts: profit and loss and cash flow. These could form the basis for your plan (or budget) that you need to control the business, although probably with some adjustments.

What you need for a budget that you use to control your business, but that is also to give you (and any employees) something to aim for, is a plan incorporating figures that you believe you may be able to achieve. Be wary of including figures that are too easy for the business, in case meeting the budget turns into the objective, rather than striving for the biggest profit possible.

As you are going to use the budget to control the business, you need to have the next year's budget prepared before the previous year has ended, otherwise there is a time gap in which the business will drift. If you employ others in the business, they should be involved in drawing up the forecasts for their particular area of the business.

How to use the budget

Every month, as soon as possible after the end of it and not later than a fortnight after, you should have the actual profit, cost and cash figures to compare with the budget. Your comparison should be for two reasons:

1 To identify what has gone wrong, and right, and to derive lessons for the future.
2 To identify problem areas for the future, which may emerge only as your actual performance fails to keep up with budgeted performance.

Keeping in touch with the business

Once you start employing others, you will no longer be dealing with every single aspect of the business yourself. Once others have areas of responsibility, you will need to devise a system of management reporting. There is no one system that is perfect for a particular business, but it should include some of the following elements:

■ *weekly reports*: these could be verbal, for example a meeting. They need to be sufficiently detailed so that everyone in the business knows as a result their objectives for the next week and what is on the critical path to allow sales to be made and products to be purchased or made ready for sale.

■ *monthly reports*: these should be written by the person responsible, for example salesperson, manager or production staff. They should cover two aspects. First, what has been achieved over the past month, how it compares with budgeted figures and the objectives set in the weekly reports plus any explanations or lessons to be drawn from successes and failures. Second, the reports should consider the outlook for the next month, what should be achieved and what the objectives are.

While management reports allow you to keep informed about the business, they have an important side-effect. They force your employees to concentrate on the objectives of the business, their own performance against budgeted performance, and their own priorities for action in the weeks and months ahead.

Cash

If your cash runs out, your business will fail. It is as simple as that. Your cash can run out for several possible reasons:

■ you do not sell enough.

■ your costs are too high for the sales you make.

■ you do not have enough cash to fund the increased number of debtors and stock quantities that extra business brings.

■ you fail to collect the debts you are owed.

How to conserve cash

There are three important steps in conserving cash:

1 Knowing how much cash you have and how much you will need.
2 Speeding up the cash inflow from your customers (p. 314).
3 Slowing down the cash outflow to your suppliers (p. 319).

The cash budget

Preparing your business plan (p. 63) will have taken you some way towards knowing how much cash you will need in the business; indeed, the most important purpose of preparing the business plan may have been to raise the cash your forecasts show will be required. Once the business is trading, the cash flow forecasts need to be turned into monthly cash flow budgets.

You can help to conserve cash by paying by instalments as much as possible. For example, consider leasing cars or furniture rather than buying outright (p. 199).

Your aim should be not just to match your budget but to do better than it says. Never despise a penny or a pound that can be saved; very small savings build up over time into very large savings. This penny-pinching attitude applies just as strongly if you have raised money.

Comparing the actual cash performance with the cash budget is an important tool in controlling your cash. It enables you to learn from mistakes and plan your cash requirements in the future.

What else controls cash?

When cash is tight, you will take much more stringent measures than when you are cash rich. For example, you could consider instituting the following control system:

- daily cash balance.
- weekly or daily bank statement.
- weekly forecast of each individual cash payment in (from customers) and planned cash payment out (to suppliers). This could be set up as a sheet with each named customer and supplier. Each day check what money you have received and tick off on your forecast sheet. Do not pay any cheques until you have received the money you need.

Obviously, when cash is short, you need to put your cash receipts in the bank as quickly as possible; and when you pay people, send the cheque by second-class post. You can say honestly that the cheque has been sent.

Clearly, the system does not work for every business; it is a good control tool for businesses that have a number of large receipts and payments. A retail business would not be able to operate in this way. However, a control sheet for a shop could consist of a weekly forecast of daily takings plus a list of those suppliers you intend to pay that week. Again, the suppliers will not be paid until the forecast cash comes in. For what happens when things are out of control, see p. 335.

A cash system like this is a nuisance to operate, so if cash is not particularly short, you could use a variant of:

- weekly cash balance.
- weekly bank statement.
- monthly payment cycle, that is, set aside one day in each month on which you pay the bills you plan for that month. This means that there is only one day in each month devoted to writing cheques. If a bill is not paid on that day, it does not get paid until a month later.

Important note: no cash control system can operate if you do not keep proper cash records, for example a cash book. This is explained on p. 340.

Making cash work for you

Your problem may not be shortage of cash; on the contrary, you may have extra cash sitting around. In this case, do not leave it all in the current account. Instead, have sufficient handy to keep the business ticking over and put what you can in a seven-day notice or call account that earns interest. Remember to give the required notice so that you can transfer what you need to cover your payments in your once-a-month cheque cycle. There are also a few of the high-interest cheque accounts that can be used by small businesses.

Operating your bank account

Most banks have readily available leaflets detailing the charges on your business bank account. If your bank doesn't, ask for the information, so you can work out in advance how much your bank charges are likely to be. Some banks will now tell you in advance what your next month's charges will be based on the current month's account usage. Most banks now make a standard charge for main account services, such as cheques, standing orders, direct debits and cash machine withdrawals. Charges may be lower for Internet banking. One way to economize is to use a credit or charge card for business expenses, as this is paid with a single payment, instead of lots of little ones.

However, it needs careful consideration before a card is given to an employee. Additionally, in the case of companies, use of a credit or charge card is a fringe benefit for employees, which would include you as a director; check how it would affect your individual tax bill.

If your business is on a very small scale, you should consider whether it is possible to run it using a building society account, rather than a bank account, bearing in mind there are limitations, such as no overdraft facility or business advice.

Some banks offer free banking for the first year (or even longer) if a small business opens an account. This can mean with some banks that there are no bank charges even if you have an overdraft.

Going into overdraft

The time to ask for an overdraft (p. 293) is not the day you realize that you will not be able to cover the bills of suppliers who are really pressing you for payment. The bank manager simply will not like it. It is much better for you to present a well-argued case one or two months before you think you will need the facility. This means planning ahead, by using your forecasts or budgets as a proper control tool.

Your customers

Selling is not the end of the story. Any old customer will not do. Making a sale to someone who does not pay their bill at all is worse than no sale at all. The ideal customer is one who pays their bill as soon as your product or service is handed over. Very few businesses are lucky enough to have that type of client. But there are steps you can take to try to ensure that you do get the cash in. First, you can check them out before you hand over the goods to them. Second, you can do everything you can to make them pay up as quickly as possible.

Giving credit to customers, that is, allowing them to become debtors and pay some time after they have received your service or product, costs you money. For example, if a bank charges 10 per cent on an overdraft, an outstanding bill of £1,000 costs you £100 if it is still unpaid after one year. Or, if it is unpaid after three months, the cost to you is £25. The more efficient you are at reducing the amount of time before you receive your payments, the lower the costs.

Investigating potential customers (credit control)

Few businesses can confine their sales to completely 'safe' customers who are guaranteed to pay what they owe and on time; usually, an element of risk is needed to meet your business objectives. But the riskiness or otherwise of customers needs to be assessed so that the risk is known and calculated. Assessment needs information, control and monitoring.

The extent of the investigation must also depend on the amount of the projected sale relative to your total sales. If it is a fairly small sale, the investigation alone may cost as much as the profit from the sale; you should establish a policy of rejecting or accepting such risks as a matter of course. But if the sale would be a significant order for you, further information is needed.

Consider the following steps:

■ if you are dealing with a large quoted company, check its payment policy. This must be published in its annual report and accounts. Since November 1998, small businesses have by law been able to claim interest for late payments from large businesses and public sector bodies. (This right has now been extended under European legislation to businesses of all sizes.) However, surveys suggest that small businesses seldom use this right, possibly because they cannot afford to lose future business from a client as a result of a payment dispute. To find out more about your right to charge interest and the amount you can charge, see The Better Payment Practice Campaign at web site *www.payontime.co.uk*.

■ ask the prospective customer for a bank reference (but this will be based only on the bank's experience, so it may indicate relatively little, but it will help in building a general picture).

■ ask for a couple of trade references. Put a specific question such as 'Up to what level of trade credit is the customer considered a good risk?'

■ ask a credit reference agency to report (p. 318).

■ ask the customer for the latest report and accounts or a balance sheet and profit and loss account. Ask your accountant to analyse them for you.

■ if you have not already done so, visit the business with a view to meeting the principals or directors. Put any questions that remain unanswered and use this visit to fill in the general picture.

Using the information you have garnered from all these sources, assess how risky you think this customer is and establish a credit limit. A common system is to have five categories of risk, ranging from the top category, who would be considered good for anything, to the bottom category, who you would sell to only on cash terms. You would draw up certain credit limits to apply to each category, for example allowed £1,000 on 30 days' credit. The actual amounts would depend on the size of debts relative to your sales and what is considered normal practice in that industry.

The payment terms you offer (credit terms)

There is a range of possible credit terms you could offer customers. These include:

■ cash with order (CWO).

- cash on delivery (COD).
- payment seven days after delivery (net seven).
- payment for goods supplied in one week by a certain day in the next week (weekly credit).
- payment for goods supplied in one month by a certain day in the next month (monthly credit).
- payment due 30 days after delivery (30 days' credit).

You have to choose the best terms you can. This means that you extend credit for as short a time as possible, but obviously industry and competitive practice may to some extent put you in a straitjacket.

There are a couple of ways you can try to encourage early payment of your bills. First, you can offer a cash discount for early payment; for example, payment within seven days of the invoice means the customer can claim a discount of one per cent. The problem with this sort of discount is that customers tend to take it (and, if your debtor control is a little sloppy, are allowed the discount) whenever they pay. Introducing a cash discount of this type needs to be accompanied by close monitoring to make it clear to customers that they are entitled to the discount only if they meet the conditions offered.

Sending out invoices

Be very prompt in sending out invoices. This is crucial to any policy of keeping tight credit control. Failure to do this will give the impression to debtors that you do not mind how long you wait for your money, and as we have seen, giving credit costs you money. No matter how busy you are keeping up with the work you do, sending out invoices, as soon as goods are delivered or services supplied, must take precedence.

The records you need for control

There is more detail on how to set up the records you need on p. 340, but the records need to provide you with the following information:

- how much you are owed in total at any time.
- how long you have been owed the money and by whom; this information is known as an aged analysis of debts.
- a record of sales and payments including the date made for each customer. This allows you to build up your own picture of the credit-worthiness of individual debtors.

How to chase money you are owed

1 Make sure your credit terms are known to your customer. The best way is to print them clearly on the invoice.

2 As soon as your customer has overstepped the mark and the bill is overdue, ask for the money you are owed. This should be done politely in writing, preferably by fax, with a follow-up in the post.

3 If there is no reply within seven days, check that the details of the invoice are correct and that you have quoted all the information the customer needs to identify it, for example the customer's own reference.

4 Fax again. Follow up with a letter sent by recorded delivery.

5 No reply within seven days? Make a phone call to find out what the problem is. Do not assume that the customer has no money; there may be queries on the account or other problems. Find out the apparent reason for the non-payment.

6 Use the phone call to find out if the customer has a weekly or monthly cheque run (p. 313) and find out the day this is done.

7 Still no payment? Keep ringing and especially two or three days before the cheque run. Try to extract a promise of payment.

8 Keep the pressure up. Do not pester and then drop for a few weeks; all your previous chasing is undone. Keep up a steady and persistent guerrilla warfare.

9 If the customer is always out or in a meeting when you telephone, and you suspect this is due to a desire not to speak to you, try pretending to be someone else who you are sure your customer will want to speak to. If you deal with an accountant or book-keeper, try speaking to the managing director of the customer's business.

10 Try different times of the day and the week: lunchtime is not usually a good time, but first thing Monday morning can be effective.

11 When you eventually manage to speak to the person you want, if he or she says 'I'll chase it up and see what has happened,' say you will keep holding until they do.

12 If the customer says 'The cheque has been posted,' ask for the date this was done, whether it went first- or second-class, how much the cheque was for and what the cheque number is.

13 If the cheque does not arrive, go to collect the money in person; this is what HMRC does. Get the cheque cashed as soon as possible, so that it cannot be stopped.

14 Check all the details of the cheque: your name, the amount, the date, the signature.

15 If all the previous steps have failed, send a formal letter, preferably from your solicitor, either threatening to take legal action to recover the debt or to start bankruptcy or winding-up proceedings (p. 337) or threatening to use a debt-collection agency. Keep the threat.

16 Consider using an agency (see below).

17 Consider issuing a writ for the debt or consider starting bankruptcy proceedings against an individual or winding-up proceedings against a company. Consider using the small claims court. Ask your solicitor's advice.

Using an agency

Once the money has been overdue for two to three months, you could hand collection over to an agency. They will write and phone and eventually either collect the money or report that it will only be collected by legal action. The usual charge for an agency is some percentage of the money recovered.

A halfway house to using the full-blown debt collection service is to use an agency to write to overdue customers pointing out that non-payment will be reported to credit reference agencies, which may harm the customer's credit rating. As this is very important to a business, it often has the desired effect. However, payment is made to you not the agency and, so long as this is done, no entry is made on the customer's file at the agency.

Selling your debts to raise cash (factoring)

Essentially, a factor buys your debts in return for an immediate cash payment. Generally speaking, factoring is available for debts from other businesses, rather than individuals. In a full service, the factor takes over your records for debtors and collects the debts. In return, you could receive a payment of up to 80 per cent of the face value of the invoices. The balance of the money will be paid when the debts are collected. Factoring occurs on a continuing basis, not for one individual set of debtors. The factor will often offer insurance against bad debts. There are also less complete services, for example:

- the factor does not take over your records.
- the customer does not pay the factor but pays you.
- invoice discounting, that is, you maintain the records and collect the debts. This means that your use of the service remains confidential and your customers are not aware of it.

While a factoring service seems to be the answer to your cash flow dreams, there are some conditions:

■ if your sales are less than £100,000 a year, you may find it difficult to factor your debtors.

■ the factor will investigate your trading record, bad debt history, credit rating procedure, customers and so on before deciding whether to offer you a factoring service.

■ some factors give automatic protection against bad debts; others do not.

■ you are likely to have to agree to a one year's contract with a lengthy period of notice.

Note that all the separate components of factoring, that is, keeping your debtor records, cash collection, invoice discounting and credit insurance, are available separately from a number of organizations. Compare costs of several factoring services and look at the cost of the individual components.

Your suppliers

Quite a lot of the way you can deal with your suppliers (or creditors when you owe them money) is simply the reverse of what you do with debtors. Taking credit from suppliers is a significant source of finance for most small businesses. However, the other side of the coin is that those suppliers may be short of funds themselves and heavily dependent on getting in the money they are owed as quickly as possible.

When you are short of cash, you may find yourself chasing your customers and cursing them for not paying up while doing exactly the same yourself to other businesses. As a starting point, your first step should be to try to negotiate improved credit terms from your suppliers rather than simply taking unapproved extended credit.

Unfortunately, being open with your suppliers does not always pay off. Saying that you are short of cash this week but you will pay next week can cause panic. Your creditor may issue a writ without delay, and your future credit terms may be affected.

Nevertheless, when the chips are down, one way of seeing yourself through a temporary shortage of cash is to push up the length of time you take to pay your creditors. However, it is a slippery road; what you fervently believe to be a temporary shortage of cash may turn into a permanent shortfall. If you cannot make good the shortfall by raising more permanent funds, you will go to the wall with a lot of unpaid bills. A lot of small businesses like yourself will also lose money as a result of your action. Somehow, you have to know where to draw the line (p. 335).

What happens when a supplier investigates you?

Any well-organized supplier will carry out the same screening of you as you do of customers who are going to place largish orders with you. Expect to be asked for:

■ permission to approach your bank for a reference.

■ two trade references.

■ a balance sheet or a set of the latest accounts.

■ further information as a result of the supplier's investigation.

The supplier will also probably approach a credit reference agency to see what it has on you and what your credit rating is. However, when you are starting in business, you can provide none of the information mentioned above. You may be forced to pay in cash initially, until you have built up some sort of record. A large supplier may even ask for a personal guarantee. You may be able to avoid this if you can demonstrate that you have sufficient funds raised to get the business through the building-up stage.

The records you need for control

Details of the records you should set up are given on p. 340. But you should be able to derive the following information from them:

■ say how much you owe in total at any time.

■ say how long you have owed the money and to whom.

■ a record of what you have paid each supplier and when.

How to delay paying what you owe

Essentially, you can use only a series of excuses, not to say downright lies; there are few honest ways of delaying payment. However, it may be some comfort to know that most successful small businesses at some stage have to delay payment.

The first step to take is not to consider paying any bills until you are asked to.

The second step is to introduce a paying schedule that involves making cheques out only once a month.

Further steps involve simply delaying paying. The sorts of excuse are those mirrored in *How to chase money you are owed* on p. 317.

Summary

1 The first stage for any new business is to get to the break-even point; after that, building up profits is needed for long-term survival.
2 Watch out for overheads; they have a nasty knack of rising with sales, thus continually pushing up the break-even point.
3 Convert your business plan and forecasts into a budget that gives you, and your employees, something to aim for.
4 Keep control of your business by comparing actual with budget performance; try to draw the appropriate lessons to be learned and plot ahead any changes in your plan that are needed.
5 If you have employees, introduce a system of weekly and monthly reporting and setting of objectives.
6 Controlling cash can keep your business afloat until break-even is reached.
7 Make your cash work for you, that is, if you have spare funds put them in an interest-earning account.
8 Operate your bank account as efficiently as possible.
9 Try to speed up the rate at which your sales are turned into cash. Do this by exercising credit control and investigating potential customers, offering the tightest credit terms you can, sending out invoices promptly and chasing overdue bills. Use *How to chase money you are owed* on p. 317.
10 Most successful small businesses have to stoop to delaying payment to their suppliers at some time during their development.

Other chapters to read

26 Moving ahead (p. 322); 27 Not waving but drowning (p. 335).

26

Moving ahead

There comes a happy stage for most entrepreneurs when the grinding and grubbing eases off. You're past the break-even stage, you're profitable, and you can start to focus your mind on what else you might achieve.

At its basic level, you might decide that all you want is to provide yourself with a good income and your ambition is limited to maximizing the income, not just in the short term but for the future too. But for others, income maximization is not sufficient. Instead, you can see opportunities to transform yourself from a small business into a larger business. You may even decide that you want to go for growth in a major way, ending up with looking to obtain a quote on one of the stock markets – the growth of the Alternative Investment Market (AIM) has been a huge success for the stock market, and more than 1,200 companies have raised money on it. After all, there are businesses in the FTSE-100 that 20 or 30 years ago were still small. And ironically some of the companies with major stock market values are not huge at all but are valued very highly by investors. Companies may have relatively small revenues, may still be unprofitable but are nevertheless worth millions because of their perceived potential by stock market investors.

Generating large capital values from a business that you start is a roller-coaster, and many businesses lose their founders along the way. Someone else with different management skills may be needed to take up the challenge on your behalf. What you want to achieve is to maximize the value that you can obtain for your efforts.

What is in this chapter?

- how to increase profits (p. 323).
- going for growth (p. 329).
- phase 2 money (p. 331).
- managing change (p. 332).

How to increase profits

The billion-dollar question is: 'How can I increase my profits?' The whole of this book should help you to do so: the sections on how to set up your business in the most efficient manner and those on how to plan and control your business, how to increase your sales and how to manage the workplace properly. All of these can help you to make bigger profits.

However, if you strip running a business down to bare essentials, there are three main ways to make bigger profits. The first two methods are what you would use for the short term; they apply particularly if you are struggling to reach break-even point. But any well-run business should constantly be on the lookout for the sort of improvement you can make. The two methods are cutting costs and increasing prices.

The third way of increasing profits will take longer to achieve the desired result. It is selling more. It will also, very often, involve you in spending more money to carry it out.

The quickest way of selling more is to try to sell more to your existing customers. This implies that your existing customers are happy with your service or product. That is the first step – focusing on and improving the quality of what you do already. Selling more may require greater investments in promotion or selling effort, but obviously your aim should be to make the existing levels of investment work more effectively for you.

You should not overlook the few occasions when you can increase profits by altering your sales mix; it may even mean selling less. This may occur if you have a range of products, one or more of which does not cover its costs. The answer: rationalize your product line. An investigation of your customers may reveal that some of the very small ones do not buy sufficient quantity to cover the cost of selling to them. This may also lead to the conclusion that selling less means higher profits. There may also be the odd occasion when you can alter your sales mix by introducing a product on which there is no profit but that improves your overall profits. For example, a loss leader encourages more purchases of higher-priced products and increases total profits.

In the longer run, there are two more moves that can result in your business showing more profits. You can sell:

1 The same product, but to new markets; or
2 A new product to new or existing markets.

Both of these may involve substantial investment by your business (see Chapter 15). If so, you cannot undertake these until you are past the break-even point and generating profits from the existing products and market.

Cutting costs

This is the most effective way in the short term of increasing your profits. You should get into the habit of thinking how many extra sales you have to make to pay for an increase in costs. For example, if your product sells for £100 and your costs for each product are £50, this means that every time you spend an extra £1,000 in your business, you have to sell another twenty of your product to stand still in terms of profit.

The best way of keeping an eye on costs is to have very strict cash control and to carry out regular audits of costs. Do not necessarily assume that because you looked at the costs last month, you will not be able to find room for cutting now. Use the audit checklist starting below to go through all the cost areas. Look at each item afresh and ignore history.

Checklist

■ *raw materials*: are there any alternative suppliers who are cheaper for the same quality and delivery? Can you renegotiate your existing terms from your present supplier? Everything is negotiable and is worth trying.

■ *stocks*: this ties up cash, which means bigger interest charges at the bank. Can you keep lower stocks by organizing yourself more efficiently?

■ *efficient systems*: are all repeated jobs standardized in your business? For example, if you have to do a lot of quotes, is there a standard form that simply needs filling in? Or are you drawing up a fresh form each time you quote? Does this apply in all business areas, financial, production and personnel, as well as selling?

■ *the range of products*: is the gross margin you get on each product satisfactory? Does one product require a much greater share of overheads than others? If you stopped selling or manufacturing one of your products, what effect would it have on costs and profit?

■ *customers and suppliers*: are your customers taking too long to pay? And are you paying your suppliers too promptly? If you're doing either of these, you are using up cash you do not need to. This means either extra interest charges on your overdraft or less interest because you have less on deposit.

Example

Jason Bottomley has a small shop selling jumpers, tops, shirts and so on. He is currently making profits of £15,000, but he does not regard this as sufficient to give him a comfortable living. He wants to increase his profits. His forecast sales and costs look like this:

Sales	£120,000
less Direct costs	£60,000
Gross margin	£60,000
less Overheads	£45,000
Net profit	£15,000

Jason wants to look at how his profit would be affected if he could cut either his direct costs by 10 per cent or his indirect costs (or overheads) by the same amount. It would look like this:

	Cut direct costs by 10 per cent	Cut indirect costs by 10 per cent
Sales	£120,000	£120,000
less Direct costs	£54,000	£60,000
Gross margin	£66,000	£60,000
less Overheads	£45,000	£40,500
Net profit	£21,000	£19,500

This shows that if Jason could cut direct costs by 10 per cent, his profit would increase by 40 per cent; if he could cut overheads by 10 per cent, profit would increase by 30 per cent. In fact, he estimates that every time he manages to cut both direct and indirect costs by only 1 per cent he would have more than £1,000 extra income. Quite small cuts can lead to a big jump in income.

■ *numbers of employees*: your payroll has the extraordinary ability to mushroom with sales; this includes not only staff directly involved in production or manufacture but also administrative staff, the so-called overheads. The trick is to keep the same number of employees while achieving higher sales. Can you improve their productivity?

■ *payroll costs*: what you pay for staff is not just their salary and benefits. You also have to pay employer's National Insurance. If a pay rise is due, would your employees consider accepting extra contributions to a pension arrangement instead? You do not pay National Insurance on this form of 'pay', and it's tax-efficient for the employee too.

■ *the right person for the job*: a lot of time and money is wasted recruiting, training and subsequently dismissing unsuitable staff. Putting a lot of effort into finding the right people in the first place, and not just grabbing what pops up, can be cost-saving.

■ *your own time*: managing your own time better can save money too. Try to sort out some system of priorities in jobs to be done. There are quite a range of time-planning systems available, often based on diaries or very small computers. See if you can find one that suits you.

Increasing prices

There is no automatic link between prices and costs. This means you do not need to feel uncomfortable about raising your prices, even if you have not had an increase in costs. And quite small increases in price can lead to a big jump in profits. There is an example in the box below that demonstrates how effective a price rise can be.

Real life is not as simple as this. Increasing your prices could lead to a fall in sales volume if you are operating in a price-conscious market. This is one of the reasons why you should think carefully about creating some sort of image or impression for your product (see p. 129), such as high quality or good service, so that the sales of your product are not so price-sensitive. To sell on the basis of price alone is a dangerous strategy (see p. 170).

Example

Jason looks at the effect of increasing his prices by 5 per cent all round. His new forecast looks like this:

Sales	£126,000
less Direct costs	£60,000
Gross margin	£66,000
less Overheads	£45,000
Net profit	£21,000

Jason can get an increase of 40 per cent in his profits for a 5 per cent price increase.

Checklist

- *discounts*: try to avoid giving discounts, or if you are giving quantity discounts, make sure you stick to the quantity set. It can be very tempting if you are competing head-on with a competitor to try to win the sale by offering a discount. Keep your nerve and try to emphasize the benefits of your product or service.

- *payment discounts*: do you give a discount for your customers paying by a certain date? Have your customers started to take the discount whether paying by that date or not? Is the discount too big? Do you need it at all, or could you achieve the same effect by better chasing?

- *price discrimination*: can you divide your customers into distinct groups and charge some groups a higher price than others? (See p. 179 for more about price discrimination.)

- *better-quality product: is there scope to upgrade your product with some improvements?* Can you charge a higher price to give a better margin?

- *inflation*: adjust your prices to allow for the effects of inflation.

- *contracts*: try including price escalation clauses in your terms and conditions for any product you are selling.

- *minimum order*: Is it too low? Small orders can take as much time to administer and carry out as large ones, so see if you can set your minimum order at a level that ensures it is at least making a contribution.

Selling more

The third way in which you can increase your profits is to sell more of your products or service – see the example in the box on page 328. This is the most difficult to achieve, and the results will not show up in the short term; however, potentially increasing your sales gives the greatest increase in profits of the three. You are unlikely to be able to double your prices or halve your costs, but you might be able to double the amount you sell.

Your first approach should be to try to sell more of the same products to the same market. You will already have invested time and money in researching this market and refining your product to meet customer needs, so the extra investment needed may be minimal.

You can increase your sales by more effective promotion or better selling. The one method of trying to increase your sales that you should avoid like the plague is cutting your prices. This achieves little except starting a price war because your competitors feel forced to follow suit, and putting pressure on your profit margins and your own profit level.

Cutting prices can increase your profits only if the increase in volume generated is enough to offset the smaller profit you make on each item sold. This could apply only in markets that are very price-sensitive; and in this sort of market, cutting prices is most likely to lead to severe price competition. Think twice before you act.

Example

Jason looks at the figures on the assumption that he could increase the amount he sells by 5 per cent, while keeping prices and overheads the same:

Sales	£126,000
less Direct costs	£63,000
Gross margin	£63,000
less Overheads	£45,000
Net profit	£18,000

Jason finds that a 5 per cent increase in the volume of the sales means a 20 per cent increase in his profits.

Checklist

- *image*: have you thought clearly about how your product is positioned? Can it be differentiated more from your competitors' products?

- *advertising*: are you aiming your message in the right place? Are you getting as much press coverage as you could? Is your advertising consistent with the style of your product?

- *selling*: have you clearly articulated your benefits? Have you prepared a detailed analysis of how your product compares with competitors? Have you developed proper scripts, either for person-to-person selling or telephone selling? Are you following up all leads, pursuing leads to turn them into quotes and converting quotes to orders? Prepare a breakdown of sales statistics, of conversion from leads to quotes to orders and analyse where you are going wrong.

- *remember*: increasing sales means increasing working capital, so your business may need more finance.

Doing all three

In practice, you will try to do all three at the same time: cut costs, increase prices and sell more. It is astonishing the effect very small across-the-board improvements can have on your profit (see Example below).

Example

Jason thinks that he could manage small improvements in all areas by cutting costs by 1 per cent, increasing prices by 1 per cent, and increasing amount of sales by 1 per cent. Doing all three would have this impact on profits:

Sales	£122,412
less Direct costs	£59,400
Gross margin	£63,012
less Overheads	£44,550
Net profit	£18,462

This means an increase in profits of 23 per cent and gives Jason an extra income of £3,462. The moral is never despise small improvements. They can transform your profit.

Going for growth

Growth businesses are the cream. They make up the top five per cent of small companies – and around 20,000 a year are started. There are several subtle differences between the growth companies and the rest. What marks them out?

The definition of a growth company will usually be based upon one of the following measurements: growth in sales, growth in employees and growth in profits. Fast-growing businesses might be aiming for sales of £500,000 in three years from a scratch start or show sales growing at over 60 per cent a year from a base sales figure of say £100,000 or so.

The motivation of the entrepreneur, the team leader, is what drives the business. If you are looking at your business solely to provide you with an income, you're unlikely to have the oomph to push the enterprise into fast growth. The same consideration applies if you have set up your own business because you prefer the lifestyle with its attendant freedom and options to that of being an employee in someone else's company. To make a success of founding a growth business, a driving force is likely to be that you have the ambition of wealth. You want to make yourself financially independent;

you want to give yourself that quantity of 'drop dead' money (that is, to know you're financially so secure that you can tell someone to drop dead if you are so minded!).

Without this extra ingredient, the determination to create wealth, there may not be enough motivation to push the business into the highest level of growth. Fast growth is uncomfortable and painful. It creates pressure points and stresses internally. It often requires an unreasonable owner to dragoon unwilling employees to produce the impossible. If your aspiration is simply to create a good lifestyle for yourself, you're unlikely to have the necessary drive to grow a business quickly.

Requirements for a fast-growing business

How do you make your business fast-growing? It's possible to identify a number of key requirements. First, the quality of the management is crucial – and that means you and your team. You need to have the character to lead your team; you need a broad set of business skills, including sales and marketing, often gained through management experience in a large company, and the ambition to grow fast. A good education, often a higher-level qualification, also helps. If you have already run and sold a successful business, this will give you a head start for two reasons: you're more experienced and less likely to make mistakes, and you may have finance available.

Your team needs to be balanced: there needs to be someone who is skilled in finance and accounting, someone in marketing and sales, someone in production, and so on. And it makes sense for the team to be offered incentives based on growth, such as share options.

As for the business, it is also possible to identify some factors that contribute to growth. Businesses that select a well-defined market opportunity, frequently a market niche, will find that their salespeople are knocking at a door already ajar. Beware the product that is unique but that as yet has no clear defined customer base. People must want to buy your product.

It is important to develop a culture within your enterprise that focuses on product quality and customer satisfaction. It can make your whole business much more confident to know that you are selling a product that people hold in high regard and that customers are satisfied. It can be very demoralizing for employees to deal with dissatisfied customers.

Businesses that are technology-based and that are constantly striving to introduce efficiencies through the clever use of technology will also have a head start on the fast-growth route. Innovative businesses, which have a competitive advantage, can also make larger strides than the average company, as long as the product is one the consumer wants to know about. Finally, many fast-growth businesses are also exporters. If you have a product with global demand, the potential market is larger.

Adapting your business

You can look at recruitment and training to improve your management style and team. Analyse your products to improve the quality and look carefully at your current market. Investigate the possibility of raising risk finance to allow you to grow faster. Focus on business planning and improve the systems infrastructure of your business.

Phase 2 money

Going for growth usually means raising more money. Not always. You may have created that elixir of business, a cash-generative model, and be able to fund your own expansion with your own resources.

In most cases, to expand you will need to raise outside money. Chapter 24 explains some of the ways you can do this. But Phase 2 money is likely to be different in that it is likely to be substantially more, come from outside sources and be risk capital rather than loans.

However, longer-term loans from your bank could provide the development capital you need for expansion. So revisit your bank manager armed with your essential business plan and forecasts.

But many businesses will be looking to raise risk capital from outside investors in exchange for shares in your company. The size you are now considering may be outside the scope of business angels. So your choices may be to approach a venture capital organization or a venture capital trust to raise development capital. Or to consider a stock market flotation.

The advantage of going to the stock market is that it enables investors to buy and sell their shares. This also means that it allows you the opportunity to expand your business by buying other companies in exchange for shares. Once your shares are publicly traded, your company should be valued higher than it would be if it were still a private company (but this is not always the case).

Which stock market?

There are several stock markets. The main London stock market is probably the least suitable. Unless you would be valued at a reasonable amount, £200 million say, small companies get lost and overlooked in favour of the blue chips. In November 1999, the London Stock Exchange started Techmark – a subgroup of companies within the main market. It includes established companies in high-tech industries, such as computers, software, telecommunications and biotechnology. There is also a facility for relatively new, fast-growing companies to join Techmark. Usually, a company needs at least a three-year track record before qualifying for listing, but special rules allow growth companies with a shorter record to join Techmark.

Your choice is probably between three markets suitable for innovative, fast-growing smaller companies. The Alternative Investment Market (AIM) is very suitable for raising sums of money for companies looking for expansion. Unfortunately, floating on the AIM can be very expensive because of the due diligence that needs to be carried out by the advisers. Generally, most of the funds would be raised from institutions rather than private investors, although private investors might buy your shares after the company is listed.

The PLUS market (formerly Ofex) is not a stock market at all but a trading facility that is privately owned. It is much less regulated than the AIM but as a consequence is an attractive way of raising funds, most of which will come from private investors. However, your shares may not be traded very frequently once listed on PLUS, and another company that you want to buy may not be too impressed with accepting your shares. A number of start-up ventures and innovative companies are traded on PLUS.

There are disadvantages in taking money from the public and becoming a quoted company. You have to meet the rules and regulations, which can be quite onerous, and accept that you have an additional layer of responsibility to your shareholders. Your business is no longer a private company, able to do what it wants with the profits and, in particular, your own rewards.

Managing change

Fast expansion gives you growing pains. Your tightly knit team becomes more loosely knit; the personal element is diluted. You will cease to know personally every bit of information, every customer, every supplier, because growth means delegation.

Managing the next stage of growth means you have to focus on four elements: people, organization structure, processes or working procedures, and technology.

Employees are scared of change. So even if it is very positive, because your business is growing fast, you have to watch out for the developing resistance to changed responsibilities, changed hierarchies of responsibility and changed chemistry for developing teams.

The structure of your organization needs to be flexible to allow for growth, but you will find it creaking at regular intervals. And one of the absorbing tasks of management is how to adapt a structure to ensure that you meet your requirements over the next phase of business growth.

Working procedures need to be documented and updated regularly. Instead of you explaining jobs to new members of staff, existing employees will be explaining them. Unless procedures are written, you can end up losing control over the efficiency of your staff.

Finally, technology plays an important role in growth. Use of technology can improve the efficiency of your workforce and enable more jobs to be done by fewer people. Constantly be on the lookout for ways that tasks can be streamlined and aided by technology.

Growing companies might consider setting up an internal web site, which could be for company data, such as price lists, purchasing details, policies, sales presentations and so on. Company knowledge is captured in this way, doesn't walk out of the door in the head of a leaving employee and is accessible by all employees from their computers at work, at home or away on a sales trip.

Summary

1 There are three ways you can increase profits: you can cut costs, increase prices or sell more.
2 The quickest way of boosting profits is to cut costs and increase prices; but the greatest long-term potential comes from increasing your sales.
3 Do not dismiss any improvement that can be made because it is too insignificant. A series of tiny changes in the right direction can lead to much bigger profits.
4 Growth can be achieved by focusing on certain key requirements, such as a balanced team, a broad skill set, a well-defined market opportunity, a focus on product quality and customer satisfaction, and an emphasis on the clever use of technology.

5 Raising Phase 2 money to fund expansion may mean risk capital from outside investors.

6 Managing change needs careful planning of employees, organizational structure, working procedures and technology.

Other chapters to read

2 Who will buy? (p. 13); 15 Building customer relationships (p. 163); 16 How to set a price (p. 170); 24 Raising the money (p. 290); 25 Staying afloat (p. 305).

27

Not waving but drowning

If you put this book's guidelines into operation at the right time, fewer of you should need this chapter than the average small business. Nevertheless, there are those who will. Some businesses will go to the wall.

Few people can appreciate before the event how traumatic the slide into failure can be. Gradually hemmed in with fewer and fewer avenues of escape, you have to come to terms with the crushing of your hopes and expectations. For natural optimists, such as entrepreneurs, it is appallingly difficult to do. At what point do you realize that your business is not going to survive? When do you accept that to carry on is to put other businesses in jeopardy and to impose the same pressures on them as on you? At what point does it become illegal to carry on?

That point may be easy to recognize for an outsider, who is calm and rational. But it is incredibly difficult to recognize when you have been fighting for weeks, or even months, to avoid it. You may find that you slid past the point so gradually that you did not have time to notice. Sometimes, matters are taken out of your hands by an outsider, such as a creditor or a bank, beginning the steps to close your business.

The problem of acceptance is made worse by the usual existence of somewhat schizophrenic behaviour. To avoid rumours and doubts emerging about the future of your business, you may well be putting on a brave face to the outside world. And you are doing this while knowing within yourself that it does not ring true. The title of this chapter is from a poem by Stevie Smith. Two lines from this poem are: 'I was much further out than you thought / And not waving but drowning.' This aptly summarizes the dilemma for someone whose business is in financial difficulties.

Further emotional difficulties are caused by society's harsh attitude towards the failure. Even though thousands of businesses failed during the recession of the early 1990s, many of them through no fault of their own, there is often little sympathy for those that do. However, since 1 April 2004, if you do go bankrupt, you will normally be discharged after just one year (instead of three as previously). For more information, contact the Insolvency Service*.

This chapter tries to help you to recognize the point at which you have to say: 'Enough is enough.'

What is in this chapter?

- the warning signs of failure (p. 336).
- the final process if you operate as a limited company (p. 337), sole trader (p. 339) or partnership (p. 339).
- what happens afterwards? (p. 339).

The warning signs of failure

Chapter 25 describes how to control your cash to avoid an ignominious end to your business. At some point, you may unfortunately find:

- you only pay a supplier when a writ is issued, and your suppliers are refusing to sell you any more goods.
- you are near or above your overdraft limit at the bank.
- you are unable to raise any more money.
- your liabilities are greater than your assets.

Once your business has reached the point that liabilities (what you owe) are more than assets (what you own), the business is insolvent. It may become insolvent at an earlier stage, when current liabilities are greater than current assets: in other words, when the amount you have in cash and debtors is less than the amount you owe to creditors. This may occur even though you have sufficient fixed assets to cover what you owe. These fixed assets may take too long to sell, at other than a knockdown price, to satisfy your creditors.

As well as insolvency occurring as a result of sales being too low or costs too high, outside events can force it on you. For example, you may be owed a large sum of money by a customer who is slow in paying and may even be unable to pay. A common complaint for small businesses is that some large companies are prone to do just that – be very slow payers – and this can start the vicious circle ending in failure.

Earlier warning signs can be detected that identify businesses that are at a high risk of failure. Studies pinpoint, among other things, these faults – not all of them relevant for the self-employed and small businesses:

■ the boss takes no advice.

■ the managing director and chairperson is the same person.

■ the board of directors does not take an active interest.

■ the skills of the business are unbalanced.

■ there is no strong financial person.

■ there is no budget, cash flow plan or costing system.

■ the business is failing to respond to change.

If your business displays some of these characteristics, while not yet being in the advanced stage of failure, get advice now, either from your professional advisers (p. 201) or your local Business Link* adviser (p. 31).

The final process

There are two constructive steps you can take: consider whether you could negotiate with creditors to pay off what you owe in instalments or to pay a smaller sum that they will accept in full settlement. Or you can enter into what is known as a formal voluntary arrangement. This is a procedure whereby you offer to pay a dividend to creditors in full settlement of your debts. You need to contact an authorized insolvency practitioner, who will require fees in advance to carry out the work. Voluntary arrangements are a formal legal procedure and have proved very effective as a means of avoiding liquidation or bankruptcy.

Limited company

You can seek to wind up your company on a voluntary basis, or you may have it imposed on you by the court or under the supervision of the court. And under the 1986 Insolvency Act there are the options of administration and voluntary arrangements. Voluntary winding-up can occur if 75 per cent of the members vote for it. The resolution for voluntary winding-up must be published in the *London Gazette*. If the directors make a statutory declaration, having investigated the company's affairs, that in their opinion the company will be able to pay its debts within twelve months, the winding-up carries on as a members' voluntary winding-up. However, if the company is not solvent, the winding-up is a creditors' voluntary winding-up. The difference between the two is that if it is a members' voluntary winding-up, the members appoint the liquidator. Otherwise, the creditors appoint the liquidator.

The liquidators will normally pay debts in the following order:

1 Loans and debts that have been secured on a fixed asset.
2 The costs of the winding-up.
3 Local authority and water rates, contributions to occupational pension schemes, wages and salaries.
4 Loans and debts that have been secured with a floating charge on the assets, that is, secured on assets in general, not a specific one (though part of the assets may be set aside for unsecured creditors).
5 Ordinary trade creditors.
6 Tax owed to Her Majesty's Revenue & Customs.
7 Shareholders.

If you do not start proceedings to wind up the company on a voluntary basis, you may find it forced on you if a creditor applies to the court for a compulsory winding-up because you cannot pay your debts. However, following a change in the law, you can no longer normally be forced down this route by a single creditor such as a bank. If you do face compulsory winding-up, the court will appoint a liquidator, who is usually the Official Receiver. The Official Receiver is an officer of the Department for Business, Enterprise and Regulatory Reform.

The secretary or director of the company must provide the Official Receiver with a statement verified by affidavit, listing the assets or liabilities of the company. The Official Receiver will call a creditors' meeting to decide whether to appoint a liquidator or whether the Official Receiver will carry on in that role. The liquidator will pay off the company's debts in the same order as that outlined for the voluntary winding-up.

The 1986 Insolvency Act strengthened the responsibilities of directors. One of the provisions could mean that a director is made personally liable for a company's creditors. This could occur if the director has allowed the company to go on trading even though there is no way it can avoid insolvent liquidation (that is, the assets of the business cannot be sold to provide a sufficient sum of money to pay all the creditors).

Sole trader

A creditor may force bankruptcy on you by beginning proceedings for payment of a debt. It is very easy for a creditor to make you bankrupt. If you owe someone more than £750 they can bankrupt you quickly. And, even if you pay the debt demanded, if the court thinks you have other debts you cannot pay, you may well still be made bankrupt. Contact the Bankruptcy Association* for more information.

Partnership

With a conventional partnership you have an added problem to that of a sole trader. Each partner is responsible for all the liabilities of the partnership, regardless of what the profit-sharing arrangements are in your partnership agreement. If you have more personal assets than your partner, it is you and your family who will suffer the most.

With a limited liability partnership, the options open to the management or to creditors are much the same as for a limited company.

What happens afterwards?

While you are an undischarged bankrupt, restrictions apply that make your chances of starting another business limited. These restrictions now normally last just a year but can be extended and last up to 15 years if you are found to have acted dishonestly. Be aware that, even though you are likely to be discharged after just one year, a note of your bankruptcy will stay on your credit record for longer – usually six years – and this will make it harder and/or more expensive for you to borrow in future.

If you are a director of a company that is wound up, you can usually be a director of another company unless you are subject to a disqualification order, bankruptcy restrictions order or undertaking.

Summary

1 Watch out for the warning signs.
2 See if your creditors will agree to your paying off what you owe by instalments or see if they will accept smaller payments in settlement.

Other chapter to read

25 Staying afloat (p. 305).

28

Keeping the record straight

Fate decrees that one of the least interesting business activities is also one of the most crucial for its continued success. Keeping records must rank fairly low in an entrepreneur's satisfaction rating. It is much more gripping to go chasing sales or to carry out a negotiation with a supplier that will lower your costs. But a complete 'seat-of-the-pants' approach to business will only keep you afloat in the short term.

If you hope to avert the dangers of sliding into failure, one thing you should try to achieve is not to allow yourself to be buried in a quagmire of bills, invoices and tax demands. Failure to organize your records from day one may mean just that. However, it is never too late to start; so if you have been pushing aside that task, now is the time to tackle it.

Allowing yourself to drift into paper chaos is understandable. Discovering a system for organizing records that is suitable for your business can be difficult. Too simple a system for your particular business may mean that you cannot derive the information from it that you need. Too complicated a system may mean that you have to spend too much time keeping it up to date. There is no one system that will apply to all businesses. You may find that you need to adjust yours with the benefit of experience until you have developed one that fits what you want.

What is in this chapter?

- why you need records (p. 341).
- which records? (p. 341).
- a very simple system (see p. 342).
- when the business is more complicated (p. 347).

Why you need records

Good accurate records are needed for two extremely important reasons. First, records are needed to substantiate what is in the accounts.

If you are self-employed or a small company (see p. 41), your accounts do not need to be audited, but they are still required for tax purposes. You do not necessarily have to send accounts in to your tax office, but you must nevertheless still have them and be prepared to produce them if asked. There are hefty fines if you can't.

Second, accurate records are needed to help you to know what is going on in your business. This, in turn, means you can keep better control and you can plan for the future. It is impossible to make realistic estimates and projections if the basic data are patchy and inaccurate.

Which records?

The first and most important record you need is for cash. You need some way of keeping information about payments into and out of your bank account and also any petty cash that you keep on the premises. The aim of your cash records is so you know at any moment how much cash you have.

For those businesses that do not sell all their goods for cash, your records will need to cope with keeping tabs on what people owe you and how long they have owed it. This allows you to forecast what money you will be getting in during the months ahead and enable you to chase debts.

Most businesses will buy goods, services and raw materials from others. Unless you are forced to pay cash for all your supplies, you will need to organize the bills that you have to pay. Following on from this, if you keep stocks of raw materials or stocks of finished goods, you need to have a tally of what there is: what has come into the business, what is currently held by the business and what has gone out.

Once you start employing people, your employee records need to be meticulous; in particular, records relating to your role as tax collector for the government (p. 240) need to be well organized and up to date.

Finally, information about fixed assets, such as cars, equipment or property, needs to be recorded.

A very simple system

If your business has only a few transactions, for example it is very small, you sell only large items or you sell your time as a consultant, the system you introduce can really be very simple. It would indeed be a mistake to get bogged down in very complicated record keeping, because it would take up a lot of time without improving the accuracy of your system. Complexities such as double-entry book-keeping can be put aside. A couple of simple accounts books may well be sufficient. Being methodical is far more important than sophistication.

Cash

You will need a cash book. This should show the cash payments you receive and make. It gives a way of recording what you have paid into the bank and what you take out of it and your petty cash position.

Diagram 28.1 on p. 344 gives an example of a way of setting up the cash book. As you can see there are two sections: one for recording cash receipts and one for recording cash payments. The cash receipts section has five columns and the cash payments section six columns.

For cash receipts, the columns are from left to right:

- the date you received the payment.
- your invoice number that has been paid.
- the name of the person who made the payment.
- the amount of the payment.
- the value of what you have paid into the bank.

If you offer discounts for prompt settlement, you will need to have an additional column to show the amount of the discount that was taken.

For cash payments, the columns are from left to right:

- the date you made the payment.
- the cheque number.
- the reference number you put on the supplier's invoice on receipt.
- the name of the person or business who has been paid.
- what you have cashed from the bank for petty cash purposes.
- the amount of the payment.

If it is normal business practice to be offered a discount, you need another column to record the amount taken. When you start paying wages, you will need a further column to record what you have cashed from the bank for this purpose. You might also find it helpful to add a 'miscellaneous' column.

Using the cash book, you should be able to work out how much cash you have and whether cash receipts are exceeding cash payments or vice versa. When you get a bank statement, which should be monthly (and when your business gets more complicated ask for a statement more than once a month), you can check that the two cash balances agree. If they do not, you should be able to identify why, that is, cheques you have sent that have not yet been cashed or cheques you have paid in that have not yet been cleared. This is called a bank reconciliation. It is useful to write your reconciliation down.

Keep all cheque books, paying-in books and bank statements.

Petty cash

You can deal with petty cash items in a number of ways. You could write a voucher or piece of paper each time you use petty cash and keep the voucher in the petty cash box. If you get a receipt for money you spend, staple this to the back of the voucher. Once a month, you could tot these up and put them in your purchases record (see p. 345).

Another approach is to carry a little notebook with you and jot down the expenses as they occur. A further alternative is to keep a sheet of paper in your office and write down the amounts spent at the end of each day, again stapling any receipts to it.

Finally, you could set up a recording system in your cash book, using perhaps the back half of the book.

Whichever way you record petty cash items, you need to record the date the cash was spent, how much it was and what it was for.

If you are registered for VAT, when you make an entry for your petty cash payments in your purchases record, you will need to know which items include the standard rate of VAT (p. 386) and to work out the amount of VAT you will be claiming.

Diagram 28.1: Cash

Cash receipts

Date received	Invoice number	Customer	Amount £	Paid into bank £

Cash payments

Date paid	Cheque number	Reference number	Supplier/ Payee	Petty Cash	Amount of payment

Sales

Every time you make a sale, you should produce an invoice (or, if you are selling for cash, a receipt). The invoices should be numbered and filed in numerical order. If there are a fair number of invoices, it might be sensible to have one file for unpaid invoices and another for paid invoices. As every invoice is paid, any documentation that comes with the payment should be stapled to it. It should then be transferred to the paid file. A separate file should be kept for every accounting period.

The next step is to write down in your accounts book a record of every sale. For every sale there should be four columns, six if you are registered for VAT. Diagram 28.2 opposite shows what it should look like. The columns are:

■ the date of the invoice.

■ the name of the customer.

■ the number of the invoice.

■ the amount of the sale, including VAT.

If you are registered for VAT, there should be two further columns:

■ the amount of the VAT.

■ the amount of the sale, excluding VAT.

You could have a further column for the payment date of your invoice.

Example 1

Peter Brown is entering the details of one of his invoices (see Diagram 28.2 below). The invoice number is 344 and the invoice is to Arnold Warehouses. Peter has charged £1,500, but VAT has to be charged. This comes to £262.50 and the total, including VAT, is £1,762.50. When the invoice is paid, Peter will enter the details in the cash book.

Diagram 28.2: Sales

Date of invoice	Description: Name of customer	Number of invoice	Amount of sale (incl. VAT)	VAT	Amount of sale (excl. VAT)
12.6.07	Arnold Warehouses	344	1,762.50	262.50	1,500.00

Purchases

If your business is simple, you can record the details of purchases in the same accounts or analysis book as your sales, perhaps using the second half of it. As every invoice comes in for goods or services that you have bought (or a receipt for items that you pay cash for), it should be numbered and filed in numerical order.

When it comes to recording purchases, a more detailed analysis than for sales can be useful for producing the accounts that you need for tax purposes. If your business is simple, your records may need to be updated only once a month.

You will probably find you use all the columns of your analysis book. The columns should read from left to right (see Diagram 28.3):

Diagram 28.3: Purchases

Date invoice received	Name of supplier	Paid	Number of invoice	Amount (incl. VAT)	VAT
12-6-07	British Telecom		222	257.83	38.40

Amount (excl. VAT)	Supplies	Car expenses	Stationery	Postage	Telephone	Heating/ lighting
219.43					219.43	

Example 2

Peter Brown has received an invoice for the telephone. He numbers the invoice 222 and enters the details in the analysis book – see Diagram 28.3 overleaf. He puts the date he received it, the supplier and the amount of the invoice including VAT, £257.83.

As he is registered for VAT, he now works out the amount of VAT, that is £257.83 less £257.83 divided by 1.175. This gives £257.83 − £219.43 = £38.40. He enters this in the VAT column and puts £219.43 in the column for the amount, excluding VAT. He puts the amount of the invoice without VAT in the analysis column.

When he pays the invoice, he ticks the appropriate column and also enters details in the cash book.

■ the date the invoice is received.

■ the name of the supplier.

■ whether the invoice is paid or not, for example a tick if paid.

■ the number you put on the invoice.

■ the amount of the invoice, including VAT.

If you are registered for VAT, you will need two further columns:

■ the amount of the VAT.

■ the amount of the invoice, excluding VAT.

The remaining columns of the book should be devoted to showing the nature of the items purchased. The exact headings you put on the columns will depend on the type of the business. Some examples could be stationery, fares, petrol, postage, heating and lighting. The amount of every invoice, excluding VAT if you are registered, should be entered in the appropriate column.

Fixed assets

If your business is a limited company, you are obliged by law to keep a record of fixed assets. If your business is fairly simple, a list in a notebook will suffice. This should show the cost of the asset and depreciation.

VAT

You are required to keep separate VAT accounts if you are registered for VAT (see Chapter 30). You can put these in your analysis book if there is sufficient room. Unless you are using the flat-rate scheme (see p. 392), this should show for each month:

- the amount of the sales, including VAT.
- the amount of VAT charged.
- the amount of the purchases, including VAT.
- the amount of the VAT paid.

When the business is more complicated

There will be many businesses for which the simple system described above will not be sufficient. This will apply to you if you make many sales or purchases each month and keep a lot of stock on the premises. An increasing number of documents and records will be needed. Your business may need to set up a system for recording information which includes some or all of the following records. And it may well be appropriate to introduce a computerized accounting system.

Purchase orders

This could be a formal document that has the name and address of the supplier plus the goods ordered and the details necessary for that. A copy of your letter may suffice, as long as they are numbered and kept in a file. This document will be needed to ensure that what the supplier sends you is actually what you ordered.

A record of what goods are received in the business

As your business grows, you will no longer know yourself exactly what has come in; there may well be employees who do this for you. The only way to keep track of what has been received is to have a formal way of recording it. This could be a specially prepared form to fill in and match against the purchase order. Or it could be a book in which you write down the details. The details are needed before a supplier invoice is passed for payment.

What have you got in stock?

You need to know at any time what raw materials or finished goods you have got in stock. Going to have a look is not the best way of doing this. Written records are the answer, because they are the best way to control and plan your business, and they will protect against staff pilfering.

If you have lots of different items that you keep in stock, stock cards may be the most suitable way of recording what there is. With fewer items, a stock book may suffice.

Sales invoices

This could be a printed form or it could be typed on business stationery and a copy kept.

Employee time sheets

For certain sorts of business, for example manufacturing or assembly, records of how many hours employees work are important and are the basis for paying wages. You could keep a time book with a simple record of when the employee started work and when the employee finished for the day. You also need to keep records for the working time regulations (see p. 242).

Petty cash vouchers

As the business gets bigger with more employees, a proper petty cash voucher will become a necessity. This should show the date, the employee who received the petty cash and what it was for. Any voucher should be signed by an appropriate responsible person with the authority to do so. Wherever possible, a receipt should be attached to the petty cash voucher.

Wages record

You have certain legal duties towards your employees (see Chapter 21). These include giving an itemized pay statement and deducting tax and National Insurance contributions from salaries and wages. Proper records need to be kept, and HMRC will send you forms to complete. You must keep the following information for all employees:

■ name and address.

■ National Insurance number.

■ PAYE reference number.

■ pay.

■ pension deductions.

■ any other deductions authorized by the employee.

The actual wages record needs to show the payments made:

■ gross pay, with a breakdown of how this is made up, for example bonuses and commission, as well as basic wage.

■ pension contributions.

■ total pay this period.

■ total pay to date.

■ tax-free pay to date (see tables from HMRC).

■ taxable pay to date.

■ tax due to date (see tables from HMRC).

■ tax paid to date.

■ tax due on earnings for this period.

■ employee's National Insurance contributions this period.

■ other deductions.

■ net pay.

■ employer's National Insurance contribution.

This is also information that needs to be set out on an employee's pay slip. You also need to keep records on statutory sick pay, statutory maternity pay, statutory paternity pay and statutory adoption pay and to keep records to show that you are meeting the requirements on the minimum wage and working time regulations.

Summary

1 You need records to back up what is in your accounts for tax purposes.
2 Planning the business and controlling it cannot be achieved if records are inadequate.
3 Keeping your records in a methodical way is more important than installing very sophisticated systems for a very small business.
4 As your business grows, you need to create control procedures to ensure that you know what has been ordered, what has been received and the supplier invoice agrees with your purchase order form.
5 You need to know who owes you what amount of money at any time so that you can chase slow or late payers.
6 As your business grows replace your accounting books with a computerized accounts package.

Other chapters to read

18 Information technology – and other equipment (p. 193); **21** Your rights and duties as an employer (p. 229); **23** Forecasting (p. 269); **25** Staying afloat (p. 305); **30** VAT (p. 382).

29

Tax

You have a choice when sorting out tax on your business: enlist a professional or do it yourself. If you operate as a company, it makes sense to use an accountant*. If you are a sole trader or partner, it can be helpful to use a professional to present your accounts and tax calculations but, provided your business is fairly simple and you have the time, you should be able to do this yourself, and the self-assessment tax system is designed to be workable by non-experts.

The starting point for working out your tax is the profit and loss accounts for your business. Whether you are a company, self-employed or a partnership, your accounts must be drawn up in accordance with Generally Accepted Accounting Practice (GAAP) for the UK. These GAAP rules are drawn up by accountancy bodies and change frequently. As a layperson, it may be hard for you to keep abreast of the changes and this is one reason why most companies are better off relying on an accountant rather than trying to draw up their own accounts. However small businesses (whether companies or not) can opt to use a short version of the accounting standards called Financial Reporting Standards for Smaller Entities (FRSSE). If you do decide to draw up your accounts yourself, make sure you comply with FRSSE and any relevant updates to it. You can download a free copy of FRSSE and check for updates at the Accounting Standards Board* web site (*www.frc.org.uk/asb/technical/frsse.cfm*).

If you do use a professional, make sure you choose someone who is suitably qualified, normally an accountant* and preferably also a member of the Chartered Institute of Taxation* or Association of Tax Technicians*. Anyone can set themselves up as a tax adviser, and unfortunately there are some with no qualifications or just not up to the job. Even if you use a professional, you are still ultimately responsible for making the correct declarations and paying the correct tax. If your adviser gets it wrong, you will be the one facing investigations, fines and interest – though you might be able to sue the adviser if they had acted negligently or fraudulently. You may also find that, although professionals will do the paperwork for you, they will not necessarily suggest ways you can save tax unless you specifically ask for their opinion on a particular measure.

To keep your tax bill to a minimum and guard yourself against advisers who are no good, it pays to know a bit yourself about the tax system.

What is in this chapter?

This chapter concentrates mainly on tax if you are a sole trader or partner. It will not answer every question you may have about how your income tax bill is calculated. But you should be able to gain a working knowledge of the system so you know the key moves to make in dealing with your tax inspector. The chapter includes sections on:

■ when you pay income tax (p. 351).

■ working out your income tax bill (p. 355).

■ business expenses (p. 356) and capital allowances (p. 361).

■ losses for the self-employed (p. 365).

■ National Insurance contributions (p. 366), capital gains tax (p. 367) and business rates (p. 368).

■ you and your tax office (p. 369).

■ drawing money out of your business if it is a company (see p. 375).

■ spare-time earnings (p. 376) and property income (p. 378).

■ the black economy (p. 379).

When you pay income tax

If you have been an employee, you'll have been used to having income tax deducted from your pay before you get it. If you are a sole trader or partner (see p. 372), you'll have to get used to setting aside part of your profits to pay tax as it falls due.

Everything to do with income tax is worked out by reference to tax years. A tax year runs from 6 April one year to the following 5 April. You pay tax for a particular tax year in three chunks: two interim payments on

31 January falling within the tax year and 31 July following the end of the tax year. These interim payments are estimates. On the following 31 January you make a final payment if the interim instalments come to less than your actual tax bill or receive a refund if you have overpaid.

Which profits are taxed?

Although tax relates to tax years, profits relate to accounting years, which do not necessarily coincide with tax years. You are usually taxed on a 'current year basis', which means that your bill for a tax year is based on profits for the accounting year ending during that tax year. For example, if your accounting year ends on 30 April, your bill for the tax year to 5 April 2008 will be based on your accounts for the year to 30 April 2007. But special rules apply in the first years of your business (see below), unless you opt for 'fiscal accounting'.

With 'fiscal accounting', your accounting year is the same as the tax year (i.e. both end on 5 April). In practice, your accounting year does not have to be exactly the same – for example, a year end of 31 March also counts.

Starting a business

If you have opted for fiscal accounting – that is, your accounting year is the same as (or nearly the same as) the tax year – there are no special rules applying to the opening years of your business. Right from the word go, you are simply taxed on the profits you make each tax year.

If you have some other year end, different rules apply for the first one, two or sometimes three tax years of your business. To find out which rules apply, follow these steps:

- *step one*: find the first tax year in which an accounting date falls that is 12 months or more after the date you started in business. Tax for that year is based on profits for the 12 months up to that accounting date. The normal current year basis applies to subsequent years.

- *step two*: there will be one or maybe two tax years before that covered in step one. In the first tax year, you are taxed on the actual profits you make in that tax year. If there is a second tax year and no accounting date falls in it, you are taxed on the actual profits for that year as well.

To decide what profits you have made in a 12-month period or your actual profits for a tax year, you take a proportion of the profits for the relevant accounting period. You do this using either days or months. For example, if your first accounting period lasts 14 months and two months fall within the first tax year, in the first tax year you are taxed on $\frac{2}{14}$ × profits for the 14-month period.

Overlap profits

Under the opening year rules for a new business, some profits are taxed more than once. In the example below, David is taxed on $\frac{2}{16} + \frac{12}{16} + \frac{12}{16} = \frac{26}{16}$ ths of the profits for his first accounting period – that is £13,000 instead of the actual £8,000 for the period. The excess £13,000 − £8,000 = £5,000 is his overlap profit. You normally do not get tax relief on overlap profits until your business finally ceases. In the meantime, overlap profits are not increased in line with inflation, so the tax relief might not be worth much in real terms by the time you finally get it.

Example: Working out profit to be taxed at the start of a business

David Weston started his business on 1 February 2007 but decides to end his accounting year on 31 May each year. To avoid a very short first period, he lets his first accounting 'year' last for 16 months. His profits are as follows:

Accounting year 1/2/07 to 31/5/08   £8,000

Accounting year 1/6/08 to 31/5/09   £12,000

Accounting year 1/6/09 to 31/5/10   £17,000

Step one: the first tax year in which there is an accounting date falling at least 12 months after the start of trading is 2008–9.

Step two: opening year rules apply to the tax years 2006–7 and 2007–8.

David's profits will be taxed as follows:

2006–7: $\frac{2}{16}$ × £8,000	£1,000
2007–8: $\frac{12}{16}$ × £8,000	£6,000
2008–9: $\frac{12}{16}$ × £8,000	£6,000
2009–10: current year basis	£12,000
2010–11: current year basis	£17,000

Choosing when to end your accounting year

You will need to weigh up a number of factors when deciding the best date on which to end your accounting year:

■ fiscal accounting – that is, ending your year on or about 5 April or 31 March – makes your tax affairs very simple but will give you the least time to draw up your accounts to meet the self-assessment deadlines.

■ a year-end early in the tax year maximizes the delay between earning your profits and paying tax on them. This is good for cash flow if your profits are rising. You also have plenty of time in which to draw up your accounts. On the other hand, a year-end early in the tax year will involve higher overlap profits. You probably won't get tax relief on these for many years and in the meantime inflation will have eroded its value.

If your business is already established, you can choose to alter your year end. In that case, you might be able to claim some or all of your overlap relief early, but whether overall the change works to your advantage depends on the pattern of profits for your particular business. Get advice from your accountant.

The self-assessment timetable

Under self-assessment, you are required to send HMRC a tax return each year and to pay your tax bill by the due dates.

You are responsible for working out how much tax to pay, though you can ask your tax office to do the sums provided you get your return back early enough. Alternatively, if you send in your return via the Internet, your tax bill is automatically worked out for you. If you send back your return late, there are automatic penalties. Similarly, if you pay your tax late, you will be charged interest and possibly fines too. Key dates for your 2007–8 tax bill are:

The year 2008

■ *31 January* First instalment (called a 'payment on account') of your tax bill for 2007–8 is due. It is usually set at half your tax bill for the previous year (2006–7).

■ *5 April* End of 2007–8 tax year.

■ *April* Receive 2007–8 tax return for the tax year just ended.

■ *31 July* Second payment on account for 2007–8 tax bill. This is usually set at half your tax bill for the previous tax year (2006–7).

■ *31 October* New deadline for sending in your 2007–8 tax return if you are using the paper version. In previous years you could choose to file a paper return by 30 September if you wanted HMRC to work out your tax bill for you, but this was optional and the final deadline was 31 January. This new 31 October deadline is different. If you miss it, you will either have to file online instead or face a late filing penalty if you stick with the paper return.

▪ *30 December* Latest date for filing your return online if you owe less than £2,000 tax and want it to be collected through PAYE (where you are also getting earnings from a job or a pension) throughout 2009–10 instead of as a single lump sum by 31 January 2009.

The year 2009

▪ *31 January* Last date for filing your 2007–8 tax return online. If your two payments on account come to less than the final bill, you must send in your payment for the remaining tax by this date.

The year 2010

▪ *31 January* Your 2007–8 tax return becomes final 12 months after the date you filed it, so this is the latest date on which your return should become final. The significance is that, if HMRC is going to open an enquiry into your return, it should tell you by the date your return becomes final. However, HMRC can still investigate your tax affairs for other reasons – for example, suspected fraud. And, if your tax return contained any estimated valuations (of, say, property or unquoted shares) which were not fully explained in the return, HMRC can still open an enquiry into that aspect of your return.

The year 2014

▪ *31 January* You can finally throw away the documents relating to your 2007–8 tax bill.

Working out your income tax bill

For sole traders and partners, you first turn your profits from your accounts into taxable profits (see the example overleaf):

1 If you have taken any items out of stock for your own use, include these in your sales figure at the normal selling price.

2 Deduct from your profits any business expenses that are normally allow-able against tax but that you have not included.

3 Add back to your profits any business expenses that are not allowable for tax purposes (p. 360).

4 Deduct the following items, which are allowable for tax purposes: capital allowances and, from 2008–9, annual investment allowance (see p. 361), any balancing allowances (see p. 364) and loss relief (see p. 365).

5 Add back any balancing charges from the sale of assets (see p. 364).

6 Deduct any income that is not part of your trading income and on which tax is paid separately, for example bank interest.

Example: Working out taxable profits

Patty Woodward, who started her business in August 2006, adjusts the profits from her accounts to provide a figure on which her tax bill will be based. Her profits according to the accounts are £7,500.

1 She has not used any stock for her own use, so no adjustment needed here.

2 She checks carefully against the list of business expenses that are normally allowed for tax purposes (see above). She realizes she has forgotten to include bank charges, which for the year total £48. The adjusted profit figure is now £7,452.

3 However, her accounting profit includes a figure for depreciation of her van of £1,000. She adds this back; her adjusted profits are now £8,452.

4 Patty now claims the allowances she can. She takes the full writing-down allowance on her van. For this year, it comes to £750. She has no losses on which to claim relief. This gives taxable profits of £7,702.

5 She has not sold any assets this year.

6 She has no business investment income. Her taxable profits are £7,702.

Business expenses

What business expenses are allowed?

You can claim, and be allowed, an item as a business expense for tax purposes if it is incurred 'wholly and exclusively' for the business. The golden rule with expenses is that if you are in any doubt as to whether an expense is allowable, claim it.

An expense incurred partly for business and partly for private reasons, for example a trip in your car to a customer, is strictly not allowed if you dropped in to see a friend on the way. However, where the business part can be clearly identified or apportioned, you are allowed to make a claim. For example, you can claim part of the cost of running a car for both business and private reasons based on records you keep of your total and business mileage. Similarly, you may be able to claim some of the expenses of using your home for business based on, say, the proportion of floor area devoted to the business and the proportion of time that space is used for business. Typical allowable home expenses will be part of the costs of heating, lighting, cleaning, telephone, insurance and security. You can also treat fixed costs, such as mortgage interest, rent, council tax, home insurance, water rates and general repairs as being partly for business if part of the home is set aside solely for business. Be aware that if part of your home is used exclusively for business, there could be capital gains tax (CGT) to pay on that proportion when you come to sell your home. HMRC makes a distinction between using part of the home 'solely' for business and 'exclusively' for business. For example:

■ you use your office solely for business from 9am to 5pm but then for other activities after 5pm. If the office represents 10 per cent of the floor space of the home, you would first work out 10 per cent of your fixed costs on the basis of floor area, then take $\frac{8}{24}$ of the result (the proportion of time the room is used for business) to find the amount you can claim. In this example, the office is used solely for business part of the time, but not exclusively for business so there would be no CGT when you sell.

■ you use your office solely for business and no other purpose. If it represents 10 per cent of the floor space of the home, you can claim 10 per cent of the fixed costs. In this case, the office is used exclusvely for business and so there could be CGT when you sell the home.

Checklist of expenses you can normally claim

1. General expenses

Claim the expenses of making your product and running your premises:

■ cost of goods you sell or use in your product.

■ selling costs, such as advertising, sales discounts, gifts costing up to £50 a year (if gift advertises your business or product and is not food, drink or tobacco).

■ office/factory expenses, such as heating, lighting, cleaning, business rate, rent, telephone, postage, printing, security, stationery, normal repairs and maintenance.

- proportion of home expenses, if used for work.

- cost of computer software, if its useful life is less than two years. If the useful life is longer, it may be treated as capital expenditure – see p. 361.

- other expenses, such as relevant books and magazines, professional fees, subscriptions to professional and trade organizations, replacing small tools, travel expenses (but not between home and work or, usually, lunches).

- running costs of a car, delivery charges, charge for hiring capital equipment, leasing payment; but special rules apply to expensive cars. In general, if you lease a car that cost over £12,000 when new, the allowable expense you can claim is limited to $(£12,000 + P)/2P$, where P is the price of the car when new. For example, if the car cost £20,000 when new, you would be able to claim only $£32,000/£40,000 = \frac{4}{5}$ of the leasing payment. However, this restriction does not apply if you are in the business of hiring your cars to, or transporting, members of the public and, from 17 April 2002 to 31 March 2008 inclusive, it does not apply to cars that are electrically propelled or have low carbon dioxide emissions. At the time of writing, the government was reviewing these rules for leased cars.

If you are not registered for VAT, include the cost of VAT in what you claim, as it is a business expense that you cannot get back through the VAT system. If you are registered for VAT, do not include it, unless it is impossible for you to claim it back from the VAT inspector because, for example, it is included in what you have purchased for part of your business that is exempt for VAT purposes.

If you have opted to use the VAT flat-rate scheme (see p. 392), you have a choice. Under the scheme, you pay VAT as a percentage of your VAT-inclusive turnover instead of working out the VAT you have charged less the VAT you can claim back. The VAT you actually hand over to HMRC may be more or less than the VAT you would otherwise have paid. Either:

- you can work out your accounts excluding VAT from both your revenue and your expenses, in which case you record any profit from using the flat-rate scheme as extra revenue or any loss as an additional expense, or

- you can work out your accounts including VAT in both your revenue and expense figures and record the VAT you actually hand over as an expense. This is the simpler method to use.

2. Staff costs

Claim the normal costs of employing people:

■ wages, salaries, bonuses, redundancy and leaving payments, pensions to former employees and dependants (but not your salary or your partner's salary), training costs, council tax paid on behalf of an employee, if a genuine part of remuneration package subject to PAYE. This includes the cost of employing family members – such as your husband or wife – provided you can show that the work is actually done and that the wage is the going market rate.

■ pension contributions made on employees' behalf. Cost of providing life, health and sick pay insurance for employees (but not yourself).

■ employer's National Insurance contributions (but not your own, see p. 366).

■ entertaining staff, for example Christmas party.

■ gifts, subscriptions and contributions for benefits for staff, but these could be regarded as employee's emoluments.

3. Financial expenses

■ bank charges on business accounts.

■ accountancy and audit fees, additional accountancy expenses needed as a result of HMRC 'in-depth' investigation but not if the investigation reveals that profits have been understated.

■ interest on loans and overdrafts for your business, and cost of arranging them (but not interest paid to a partner for capital put into the business, or interest on overdue tax).

■ charge part of hire purchase payments (that is, the interest plus additional costs).

■ business insurance.

■ bad debts that you specifically claim (but not a general reserve for bad or doubtful debts).

■ incidental cost of obtaining loan finance, but not stamp duty, foreign exchange losses, issue discounts or repayment premiums.

4. Legal and other expenses

- legal charges such as debt collection, preparing trading contracts, employee service contracts, settling trading disputes and renewing a short lease (that is, 50 years or less).

- legal costs of defending yourself against disciplinary action by a body that regulates your profession (but not any fines imposed as a result of that action).

- premium for grant of lease, but limited to the amount assessed on the landlord as extra rent spread over the term as the lease is paid.

- fees paid to register trade mark or design, or to obtain a patent.

What is not normally allowed as a business expense

1 Your own income and living expenses, ordinary clothes, medical expenses, your NI contributions (p. 366), income tax, capital gains tax, inheritance tax, fines and other penalties for breaking the law (but you could pay a parking fine for an employee), VAT surcharge.

2 Depreciation or initial costs of capital equipment, buying a patent, vehicles, computer hardware or software if treated as a capital item (see below), permanent advertising signs, buildings and the cost of additions or improvements to these (but see capital allowances). An initial lump sum paid for a franchise is not normally allowable (but should qualify for capital allowances), but any part paid for, say, trading stock or staff training (but not your own training) is normally allowable.

3 Legal expenses on forming a company, drawing up a partnership agreement, and acquiring assets such as long leases.

4 Business entertaining expenses, cost of partners' meals at regular lunchtime meetings, gifts to customers (but see p. 359), normally charitable subscriptions and donations, and donations to political parties.

5 Reserves or provisions for expected payments, such as repairs and general reserve for bad and doubtful debts (but see p. 359).

6 Wages to employees that remain unpaid 18 months after the accounting date.

Capital allowances

What capital allowances can be claimed?

Depreciation on capital equipment and its initial cost are not allowable business expenses (see above). But instead you can claim capital allowances, which are like a sort of depreciation worked out in a standard way. The main capital allowance is writing-down allowance, but up to 2007–8 sometimes you can claim extra in the year you buy equipment, and this is called a first-year allowance. From 2008–9 onwards, first-year capital allowances for plant and machinery are being replaced by a new annual investment allowance. The allowance will enable you to write off the full cost of up to £50,000 of expenditure each year. Any spending over that limit will be written off gradually through writing-down allowances.

The way in which you pay for equipment does not affect the capital allowance you can claim. But you do not claim a capital allowance for the interest on a loan or overdraft to buy equipment; this is an allowable expense, not part of the cost of the asset. If you are buying on hire purchase, the charge is also a business expense. With leased equipment, you claim the rent as an expense, not a capital allowance.

To qualify for a capital allowance, expenditure must be 'wholly and exclusively' for the business. But this does not mean you cannot claim a capital allowance for some item that you use in your private life as well as in your business. For example, if you use a car half in your business and half for private purposes, you work out the capital allowance on the cost of the car and claim half the allowance.

If you bring into your business something you already owned privately, you can claim a capital allowance (but not any first-year allowance) on its market value at the time you brought it into your business.

Maximum capital allowances in 2007–8

These are the maximum allowances you can claim for what you spend:

most plant and machinery – *small businesses*	50 per cent for spending from 6 April 2006 to 5 April 2008 25 per cent writing-down allowance thereafter (reducing to 20 per cent from 2008–9)
most plant and machinery –	40 per cent in the first year

medium-sized businesses	25 per cent writing-down allowance thereafter (reducing to 20 per cent from 2008–9)
eligible new environmentally friendly equipment, for example energy-saving boilers, refrigeration, water meters – details from Environment and Energy Helpline*	100 per cent
new low-emission cars, and natural gas and hydrogen fuel refuelling equipment	100 per cent for spending from 17 April 2002 to 31 March 2008
other cars	25 per cent, with a maximum of £3,000 (under review and likely to change in future)
industrial buildings (including hotels) and agricultural buildings	4 per cent of original cost (but being phased out from 2008–9 onwards)
industrial buildings in enterprise zones	100 per cent in first year; 4 per cent of original cost thereafter (but being phased out from 2008–9 onwards)
renovating or converting residential space over shop or other commercial property into flat(s) for rent	100 per cent in first year
loft, cavity wall and solid wall insulation up to £1,500 – residential landlords	100 per cent in first year
renovating commercial premises in assisted areas (see p. 184) vacant at least a year	100 per cent in first year
buying a patent	25 per cent (reducing to 20 per cent from 2008–9)
know-how	25 per cent (reducing to 20 per cent from 2008–9)
research and development (companies only)	100 per cent in first year

Working out the allowance for plant and machinery

In the year you first bring an item into your business, you claim a capital allowance on its cost if you bought it or market value if it is something you already owned (from 2008–9, you claim annual investment allowance on the first £50,000 of such spending).

You deduct the first-year allowance from the cost if you have newly bought the item (or writing-down allowance from the market value if it's something you already owned) and carry the remainder forward to the next year, when you claim writing-down allowance on the amount brought forward. You deduct the written-down allowance from the value brought forward to find the starting value for next year, and so on. See example below.

Example: What capital allowance can be claimed?

Adam Horsfield buys a desk for his small business on 30 September 2007; the cost of the desk is £800. At the end of the accounting year, Adam claims a first-year allowance of 50 per cent of £800, that is, £400. He deducts this from the value of the desk, giving a value of £400 at the end of the accounting year.

Equipment Adam has bought in earlier years is valued, at the start of this accounting year, at £3,450. He claims a writing-down allowance of 25 per cent of £3,450, which comes to £862.50. He deducts this from the value of the equipment to give a new value at the end of the year of £2,587.50.

In total, Adam claims capital allowances of £400 + £862.50 = £1,262.50. The closing value of his capital pool is £400 + £2,587.50 = £2,987.50.

Where you have more than one item, you pool the brought-forward values and claim writing-down allowance each year on the remaining value of the pool. Some types of item have their own separate pool (see below).

The table on pages 361–2 shows the maximum capital allowances available in 2007–8, and you can claim less. For example, if you already have other deductions that are enough to reduce your profits to zero or to the level of your personal allowance, there is no point claiming capital allowances too. If you claim less than your maximum capital allowances this year, you carry forward a higher level in your pool, which means you can claim more in capital allowances in the next and subsequent years.

When it comes to selling an asset on which you have claimed capital allowances, you have to reduce the value of your pool by the lower of the sale proceeds or the original cost. Do this before working out the amount of the allowance you can claim for the accounting year in which you sell the asset. If the sale proceeds are more than the value of the pool, the difference (the balancing charge) will be taxable as if it were extra profit for the year. Note that this also applies to an asset that has formed its own separate pool (see below). If the sale proceeds come to less than the pool value of an asset you sell, you can't normally get any tax relief on the residue, unless it was a short-life asset (see below). However, when your business stops trading for good, if the proceeds from getting rid of all the assets in the pool come to less than the value of the pool, you can claim the difference as a balancing allowance that will reduce your tax bill for that year.

What is not included in the pool

These items have separate pools of expenditure:

- cars costing more than £12,000 at present must each have their own separate pool (except low-emission cars, defined as emitting no more than 120 g/km of carbon dioxide). Cars costing £12,000 or less are included in your main expenditure pool. However, at the time of writing the government is consulting on changing the capital allowance rules for cars. The suggestion is that all cars (even those costing £12,000 or more) should go into a car pool with reduced writing-down allowances. Energy-efficient cars would qualify for higher first-year allowances.

- anything used partly in your business, partly in your private life.

- if you choose, any piece of plant and machinery (but not cars) that you expect to sell or scrap within five years of buying. With these short-life assets, for example tools or a computer, you have to choose to put it in a separate pool within two years of buying it. If, when you sell the equipment, you sell it for less than its value after deducting the capital allowances you have claimed on it, you will be able to write off the difference in that year. If you sell it for more than the value, the difference will be taxable as if it were extra profit. If you do not sell it in five years, its value will be added to your main pool as if it had never been treated separately.

- 'long-life assets' are pooled separately and qualify for reduced allowances of six per cent a year. These are assets that have an expected working life when new of 25 years or more. But there are various exclusions, including cars and any machinery or plant in a building that is used wholly or mainly as a home, shop, showroom, hotel or office. Importantly, the long-life asset rules do not apply to businesses spending less than £100,000 a year on such assets, so the vast majority of small and medium-sized businesses are not affected and can continue to claim the higher allowance (50 or 40 per cent initially, 25 per cent thereafter in 2007–8) on such assets.

Losses for the self-employed

If you have made a loss in your business, you normally claim tax relief on it by deducting it from other income or a capital gain, or by carrying the loss forward and deducting it from future trading profits from your business.

Deducting the loss from other income and capital gain

You can either deduct your trading loss from any other income or capital gains that you have in the tax year in which your loss-making accounting year ends, or you can carry the loss back and set it against other income or gains for the previous tax year. Other income could be, for example, dividends from shares or earnings from a job.

You must claim this relief within 12 months of the 31 January following the end of the tax year to which the loss relates. For example, suppose you have been in business for some time, your accounting year ends on 31 July and you made a loss in your 2006–7 accounting year. These accounts form the basis of your tax bill for the 2007–8 tax year. Your tax return and final tax settlement for 2007–8 are due on 31 January 2009. You then have a further 12 months – in other words, until 31 January 2010 – to elect to deduct your losses from other income and gains either for 2007–8 or for 2006–7.

If you have other deductions that will reduce the tax bill on your other income and gains to nil in one of the tax years, opt to deduct the loss in the other year. If after setting the loss against income and gains for one or both years, there is still some loss left over, you can carry the excess forward to set against future profits (see below).

Deducting the loss from future trading profits

If you make this choice, you carry forward the loss and set it against the next future profits from the same trade. If you have any losses left over, you carry them forward against future profits *ad infinitum*, until they are used up. If you are going to use your loss in this way, you have to use the whole of the loss before you can use any other deductions, such as outgoings or allowances, that you may have. The main disadvantage of making this choice to use up your loss relief is that it takes a while to turn it into cash.

To use this option, you must tell your tax office within five years of the 31 January following the tax year to which the loss relates. For example, if the loss was made in the accounts being assessed for the 2007–8 tax year, you have until 31 January 2014 to make your claim.

If you are starting a new business

If you spend money before your business actually starts, it may count as pre-trading expenditure. It will be set against the earnings of your business in its first year and, if it creates a loss, you can get loss relief. You can get tax relief on expenditure going back seven years.

There is special tax treatment for any losses you make in the first four tax years of a new business (as long as your inspector believes it was reasonable to plan for profits during that period). You can get a tax refund by setting the loss against any other income (for example, wages from a job) that you had in the three years before the loss. Set the loss off against the earliest year of income first, then the next earliest, and so on.

If you want to set off your loss in this way, you need to tell your tax office in writing within 12 months of the 31 January following the end of the tax year to which the loss relates.

Other taxes you might pay

National Insurance

If you are self-employed, you normally have to pay Class 2 National Insurance contributions. If your earnings from self-employment are expected to be less than a certain amount, £4,635 in 2007–8, you can claim exemption from payment, but this is seldom worth doing given the value of the state benefits you lose. Class 2 NI is paid at a flat rate of £2.20 a week in 2007–8, which you can pay monthly by direct debit or you will be sent a bill each quarter. Paying Class 2 contributions means you may be able to claim incapacity benefit, basic maternity allowance and basic retirement pension, and your spouse or civil partner might get bereavement benefits in the event of your death.

If your earnings from your business are above a certain amount, £5,225 in 2007–8, you will have to pay Class 4 contributions. These are earnings-related, collected along with income tax and are 8 per cent of your profits between the lower limit up to a specified maximum, £34,840 in 2007–8, and 1 per cent of all earnings above the upper profit limit.

Example: Class 4 National Insurance

Carolyn Harbury has profits of £42,000 for her accounting year ending in 2007–8. Class 4 National Insurance contributions are payable at 8 per cent on profits between £5,225 and £34,840 plus 1 per cent of £42,000 − £34,840 = £7,160. For Carolyn, this means paying contributions of (£34,840 − £5,225) × 8% + £7,160 × 1% = £2,440.80.

Capital gains tax

You do not normally pay capital gains tax (CGT) on business stock you sell, but you might have to pay it when you dispose of land and buildings, plant and machinery or goodwill. Disposing includes selling, giving away, exchanging or losing.

However, gains made on assets used in your business qualify for 'taper relief' at a very favourable rate. For assets disposed of from 2002–3 onwards, the gain is reduced by half provided you have held it for at least a year and by 75 per cent if you have held it for at least two years. (The rules are more complicated if you first owned the asset before 6 April 1998.) There is no tax in 2007–8 on the first £9,200 of net capital gains. To find out more about capital gains tax, contact HMRC*.

In general, you pay no CGT on your home if you claim some of the costs of running your home as a business expense because you work from home. But if you use part of your home exclusively for business purposes, you may pay tax on a gain from that part.

If you sell or otherwise dispose of assets from your business, and make a gain, you could pay capital gains tax on the gain. But if you replace the assets in the three years after the sale or one year before the sale of the old one, you can claim roll-over relief and defer paying capital gains tax. You can also claim relief if you do not replace but use the proceeds to buy another qualifying business asset. You usually get the relief by deducting the gain from the old asset from the acquisition cost for the new one. So when you sell the new one, the gain on it has been increased by the size of the gain on the old one. However, if you replace again, you can claim further roll-over relief. And so on. Capital gains tax will not have to be paid (under current legislation) until you fail to replace the business asset.

Not every business asset qualifies for the relief. But if it is land or a building used by the business, goodwill, fixed plant or machinery, for example, it will qualify for roll-over relief.

Business rates

If you occupy business premises, you must normally pay business rates. Your bill is worked out by multiplying the rateable value of your property by the appropriate multiplier. Rateable values are assessed every five years by the government and aim to reflect the commercial rent you would pay for your premises. The latest revaluation came into effect from 1 April 2005. For the year from 1 April 2007, the multiplier is 44.4p, or 44.1p if you qualify for a new small business rate relief. There are a range of reliefs that you might be able to claim from your local authority, including:

- *transitional relief*: if the revaluation has resulted in a significant rise in your bill, you may be able to claim transitional relief to spread the increase over up to four years.

- *small business rate relief*: the lower multiplier applies if the rateable value of your property (or combined value if you have more than one) is under £15,000 (or £21,500 if your only or main property is in London). In addition, you may qualify for a reduction in the bill for your only or main premises of up to 50 per cent if the rateable value is less than £5,000. The reduction decreases by roughly one per cent for each £100 of rateable value over £5,000. There is no reduction if the rateable value is over £10,000. If you have more than one property, you are eligible for the reduction only if your additional properties each have a rateable value of less than £2,200 and the combined value of all your properties is less than £15,000 (£21,500 in London). You must apply for this relief each year within six months of the end of the financial year – for example, by 30 September 2007 for the year ending 31 March 2007.

- *rural village with population under 3,000*: you can claim a 50 per cent reduction in your bill (more at the discretion of your local authority) if you run the only village store or post office and your rateable value is under £7,000, you run the only village pub or petrol station and your rateable value is less than £10,500, or you run a food shop with a rateable value under £7,000.

Example: Small business rate relief

Arif Patel works from a small workshop with a rateable value of £3,000 a year. His basic rates bill for 2007–8 is £3,000 × 44.1p = £1,323. But he can claim small business rate relief of 50 per cent, which reduces his bill to 50% × £1,323 = £661.50.

If the property is partly for business and partly for private use – for example, a shop with a flat above – business rates are payable on the business part of the property and council tax on the rest. The same treatment may apply where you use part of your home for business purposes, but this has until recently been something of a grey area. However, in 2003 a tribunal case (*Tully* v. *Jorgensen*) ruled that, where home-based work involves using furniture and equipment normally found in a home, residential use is not compromised and business rates are not due. But business rates are likely to be chargeable if you make structural alterations to your home, hire staff, use specialist equipment or have customers visiting your home.

You and your tax office

When you first start in business

When you first start working for yourself, you need to inform your local tax office, which is your contact point for both income tax and National Insurance contributions. You must normally do this within three months of the end of the month you started up or face a £100 fine. Fill in form CWF1, which is available from HMRC* and contained in its leaflet SE1 *Thinking of working for yourself?* You can also register over the Internet if you have the appropriate computer equipment. Your tax office will pass details to the VAT section of HMRC, which will then contact you to find out whether you need or want to register for VAT (see Chapter 30).

If you have finished a job as an employee, you will have form P45, which should be sent to your tax inspector so that the amount of your personal allowances and the amount of tax to be paid for that tax year can be sorted out. If you start self-employment part way through the tax year, having been an employee before, you can ask for a refund of part or all of the tax paid under PAYE if you can show that you will otherwise pay too much tax. This can help with the cash flow problems of starting the business.

Once you have started a business

When you first start in business, there are no interim payments of tax for the first year or so, because there is no track record from a previous year on which to base any payments. You'll be sent a tax return in the April following start up and, as usual, you have until the following 31 January to send in your return and to pay the tax due. For example, you might start in business in, say, June 2007. You'll get a tax return in April 2008, and your first tax payments must be made by 31 January 2009. At that time, you'll pay all the tax due for the 2007–8 tax year plus the first interim payment for 2008–9 which will be set at half the amount due for 2007–8.

Your tax return

If your business is very small and the rest of your tax affairs uncomplicated, you may receive a short four-page tax return. HMRC will have selected you for the short return on the basis of your previous years' affairs, but it is up to you to make sure that you are eligible to use the form. If not, you need to contact HMRC* to get the full tax return. Anyone with more complicated business affairs will in any case be sent the full return.

In 2006, HMRC piloted a new tax return with a shorter, simpler self-employment section suitable for businesses with a turnover of less than £40,000 a year. The aim is to roll it out nationwide in 2008.

The full tax return includes supplementary pages for self-employment, which ask for name, address and description of your business, the period on which your tax bill is based and details of the business's income, expenditure and profits. You must also fill in the details required in the main section of the tax return and fill in the orange-headed supplement 'Self-employment'. Exceptionally, you might not have all the information you need to complete the return on time – for example, if you have not yet made up your first set of accounts. In this case, you should estimate what your profits will be and enter provisional figures on the supplementary pages. These should be as realistic as possible, taking into account all the information you have to date. Your tax office wants to know why figures are not yet available and when you think they will be.

Normally, if your tax return is incomplete, you will be treated as having missed the deadline and will face a penalty if tax is paid late as a result. However, HMRC says that a return containing provisional figures will not be treated as incomplete, provided you have taken all reasonable steps to obtain the final figures and you make sure you send final figures to your tax office as soon as they become available. There will be interest to pay if the finalized figures show that more tax was due than the provisional figures indicated.

Being investigated

During the 12 months after you have sent in your tax return together with your self-assessment (if you are working out your own tax), HMRC can choose to audit your return and assessment. After the 12 months has passed, HMRC can still investigate you, but only if it suspects fraud or discovers an error.

If you have been selected for audit or investigation, HMRC must by law write to you telling you that this is the case. It does not have to tell you why you are being investigated, but it must say whether your whole return is being investigated or just some aspect of it, for example how you calculated your capital allowances. The tax officer has wide-reaching powers to ask for any relevant documents, and the self-employed are required, by law, to keep documents for five years after 31 January following the end of the tax year to which they relate. If you fail to produce the documents asked for, you will be fined.

The tax officer may request an interview, the purpose of which will probably be to establish:

■ why your business, and hence profits, are different from other similar businesses.

■ whether you have correctly calculated adjustments for tax purposes.

■ if you have assessed your own tax bill, whether you have made any errors or omissions.

■ if the amount shown for what you have taken out of the business seems adequate to support your lifestyle. You may need to work out an estimate for your living expenses, for example general household expenses, as well as leisure expenditure and so on.

If the tax officer is satisfied with your records and explanation, there will probably be a fairly minor, or even no, adjustment to your accounts. However, if a more serious view is taken, you may find that your figures for profit for this and previous years are increased.

Either following or during the investigation, you will be sent an assessment if extra tax is deemed to be due. You will have to pay interest on the tax, and there may also be penalties.

Do you count as self-employed?

It may be obvious that you are self-employed, but sometimes it is not clear-cut. You cannot simply declare yourself self-employed; you will have to convince your tax inspector that you are. And recently, HMRC has been taking a closer look at those claiming to be self-employed, particularly sub-contractors working in the construction industry, and people ceasing to be employees but returning to the same work as consultants, and reclassifying them as employees. The sort of points that will help you to establish self-employment are:

1 Working for more than one customer.
2 Showing that you control what you do, whether you do it, how you do it and when and where you do it.
3 Providing the major items of equipment you need to do your job.
4 Being free to hire other people, on terms of your own choice, to do the work that you have agreed to undertake.
5 Correcting unsatisfactory work in your own time and at your own expense.

If you do the above, there will probably be little difficulty in persuading an inspector that you are self-employed. You can check whether you are likely to be classified as employed or self-employed, by using the HMRC online employment status indicator tool at *www.hmrc.gov.uk/calcs/esi.htm*.

Partners

If you decide to take a partner, your tax treatment becomes a bit more complex because as well as individual tax returns for each partner, you also have to complete a partnership tax return.

What is the taxable income?

The taxable income for your partnership is worked out in much the same way as if you were working on your own and taxed as a sole trader. From your sales figure, you can deduct business expenses that are allowable for tax purposes (p. 355). Your partnership can get tax relief on capital expenditure (capital allowances, see p. 361) and losses (p. 365). Each partner can set their allowances against their share of the profits.

If your partnership has any non-trading income, such as interest, this will not be included in the taxable profits of the partnership but taxed as investment income. In practice, partnership investment income is normally allocated in the same ratio as the profit share, and each individual partner is given a tax bill for the investment income. Any capital gains of the partnership will be subject to capital gains tax.

If a partner has other income or gains that do not come as a result of the partnership, the partner will be taxed on these as an individual in the normal way.

Who pays what tax?

■ profits are normally taxed on a current year basis (see p. 352). For example, the tax bill for 2007–8 will be based on profits for the partnership accounting year ending in 2007–8.

■ profits are divided between the partners according to their profit-sharing agreement for the accounting year being taxed – that is, there is no mismatch between your share of the profits and the tax bill.

■ tax is worked out for each partner individually based on each share of the profits as if each of you were running your own separate business. If the partnership is new or you have newly joined an existing partnership, opening year rules (see p. 352) apply to you personally.

■ tax on investment income is also worked out for each partner individually. For this purpose, untaxed investment income is allocated to each partner as if it were income from a second business but based on the same accounting period as the partnership's mainstream business. Taxed investment income is allocated to each partner but on the basis of the amount received in each tax year.

■ each partner is responsible only for their own tax bill on their own share of the profits. You can't be asked to stump up the money if other partners don't pay their tax bills.

Tax returns

In April each year, both the partners and the partnership as a whole receive a tax return. The partnership tax return is completed on behalf of the partnership as a whole and shows the income, expenses and so on for the partnership. The partnership return must be returned to the tax office by the normal deadline of 31 January following the end of the tax year but, in practice, it will need to be ready much earlier than that.

Each partner has his or her own tax return to complete and return to the tax office by the deadlines described on page 354 (30 September 2007 or

31 January 2008 for the 2006–7 tax return and 31 October 2008 or 31 January 2009 for the 2007–8 return). The partner's tax return includes supplementary pages relating to his or her partnership income. The details that must be included are based on information contained in a 'partnership statement'. The partnership statement is a copy of information given in the partnership return.

Therefore, the partnership return must be completed early enough for partners to complete their own paperwork in good time. Timing could be very tight if the partnership has an accounting date late in the tax year. An early accounting date gives the maximum time for getting the accounts prepared ready for early completion of the partnership return.

Changing partners

Each partner is treated as if they were running their own business, so normal opening year rules (see p. 352) apply to you personally when you join a partnership. Similarly, there are closing year rules, which are applied individually to you if you leave a partnership.

Losses for partners

Losses can be treated in much the same way as if you were a sole trader (p. 365). You and your partners share the losses on the same basis as you would share any profits; the losses are apportioned on the basis applying in the year in which they arise.

You can each treat your losses as you want. One of you can set them off against other income, while the other can carry them forward and set them off against future partnership profits.

However, from 10 February 2004 onwards, if you are a non-active partner who does not spend much time running the business, the amount of losses for which you can claim relief by setting them against other income and gains (see p. 365) or setting them against profits for earlier years (see p. 366) is limited to the amount you have contributed to the partnership. And, for investments you make from 2 March 2007 onwards, this 'sideways loss relief' is further restricted to the lower of the eligible amount as described above and £25,000. You will count as a non-active partner if you devote on average less than 10 hours a week to the business. There is an exception: the £25,000 limit will not apply where you are investing in a partnership carrying on a film-related trade. You can still claim relief without any restriction by carrying losses forward to set against future profits from the same business.

Drawing money out of your company

If you operate your business as a company, you are strongly advised to get the help of a professional in drawing up your accounts and handling your tax affairs. The aim of this section is not to explain how companies are taxed but to highlight the main points to consider when thinking about how to draw money out of the company for your private use.

Your company has a separate legal identity from you and is subject to its own tax regime – corporation tax. The profits the company makes belong to its shareholders and not directly to you, so you have two main ways in which you can transfer money from the company to yourself:

1 *Salary and fringe benefits*: as a director of the company, you count as an employee. You are subject to income tax and employee's Class 1 National Insurance contributions on any salary (but not fringe benefits) in the normal way. In addition, your company has to pay employer's National Insurance on your salary and many types of fringe benefit. Your company will have to collect these taxes by operating the PAYE system.
2 *Dividends*: you can receive these if you are a shareholder in the company. Dividends are normally subject to income tax but not National Insurance contributions. But see below for various ways in which the HMRC might challenge your dividend payments.

There is no income tax or National Insurance on salary up to the level of the personal allowance (£5,225 in 2007–8). But, provided you receive an amount at least equal to the lower earnings limit (£4,524 in 2007–8), you will be building up entitlement to certain state benefits such as state basic and additional retirement pensions. So it is worth paying yourself a salary of at least £5,225. Provided your pay is not excessive for the work you do, the company should be able to claim your pay as an allowable expense when working out the level of profit on which corporation tax will be due.

On some fringe benefits, neither you nor the company pay any tax or National Insurance. In particular, this applies to pension scheme contributions. So, if your company pays into a pension scheme for you, that can be a very tax-efficient form of pay. Once again, your company is able to claim corporation tax relief on the amount it pays into the pension scheme for you, but only if the contributions are 'wholly and exclusively' for the purpose of the business. In practice this means that your whole remuneration package, including salary and pension, must be in proportion to the value of the work you do for the company. If you would prefer to take a large proportion of your remuneration in the form of pension contributions rather than pay, you could arrange a 'salary sacrifice' where you formally give up part of your pay in return for pension benefits.

Often you will save tax by putting the rest of your 'pay' in the form of dividends, but get advice from your accountant* or other tax adviser*, especially if you provide your personal services to clients, e.g. as an IT contractor. Under legislation referred to as 'IR35', HMRC may argue that despite your personal services company you are in effect an employee of your client(s). In that case, HMRC can charge tax and National Insurance on a notional salary you are deemed to receive even if in fact your company pays you in dividends.

Following a change in the law in respect of shares you started to own from 2 December 2004 onwards, where you are an owner/manager of your own company and pay yourself mainly in the form of dividends, HMRC might seek to tax the dividends as if they are earnings if it can show that the main purpose of your mode of payment is to avoid paying tax or National Insurance.

It is common for companies owned and run by a husband and wife to minimize tax by paying dividends to both spouses, especially where this results in one or both paying income tax at less than the higher rate. However, through a test tax case generally referred to as *Arctic Systems*, HMRC has been trying to tax dividends paid to one spouse as income of the other if the latter earns all or most of the income coming into the company. HMRC argues that there is a gift from the main earner to the other spouse, which is caught by anti-avoidance 'settlements' legislation. In the most recent judgment concerning the case, the Court of Appeal did not agree with the HMRC's thinking and found for the taxpayer. But, at the time of writing, HMRC is appealing to the House of Lords which could either agree with or overturn the Court of Appeal ruling. For more information, see the HMRC* web site.

Spare-time earnings

There is no quick answer to the question of how you will be taxed if you have spare-time earnings. It will depend mainly on whether your income counts as starting a business. You might find yourself in a dilemma as to how your spare-time earnings will be taxed if:

■ you are still employed but earning some extra money in your spare time. You might be doing this either because you have started your business in a small way to see how it goes before you take the plunge and hand in your notice; or because you are doing the occasional bit of freelance work to boost your income.

■ you are not employed, but you are starting your business on a part-time basis. This could be the case if you are at home looking after young children, for example. Some people who earn extra income in this way hope that they will be able to keep it out of the clutches of the HMRC. Very often they ask for payment in cash. In the section *the black economy* (p. 379), you will see how HMRC can catch you and what the penalties are if you are caught.

What you must do

By law, you must notify your tax office when you get income from a new source. You have to do this within six months of the end of the tax year in which the income first arose. The onus is on you to tell your tax office, and you cannot plead as an excuse that you did not receive a tax return. Nor does it make any difference whether you are making a profit or a loss; what matters is that you are receiving payments from a new source that your inspector does not know about. If you do not tell your tax office about a new source of income, not only will you have to pay the tax due on that income but you will usually have to pay a penalty on top – up to the same amount again – plus interest on any tax paid late. The penalty will only be imposed if you haven't paid the tax by 31 January following the end of the tax year in question.

Bear in mind that, if the new source of income amounts to business income, you must in any case tell your tax office that you have started in business within three months or risk a fine (see p. 47).

You need to convince the inspector that your activities amount to a business, rather than just casual earnings. So follow this checklist.

1 Describe your activities as a business or profession.
2 Do not describe your income as 'occasional' or 'casual'.
3 Let your tax inspector know that you believe your sales will repeat and grow.
4 Register for VAT, even if you don't have to, if you consider it appropriate and it won't cost you money (see Chapter 30, 'VAT' (p. 382), for more details). You may have to persuade the VAT people to let you do this.
5 Get headed notepaper for your correspondence.
6 Be careful if your business is writing or consultancy. Explain to your tax office why you regard it as a business – for example, because your work

covers other aspects such as research and collation of information or because you carry out your profession or vocation on a regular basis.

7 Keep your accounting records carefully and on a businesslike basis. This is not just good business sense. It is a legal requirement that you keep records and documents used as a basis for working out your tax bill for five years and ten months after the end of the tax year to which the records relate. If you do not keep these records, or fail to produce them on request, you can be fined.

Casual income

If you don't succeed in convincing the tax office, your income could be treated as casual. Casual income will generally be taxed on an actual basis – that is, tax for any tax year will be based on the actual income you have from that source during the tax year. This contrasts with self-employment, where tax is based on the profits for an accounting period ending during the tax year. Self-employment gives you more scope for building in a time lag between making the profits and paying tax on them.

A disadvantage if your income counts as casual is that the treatment of losses is less favourable than if you are taxed as being self-employed. If you make a loss, it can only be deducted from profits taxed in the same way, made either in the same tax year or in the future. It cannot be deducted from any other income you have, for example from your job if you have one.

Property income

The tax treatment of property income is generally outside the scope of this book. However, if you run a hotel or guest house, your income will normally count as earnings from self-employment and be taxed as described on p. 355.

Income from other types of letting is not business income but is treated in a similar way. However many properties you rent out, the income is pooled and treated as a single source of income for tax purposes. You are taxed on the amount of this type of income you get during the tax year. In working out how much income you pay tax on, you use normal accounting rules and can deduct expenses – including interest on a loan to buy the property – in the same way as if you were running a business – see p. 352. However, you can't normally claim capital allowances for equipment and furnishings you provide. Instead, you can claim an allowance for wear and tear. This is based either on items you have actually replaced during the year – called the renewals basis – or on a proportion (usually 10 per cent) of the rents you get less council tax and water rates. You choose which basis to use. See p. 361 for the capital allowances you can claim.

Although your income from letting property is now treated in a similar way to earnings from a business, it still counts (as in the past) as investment income. This means, for example, that you can't use this income for making tax-efficient payments to a pension plan (see p. 398). However, see below for the special treatment of furnished holiday lettings.

If you let furnished holiday accommodation

If the property (including caravans) is let as furnished holiday accommodation for part of the year, the income will be treated as earned income, subject to certain conditions. This means, for example, that you will be able to get tax relief on these earnings for pension payments (p. 398), and you can get capital allowances for what you spend on equipment and furnishings you buy and use in your letting (p. 361).

To be treated as earned income, the property must be available for letting to the general public at a commercial rent for at least 140 days in any twelve-month period. It must also be let out as living accommodation for at least 70 of those days and not normally occupied by the same tenant for more than 31 days at a stretch during a seven-month period.

The black economy

It is illegal to try to conceal any earnings from your tax office. The tax officer has various ways of discovering that you are earning money. Employers who make use of freelance staff, such as consultants, writers and caterers, can be made to give details to HMRC of the payments made. There is also a department in HMRC that keeps an eye on advertisements in the press to make sure that any source of income has been declared. And if you annoy any neighbours, acquaintances or customers who suspect what you are doing, you also run the risk that they might inform on you to your tax office.

Once your tax office has started an inquiry into your affairs, you will find it very time-consuming. You may find you end up paying interest on unpaid tax from the day it was due until the date of payment; the current rate of interest is 6.5 per cent. On top of that, the tax officer can slap on penalties, for example:

- failure to tell your tax office about taxable income or gains within six months of the end of the tax year – up to the amount of the tax unpaid if it has not been paid by 31 January following the end of the tax year.

- failing to send in your tax return by 31 January following the end of the tax year – automatic penalty up to £100 with a further automatic £100 fine if the return is still outstanding six months later. After one year, a further fine equal to the amount of tax unpaid. If the failure persists, further penalties up to £60 a day can be imposed.

- fraudulently or negligently sending in an incorrect return – up to the amount of the tax unpaid.

- failure to produce documents requested by HMRC – initial penalty of £50 plus further penalties up to £30 a day if the failure continues.

- failure to retain and preserve records – a penalty of up to £3,000.

At the time of writing, the penalty system was under review and a new system is expected for tax returns filed from April 2009 onwards. Under the new system, there will be four levels of penalty, ranging from nothing for a genuine mistake to a hefty fine if you deliberately underpay tax and try to conceal it. The penalties may be reduced in line with the extent to which you own up and cooperate with HMRC.

Summary

1 Consider an accounting year end that will give the greatest delay between earning the profits and paying the tax if you expect profits to rise year by year. Choose fiscal accounting to keep your tax affairs simple.

2 Remember to claim all your business expenses. Where possible, get invoices and receipts to back up your claims.

3 If you use your car partly for business, you can claim part of your car expenses (and capital allowances). If you work from home, you can claim part of the running expenses, but watch out for CGT.

4 Try to cut down the risk of being investigated by your tax office. For example, do not omit items from your tax return, such as bank interest. If you know your profit margin is lower than others in the same business, or if you make a loss, explain why.

5 To avoid fines, keep an eye on the various tax deadlines: 31 October if you are filing a paper 2007–8 return, 31 January if you file online, and pay any outstanding tax by 31 January following the end of the tax year.

6 You must by law keep documents relating to your tax return and assessment for nearly six years. You'll be fined if you can't produce the necessary documents when asked.

7 Tell your tax office about any new source of earnings within six months of the end of the tax year in which the earnings first arose.

30

VAT

One subject that is guaranteed to raise ire among small businesses is VAT. Essentially, the VAT system is operated by businesses acting as tax collectors for the government. As far as the consumer is concerned, it is what is called an indirect tax. It is only paid by the consumer when something is bought, but the amount of VAT cannot be claimed back by a consumer. As far as you the business person are concerned, you pay tax when you buy goods from someone else and charge the tax when you sell them on. Broadly speaking, you hand over to Her Majesty's Revenue & Customs (HMRC) the difference between the amount of tax you charge your customers and the amount of tax you have paid your suppliers.

What is in this chapter?

- how the VAT system works (p. 383).
- who has to register? (p. 383).
- what rate of tax? (p. 386).
- voluntary registering (p. 387).
- how is the tax worked out? (p. 388).
- the records you need (p. 390).
- paying the tax (p. 393).

VAT is a complex tax, and this chapter can only outline the principles. The examples given are deliberately simplified. You are advised to ask for professional help with VAT if your affairs are at all complicated.

How the VAT system works

The principle of the system is that tax is paid on the value added at each stage of the business process.

Example

Jason King grows timber. He sells £1,000 of oak to A. J. Furniture, which will turn the oak into hand-crafted timber. He charges £1,000 for the timber and adds on 17½ per cent to the invoice for VAT. The total A. J. Furniture pays to him is £1,000 plus £175 VAT, £1,175 in all. Jason pays the £175 tax collected (called output tax) to HMRC.

A. J. Furniture makes the oak into ten tables. These are sold on to a furniture shop run by Doris Bates. Doris is charged £250 for each table plus VAT. On the invoice, this is shown as £2,500 plus £437.50 VAT. A. J. Furniture claims back the VAT charged by Jason King (called input tax), that is, £175, and hands over the VAT Doris pays to them, £437.50 (called output tax). This means a net payment of £437.50 − £175 = £262.50 to HMRC.

Doris sells the tables in her shop at a price of £500 plus VAT. She receives in total for the tables, £5,000 plus VAT of £875. When she makes her VAT return, she claims back the £437.50 VAT (called input tax) she paid to A. J. Furniture, while handing over the £875 VAT paid by the customers (called output tax), a net payment of £875 − £437.50 = £437.50.

The customers cannot claim back the VAT they have paid on the tables, but all the businesses are registered for VAT and can do so.

VAT is charged on what is called taxable supplies. In the example above, Jason King makes taxable supplies (the timber) of £1,000, A. J. Furniture makes taxable supplies (the tables) of £2,500 and Doris makes taxable supplies of £5,000 (the tables). Not all goods supplied to businesses are taxable; some are known as exempt, and VAT is not charged on those (see p. 384).

In VAT terms, the VAT that you charge on what you sell is called your 'output tax'. If registered for VAT, the business to which you sell claims back the VAT that it pays you as its 'input tax'. This is done when it makes its VAT return to HMRC.

Who has to register?

It is the person, not the business, who is registered for VAT. Each registration covers all the business activities of the registered person. For VAT purposes, a company is treated as a person. There are a number of reasons why you might not have to register. These include:

■ your sales (strictly, the amount of your taxable supplies, see overleaf) are too low, but you might still wish to register for VAT purposes and charge it on your sales (see below).

■ your business operates outside the VAT area (see below).

■ you make only exempt supplies (see below).

■ you carry out non-business activities (but you would still charge VAT on what counts as your business activities) (see opposite).

If you fail to register when you should do so – and you have 30 days' grace – HMRC can impose financial penalties. The penalty is five per cent of the tax due if registration is up to nine months overdue, 10 per cent if registration is more than nine but not more than 18 months overdue and 15 per cent if registration is more than 18 months late.

Your level of sales

You must register your business for VAT if your sales are above a certain limit (strictly, the limit is for the value of your taxable supplies, see below, rather than sales). The limit increases each year in line with the rate of inflation. From 1 April 2007, you must register if:

■ your sales in the previous year were more than £64,000 (but not if you can show that your sales will be less than this in the next year).

■ your sales in the next 30 days are likely to be more than £64,000.

Should your sales fall below the limit above, you can ask to have your registration cancelled. You would have to establish that your sales, excluding VAT, will be £62,000 or less for the next twelve months.

The area for VAT

VAT applies to England, Scotland, Wales, Northern Ireland and the Isle of Man. It does not include the Channel Islands. If you have customers or suppliers there, the goods you buy or sell will be treated as imports or exports.

What are taxable supplies and what are exempt?

Broadly speaking, if you supply goods and services in your business (including anything you take for your own use or sell to your staff), these will be taxable unless the government has specifically laid down that they are not. If they are not taxable, they are called exempt.

If all the goods or services that you supply are exempt, you cannot normally be registered for VAT. What this means for you is that you cannot claim back the VAT on any of the things you have bought for your business.

On the other hand, with a business composed of some taxable and some exempt supplies, you will still have to comply with the registration limits for the value of your taxable supplies. You will be able to claim back the VAT you have paid for the whole of your business if the value of your exempt input tax (that is, input tax relating wholly or partly to your exempt supplies) is not more than £625 per month on average and comes to no more than half your total input tax.

The main items that are exempt as far as VAT is concerned are, broadly speaking:

■ most sales, leases and lettings of land and buildings (but not lettings of garages, parking spaces or hotel and holiday accommodation). Landlords of non-domestic buildings will be able to charge VAT on rent if they choose to do so.

■ providing credit.

■ insurance.

■ certain education and training.

■ most healthcare.

■ postal services.

■ most betting, gaming and lotteries.

■ certain supplies by undertakers.

■ membership benefits provided by trade unions and professional bodies.

What is business and what is non-business?

As far as the VAT system is concerned, business is supplying goods or services to someone else in return for something that could be regarded as payment; it does not need to be money. You must be supplying the goods on a continuing basis to be a business activity.

If you are carrying out only non-business activities, you cannot be registered for VAT; if you have some non-business activities, the VAT you can reclaim is reduced.

When is your registration cancelled?

Apart from you requesting it to be cancelled (see p. 384), your registration will be cancelled if:

- the business is closed down.
- the business is sold.
- you take a partner or become a sole trader rather than a partner.
- as a sole trader or partner, you change the business into a company and vice versa.

What rate of tax?

For taxable supplies, there are at present three rates of tax:

- the standard rate, currently 17½ per cent.
- a special five per cent rate applying to domestic fuel, installation of energy-saving materials in homes and women's sanitary products.
- the zero rate.

The standard rate is charged unless the government specifies otherwise.

These are the main supplies that are zero-rated at present:

- most food and drink, but not if supplied for catering, or certain items like chocolate, crisps and so on, which are regarded as 'non-essential', or 'hot food' to be taken away.
- books and newspapers.
- young children's clothing and footwear.
- public transport, but not taxis, hire cars or 'fun' transport, such as steam railways.
- exports.
- sales of, and the construction of, new domestic buildings only.
- dispensing prescriptions.
- mobile homes and houseboats.

Do not confuse exempt and zero-rated. The effect of the two categories is quite different. Neither charges VAT on what they sell, but the exempt category cannot claim VAT back on what they have paid, while the zero-rated category can. Costs for the exempt category are likely to be up to 17½ per cent higher than the costs for the zero-rated category.

Voluntary registering

You can apply to register even if the value of your taxable supplies is below the limit. You have to satisfy HMRC that you are making taxable supplies in your business. There are two reasons why you might apply to register even if your sales are likely to be below the limit (p. 384). In both cases, registering will mean lower costs.

The first instance would be if you sell to businesses that can claim back VAT, so charging the 17½ per cent on your sales will not mean you lose business. If this is the case with you, consider applying to register. You may still decide not to if the administrative set-up is too difficult, for example if you sell a large number of low-value items. But if you register, your costs could be as much as 17½ per cent lower than they otherwise would be. See Example 1 below.

Example 1

Susan Hammond runs a car hire service. Her main customers are businesses. She considers whether she should apply to register for VAT, although her present sales of £25,000 are below the limit. Her costs are £10,000 including VAT of £1,000 (she is not charged VAT on all the goods and services she purchases).

If she registers, she will have to charge VAT of £4,375 on her sales of £25,000, but her customers can claim this back. She can claim back the £1,000 of VAT (input tax) she has paid on her purchases. The net result is that she receives £25,000 from her sales, claims back £1,000 VAT and pays £10,000 to her suppliers. Her income goes up from £15,000, before registering, to £16,000, after registering.

An alternative would be to lower her prices as her costs are now lower, but this does not seem necessary as she is not losing sales because of the price she charges.

The second instance when registering is beneficial if your sales are zero-rated but you are paying VAT on the goods you buy in. See Example 2 below.

Example 2

Barbara Croft runs a business making bibs and similar items for babies. Consumers cannot claim VAT back, but clothing for children is zero-rated, so she does not charge VAT. Her sales are £15,000 and her costs are £5,000, including VAT of £500. If she did not register, her income would be £15,000 − £5,000 = £10,000. This would be increased by £500 to £10,500 if she can register voluntarily.

How is the tax worked out?

What do you charge VAT on?

You charge VAT on the taxable sales you make; this is known as output tax. The amount of VAT is worked out on the price for the goods or services you are supplying. Occasional sales of second-hand goods are treated in the same way as new goods, but if your business involves buying and selling second-hand, you'll usually be covered by a special scheme.

You cannot escape charging VAT if you decide to take other goods, for example, rather than money in full payment or in part exchange. In this case, you have to work out the VAT to add on the basis of the open-market value of the goods or services you are supplying.

With discounts, the treatment varies depending on the type of discount. If the discount is unconditional, the VAT is charged on the discounted amount. This is also what applies if the discount is for prompt payment. Whether the customer pays promptly or not, VAT is worked out on the discounted amount. If the discount you offer is dependent on something happening later, for example the customer buying more, VAT is worked out on the full amount for the first payment. If the discount is subsequently taken, the VAT is adjusted at that time. Packaging is treated as part of what you are selling, so there will normally be no extra VAT to pay; and if the thing you are selling is zero-rated, that also applies to the packaging. With delivery, if you charge extra for it, VAT is due on that extra amount. But if the delivery is included in the selling price, no extra VAT is due.

Exports of goods are normally zero-rated, and this also applies to many exports of services, although some are standard-rated.

What you can claim VAT back on

You can claim back VAT on the goods and services you use in your business; these include imports and goods you remove from bonded warehouses. However, there are some supplies on which you cannot claim back the VAT. These include:

■ motor cars (but private taxi and self-drive hire firms and driving schools can recover the VAT they pay on cars purchased for their businesses; however, they will have to pay VAT on any private use. And businesses that lease cars to them can claim back the VAT on cars bought on or after 1 January 1994. In both cases, VAT has to be paid on the ultimate sale of the car).

■ business entertainment expenses.

■ if you are a builder, on certain things you install in buildings.

■ on some imports if you do not wholly own them.

■ on assets of a business transferred to you as a going concern (because you should not have been charged VAT if the going concern conditions have been met).

■ on goods that are zero-rated or are exempt supplies (because you have not been charged VAT).

Working out the amount of input tax you have paid

In Chapter 28, 'Keeping the record straight' (p. 340), you can see how to organize your records to obtain the information you need for VAT purposes. There are also guidelines overleaf on some of the records you need. Basically, if your business is very simple, you can work out the input tax like this:

1 Get all your purchase invoices in date order.
2 In your records (p. 345), you will have some way of showing the VAT you have paid on each invoice.
3 You cannot claim back VAT on exempt or zero-rated supplies.
4 Some invoices show the amount of VAT you are charged, so these are quite straightforward. Enter the amount in the column marked VAT.
5 Other invoices are not so detailed and you will have to work out the amount of VAT yourself. See example below for how to do this.
6 Remember you can claim back only the proportion of VAT for goods that you use partially in your business. For example, if you run your business from your home, you could claim back the VAT only on the part of your telephone bill that was due to your business.

Example

Peter Taylor is working out what VAT he can claim back on some stationery he has purchased for his business. The amount of the VAT is not shown on the receipt he has from the shop. The stationery cost him £4.75. He needs to know the amount of the VAT and the net cost of the stationery.

He divides £4.75 by 1.175 or he does this sum: £4.75 × 1,000/1,175

Both calculations give the same figure, £4.04, which is the net cost; the amount of VAT he can claim back is £4.75 − £4.04 = £0.71.

The records you need

These are the main additional records you need for VAT purposes, and these must be kept for six years:

■ the tax invoice.

■ a VAT account showing the results for each tax period.

■ the returns to HMRC showing the VAT payable or repayable.

If you fail to keep your records properly, you can be charged a financial penalty. VAT inspectors will come to see you every so often to check that your records are satisfactory. Although you are still required by law to keep your records for six years, in the normal way, HMRC can go back only three years to review the amount of VAT you should have paid. However, in cases of fraud, HMRC can go back 20 years.

There are special rules about petrol used for your private motoring – check with your VAT inspector. But, broadly speaking, you must keep detailed records of your business and private mileage to support claims that the cost of your private mileage is not included in the business accounts.

Tax invoice

When you supply goods, you should send a tax invoice and keep a copy of it. Your ordinary invoice will do, as long as it includes the following details:

■ invoice number.

■ tax point (see opposite).

■ your name and address.

■ your VAT registration number.

■ your customer's name and address.

■ a description of the goods or services you have supplied. This should include the quantity supplied, the charge without VAT, the rate of VAT, the rate of any cash discount and the total VAT charged.

■ the unit price of the goods or services.

If you are supplying goods and services direct to the public, for example as a shop, you don't need to give a tax invoice unless you are asked for one. And you do not need to provide such detailed invoices for items that are £100 or less, including the VAT. Nor do you need to keep copies of these. There are a number of special schemes for retailers, as it would be very time-consuming to keep records of every single sale, although the use of these schemes is being restricted in the light of new technologies that do now enable shopkeepers to work out the precise amount of VAT due on their sales.

A tax point is nothing more than the date on which you are liable to account for the VAT to HMRC; this is the date on which you provide the goods or services. However, if you issue a tax invoice or receive a payment earlier than this, the tax point is the date you issue the invoice or receive the payment, whichever happens first. If you issue a tax invoice up to 14 days after supplying the goods or services, and no earlier tax point has been created by a previous invoice or payment (as above), the date when you issue the invoice becomes the tax point. Finally, if you want to invoice monthly, you can use a monthly tax point, but you must have written approval from HMRC first.

VAT account

The results for each VAT period need to be summarized separately in your accounting records. This should show the totals of input tax and output tax and the difference between the two, either a repayment to you or the amount due to HMRC.

VAT return

This is the form which you need to fill in at the end of each VAT period, normally every three months, although if you are constantly claiming a repayment, for example because you are zero-rated, you can arrange monthly returns. In the return, you show the information you put in your VAT account; see above. You also enter any bad debts you may have. As a check for HMRC, you have to enter the figures for your total purchases and total sales for the period.

By 2009–10, all companies and self-employed businesses with annual turnover exceeding £100,000 will have to file VAT returns online (see p. 394).

The VAT period can be arranged to coincide with your accounting year end, which can make keeping your records much more convenient. And to simplify it even more, you can go over to a system of annual accounting for VAT – see overleaf.

There is a misdeclaration penalty that can be imposed. If you make an error in your VAT return of 30 per cent of the gross tax (output and input tax) or

£1 million, the penalty charged could be 15 per cent of the VAT due. However, you will not normally have to pay this unless the net tax you have under-declared or over-claimed is more than £2,000 in the period and you have made a voluntary disclosure. However, you will have to pay interest on under-declared VAT.

VAT flat-rate scheme

Businesses with a taxable turnover up to £150,000 can opt to join a flat-rate VAT scheme. This can cut the administration involved. Instead of keeping a record of your inputs and outputs and calculating the VAT due to be paid or reclaimed, under the flat-rate scheme you simply pay VAT as a percentage of your tax-inclusive turnover (including all reduced, zero-rated and exempt income). In most cases, the only VAT records you will need to keep are the relevant turnover figures and the flat percentage rate being used. However, you will still have to send out VAT invoices, and you might want to continue calculating your VAT in full to keep an eye on whether you are paying more or less VAT under the flat-rate scheme. If you find you are persistently paying extra, consider opting back out of the scheme.

The flat rate to be used is set by HMRC and depends on the type of business you are in. The rates vary from two per cent for food retailers up to 13.5 per cent for building labourers, though there is a one per cent reduction for newly VAT-registered businesses during their first year. The rates are designed to reflect the average VAT payable by firms in the particular sector. Whether you'll pay more or less VAT if you join the scheme depends on whether your VAT payments are usually more or less than the average for your particular industry. For more information, see HMRC leaflet 733 *VAT flat rate scheme for small businesses.*

Annual accounting

Instead of filling in a VAT return every three months, relatively small businesses can instead switch to annual accounting. This offers three advantages:

1 More predictable cash flow because you make regular payments on account throughout the year.
2 A possible cash flow advantage, especially if your turnover is tending to increase each year.
3 Less paperwork – and lower fees if you use an accountant – because you send in just one VAT return a year.

Annual accounting is open to your business if you have a yearly taxable turnover of no more than £1,350,000. You can continue in the scheme until your taxable turnover reaches £1,600,000 a year.

The basic scheme works as follows: you and the VAT office agree an estimate of your likely VAT for the forthcoming year – usually this will be based on what you paid last year. You pay $\frac{1}{10}$ of this amount by direct debit from the fourth month through to the 12th month of your VAT year. Within two months of the end of the year, you send in your annual VAT return, making a final balancing payment if further VAT is due or claiming a repayment if the instalments came to more than the total for the year.

If you prefer, you can opt to pay by three larger interim instalments plus a final balancing payment.

Whichever system of annual accounting applies, both you and the VAT office can adjust the interim payments during the year if new information suggests they are no longer appropriate – for example, if your turnover is well below the previous year, you might request that the interim payments be reduced. You can withdraw from an annual accounting scheme at any time by writing to your VAT office.

Paying the tax

Any VAT that is due to HMRC is payable within one month of the end of the quarterly accounting period or within two months of the end of an annual period. This is regardless of whether you have actually yet received the money from your customers for the VAT due.

If you fail to pay your VAT on time, you are given a warning and could face surcharges. However, penalties are not automatically applied if yours is a small business (with a turnover up to £150,000). Instead, HMRC will initially offer you help and advice to remedy your late payment problem.

Small businesses can pay VAT on a cash accounting basis. With this you pay VAT due only when you have been paid by your customer and claim it back only when you have paid your supplier. You don't have to pay VAT on bad debts. You can opt to use this scheme if your taxable turnover is £660,000 or less, you don't owe any VAT (or, if you do, you have made arrangements with your VAT office for its payment), your VAT returns are up to date, and you haven't been convicted of a VAT offence or assessed for dishonest conduct. You can remain in the scheme until your taxable turnover reaches £825,000.

The government has proposed to increase the turnover threshold for businesses joining the scheme from £660,000 to £1,350,000, but is awaiting EU approval for the change.

You can claim relief from VAT for bad debts that are six months old and that you have written off in your accounts. You can go back three years to claim bad debt relief. However, if you adopt the cash accounting scheme, you automatically get relief from bad debts by never having to pay VAT on them at all.

If you have paid too much VAT as a result of an HMRC error, you have the right to ask for interest on the amount of the incorrect payment. You can go back three years to claim back overpaid VAT.

Compulsory online filing

At present, you can choose whether to file your VAT returns online or to carry on sending your returns in by post. But, by 2009–10, all companies and self-employed businesses with annual turnover exceeding £100,000 will have to file VAT returns online. The intention is that, progressively, all businesses will be brought into the compulsory online filing scheme, though the government has said that the earliest this will affect the smallest existing self-employed businesses is 2012.

If you file your VAT returns online, you must pay the VAT due electronically. For example, you can set up a direct debit arrangement and initiate the payment online at the same time as you file the return. Alternatively, you can instruct your bank when each payment is due to make the transfer by BACS.

Summary

1 You do not need to register if the value of your sales is too low, but it could still be worthwhile to apply to do so if you sell to businesses that can claim back the VAT or if you are zero-rated.

2 Do not confuse zero-rated with exempt supplies. If you supply only exempt goods, you cannot claim back VAT on goods you purchase.

3 If the level of your sales falls below a certain limit (£62,000 from 1 April 2007) you can ask to have the registration cancelled.

4 You may save on administration and may also save tax if you switch to the VAT flat-rate scheme. You do not have to stay in the scheme if you find it results in your paying extra tax.

5 You can save on administration and may benefit from cash flow advantages if you opt for the annual accounting scheme.

Other chapter to read

28 Keeping the record straight (p. 340).

31

Pensions and retirement

No doubt all your thoughts and energies are devoted to making your business successful, but spare a thought for what will happen when you retire. Your business might be the sort that you will be able to sell when it comes to retirement. This means you could have a lump sum that you can invest to give yourself an income to live on.

But with lots of self-employed people this is not so; if they retire, the business retires too, because their skills are essential to the success of their enterprise. Even if you hope that you will be able to sell your business on retirement, there is no certainty of this, and you should show some caution in relying on it. You may be forced to retire earlier than you had intended because of ill health, and this might coincide with a bad patch in your business fortunes. Or you may simply not be successful in building your business sufficiently to be able to sell for the sort of sum of money you need. The prudent course is to make separate arrangements to provide yourself with a pension.

This chapter looks at how to build up a pension during your working life. It also looks briefly at what happens from a tax point of view if you sell or give away your business on retirement.

What you get from the state

If you are self-employed, you will pay Class 2 National Insurance contributions. If you have set up a limited company and count as an employee of the company, you will pay Class 1 contributions (and the company will pay employer's contributions), assuming you are paid a salary of more than a given amount. Both these contributions will entitle you to the basic state pension, assuming you have paid sufficient contributions during your lifetime. The Class 4 contributions you make as a self-employed person do not increase your pension.

If you count as an employee of your company, even if you are a director, you may be building up an entitlement under a state additional pension scheme. Formerly this was the State Earnings Related Pension Scheme (SERPS) but was replaced from April 2002 onwards with the state second pension (S2P). Both you as an employee and your company as an employer will pay additional National Insurance contributions. This is known as being 'not contracted-out'. If you contract out, the contributions are either reduced or partially rebated and instead of building up S2P, you build up a pension in either an occupational pension scheme or your own personal plan.

S2P is currently an earnings-related pension. It is much more generous than its predecessor, SERPS, for some groups of people: employees earning at least £4,524 but less than £13,000 in 2007–8; many people caring for young children or, say, an elderly relative, and some people who are long-term sick or have a disability. All these groups build up S2P as if they have earnings equal to £13,000 in 2007–8.

At the time of writing, a Pensions Bill was being considered by Parliament that, if passed, makes the following changes to the state pension system:

■ *raise the state pension age in stages to 68:* overall, people are tending to live longer. Therefore, with an unchanged pension age, they would spend longer in retirement and so their pensions would cost more. To contain the cost, state pension age is being increased – see the table on p. 398.

■ *make it easier to build up the full state basic pension:* at present, with a state pension age of 65, you need 44 years of National Insurance contributions and/or credits to qualify for the full basic pension. The Pensions Bill reduces this to just 30 years. It also simplifies and extends the system of giving credits to people who are caring for children or dependent adults. These measures will help women in particular to achieve higher state pensions.

■ *increase the basic state pension in line with earnings once it starts to be paid:* since 1979, state pensions have been increased only in line with price inflation. This means that, although the pension retains the same buying power year after year, pensioners have not shared in the growing prosperity of the economy. While people in work have enjoyed above-inflation increases in their wages, pensioners dependent purely on the state have become poorer relative to the working population. From a date expected to be April 2012 onwards, the measures in the Pensions Bill will link the state basic pension to earnings to prevent further erosion of the basic pension.

■ *turn the state second pension into a flat-rate scheme*: the way S2P is structured, it would eventually have automatically become a flat-rate scheme paying a pension to all based on earnings equivalent to £13,000 today. The Pension Bill measures speed up the rate at which this change happens. It means that middle and high earners will get less S2P in future. The Bill also includes measures to abolish contracting out except for people who instead of S2P build up a pension in a salary-related occupational scheme.

Your state pension age

Sex and date of birth	State pension age
Woman born up to 5 April 1950	60
Woman born 6 April 1950 to 5 April 1955	Between 60 and 65
Woman born 6 April 1955 to 5 April 1959 Man born up to 5 April 1959	65
Man or woman born 6 April 1959 to 5 April 1960	Between 65 and 66
Man or woman born 6 April 1960 to 5 April 1968	66
Man or woman born 6 April 1968 to 5 April 1969	Between 66 and 67
Man or woman born 6 April 1969 to 5 April 1977	67
Man or woman born 6 April 1977 to 5 April 1978	Between 67 and 68
Man or woman born 6 April 1978 onwards	68

If you are self-employed

The simplest way of increasing your pension is to start paying money into a personal pension. Because you can get tax relief on what you pay at your highest rate of tax and your money is put into a largely tax-free fund, doing this may be the best way of saving for retirement. Stakeholder pension schemes are personal pensions that meet certain conditions on low costs and flexibility:

■ *low charges*: charges must total no more than one per cent a year of the value of your pension fund where you started the scheme before 6

April 2005. For schemes started on or after that date, the maximum charge is 1.5 per cent a year for the first 10 years and one per cent thereafter.

■ *flexibility*: the minimum contribution can be no more than £20. You decide when or how often to pay.

■ *portability*: you can transfer out of a stakeholder scheme without penalty. Stakeholder schemes must accept transfers from other pension schemes and plans.

■ *simplicity*: the scheme must include a default investment option, if you don't want to choose an investment fund for yourself.

■ *information*: you must get a statement at least once a year showing you the value of your scheme. If charges alter, you must be informed within one month of the change.

A personal pension will pay out an income; the size depends on how long and how much you have saved, although there are limits imposed on how much you can save (see p. 400). It also depends on how well the investments in the pension fund have done and the level of annuity rates when you retire. You can choose when you want to start receiving the benefits from the plan, but currently it must be somewhere between ages 50 (rising to 55 by 2010) and 75.

Under the government's package of measures aimed at increasing future retirement incomes, it intends to establish a new system of low-cost personal pension accounts from 2012. Employees will be automatically enrolled into this system (but can opt out) and both they and their employer will contribute to their accounts. Self-employed people will not be automatically enrolled and there will be no compulsory contributions for them, but they can choose to join the system if they want to.

Personal pensions

Personal pensions can be very flexible, provided you choose the right plan. For example:

■ you can invest a lump sum when you want or save on a regular basis.

■ you can alter the premium from time to time.

■ the pension can be level or start off lower but increase each year.

■ you can choose a smaller joint-life pension, which will be paid as long as either of two people is alive.

■ most plans offer an 'open-market option', which allows you to shop around to see if you can use the sum of money you have built up with one company to get a higher pension from another company.

■ you can normally choose to take a lower amount of pension and have a tax-free lump sum as well.

■ some schemes let you put off buying a pension (an 'annuity') at the time you retire and draw an income direct from your pension fund instead. This is useful if annuity rates are poor at the time you retire, but it is an option only suitable for large pension funds of £250,000 or more, say.

■ generally, you can use your pension scheme to back up a mortgage in much the same way as an endowment mortgage.

■ most of the plans have loanback facilities, which allows you to use your pension to get a loan.

■ self-invested personal pensions (SIPPs) give you wide freedom to choose how your pension fund is invested, including investment in commercial property, which opens the way for your pension fund to own your business premises and lease them back to you.

Getting tax relief

Personal pensions are efficient ways to save for retirement because they have the benefit of several tax advantages. You get tax relief on what you pay in, your investment builds up largely tax-free, and you can take part of the proceeds at retirement as a tax-free lump sum.

Because of these tax breaks, the government limits the amount you can invest. But under new rules, which came into effect from 6 April 2006, the limits are fairly generous and enable most people to invest as much as they wish through pension schemes. The main limits – which apply to the total of your savings through any number and types of pension scheme – are as follows:

■ *annual limit for tax relief*: you can pay as much as you like into a pension scheme but the maximum contributions on which you can get tax relief are the greater of £3,600 a year or 100 per cent of your UK earnings. Included in your UK earnings are profits from self-employment or working in a partnership, salary (but not dividends) you pay yourself if you operate as a company, and profits from renting out furnished holiday lettings (but not most other types of rental property). Anything paid into your pension scheme(s) by an employer (say, your company) does not count towards this limit.

Tax year ending 5 April	Lifetime allowance, £ million	Annual allowance, £
2008	1.6	225,000
2009	1.65	235,000
2010	1.75	245,000
2011	1.8	255,000

- ■ *annual allowance*: this is a cap on the increase over a year in the total value of your pension savings and is set at £225,000 for 2007–8. The table above sets out the allowance for subsequent years. If, as is likely, you are saving through the types of pension schemes where you build up a fund to be used at retirement to provide your pension (called money purchase schemes), this means that the total contributions paid in by you, your employer (if applicable) and anyone else should not come to more than £225,000 in 2007–8. If you break the limit, tax at 40 per cent is charged on the excess paid in. The annual allowance does not apply in the tax year in which you start to draw your pension, giving scope for large, last-minute contributions – perhaps following the sale of your business.

- ■ *lifetime allowance*: the total of your pension savings should not exceed this limit, which is set at £1.6 million in 2007–8 and increased in subsequent years broadly in line with inflation (see table above). Savings in excess of the lifetime limit are subject to tax at 55 per cent at the time they are drawn out of the scheme as a lump sum or 25 per cent if drawn out as taxable income.

If you are paying into a company pension scheme, your contributions are deducted from your pay before tax is worked out, so you automatically get income tax relief up to your highest rate on the contributions you make. There is no National Insurance relief on the contributions.

If you are paying into most other types of scheme, including personal pensions and stakeholder schemes, you get tax relief at the basic rate at source by handing over an amount from which you have already deducted the basic rate tax relief – see the example on p. 402. The pension scheme provider then claims the amount of basic rate relief from HMRC and adds it to your scheme. You get this basic rate tax relief even if you are a non-taxpayer or pay tax only at the starting rate. If you are a higher-rate taxpayer, you can claim extra tax relief through your tax return.

If you have a retirement annuity contract (a type of personal pension started before 1 July 1988), you may have to pay gross contributions of the full amount and then claim all the tax relief due through your tax return.

Example

Daniel Patterson is considering putting money aside for retirement. His self-employment earnings in 2007–8 are £60,000. This means the maximum he can pay into one or more pension schemes this year is £60,000. In fact, he needs some of his earnings to live on and decides he can afford to pay £7,800 into a personal pension.

The £7,800 is treated as a net contribution from which tax relief at the basic rate of 22 per cent has already been deducted. The pension provider claims £2,200 from HMRC and adds this to Daniel's scheme. This means that a gross contribution of £7,800 + £2,200 = £10,000 goes into the scheme.

Daniel pays tax at the highest rate of 40 per cent on at least £10,000 of his 2007–8 earnings, so he can claim further tax relief through his tax return. Tax relief at 40 per cent on the £10,000 contribution comes to £4,000. But Daniel has already had basic rate relief of £2,200. So he gets further relief of £4,000 − £2,200 = £1,800.

A total of £10,000 has gone into Daniel's pension scheme at a cost to him of £7,800 − £1,800 = £6,000.

From 2008–9, the basic rate of tax falls to 20 per cent. If Daniel continues to pay £7,800 into the scheme, he will get basic rate relief of only £1,950. This brings the gross contribution to £7,800 + £1,950 = £9,750. Daniel can claim higher rate relief of (40% × £9,750) − £1,950 = £1,950. If Daniel still wants £10,000 in total to go into his scheme, he will need to increase his net contribution to £8,000.

Choosing a personal pension

Many schemes are available, and it is very difficult to choose which is the right personal pension. An independent financial adviser (IFA)* can help, but they have differing levels of expertise, so you should shop around in the same way as you do for your business insurance.

You can choose between a pension plan from, say, an insurance company, bank, building society, unit trust manager, fund supermarket or discount broker. There are different types of personal pensions, including:

■ *with-profits*: the insurance company invests your money as it thinks fit, often in bonds, shares and property. The company will guarantee a minimum pension or lump sum of money you will get, but this will be fairly low. However, you stand the prospect of receiving a higher pension in the end, because the company adds bonuses to your pension, depending on the profits it makes on its investments. The company aims to smooth the bonuses by holding back some profits from good years to hold up the bonus rate in lean years, but there is no guarantee that a bonus will be paid every year. Usually, annual bonuses once added to your plan can't be taken away, but you might lose some of these bonuses if you transfer your plan to another company.

■ *unit-linked*: with this type of policy, you have some choice as to how your money is invested. Commonly, you can choose for the money to be invested in property, shares, fixed-interest investments such as gilts, cash investments such as bank deposit accounts or you can choose to invest in a mixture of all these. With a unit-linked plan, the value of your pension is directly linked to the value of the investments, so it can fluctuate. This could be a problem if values happen to be low when it comes to retirement.

■ *deposit-administration scheme*: these give a safe, if unexciting, return similar to a bank or building society account.

■ *self-invested*: you build your own portfolio of investments. These might be individual shareholdings, some unit trust holdings, gilts, corporate bonds – you choose. Charges for self-invested plans are often higher than for fund-based plans.

Nearly all personal pensions expose you to investment risk. This means the value of your pension fund – and so the pension you can buy with it – can fall if share prices or other investments tumble. Bear in mind that a pension is a long-term investment, so a short-term slide in the stock market need not necessarily concern you (and could in fact be a good opportunity to pay extra into your pension). However, a fall in share prices shortly before retirement could be disastrous, so in the ten years or so before retirement, you should aim progressively to shift your pension fund away from shares and into safer investments, such as bonds and deposits.

If you are the director of a company

If you are a director of a small company, you can take out a personal pension in the same way as if you were self-employed.

The company could set up a special sort of occupational pension scheme (called a small self-administered scheme or SSAS) for you and other employees of the business. But, since 6 April 2006, when a single uniform set of rules started to apply to all types of pension scheme, there is little to choose between a SSAS and a self-invested personal pension (SIPP). With both:

■ *you can choose how the pension scheme invests its fund*: this can include for example buying commercial property or other assets to be used by the company.

■ *the scheme can make a loan up to half the value of its assets to your business*: the loan must be secured, interest must be charged at a commercial rate, repayments must be made regularly, and the maximum term is five years.

This area of pensions is very specialized. If you do want to go ahead, consult an independent financial adviser* or other adviser with specialist knowledge, but don't be rushed into decisions by salespeople. Consider straightforward ideas too, like a personal pension.

When you retire or sell

If you retire and sell, give away or dispose of your business you may have to pay capital gains tax. However, taper relief, which is particularly generous for business, was introduced from 1998–9 onwards and was made significantly more generous from 2000–1 and 2002–3 onwards. Full relief is available once you have held a business asset for just two years or more. At that stage, your gain is reduced to one-quarter of its original amount. For example, if you bought an asset in April 2006, you will qualify for the maximum relief on its disposal, provided you hold on to it until April 2008.

If you give away business assets (doesn't need to be at retirement), your gift can be free of inheritance tax. Business relief means that there will be no inheritance tax to pay on business assets such as goodwill, land, buildings, plant, stock and patents. If the business is a company, you can also get 100 per cent business relief on transfers of the shares. Agricultural relief can mean no inheritance tax on owner-occupied farmlands and farm tenancies (including cottages, farm buildings and farm houses). Get advice from an accountant* or other tax adviser*.

Summary

1 Saving for retirement through a pension scheme can be very cost-effective. This is because you can get tax relief at your highest rate of tax.

2 A self-invested personal pension (SIPP) or small self-administered scheme (SSAS) can give tax-efficient support to your business by, for example, owning its property or lending it money.

3 Taper relief reduces capital gains tax when you dispose of your business or shares, if you meet certain conditions.

4 There may be no inheritance tax to pay on your business when you give it away or leave it on your death.

References

This section provides a handy list of further reading and names and addresses of organizations. The inclusion of any commercial organization in this section is not to be taken as a recommendation. You must rely on the usual precautions, for example taking up references.

Useful web sites

The Internet is a handy source of information, news and advice. Two sites worth investigating are my company's web sites *www.smallbusiness.co.uk* and *www.growthbusiness.co.uk*. Also have a look at:

www.britishchambers.org.uk
www.businesslink.gov.uk
www.bvca.co.uk (funding)
www.bbaa.org.uk (business angels)
www.companies-house.gov.uk
www.dberr.gov.uk/employment (employment law)
www.hmrc.gov.uk (tax and VAT)
www.frc.org.uk/asb/technical/frsse.cfm (accounting rules for small businesses)

Directory web sites

Kellys: *www.kellysearch.co.uk*
Kompass: *www.kompass.com*
Yell: *www.yell.co.uk*
Thomson Directories: *www.thomweb.co.uk*

Search engines

www.alltheweb.com
http://uk.ask.com
www.google.co.uk

www.lycos.co.uk
www.ukdirectory.co.uk
www.ukplus.co.uk
www.webcrawler.com
www.yahoo.co.uk

Web sites with businesses for sale

Business For Sale: *www.businessforsale.com*
Business Base: *www.ukbusinessbase.com*
Dalton's Weekly: *www.daltonsbusiness.com*
Exchange and Mart: *www.exchangeandmart.co.uk*
Nationwide Business: *www.nationwidebusiness.co.uk*

Web sites with information about vacant premises

www.startinbusiness.co.uk

Web sites selling mailing lists

www.marketingfile.com
www.businessmailing.co.uk

Contacts

Advisory, Conciliation and Arbitration Service (ACAS). Helpline (employment queries): 08457 47 47 47. Equality Direct Helpline (small business queries on equality): 08456 00 34 44. Publications: 08702 42 90 90. *www.acas.org.uk*

Accountant: to find one, look in *Yellow Pages* under 'Accountants'; or for a list of members in your area, see separate entries for Association of Chartered Certified Accountants and the Institute of Chartered Accountants.

Advertising Standards Authority (ASA), Mid City Place, 71 High Holborn, London WC1V 6QT. Tel: 020 7492 2222. *www.asa.org.uk*

Angel Bourse, 35 Park Lane, Mayfair, London W1K 1RB. Tel: 020 7355 7820. *www.angelbourse.com*

Association of British Insurers (ABI), 51 Gresham Street, London EC2V 7HQ. Tel: 020 7600 3333. *www.abi.org.uk*

Association of Chartered Certified Accountants, 29 Lincoln's Inn Fields, London WC2A 3EE. Tel: 020 7059 5000. *www.acca.co.uk*

Association of Consulting Actuaries, Warnford Court, 29 Throgmorton Street, London EC2N 2AT. Tel: 020 7382 4594. *www.aca.org.uk*

Association of Tax Technicians, 12 Upper Belgrave Street, London SW1X 8BB. Tel: 020 7235 2544. *www.att.org.uk*

Audit Bureau of Circulations, Saxon House, 211 High Street, Berkhamsted, Hertfordshire HP4 1AD. Tel: 01442 870800. *www.abc.org.uk*

The Bankruptcy Association, FREEPOST LA1118, 4 Johnson Close, Lancaster LA1 5BR. Tel: 01524 782713 (weekdays 10am–12.30pm). *www.theba.org.uk*

British Bankers' Association (BBA), Publications Unit, Pinners Hall, 105–108 Old Broad Street, London EC2N 1EX. *www.bba.org.uk*

British Business Angels Association (BBAA), New City Court, 20 St Thomas Street, London SE1 9RS. Tel: 020 7089 2305. *www.bbaa.org.uk*

British Chambers of Commerce, 65 Petty France, London SW1H 9EU. Tel: 020 7654 5800. *www.britishchambers.org.uk*

British Exporters Association, Broadway House, Tothill Street, London SW1H 9NQ. Tel: 020 7222 5419. *www.bexa.co.uk*

British Franchise Association (BFA), Thames View, Newtown Road, Henley-on-Thames, Oxfordshire RG9 1HG. Tel: 01491 578050. *www.thebfa.org*

British Insurance Brokers' Association (BIBA), 14 Bevis Marks, London EC3A 7NT. Consumer Helpline: 0901 814 0015 (charged at 25p per minute). *www.biba.org.uk*

British Library Business Information, 96 Euston Road, London NW1 2DB. Tel: 020 7412 7454. Document Supply: Customer Services, Boston Spa, Wetherby, West Yorkshire LS23 7BQ. Tel: 01937 546060. *www.bl.uk*

British Rate and Data (BRAD). Tel: 020 7505 8458. e-mail: sales@brad.co.uk. *www.intellagencia.com*

British Standards Institute (BSI), 389 Chiswick High Road, London W4 4AL. Customer Services Tel: 020 8996 9001. *www.bsi-global.com*

British Venture Capital Association (BVCA), 3 Clements Inn, London WC2A 2AZ. Tel: 020 7025 2950. *www.bvca.co.uk*

Business in the Community, 137 Shepherdess Walk, London N1 7RQ. Tel: 0870 600 2482. *www.bitc.org.uk*

Business Eye (Wales). Tel: 08457 969798. *www.businesseye.org.uk*

Business Gateway. Tel: 0845 609 6611. *www.bgateway.com*

Business Link (England): to find your local Business Link, see *Phone Book* or Tel: 0845 600 9006. *www.businesslink.gov.uk*

Chamber of Commerce (or Trade): to find local branch, see *Phone Book* or contact British Chambers of Commerce (see separate entry).

Chartered Institute of Patent Agents, 95 Chancery Lane, London WC2A 1DT. Tel: 020 7405 9450. *www.cipa.org.uk*

Chartered Management Institute, Management House, Cottingham Road, Corby, Northants NN17 1TT. Tel: 01536 204222. *www.managers.org.uk*. CMI runs more than 40 courses a year. It also has a very comprehensive library of management-related data, including electronic databases. Some of its services carry charges.

The Chartered Institute of Taxation (CIOT), 12 Upper Belgrave Street, London SW1X 8BB. Tel: 020 7235 9381. *www.tax.org.uk*

Commission for Racial Equality (CRE), St Dunstan's House, 201–211 Borough High Street, London SE1 1GZ. Tel: 020 7939 0000. *www.cre.gov.uk*

Companies House, Tel: 0870 333 3636. *www.companieshouse.gov.uk*

- England and Wales: Crown Way, Maindy, Cardiff CF14 3UZ.

- Scotland: 37 Castle Terrace, Edinburgh EH1 2EB.

Co-operatives UK, 1st Floor, Holyoake House, Hanover Street, Manchester M60 0AS. Tel: 0161 246 2900. *www.cooperatives-uk.coop*

Department for Communities and Local Government, Eland House, Bressenden Place, London SW1E 5DU. Tel: 020 7944 4400. *www.communities.gov.uk*

Department for Business, Enterprise and Regulatory Reform (DBERR), Ministerial Correspondence Unit, 1 Victoria Street, London SW1H 0ET. Tel: 020 7215 5000.

- Employment law: *www.dberr.gov.uk/employment*

- DBERR does not provide service direct to businesses. Instead contact Business Link (see separate entry).

DirectGov. *www.direct.gov.uk*. This web site is intended to be a one-stop shop for all government information and services.

Direct Marketing Association (DMA), DMA House, 70 Margaret Street, London W1W 8SS. Tel: 020 7291 3300. *www.dma.org.uk*

Disability Rights Commission (DRC), DRC Helpline, Freepost MID02164, Stratford-upon-Avon CV37 9BR. Tel: 0845 7622 633. *www.drc-gb.org*

E-mail Preference Service, *www.dmaconsumers.org/emps.html*

English Heritage, Customer Services Department, PO Box 569, Swindon SN2 2YP. Tel: 0870 333 1181. *www.english-heritage.org.uk*

Environment and Energy Helpline, Tel: 0800 585794. *www.envirowise.gov.uk*

Equality Direct, Tel: 0845 600 3444. *www.equalitydirect.org.uk*

Equal Opportunities Commission (EOC), Arndale House, Arndale Centre, Manchester M4 3EQ. Tel: 0845 601 5901. *www.eoc.org.uk*

Euro Info Centres. To find nearest centre see *www.europe.org.uk*. These centres have been set up by the European Commission. They are designed to help the public and businesses get information on what the EU does.

Export Marketing Research Scheme. Contact British Chambers of Commerce (see separate entry).

Fax Preference Service Registration Line, Tel: 0845 070 0702. *www.fpson line.org.uk*

Federation of Small Businesses (FSB), Sir Frank Whittle Way, Blackpool Business Park, Blackpool, Lancs FY4 2FE. Tel: 01253 336000. *www.fsb.org.uk*

Finance and Leasing Association, 2nd Floor, Imperial House, 15–19 Kingsway, London WC2B 6UN. Tel: 020 7836 6511. *www.fla.org.uk*

Financial advisers: to find firms that can help you raise finance, ask your local Business Link (England), Business Eye (Wales), Scottish Enterprise or Highland and Islands Enterprise or InvestNI (Northern Ireland).

Financial Services Authority (FSA), 25 The North Colonnade, London E14 5HS. Consumer Helpline: 0845 606 1234. *www.moneymadeclear.fsa.gov.uk*. FSA Register: *www.fsa.gov.uk/register*

Food from Britain, 4th Floor, Manning House, 22 Carlisle Place, London SW1P 1JA. Tel: 020 7233 5111. *www.foodfrombritain.com*

Forum of Private Business (FPB), Ruskin Chambers, Drury Lane, Knutsford, Cheshire WA16 6HA. Tel: 01565 634467. *www.fpb.org*

Franchise directories: *Franchise World Directory* (£29.50) published by Franchise World, Highlands House, 165 The Broadway, London SW19 1NE. Tel: 020 8605 2555. *www.franchiseworld.co.uk*. For a constantly updated directory of all franchises available in the UK and Republic of Ireland. *www.franchiseadvice.com*

Growth Company Investor, Octavia House, 50 Banner Street, London EC1Y 8ST. Tel: 020 7250 7010. For information about the Alternative Investment Market (AIM) and PLUS. *www.growthcompany.co.uk*

Health and Safety Executive (HSE), Rose Court, 2 Southwark Bridge, London SE1 9HS. HSE Infoline: 0845 345 0055. *www.hse.gov.uk*

Highlands and Islands Enterprise, Cowan House, Inverness Retail and Business Park, Inverness IV2 7GF. Tel: 01463 234171. *www.hie.co.uk*

HM Revenue & Customs. For local tax office, see *Phone Book*. National Insurance Registration Helpline: 0845 915 7006. Helpline for Newly Self-Employed: 0845 915 4515. Self-Employed Contact Centre: 0845 915 4655. New Employer Helpline: 0845 60 70 143. Self-Assessment Helpline: 0845 900 0444. VAT National Advice Service: 0845 010 9000. Publications Orderline: 0845 9000 404. *www.hmrc.gov.uk*

Independent financial adviser (IFA) (to find one).

- IFA Promotion: Tel: 0800 085 3250. *www.unbiased.co.uk*
- The Institute of Financial Planning, Whitefriars Centre, Lewins Mead, Bristol BS1 2NT. Tel: 0117 945 2470. *www.financialplanning.org.uk*
- MyLocalAdviser. *www.mylocaladviser.com*
- The Personal Finance Society, 42–48 High Road, South Woodford, London, E18 2JP. Tel: 020 8530 0852. *www.thepfs.org*

Information Commissioner, Wycliffe House, Water Lane, Wilmslow, Cheshire SK9 5AF. Helpline: 08456 306 060. *www.informationcommissioner.gov.uk*

Insolvency Service. Enquiry line: 0845 602 9848. *www.insolvency.gov.uk*

Institute of Business Advisers (see Institute of Business Consulting)

Institute of Business Consulting (formed in April 2007 by the merger of the Institute of Business Advisers and Institute of Management Consultancy), *www.ibconsulting.org.uk*. While the new Institute is being created, see also:

■ Institute of Business Advisers, Chartered Management Institute, Management House, Cottingham Road, Corby, Northants NN17 1TT. Tel: 01536 207403. *www.iba.org.uk*

■ Institute of Management Consultancy, 3rd Floor, 17–18 Hayward's Place, London EC1R 0EQ. Tel: 020 7566 5220. *www.imc.co.uk*

Institute of Chartered Accountants in England and Wales, Chartered Accountants' Hall, PO Box 433, London EC2P 2BJ. Tel: 020 7920 8100. *www.icaew.co.uk*

Institute of Chartered Accountants in Ireland, CA House, 83 Pembroke Road, Dublin 4, Republic of Ireland. Tel: (00 353) 1 637 7200. *www.icai.ie*

Institute of Chartered Accountants of Scotland, CA House, 21 Haymarket Yards, Edinburgh EH12 5BH. Tel: 0131 347 0100. *www.icas.org.uk*

Institute of Directors, 116–123 Pall Mall, London SW1Y 5ED. Tel: 020 7839 1233. *www.iod.com*

Institute of Management Consultancy (see Institute of Business Consulting).

Institute of Patentees and Inventors, PO Box 39296, London SE3 7WH. Tel: 0871 226 2091. *www.invent.org.uk*

Institute of Trade Mark Attorneys, Canterbury House, 2–6 Sydenham Road, Croydon, Surrey CR0 9XE. Tel: 020 8686 2052. *www.itma.org.uk*

Insurance broker (to find one). See *Yellow Pages*. For members of British Insurance Brokers' Association, see separate entry. To check authorization, see entry for Financial Services Authority.

Invest Northern Ireland, Bedford Square, Bedford Street, Belfast BT2 7ES. Tel: 028 9023 9090. To find local office, see *Phone Book* or web site. *www.investni.com*

Jobcentre Plus. For local office, see *Phone Book* or web site. *www.jobcentre plus.gov.uk*

The Law Society of England and Wales, 113 Chancery Lane, London WC2A 1PL. Find a solicitor Tel: 0870 606 2555. *www.lawsociety.org.uk*

Law Society of Northern Ireland, 40 Linenhall Street, Belfast BT2 8BA. Tel: 028 9023 1614. *www.lawsoc-ni.org*

Law Society of Scotland, 26 Drumsheugh Gardens, Edinburgh EH3 7YR. Tel: 0131 226 7411. *www.lawscot.org.uk*

Lawyers for Your Business (England and Wales). For a list of lawyers in your area, e-mail: *lfyb@lawsociety.org.uk www.lawsociety.org.uk/choosingandusing/ helpyourbusiness/foryourbusiness.law*

Learn Direct. Tel: 0800 101 901. *www.learndirect.co.uk*

Learning and Skills Council – apprenticeship schemes. Tel: 08000 150 400. *www.apprenticeships.org.uk/employers*

Local authority. See *Phone Book* under the name of your authority or ask at your public library.

Local Enterprise Agency (LEA). To find a local agency, contact the National Federation of Enterprise Agencies or Business Link (see separate entries).

Local Enterprise Company (LEC) (Scotland). To find a local office, see *Phone Book* or Tel: 0845 607 8787. *www.scottish-enterprise.com*

London Stock Exchange, 10 Paternoster Square, London EC4M 7LS. Tel: 020 7797 1000. *www.londonstockexchange.com*

Mail Order Protection Scheme (MOPS). See entry for the Safe Home Ordering Protection Scheme.

Mailing Preference Service, DMA House, 70 Margaret Street, London W1W 8SS. Tel: 020 7291 3310. *www.mpsonline.org.uk*

Market Research Society, 15 Northburgh Street, London EC1V 0JR. Tel: 020 7490 4911. *www.mrs.org.uk*

National Association of Commercial Finance Brokers, 17 Gandy Street, Exeter, Devon EX4 3LS. Tel: 01392 491551. *www.nacfb.org*

National Business Register, Somerset House, 40–49 Price Street, Birmingham B4 6LZ. Tel: 0121 678 9000. Offers free information, advice and support on setting up a new business, new company, trade mark or brand and domain name. *www.start.biz/home.htm*

National Federation of Enterprise Agencies, 12 Stephenson Court, Fraser Road, Priory Business Park, Bedford MK44 3WJ. Tel: 01234 831623. *www.nfea.com*

Natural England, Northminster House, Peterborough, PE1 1UA. Tel: 0845 600 3078. *www.naturalengland.org.uk*

Newly Self-Employed Helpline (HM Revenue & Customs). Tel: 0845 915 4515.

Nominet UK, Sandford Gate, Sandy Lane West, Oxford OX4 6LB. Tel: 01865 332244. *www.nominet.org.uk*

Office for Harmonization in the Internal Market (OHIM), Avenida de Europa, 4, E-03008 Alicante, Spain. Tel: 00 34 96 513 9100. *http://oami.eu.int*

Office of Fair Trading, Fleetbank House, 2–6 Salisbury Square, London EC4Y 8JX. Tel: 08457 22 44 99. Publications: 0800 389 3158. *www.oft.gov.uk.* (But for consumer advice, information on specific consumer rights or to make a consumer complaint against a trader, call the Consumer Direct advice service on 08454 04 05 06.)

OneLondon Business Angels Network (OLBAN), GLE oneLondon, New City Court, 20 St Thomas Street, London SE1 9RS. Tel: 020 7403 0300. *www.gle.co.uk/commercialfinance*

Patent agent (to find one): consider a member of the Chartered Institute of Patent Agents or contact the Institute of Patentees and Inventors (see separate entries).

Planning officer: contact the planning department of the local authority (district, borough, unitary or metropolitan) for your area. See *Phone Book* under the name of your authority.

Postcomm, Hercules House, 6 Hercules Road, London SE1 7DB. Tel: 020 7593 2100. *www.psc.gov.uk*

Prince's Initiative for Mature Enterprise (PRIME), Astral House, 1268 London Road, London SW16 4ER. Helpline: 0800 783 1904. *www.primeinitiative.org.uk*

- PRIME Cymru, 16 Stone Street, Llandovery, Carmarthenshire SA20 0JP. Tel: 0845 601 8693. *www.prime-cymru.co.uk*

The Prince's Trust, 18 Park Square East, London NW1 4LH. Tel: 020 7543 1234 or Freephone: 0800 842842. *www.princes-trust.org.uk*

Professional Contractors Group, Heathrow Boulevard, 280 Bath Road, West Drayton UB7 0DQ. Tel: 0845 125 9899. *www.pcg.org.uk*

Recruitment and Employment Confederation, 15 Welbeck Street, London W1G 9XT. Tel: 020 7009 2100. *www.rec.uk.com*

Regional Development Agency (RDA), RDA National Secretariat, Broadway House, Tothill Street, London SW1H 9NQ. Tel: 020 7222 8180. *www.england rdas.com*

Royal Institution of Chartered Surveyors (RICS), Contact Centre, Surveyor Court, Westwood Way, Coventry CV4 8JE. Tel: 0870 333 1600. *www.rics.org.uk*

Royal Mail. To contact your local business sales centre Tel: 08457 950950. *www.royalmail.com*

Safe Home Ordering Protection Scheme (SHOPS) (formerly the Mail Order Protection Scheme), 18a King Street, Maidenhead SL6 1EF. Tel: 01628 641930. *www.shops-uk.org.uk*

Scottish Enterprise. To find local office, see *Phone Book* or Tel: 0845 607 8787. *www.scottish-enterprise.com*

Shell *Live*WIRE, Design Works Unit 15, William Street, Felling, Gateshead, Tyne & Wear NE10 0JP. Tel: 0845 757 3252. *www.shell-livewire.org*

Small Business Advice Service. *www.smallbusinessadvice.org.uk/sbas.asp*. Online advice service from the National Federation of Enterprise Agencies.

The Small Business Bureau, Curzon House, Church Road, Windlesham, Surrey GU20 6BH. Tel: 01276 452010. *www.smallbusinessbureau.org.uk*

Small Firms Enterprise Development Initiative (SFEDI), PO Box 159, Newton Aycliffe, DL5 6WE. *www.sfedi.co.uk*. Provides learning and skills support for small and home-based business owners.

Solicitor (to find one): look in *Yellow Pages* or for a list of their members in your area, see separate entries for the Law Societies.

Tax adviser (to find one): for tax compliance work consider a member of the Association of Tax Technicians or Chartered Institute of Taxation (see separate entries). For advice, consider a member of the Chartered Institute of Taxation.

Telephone Preference Service (TPS), DMA House, 70 Margaret Street, London W1W 8SS. TPS Registration line: 0845 070 0707. *www.tpsonline.org.uk*

UK Business Incubation, Faraday Wharf, Aston Science Park, Holt Street, Birmingham B7 4BB. Tel: 0121 250 3538. *www.ukbi.co.uk*

UK Intellectual Property Office, Concept House, Cardiff Road, Newport, South Wales NP10 8QQ. Tel: 08459 500505. Publications include *Patent protection, How to prepare a UK patent, Design registration, Applying to register a trade mark. www.ipo.gov.uk*

UK Science Park Association, Chesterford Research Park, Little Chesterford, Cambridge CB10 1XL. Tel: 01799 532050. *www.ukspa.org.uk*

UK Trade and Invest Information Centre. Trade & Investment Enquiry Service, Tay House, 300 Bath Street, Glasgow, G2 4DX. Tel: 020 7215 8000.

This is a government organization that supports businesses trading internationally. *www.uktradeinvest.gov.uk*

Valuation Office Agency, New Court, 48 Carey Street, London WC2A 2JE. Tel: 020 7506 1801. *www.voa.gov.uk*

Welsh Assembly Government, Cathays Park, Cardiff CF10 3NQ. Tel: 0845 010 3300. *http://new.wales.gov.uk*

■ Department for Education, Lifelong Learning and Skills (DELLS), *http://new.wales.gov.uk/topics/educationandskills*

■ Department for Enterprise, Innovation and Networks, *http://new.wales.gov.uk/topics/businessandeconomy*

Women Into Business, Curzon House, Church Road, Windlesham, Surrey GU20 6BH. Tel: 01276 452010. *www.smallbusinessbureau.org.uk*

Useful books and literature

As reference books:

Tolley's Capital Gains Tax 2007–8, £99.95 (LexisNexis)

Tolley's Corporation Tax 2007–8, £99.95 (LexisNexis)

Tolley's Value Added Tax 2007, £129.95 (LexisNexis)

Tolley's Employment Handbook, £92.00 (LexisNexis)

Tolley's National Insurance Contributions 2007–8, £109.95 (LexisNexis)

Tolley's Company Law Service (LexisNexis, looseleaf edition) £719.00 a year by subscription, covers the legal requirements of limited companies in great detail.

Forming a Limited Company by Patricia Clayton, £15.99 (Kogan Page)

The Company Secretary's Handbook by Helen Ashton, £16.99 (Kogan Page)

Law for the Small Business by Patricia Clayton, £15.99 (Kogan Page)

FT Guide to Personal Tax by Sara Williams and Jonquil Lowe, £12.99 (FT Prentice Hall) has a more detailed exposition of tax treatment for the sole trader, capital gains tax and dealing with self-assessment. Tel: 020 7250 7010 to buy copies over the phone. Also see the web site *www.taxguide.co.uk*, which has information and tips.

Bankruptcy Explained by John McQueen, £16.94 (Bankruptcy Association)

Discipline and Grievances at Work £4.95 (Advisory, Conciliation & Arbitration Service). Order from *www.acas.org.uk*

Successful Marketing for Small Business by Dave Patten, £9.99 (Kogan Page)

A useful book for those interested in permanent toe-dipping is the *Which? Guide to Working from Home* (latest edition is 2003) by Lynn Brittney, £4.74 from *www.amazon.co.uk*

The Business Plan Workbook by Colin Barrow, £19.99 (Kogan Page)

More details about franchises, including if you want to become a franchiser:

How to Choose a Franchise by Iain Murray, £9.99 (Kogan Page)

Tottel's Payroll Management Handbook, £68.95 (Tottel Publishing)

Index

accident book 245
accountants 105, 202–3
  and balance sheet 279
  and business plan 65
  and buying a business 83, 84, 87
  choosing 202–3
  and forecasts 289
  tax advice from 350, 376
accounting expenses, and tax 359
Accounting Standards Board 350
accounts 41–2, 72
  auditing 42, 202, 203
  of business for sale 86–7
  computerized 41, 194, 347
  franchisor 108
  help with 202–3
  taxation and 41–2, 350, 352
  year end 45, 72, 352, 353–4, 377, 380
adoption
  leave 232, 251
  pay (SAP) 232, 236, 251, 252, 254, 349
ADSL 196–7
advertising 136–48
  agencies 143, 207
  content of 142–3, 217–18
  direct response 139–44, 148
  and discrimination law 215, 218, 232–3
  for employees 215–19
  franchises 104, 108, 112, 117
  legal aspects 143–4
  media 141–3
  and reputation 135
Advertising Standards Authority 144
advertising strategy, aims 139
advisers 71, 72, 201–9, 350–1
  see also accountants; financial advisers; solicitors
Advisory, Conciliation and Arbitration Service (ACAS) 229, 235, 243, 251, 258, 261
age and business start-up 77–8
age discrimination 231, 245, 246, 248–50
  and dismissal 234
  in interviews 232, 233
  job adverts 218
  and pay 240
  and redundancy 260
agencies/agents
  advertising 143, 207
  business transfer 83
  company formation 40–1
  credit reference 315, 318
  debt collection 318
  enterprise 201
  patent 121, 124
  recruitment 219–20
  sales 161–2
  workers from 214
Alternative Investment Market (AIM) 208, 294, 322, 332
Angel Bourse 300
Arctic Systems 376
articles of association 50
assets
  of business for sale 84, 85, 90–1, 94, 96
  cash flow forecast 273
  current 281
  fixed 280–1, 346
  personal 39, 48
assisted areas 184, 192
Association of Charterd Certified Accountants 203
Association of Tax Technicians 350
attachment of earnings 236
Audit Bureau of Circulations (ABC) 142
auditing of accounts 42, 202, 203

balance sheet forecast 280–3, 288
bank 32, 203–5
  advice/guidance from 203–5
  charges and interest 275, 279, 313
  choice of 204–5
  Internet 313
  loans 46–7, 279, 294, 298–9, 331

operating your account 313–14, 321
overdrafts 283, 293–4, 298–9, 304,
    313–14
reconcilliation 343
statements 312, 343
bankruptcy 39, 52, 336–9
Bankruptcy Association 339
bereavement benefit 44
Better Payment Practice Campaign 315
black economy 377, 379–80
book-keepers 202–3
brand image 129, 133, 135
    building 138–9
    franchised product/service 103
break-even point 305, 306–9, 321
    calculating 307–9
    fixed costs increase and 307
    staff costs and 226–8
British Bankers' Association 205
British Business Angels Network 300
British Codes of Advertising and Sales
    Promotion 144
British Franchise Association 105, 113,
    117
British Insurance Brokers Association
    263
British Rate and Data (BRAD) 142, 219
British Venture Capital Association 301
broadband 196–7
brochures 72, 138, 207
budgets 310, 321
    cash 311–12
building societies 313
business angels 47, 81, 294, 300
    shareholder agreements 98–9
business entertainment expenses 360
Business Eye 27, 31, 33, 298
Business Gateway 27, 31, 33, 298
business ideas 9–11
    brainstorming session 11
    checklist analysis 61–2
    defining 11
    market based 10–11
    for part-timers 76, 79
    portfolio work 78–9
    skills-based 9–10
    see also buying a business
business incubators 188
business interruption insurance 265
Business Link 27, 29, 32, 33, 37, 65, 72,
    201
    and funding 298
    and potential failure 337
    and premises 184, 185, 189
    services offered 31, 289
    web site 230
business name see name, business

business plan 63–8, 70, 71
    content 65–7, 68
    help with 65, 68
    length 67
    number of plans 64, 64–5, 68
    objectives 63–4, 68
    presentation 67–8, 68
    who should write 65
Business Premises Renovation
    Allowance 184
business profile 81–2, 100
business rates see rates
Business Support Team 47
buy-ins and buy-outs 81, 99–100
buying a business 50, 80–100
    accounts 86–7
    assets 90–1, 94, 96
    changing 93
    debtors 90
    earnings multiple 96
    employees of 92
    goodwill 85, 90
    investigating 84–92, 100
    land and buildings 87–90
    liabilities 91
    negotiation 94, 96–8, 100
    plant and equipment 89
    professional advisers 202–3
    return on capital employed 96
    sales potential 91–2
    search for, guide 81
    searching for 82–4
    setting a price 93–6
    stock 89–90

capital
    balance sheet forecast 282
    cash flow forecast 273, 275
    expenditure 275
    start up 109
    working 293
capital allowances 361–5
    2007–8 361–3
    annual investment allowance 361
capital gains tax 187, 367–8, 404, 405
    roll-over relief 367–8
cars see vehicles
cash
    book 342–3, 344
    of business for sale 90
    conserving 311–12
    controlling 306, 311–13, 321, 324
        records 313, 341, 342–4
    daily balance 312
    forecasting requirements 291–2
    interest on 313, 321
    payments 342–3

receipts 342, 343–4
cash on delivery 316
cash discount for early payment 316
cash flow
  budgets 311–12
  forecast/s 68, 270–6, 284–5, 289,
    311–12, 321
cash with order 315
certificate of incorporation 51
chambers of commerce 27, 32
change management 332–3, 334
character: for business start-up 1–5
  checklist 54–6
charge card 313
charities and finance 297–8
Chartered Institute of Taxation 350
Child Support Agency 236
collective agreement 235
Commission for Racial Equality (CRE)
    230, 235, 245
communications 136, 193
  cost-effective 137–8
  equipment 195–7, 199
  Internet 196–7
  and location 183
community development finance
    initiatives (CDFIs) 297
Companies Acts 41, 52
Companies House 39, 41, 132, 133
  filing accounts 42
  name change 51
  registering with 40–1, 50
company law reforms 41, 50
company secretary 41, 49–50
competitive advantage 130, 331
competitors 20–1
  and pricing 174–5
complaints handling 164–5, 169
compulsory winding-up 338
computer systems 194–6, 199, 209
  network 196
constructive dismissal 229, 260
consultants 78, 79
Consumer Credit Act (2006) 144
Consumer Protection (Distance Selling)
    Regulations (2000) 144
contract hire 199
contracts 205
  employment 72, 215, 225, 233,
    234–5, 236
  franchising 103, 104, 105, 109,
    114–17
  and insurance 264
  price escalation clauses 327
contributory jobseeker's allowance 44–5
Cooperative Union 53
cooperatives 38

formation and principles 52–3
  legal forms 53
copyright 125–6
  cost 126
  design 125–6
  protection 126
corporate venturing scheme 302–3
corporation tax 274, 375
  relief for coprorate venturing schemes
    302–3
costs
  franchising 101, 106–9, 115
  reducing 324–6, 333
  of sales 276–8
  of staff 225–8, 279, 326, 359
    recruiting 225–8
counselling 30–2, 37, 65
credit 72, 315
  of business for sale 90
  controlling 266, 314–19, 321
    records 316, 349
  for customers 314–16
  from suppliers 319–21
  insurance 266
  terms 315–16, 321
credit card 313
credit reference agency 315
creditors 282, 283, 306
creditors' voluntary winding-up 338
criminal convictions and employment
    250
current assets 281
customers
  attracting 149–62
  complaints handling 164–5, 169
  customer care 164–5
    club concept 165
    response times 164, 169
  data gathering 166–8, 169
  giving credit to 314–16
  individual records 166–7
  information about 17
    databases 17, 166–8
    legal aspects 167–8
  lists of 150–1, 152, 154
  needs 13, 159
  new offers 168
  potential 17, 18
  and price 175–6, 181
  referrals 165
  relationships 163–9
  repeat purchases 169
  retaining 163
  using questionnaires 168

Daily Express 33
Dalton's Weekly 83

data gathering 166–8, 169, 195
data mining 166
data protection 167–8, 195, 224
Data Protection Act (1998) 195, 224
data sheets 139, 148
data warehousing 166
databases 209
  for acquisitions 84
  customer 17, 166–8
  marketing 148
  software packages 194–5
death of franchisee 106
debentures of business for sale 91
debt 306, 359
  age analysis 90
  of business for sale 90
  collection 317–19
    service 318
  delaying payment 319, 320–1
  factoring 318–19
  insurance against 266
  order of payment by liquidator 338
  and winding-up 338
debtors, and cash flow forecast 271
demonstrations 138, 158, 160
Department for Education and Lifelong
    Learning and Skills (DELLS) 27
Department for Business, Enterprise and
    Regulatory Reform 235, 243, 254,
    256, 261, 299
depreciation 279, 289, 346, 360
design 119, 122–4
  consultant 207–8
  protection 122–3
  registration 122–4
desk research 23–4
direct mail 25, 150–3
Direct Marketing Association 144
direct selling 19, 20
directories 144–2, 152
  franchise 113
directors 41, 301
  and insolvency 338, 339
  non-executive 78, 301
  obligations 51–2
  personal pensions 403
  state benefits 44–5
  tax liabilities 375–6
disability discrimination 230, 231, 232,
    234, 245, 246, 247, 251
Disability Discrimination Act (1995)
    247
Disability Rights Commission 235, 245,
    247, 251
disciplinary procedure 258
disclosure requirements 41
discounts 140, 151, 174, 316, 327, 342–3

discrimination 215, 231, 232–3, 245–51
  age 218, 231, 232, 233, 234, 240, 245,
    246, 248–50, 260
  criminal convictions 250
  disability 230, 231, 232, 234, 245,
    246, 247, 251
  equal pay 231, 235, 239–40
  guidance 251
  health 250–1
  and job adverts 218
  marital status 232, 234, 245, 246
  part-time employees 231
  racial 230, 231, 232, 234, 245, 246,
    247–8
  religious beliefs 231, 232, 245, 246,
    248
  sex 229–30, 231, 232, 233, 234, 245,
    246
  sexual orientation 231, 232, 245, 246
  trade union membership 231, 245,
    246, 250
dismissal of employees 210, 232,
    256–61
  amount of notice 260–1
  appeals 259
  constructive 229, 260
  and health of employee 250–1
  and incompetence 245
  instant 259
  and pregnancy 251, 252
  reasons for 257–8, 260
  three-step procedure 257, 258–9
  unfair 234, 256–7, 260
distance selling 144, 164–5
  cooling off period 165
Distance Selling Regulations 144
distributors 162
dividends 43–4
  tax 375–6, 376
documents – retention for tax purposes
    378, 380, 381
driving licence and recruitment 225,
    228
  criminal convictions 250
due diligence 301, 332
Dun & Bradstreet survey 305

e-commerce 70
e-mail 72, 193, 196
Early Growth Funds 302
earnings, spare-time 376–8
earnings multiple of business for sale 96
employees/staff 72, 210–28
  agency workers 214
  of business for sale 92
  and change 333
  commission-only 214–15

competence 244–5
contracts 72, 215, 225, 233, 234–5, 236
costs 225–8, 279, 326, 359
dismissal *see* dismissal of employees
emoluments 359
family members 213
fixed term contracts 215
freelance staff 213–14
fringe benefits 225, 241–2
health of 250–1
improving productivity 326
leave entitlement 231–2
    for dependents 254–5
legal life cycle 231–2
notice period 234
part-time 214, 231
probationary period 256
records 341, 348–9
recruitment 210, 210–28
    advertising 215–19
    break-even point 226–8
    costs 225–8, 228
    and discrimination law 232–3
    health and disablement 250–1
    job definition 211–12
    job offer 225
    medical 225, 228
    profile of candidate 215–16, 228
    through contacts 220
redundancy 231, 232, 249, 257, 260
rights 230
and tax 359
terms and conditions – written
    statement 232
time sheets 348
working time regulations 242, 349
see also dismissal
employer
    advice/guidance for 230, 235
    liability insurance 243, 263
    rights and duties 229–61
Employment Appeal Tribunal 252
employment bureaux 219, 220
employment law 229, 230
employment and support allowance 44
enterprise agency 201
enterprise areas 184, 192
Enterprise Capital Funds 302
enterprise investment scheme 47
entrepreneurs 3–4
environmental health 192
    working from home 187
Equal Opportunities Commission
    229–30, 235, 243, 245, 251
equal pay 231, 235, 236, 239–40
Equality Bill 2006 230

Equality Direct 246
Equality and Human Rights
    Commission 230, 246
equipment 72, 198–9
    of business for sale 89
    capital allowance 361–5
    hire purchase 198–9
    and insurance 264
    IT 194–7
    leasing 199
    outright purchase 198
        and investment allowance 198
estate agents 83, 188, 206
ethnic minorities, help for 35
European Investment Bank 302
European Patent Convention 120
European Union
    and design 123
    funding 297, 298
    patent/trade mark 120, 125
Exchange and Mart 83
expenses allowable against tax 356–60
    financial expenses 359
    general expenses 357–8
    legal expenses 360
    not normally allowed 360
    staff costs 359

factoring 318–19
failure 5, 335–9
    contributing factors 305
    family plan for 296
    reasons for 8
    warning signs 306, 336–7
family 69, 70, 185, 296
    checklist 56–7
    as employees 213
    insurance 268
    investment from 296
faxes 196, 197
FE colleges, direct recruitment from 220
Federation of Small Businesses 33–4
finance
    advice 202
    amount 291–2, 304
    and business plan 64–5
    in business plan 67
    franchising 109
    Phase 2 money 331–2, 334
    professional advisers 65, 202–3,
        208–9, 402, 404
    raising 46–7, 290–304
        from family 296
        government and local authorities
            297–8
        large sums 292
        overdrafts 293–4, 304

presentation 303–4
private investors 300
selling shares 294–5
for setting up 292
taking partners 295
for working capital 293
software packages 194
tax relief on interest paid 296
see also bank
Finance and Leasing Association 299
financial adviser 65, 208–9
and insurance 268
and pensions 46, 402, 404
financial control system 72
financial expenses, allowable against tax 359
Financial Reporting Standards for Small Entities 350
Financial Services Authority (FSA) 53, 144, 263
financial skills 57–9
Financial Times 33, 83, 300
fire
insurance 264–5
risk assessment 244
first-aid officer 244
fiscal accounting 352, 354, 380
fixed assets 280–1, 346
flexible working 232, 251, 252, 254, 255–6
floating charge on assets 47
flyers 139, 148, 151
forecasts 269–89
balance sheet 280–3, 288
cash flow 270–6, 284–5, 289, 311–12
profit and loss 276–80, 286–7, 289
formal voluntary arrangement 337
forms
10 and 12 50
117 50
CWF1 47, 369
LLP2 49
P11D 241–2
P45 233, 241, 261, 369
P46 233, 241, 261
P60 240
Forum of Private Business 34
franchising 80, 101–18
contract 103, 104, 105, 109, 114–17
costs 101, 106–9, 115
advertising levy 108
initial cost 107
service fee 107–8
duration 115
ending agreement 116
finding and buying 113–14
guide to choosing 105–6

how they work 102–3, 106–12
ongoing support 111–12, 118
opening business 110–11
operations manual 110
pilot operation 102, 105, 117
pluses and minuses 103–4, 117–18
premises 110
and pyramid selling 112
sale of business by franchisee 116
territory 109, 115
training 110
franchisor, setting up as 117
freelance staff 213–14, 228
fringe benefits 225, 241–2, 375–6
funding 46–7, 70, 71, 72, 290–304
assistance with premises 184–5
EU 297, 298
see also finance
furnished holiday accommodation, income from 379
furniture 197, 199

GAAP (General Accepted Accounting Practice) 350
Gauntlet, The 304
gifts, business 359
going concern, sale of business as 81
goods received, records for 345–6, 347
goods in transit insurance 266
goodwill of business for sale 85, 90
government and local authority assistance 184–5, 302
grey business 77
growth 329–33
Phase 2 money 331–2, 334
requirements 330–1
guarantee, money-back 165
guarantee payments 239
Guardian 33, 300

hardware, computer 195, 209
health
of employee 250–1
recruitment 250
health and safety 243–5
paperwork 245
risk assessment 245
Health and Safety Executive 243, 245
heating and lighting 275, 279
Highlands and Islands Enterprise 27, 31, 298
hire purchase 198–9
HM Revenue and Customs (HMRC) 73, 254
employment status 79
guidance booklets 242–3
and PAYE 45, 236, 240–1

registering with 40
Tactical and Information Packages 24
wages record 348–9
see also tax
holiday entitlement 234
holiday pay 232
home, working from 72, 186–7

ideas *see* business ideas
identity of business 38
illegal economy 377, 379–80
image 207
  brand 129, 133, 135, 138–9
  of business 72, 152
  of product/service 326, 328
incapacity benefit 44
income
  from property 378–9
  personal 5
  spare-time earnings 376–8
income tax 236, 355–6, 369
  payment dates 351–2, 354–5
Incorporation Document 49
independence 6
independent financial adviser *see*
    financial adviser
indirect selling 161–2
induction and training 225, 228
Industrial and Provident Societies Act
    (1965) 53
Information Commissioner 152, 167,
    195
information technology 78, 193–200
  specialists 196, 209
  strategy 71
insolvency 336–9
  voluntary winding-up 337–8
Insolvency Act (1986) 337, 338
Insolvency Service 336
Instant Muscle 35
Institute of Business Consultancy 203
Institute of Chartered Accountants
    202–3
Institute of Directors 52
insurance 262–8
  against theft 265–6
  broker 262–3, 265, 268
  business interruption 265
  business specific 267
  credit 266
  employer's liability 243, 263
  and equipment 264
  fire 264–5
  goods in transit 266
  intermediaries 263–4
  keyman 267
  legal expenses 267

for loss of profits 265
  motor 264
  personal 268
  professional advisers 268
  professional indemnity 267
  public and product liability 266
  and working from home 187
Intellectual Property Office (UK) 121,
    122
intellectual property protection 205
intermediaries 19–20
Internet 19, 20, 193
  banking 313
  communications 78
  connecting to 196–7, 199
  filing tax 240–1, 354, 381, 394
  and loans 299
  marketing 145–7
  for recruiting employees 219
  selling 195
  VAT filing 394
interviewing prospective staff 221–4, 228
  guidance for 221–4
  setting tests 221–2
  useful questions 222–3
interviews, market research 24–5
inventions 119, 120–2
  patenting 120–2
investments, of business for sale 90
InvestNI 27, 32
investors 295–303
  and business plan 64–5
  see also finance
invoices
  credit control 316, 321
  purchases 345–6
  sales 348
  VAT 390–1
IR35 legislation 376

job description 211–12, 228, 232, 233
Jobcentre Plus 72, 214, 216, 219, 220,
    230

keyman insurance 267

labels 134, 135
land and buildings, of business for sale
    87–90
Law Society 206
Lawyers for Your Business scheme 205
leaflets 138–9, 148, 207
Learn Direct 27, 29, 30
Learning and Skills Council 221
leasing
  equipment 199
  premises 191–2

legal advice 205–6
legal aspects
  advertising 143–4
  business names 132–3
  data protection 167–8, 195, 224
  employees 231–2
    mail shots 152
    premises 191
legal fees, venture capital 301
legal forms of business 38, 71
    choice of 39–47
    cooperatives 53
  letterheads 71, 72, 133–5, 196, 207
legal expenses
  insurance 267
  and tax 360
letterheads 71, 72, 133–5, 196, 207
liabilities
  balance sheet forecast 282–3
  of business for sale 91
liability 39–40
limited company 38, 53
  accounts 42
  buying 85
  cooperative 53
  credibility 39
  disclosure requirements 41
  information requirements 51
  insolvency 337–8
  liability 39–40
  losses 45
  name 41, 51, 71, 132
  name change 50–1
  paying tax 45
  and pensions 46
  public see public limited company
  raising money 47
  registered office 50, 51
  registration with Companies House
      40
  selling part of the business 47
  setting up 40–1, 49–52
limited liability partnership 38, 295
  accounts 42
  agreement 48–9
  credibility 39
  insolvency 339
  liability 39–40
  name 132
  setting up 40, 49
  see also partnership
liquidation 337, 338
  order of payment of debts 338
literature mailers 72
loans 298–9
local authorities 368–9
  and market research 23

planning permission 186, 192
  and premises 184–5, 189, 192
  and raising money 297–8
local enterprise agencies 27, 31, 33, 298
local enterprise companies 27, 31, 33,
      298
Local Enterprise Growth Initiative
      (LEGI) 185
location of business 182, 183–5, 192
  accessibility 183, 189
  assistance 184–5
  communications 183
  constraints 183
  labour 183–4
  proximity to suppliers 184
logo 124, 131, 134, 135, 207
London Stock Exchange 208, 332
losses 45–6, 374

magazines see newspapers and
      magazines
mail shot 139, 150–3
  envelope 151, 152
  legal aspects 152
  list broker 152
  lists 150–1, 152
  mailer 151, 153
  offer 151
  organizing 152–3
  pilot 25
Mailing Preference Service 168
managed service companies 44
managed workshops 188
management
  in business plan 66
  buy-ins 81, 99–100
  buy-outs 81, 99–100
  consultancy 203
  reporting 310–11, 321
  skills 60–1, 66, 68
marital status discrimination 232, 234,
      245, 246
market 13
  and business plan 65, 66
  choice of 10–11
  identifying 14–17
  leaders 176, 177, 181
  market research 13, 14–15, 22–5, 70,
      83
    before start-up 75
    desk research 23–4
    and location 184
  niche 14, 15, 18
  and pricing 170, 176
  sector 70
  segmentation 14–15, 179–80, 327
  share 20–1, 178–9, 181

size 19
structure 19–20
target 18, 136, 137–8, 151
trends 21, 70
web research 22–3
when buying a business 82
market groupings, analysis – step-by-
step 16
marketing 136
database 148
and design protection 125
franchised product/service 103, 105,
108
Internet 145–7
skills 59–60
test 25
and trade mark protection 125
maternity/pregnancy
ante-natal leave 231, 252
guidance 254
maternity allowance 44
maternity leave 231, 251–2, 252–3
pay (SMP) 232, 236, 251–2, 253, 349
right to return to work 232, 251, 252,
254
unfair dismissal 231, 232, 251, 252
media
advertising 141–3
buyers 140–1
members' voluntary winding-up 338
memorandum of association 50
minimum wage 236, 249, 349
Moneyfacts 205
motives 4–5

name
business 50–1, 71, 128–35, 149
choosing 128–33
legal considerations 132–3
franchise 106
product/service 71, 128–9
National Association of Commercial
Finance Brokers 299
National Federation of Enterprise
Agencies (NFEA) 31
National Insurance contributions 43–4,
236, 240, 241, 359, 366–7, 369
and cash flow forecast 273–4
and maternity pay 253
and pensions 396–7
records 348–9
registering 47
national minimum wage 231
negotiations
buying a business 96–8, 100
for premises 190–2
sales 160–2

Neighbourhood Renewal Fund areas
185
New Deal 214
Newly Self-Employed Helpline 47
newspapers and magazines 33
advertising in 140, 141–3
for employees 216–17, 219
business for sale 83
Nominet UK 135
non-executive directors 78, 301
notice periods 232

Office of Fair Trading 144
Official Receiver 338
operational skills 60
overdrafts 293–4, 298–9, 304, 313–14
security for 293–4
overheads 278–9, 321
and break-even point 306–9
overlap profits 353, 354
overtime 236
ownership change 93, 98

packaging 134, 135
parental leave 251, 254–5
part-time employees 214, 231
partnership 38, 295
accounts 41–2
agreement 48–9, 53, 86
bankruptcy 339
buying into 80, 85, 86
changing partners 374
co-operative 53
credibility 39
liability 39, 48
losses and tax 374
NI contributions 42, 43, 44
setting up 40, 48–9, 53
tax 43, 355–6, 372–4
see also limited liability partnership
Patent Office 120, 121, 124
patents 71, 120–2
of business for sale 90
costs 121
defined 120
Europe 120
UK 120–2, 121–2
paternity
leave 232
pay 232, 236, 252, 254, 349
pay 234, 236–42
adoption 232, 236, 251, 252, 254, 349
attachment of earnings 236
bonuses 236
commission 236
deductions 236, 237
equal 231, 235, 236, 239–40

fringe benefits 241–2
holiday 232, 236, 238
itemized statement 231
maternity 232, 236, 251–2, 253, 349
overtime 236
paternity 232, 236, 252, 254, 349
sick 231, 234, 236, 238–9, 349
when no work for employee 232, 239
written statement/slip 237, 349
PAYE system 45, 236, 240–1, 348
and cash flow forecast 273–4
payment to suppliers, and cash flow
forecast 271
pensions 231, 234, 235, 396–405
changes from 2012 398, 399
contracting out 235
employers' contributions 241
personal 398–403
choosing 402–3
retirement annuities 400, 401
stakeholder 398–9, 401
tax relief 46, 400–2
types of 402–3
professional advisers 46
self-invested personal pension (SIPP)
400, 403, 404, 405
small self administered scheme
403–4, 405
state 44
changes to 397–8
contracting-out 397
second pension (SP2) 397
for self-employed 396–9
tax relief 46, 359, 405
personal characteristics 1–5, 7–8, 76
personal relations 7
personal service companies 44
petty cash 341, 343–4, 348
Phase 2 money 331–2, 334
place of work 234
planning regulations 48, 93, 186
plant and equipment
of business for sale 89
capital allowances 361–2, 363, 364
PLUS 208, 332
portfolio work 78–9
Preference Services 168
pregnancy see maternity/pregnancy
premises 72, 182
appearance 187
changing use 93
checklist 189–90
costs 187, 190, 190–1
franchises 110
investigating and negotiating 190–2
lease 191–2
legal aspects 191

parking and transport 187
physical environment 187, 189
search for 188–90
services and facilities 189
shared facilities 188
size and layout 187
and tax 184, 357
valuation 88
see also location of business
press releases 144–5
price-sensitivity 175, 181
price-skimming strategy 171, 175
and product life cycle 175
range of prices 179–80
price/s and pricing 71, 170–81
cutting 172–3
discrimination 179–80
high pricing 170, 171, 177–8, 181
increasing 326–7, 333
level costs method 170, 173–4, 180
lowest 172–3, 180, 181
more than one price 179–80, 181
and non-price benefits 177–8, 179, 181
penetration policy 175, 178
prestige pricing 171
price-cutting war 179, 181
range of prices 170, 171–4
setting 174–80
specialist niche 171
Prince's Trust 36, 297
printers 196
private investors 300
product/service 66
of business for sale 92
differentiation 14, 18
information 138–9
knowledge of, in selling 155, 156
liability insurance 266
name 128–9
new 168–9
repeat purchase 169
sales package 17–18
Professional Contractors Group 34
professional indemnity insurance 267
profit and loss forecasts 276–80, 286–7,
289
profits 306
checklists 324–6, 327, 328
increasing 93, 306, 322–9, 333
overlap 353, 354
and tax 43, 45, 352–4, 355–6
property income 378–9
property renovation 78
Public Interest Disclosure Act (1998) 256
public liability insurance 266
public limited company (PLC) 39, 49–52
public relations 135, 144–5

purchase records 345–6, 347, 349
pyramid selling 112

racial discrimination 230, 231, 232,
        234, 245, 246, 247–8
rates 88, 187, 274, 278, 368–9
    rural village 368
    small business rate 368
    transitional relief 368
records 340–9
    cash control 341
    computerised 347, 349
    employees 348–9
    purchases 345–6, 347, 349
    sales 344–5
    stock 347
    wages 348–9
recruitment *see* employees/staff
recruitment, and discrimination law
        232–3
recruitment agencies and consultants
        219–20
Recruitment and Employment
        Confederation 220
redundancy 249, 257, 260
    consultation with trade union 231
references 224–5
    for customer credit 315
    recruiting staff 224–5, 228
Regional Development Agencies 185,
        192
Regional Venture Capital Funds 302
religious beliefs discrimination 231,
        232, 245, 246, 248
rent 274, 278
reporting, management 310–11, 321
reporting system for staff 73
reputation 129, 133–5, 137
    and pricing 178
retirement
    age 248, 249–50
    and sale of business 404
return on capital employed 94
risk capital 98, 331
risks 6, 71
Royal Institution of Chartered
        Surveyors 191
Royal Mail: mailing options 151, 153

safety 243–5
sales 70, 135, 276
    agents 157, 161–2, 214–15
    back-up organization 156, 162
    in business plan 66, 67
    of business for sale 91–2
    and cash flow forecast 271
    closing 161

cost of 276–8
dialogue 72
direct mail 150–3, 162
distance selling 144, 164–5
estimating 21–2
face-to-face 153, 154–61
forecasting 70, 276–8
increasing 323, 327–8
indirect 161–2
Internet 195
invoices 348
leads 154
lists 154
mix 323–4
open questions 159–60
package 17–18
qualifying potential customers 154,
        162
records 344–5
referrals 154
representatives 155–7, 162
    pay 155–6
    training 156
role-play 158
skills 157–8
stages of 158–61
strategy 157
techniques 158–61
telephone 19, 20, 138, 158, 162
sales of assets, and cash flow forecast 273
scamp form 207
science parks 188, 192
search engines 22–3, 146, 406–7
self-assessment tax system 350, 354–5,
        381
self-discipline 186
self-employment
    accounts 42
    suitability checklists 54–62
    tax relief on loss 365–6
self-invested personal pension (SIPP) 46,
        400, 403, 404, 405
selling part of business 47
service *see* product/service
sex discrimination 229–30, 231, 232,
        233, 234, 245, 246
sexual orientation discrimination 231,
        232, 245, 246
shared accommodation 188
shareholder agreements 98–9
shareholders
    liability 39
    and tax 43–4
shares, selling 294–5
Shell *live*WIRE 36
sick pay 231, 234, 236, 238–9, 349
size

of business 8
of market 19
skills
    analysis of 69
    assessment checklists 57–61
    financial 57–9
    management 60–1
    marketing 59–60
    operational 60
    personal 9–10
    sales 157–8, 162
    weak areas 70, 201
sleeping partner 48
Small Business Advice Service 31, 33
Small Business Bureau 34
small business centres 188
small claims court 318
Small Firms Loan Guarantee Scheme
    299–300
small self-administered schemes (SSASs)
    46
software, computer 194–5, 209
sole trader 38, 53
    accounts 41–2
    bankruptcy 339
    buying business 85
    credibility 39
    liability 39
    NI contributions 42, 43, 44
    setting up 47–8
    tax 44, 355–6
solicitors 105, 205–6
    buying a business 83, 86, 99
    choosing 206
    and premises 191–2
spare time earnings and tax 376–8
starting up
    capital 109
    checklist analysis before 54–62
    notifying tax office 369
    opening year tax rules 352–3
    part-time 74–9
    preparation 69–73
    timing 69–73
    while employed 69, 71, 72, 74, 75–6, 79
state benefits 44–5
state second pension (SP2) 397
stationery 72, 133–4, 149
statutory maternity/paternity/sick pay
    see under pay
stickers 134, 135
stock 306
    of business for sale 89–90
    cards 347
    control 195
    initial 72
    records 341, 347

stock market flotation 322, 331–2
    prospectus 202, 205
stress 6
success criteria 2, 7–8
Sunday Times 83, 300
suppliers 71, 184
    investigations by 320
    payments to 319–21
        cash flow forecast 271
        delaying 319, 320–1
surveyor 206–7
survival rates 5
SWOT analysis 67
syndication 302

target market 18, 136, 137
    communicating with 137–8
    mailers 151
tax 43–4, 350–81
    accountancy expenses 359
    advice 202, 376
    agricultural relief 404
    asset pool 363–5
    balance sheet forecast 282, 283
    being investigated 371, 380
    business expenses 356–60, 380
    and business premises 184
    business rates 368–9
    capital allowances 361–5
    capital gains 187, 367–8, 404, 405
    and cash flow forecast 273–4
    casual income 378
    corporation 274, 302–3, 375
    dividends 375, 376
    establishing self-employment 372
    financial expenses 359
    inheritance 404, 405
    inspector 369–72
    Internet filing 240–1, 354, 381
    and leasing equipment 199
    legal expenses 360
    and new employees 233
    opening year rules 352–3
    partnership 372–4
    payment on account 354
    and pensions 46, 400–2
    pre-trading expenditure 366
    on profits 43, 45, 352–4, 355–6
    property income 378–9
    relief on losses 365–6
    retention of documents 378, 380, 381
    returns 370–1
        deadlines 381
        late penalties 354, 370, 380
        partners 373, 374
        self-employed 42
    salary and fringe benefits 375–6

self-assessment 350, 354–5
and shares 43–4
spare time earnings 376–8
staff costs 359
starting a business 352–3, 366, 369
taper relief 367, 404, 405
timetable 2008–2014 354–5
vehicle expenses 356–7, 358
years 351–2, 353–4
  2008 354–5
see also PAYE system
tax adviser 350–1
Techmark 332
technology 79, 333, 334
telephone 193
answering 135, 149
bills 275, 279
phone scripts 72
response times 164
selling 138, 153–4, 158, 162
sifting potential employees 218
systems 196–7
Telephone Preference Service 168
terms and conditions of sale 72
test-marketing 25, 71
Times, The 33, 83, 300
timing of start 69–73, 72
trade associations 23
trade exhibitions 23
trade journals/magazines 83, 142
trade mark 124–5, 131, 133
of business for sale 90
definition 124
registration 124–5
trade union membership 231, 245, 246,
  250
trade unions, and redundancy 231
Trading Schemes Act (1996) 112
training courses 27–30, 37

undischarged bankrupt 339
unemployed people, help for 35, 36, 297
unfair dismissal 234, 256–7, 260

Valuation Office Agency 187
VAT (Value Added Tax) 282, 283, 289,
  382–95
account 391, 392–3
annual accounting 392–3, 395
cancelled registration 386, 394
and cash flow forecast 271–3, 274, 275
claiming back 388–9
compulsory online filing 394
exemptions 383–5
flat-rate scheme 358, 392, 394
input tax 383, 389
misdeclaration penalty 391–2

output tax 383, 388
paying 393–4
period 391
and petty cash 343
and profit and loss forecasts 276
rates 386
receipts 271–3
records 346–7, 390–3
registering 40, 383–6, 387
return 391–2
and sales records 344
tax invoice 390–1
turnover threshold 384, 394
voluntary registration 387
zero-rate and exempt 386, 394
vehicles 197–8, 200
contract hire 200
livery 207
motor insurance 264
and reputation 135
and tax 356–7, 358, 362, 364, 380
and VAT 388
venture capital 47, 294, 300–2
trusts 300–1
virtual business 74, 78, 182, 192, 193
voluntary winding-up 337–8

wages
and cash flow forecast 273
records 348–9
see also pay
wages order 236
web research 22–3
web site/s 134–5, 145, 148, 209
businesses for sale 83
cost 145, 146
designing 147, 207–8
internal 333
links with others 146, 147
registering name 135
useful 406–7
for vacant premises 188
whistle blowing 256
wholesalers 162
winding-up, voluntary 337–8
word processing 194
working capital 293
working hours 5–6, 234
working time regulations 242, 349
workplace 182–92
see also location; premises
written statement of employment 233,
  234–5

Yellow Pages 83, 84, 142
young business 77–8
Young Enterprise UK 77